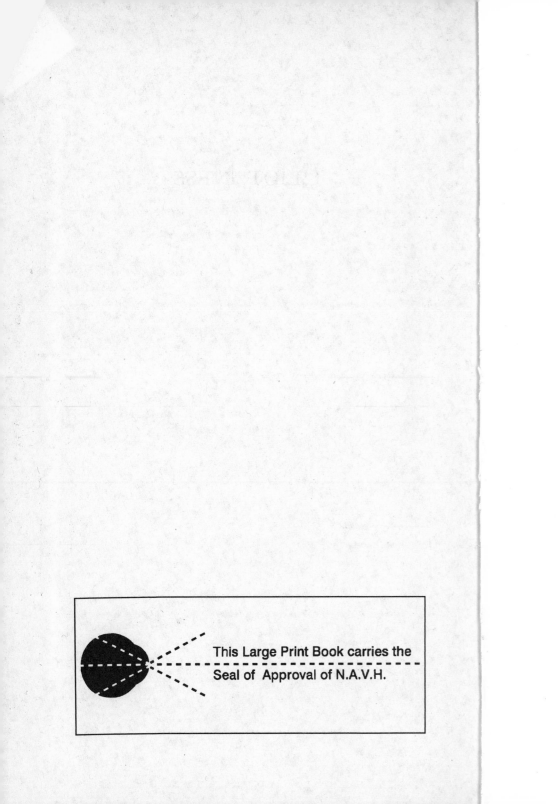

ELIOT NESS

ELIOT NESS

THE RISE AND FALL OF AN AMERICAN HERO

DOUGLAS PERRY

THORNDIKE PRESS
A part of Gale, Cengage Learning

GALE
CENGAGE Learning·

Farmington Hills, Mich • San Francisco • New York • Waterville, Maine
Meriden, Conn • Mason, Ohio • Chicago

GALE
CENGAGE Learning®

Copyright © 2014 by Douglas Perry.
Photograph credits:
Pages 24: ATF promotional pamphlet; III: Courtesy of Cleveland Public Library; 494: Author's collection.
Insert credits:
pages 1, 3, 4, 7, 8: Author's collection; 2: University of Chicago, Special Collections Research Center; 5 (bottom), 6, 9 (bottom), 10: Cleveland Public Library; 5 (top): Ohio Historical Society; 9 (top): The Cleveland Museum of Art-Ingalls Library.
Thorndike Press, a part of Gale, Cengage Learning.

LIBRARY OF CONGRESS CATALOGING-IN-PUBLICATION DATA

Perry, Douglas, 1968–
    Eliot Ness : the rise and fall of an American hero / by Douglas Perry. —
Large Print edition.
        pages cm. — (Thorndike Press large print crime scene)
    Includes bibliographical references.
    ISBN 978-1-4104-6870-3 (hardcover) — ISBN 1-4104-6870-4 (hardcover)
    1. Ness, Eliot. 2. Detectives—United States—Biography. 3. United States.
Federal Bureau of Investigation. I. Title.
HV7911.N45P47 2014
363.25092—dc23
[B]   2014006522

Published in 2014 by arrangement with Viking, a member of Penguin Group (USA) LLC, a Penguin Random House Company

Printed in the United States of America
1 2 3 4 5 6 7 18 17 16 15 14

For my mother

CONTENTS

INTRODUCTION:
THE REAL ELIOT NESS

When Walter Taylor arrived, Betty was still in the kitchen, standing over her husband's body. She was sobbing fitfully, in a daze. Her ten-year-old son stood nearby, paralyzed by fear. A doctor was there, too, and someone else, a business partner of the man sprawled on the floor.

Taylor had witnessed this ghastly tableau many times over the years. He was the town's deputy coroner and the editor of the local newspaper. But this time was different.

The dead man was lying on his back, his white shirt twisted across his bulk. In the sink basin, smashed glass sparkled in the dissipating light. He'd been getting a drink of water when the coronary hit. Betty had come in from the garden and turned the faucet off before she saw her husband there on the floor. She screamed, high and long and loud — loud enough to bring their son running from the neighbor's yard. She continued to sob now, a guttural sound, too deep and raw for such a pretty woman. "It will be all right, Betty," someone said, and that was as much as she could take. She started to collapse. The business partner grabbed her before she fell.

Taylor turned away. He'd seen enough. He walked out of the kitchen, past the soot-stained mantel in the living room with the cherubic white angel suspended above it. The angel, its wings aflutter, gazed toward the trauma unfolding in the kitchen. Betty had made the piece. Someone had once told Taylor that she had been a student of a famous sculptor. Outside, Taylor found the neighbors milling about. The poor man had been sweating when he came up the walk, one of them said. He looked like he was in pain, another offered. Taylor moved away from the bystanders and picked up his pace. It was a warm, humid evening, and he was wearing a suit, but he ran all the way back to the office. He was a newsman. He had to let the world know it had just lost Eliot Ness.

The world didn't much care. Taylor's report went out on the Associated Press wire on that balmy spring day in 1957, but few newspapers bothered publishing an obituary. The *New York Times,* America's paper of record, did not take note of Ness's death. In Chicago, the place of his birth and where he raised the once-famous "Untouchables" squad, the *Tri-*

bune gave his life barely one hundred words. It got his age wrong. Arnold Sagalyn, despite being a newspaper executive in the Washington, DC, area, heard about Ness's death only because Betty called him a few days later. Sagalyn made a small noise, a kind of pained grunt, when Ness's widow gave him the news. He thought of Eliot like a big brother. Ness had taught Sagalyn how to carry a gun, how to unnerve a suspect, how to mix a drink. The call couldn't have been easy for Betty, either. The reality of her husband's death had settled on her by then, but she didn't know Sagalyn well. He'd worked with Ness before she came on the scene. He'd been close with Eliot's previous wife, Evaline. Betty called him because she had nowhere else to turn. Her husband had left her nothing but debts and dreams. Sagalyn sent her some money.

Not everyone was so sympathetic. David Cowles, the superintendent of criminal identification for the Cleveland Police Department, had also worked with Ness during the glory years. But unlike Sagalyn, he didn't owe his career to the "fair-haired boy." He thought Ness had hogged the headlines. "The last time I saw Eliot, he didn't have two pair of shoes to wear," Cowles would recall when asked about his former boss. "He was a heavy drinker. . . . I think he had four or five wives, didn't he?"

Broke, alcoholic, and dead from a massive

13

heart attack at just fifty-five. Such a fate for Eliot Ness was inconceivable to most everyone who knew him during his long law-enforcement career. This was the golden boy who crashed Al Capone's party in Chicago. The young, irrepressible top cop in Cleveland who announced "there was no room for traitors in the police department" — and then set out to prove it. The detective savant who, like his fictional hero Sherlock Holmes, could stun a stranger by deducing some core aspect of his character simply by observing the twitch of his lip. (As one of the resident experts on the crime quiz show *Masterminds, Attention!,* he solved the mysteries so quickly the radio program burned through its material at twice the expected rate and had to go off the air.)

"He really captured the imagination of the public in his early years," John Patrick Butler, a former aide for Cleveland mayor Thomas Burke, would recall years later.

By the time of Ness's death, however, that hero worship was long gone. He hadn't been a lawman for more than a decade. Desperate for money, his ambitious business plans in shambles, Ness had been working on a memoir when he collapsed in his kitchen in the tiny town of Coudersport, Pennsylvania. The book hadn't been his idea. His business partner, Joe Phelps, was a childhood friend of Oscar Fraley, a hack for United Press

International. On a trip to New York, Phelps and Ness met the journalist at a bar, and Ness sat quietly while the two old pals played "remember when." During a lull in the conversation, Phelps had jerked a thumb at Ness and said, "You'll have to get Eliot to tell you about his experience as a Prohibition agent in Chicago. He's the guy who dried up Al Capone. Maybe you never heard of him, but it's real gangbuster stuff: killings, raids and the works. It was plenty dangerous."

Ness smiled bashfully and shrugged. "It was dangerous," he said.

At Phelps's urging, Ness offered up some old stories. Fraley, fascinated, told his new drinking companion he should write a book, that it could bring him a nice chunk of change. Ness shrugged again, but Fraley wouldn't let it go. He said he'd write it for him. Some weeks later, Fraley called Ness at home in Coudersport. He told him he had pitched a book proposal to New York publishers, and he'd found one that wanted a memoir about the Untouchables. Ness stared at the telephone receiver. "I can hardly believe it," he finally said. "You think it will be interesting?"

Fraley had no doubt that it would be. Ness thought of himself as a failure — it had been a long time since the Capone days — but Fraley knew Ness was an American icon waiting to be discovered. Or, more accurately, rediscovered. Not that Fraley was concerned about accuracy. He would take a series of conversations he had with Ness, along with an outline Ness wrote for him, and stretch them like Silly Putty. He added a lot of *biff!*s and *pow!*s and tommy guns going *rat-a-tat-tat!* He threw in some hard-boiled dialogue cribbed from private-dick movies. He wrote a pulp novel. Worried about what he considered Ness's "fetish" for honesty, he tried to convince him that this was the way things were done in publishing, that they had "literary license."

The truth about Eliot Ness has been up for grabs ever since. Thanks to Fraley's *The Untouchables,* published seven months after Ness's death, Ness received more credit for taking down Al Capone than he deserved. This has rankled many Capone stakeholders over the years, as Fraley's book begat a top-rated TV series in the 1960s, which begat a blockbuster movie in the 1980s, which begat more TV shows and novels and comic books and movies that continue to appear. George E. Q. Johnson Jr., son of the U.S. attorney who hired Ness to harass Capone's operations, told an interviewer that the Untouchables' work "was damaging to Al Capone, an annoyance, but resulted in no convictions. There were no convictions of any conse-

16

quence for violations of Prohibition laws, because it was unenforceable." An income-tax case, he pointed out, got Capone.

The professional debunkers followed hard and fast. They slathered their own counter-myth onto Ness, insisting he was an incompetent and a glory hound, a liar and a drunk. Some even suggested that the Capone hunt turned him into a wild man, a rogue agent. "Eliot changed. The niceties of the law no longer meant all that much to him," said Al Wolff, a former federal Prohibition agent in Chicago. "He bent a few rules and even broke a few. We didn't always see eye to eye on that."

All of this has taken a toll. Thirty years after Ness's death, the *Los Angeles Times* wrote that the Untouchables' leader had committed suicide. A reader had to call the paper and demand a correction. Ken Burns, promoting his 2011 television documentary about Prohibition, said that Ness was nothing but "a PR invention." Burns's codirector, Lynn Novick, added: "He raided a few old breweries and busted up some stale beer. Then, after he retired, he wrote a book in which he just made stuff up."

The thing that gets overlooked, even after all these years, is that Ness didn't need Oscar Fraley's help to be a hero. Fans of the Robert Stack TV series and the Kevin Costner movie and the various novels and comic books can all legitimately lay claim to Ness being one of the most influential and successful lawmen of the twentieth century. Scarface Al is only one small reason for this. Ness was just thirty years old when Capone was marched off to prison and the Untouchables disbanded. It was the beginning of Ness's career, and far from the highlight. Three years later, in the heart of the Great Depression, he moved to Cleveland. The *Cleveland Press,* in announcing Ness's appointment as the city's public safety director, pointed out that he had nothing to do with the case in Chicago that sent Capone to prison. This was not a criticism. The newspaper presented Ness as a savior, the man they had all been waiting for. Cleveland was the sixth-largest city in the country and arguably the most corrupt. Ness announced he would clean up the town — all by himself, if he had to. "I am going to be out (in the field). And I'll cover this town pretty well."

Marion Kelly, a longtime Cleveland police reporter, would remember him as "the sexiest man I'd ever known." She insisted "he wasn't handsome or flashy, but women were drawn to him." Louise Jamie, who was related to Ness through marriage, believed he personified the very best the country had to offer. "He never carried a gun," she said. "He was very private. He was typical of the English-Norwegian, the backbone of America. Even the gangsters knew it. There is honor among thieves, you see, if they respect you. Nobody ever shot Eliot for that reason."

Novelists and screenwriters have used these images to conjure up the man they wanted Ness to be. He was the tough, golly-gee G-man, quick to blush, even downright priggish, but willing to do what needed to be done for God and country. It's a compelling, all-American portrait, but it's also wrong. Or, at least, woefully incomplete.

Like the comic-book superheroes popularized during his career, Ness had an earthbound alter ego. In his case, it was his real self. He was, by all accounts, modest, kind, shy. Which only seemed to make his actions on the job all the more impressive. There was simply no explaining them. "There is nothing about Ness' appearance to inspire fear," the *Cleveland News* wrote in 1940 during the racketeering trial of a union boss. "But the shadowy characters who sometimes drift into the Criminal Courts Building point him out with awe. 'There goes Ness,' they say as though they were indicating Wyatt Earp, the two-gun sharpshooter of the gold rush days." During another racketeering trial, Ness's reputation and its possible effect on jurors so unnerved the defense attorneys they tried to get him banned from the courtroom.

Work obsessed Eliot Ness, so much so that he couldn't help but ruin his marriages with

19

it. He never could separate his public self from his private self. The two inevitably rolled together. He could be a heroic figure in his personal life as well as his professional one; he found scandal in both as well. Women fell in love with him on trains and from across crowded rooms. He loved to shoot guns and to dance, and he was good at both. (He was good at everything he did; he steered clear of activities that didn't come naturally to him.) He was a hard partier — so hard that he never figured out how to come down from the high. So hard that it undermined his reputation and, ultimately, helped end his life at what should have been not much more than the midway point.

Once he was dead and gone, the rest of the world caught up with Chicago and Cleveland, and became fascinated by Ness. Everyone, it seemed, wanted to know about the "real" man. "Tell me, what kind of guy was this Eliot Ness?" the mobster Lucky Luciano asked Oscar Fraley in the early 1960s. Fraley fielded this question frequently.

Back on that night when the reporter had first met Ness, the former Prohibition agent had described his Untouchables' adventures as "dangerous." That word had stuck with Fraley, and it was how he now liked to describe Ness to anyone who asked. It was true enough — Eliot Ness had been danger-ous in many ways — so Fraley usually left it at that. Even though he knew there was so much more to say about the man.

■ ■ ■ ■

PART I
RISING STAR

■ ■ ■ ■

Photos of employees collectively make up Eliot Ness's face in artwork at the headquarters of the Bureau of Alcohol, Tobacco, Firearms and Explosives in Washington, DC.

CHAPTER 1
HARDBOILED

Edna Stahle opened her eyes and looked at the ceiling. She had no idea where she was. She'd been warned that might happen.

She was on the floor, that much was obvious. She rolled onto her side, got her knees under her, and rose slowly. She realized she was sweating. A wall heaved into view, and she reached out to steady herself.

She noticed other women in the room. Everyone was moving slowly, with measured steps. One of them let out a moan. They were beginning to understand what had happened to them.

Just the day before, Edna and the five other girls from the office thought they were being so grown-up. They had rented this cottage on Lake Michigan. They'd picked it out themselves, paid for it themselves, stocked it themselves. They didn't tell anyone what they were up to. It was their secret.

The weekend had started innocently enough. The first thing they did was go for a swim. They banged into the lake like children, laughing and splashing one another, unselfconscious with no men around. They stood up to their waists, heat dazed, and looked out at the horizon, at the boats backlit along its edges. There were beautiful yachts on the lake all day. The girls didn't know it, but bootleggers owned the grandest ones. The gangsters had figured out that the big, gaudy vessels, laid out in rosewood, with "gold handles on the toilets and all that jazz," were better for business — at least for now. The Coast Guard was suspicious of any fast little boat zipping across the lake, but it paid no mind to the pleasure cruisers, home to industrialists and politicians at play. "So [gangsters] took these yachts and decorated them with pretty girls in bathing suits, like going out for a little sail. Load up and come back," one of those pretty girls confided years later. This was a good time for them to be out there. It was a hot summer day — perfect for a little sail. Perfect for a drink. Back in the city, the bootleggers' thirsty customers sat on shiny wooden barstools, sweat running down their faces. Nineteen twenty-eight had been surprisingly warm so far, starting early and building to a record-breaking heat wave in July. Some club owners brazenly propped their doors open, allowing the pungent smell of beer to waft onto the sidewalks. Most of them kept a wad of cash ready in case a dry agent walked in

— and a truncheon behind the bar in case he was honest.

None of the women at the rented cottage ever went to those "private clubs." Pretty girls were always welcome; Prohibition had brought women into what long had been a male-only domain. But for the respectable ones, it was a dangerous game. A young woman couldn't get away with drinking on her own or even with a girlfriend. She was going to be approached, time and again. And if a girl did accept a drink from a man? One saloon regular put it succinctly: "If she had two drinks with him, and she didn't lay her frame down, she was in a serious matter." Worse yet for these particular young women now enjoying their lakeside holiday: at a saloon they might run into one of the men they worked for. After all, they didn't slave away at just any office. They were all secretaries in the Chicago office of the Prohibition Bureau. That was why they had planned this secret drinking weekend at an out-of-the-way cottage way up on the lake, where no one would see them, let alone recognize them.

Now they realized they might have made a mistake. There was no way to tell what you were going to get from a bootlegger. How many times had they heard that? Coal tar dyes, industrial solvents, paint thinner, rat droppings. Anything could be in there. They'd read reports about men dying or going blind from drink. *One* drink. Women just like them had gone mad and killed their lovers. Of course, those were extreme cases. No one would say otherwise. The fact was, everyone they knew drank bootleg liquor. Everyone but them.

Edna settled herself at the kitchen table. Until this summer, the petite twenty-one-year-old had never tasted alcohol. The way her head felt now, she figured it would be a long time before she tried it again. The other women at the table had already resolved to take it easy all morning. Read books and sit on the beach.

Maybe they should drink some more, one of them said. Hair of the dog.

The women stared off into space, pondering that one. Maybe later, they decided. For now, they would do nothing, enjoy the quiet.

Early afternoon brought a knock on the door. One of the secretaries, decked out boyishly in a shapeless shift and bangs, opened up and found Eliot Ness standing on the porch, kneading his hat in his hands. She almost cried out. The women had cleaned themselves up by then. They'd come to terms with the previous night and begun to relax about it. The liquor hadn't been poisonous after all. They were chatting and laughing, talking about giving it another go. But now silence gripped the cottage. The women exchanged glances, their eyes wide. They invited Eliot in — they *had* to invite him in — but, as the nephew of one of the secretaries would remember the story, "with him there they were afraid to break out the booze. He was the kind of guy who probably would have arrested them."

They actually weren't too worried about that. True enough, he was the new agent on the special squad, the most hardcore unit in the office. But they were pretty sure he hadn't driven all the way up there to bust them. He'd come because he was "sweet on one of the girls." Which was just fine with them. In fact, it was exciting. Because all of the girls were sweet on him.

Eliot stepped into the room, into the light. The women watched him with sucked-in breath. It wasn't that he had matinee-idol looks. He didn't. He had a soft, indistinct face, a face that blended into the background of photographs. But he was tall — easily six feet in his stocking feet — with a rangy, athletic build. And there was such sadness in his eyes, even when he was smiling. Those blue eyes told everything. They told you he was cerebral and sensitive and maybe a little troubled down deep in his soul. Women could see this — or feel it. He just gave off a vibe.

Edna had caught it right off. Eliot would always pause by her desk when he was in the office and give her a smile. She loved the way he talked to her. He was amiable and jokey with the men, slapping backs and all that, but he would settle down as soon as he turned his gaze on the assistant administrator's secretary. He'd sit on the edge of her desk, his voice muted, those sad eyes at half-mast, and Edna would gaze up at him as the rest of the bustling office hurtled off into the cosmos. She couldn't understand why this incredible man was interested in her.

Edna Margaret Stahle was not beautiful. She knew it. She hated her mousy brown hair and her bony, plain face. She had a nice figure going for her — a long torso and boyish curves, the body of a natural-born flapper — but she didn't know that. No one else did, either. The social revolution that had brought women the vote and the Charleston hadn't yet made it out to Kensington, the far South Side neighborhood where Edna had grown up in a squat, cramped house on Union Street, just a few blocks from the Ness home. Edna wore high-collared blouses and calf-length wool skirts, usually topped with a heavy overcoat. Nobody saw her curves. She rode the streetcar to the Prohibition Bureau offices every day, her head always down, too shy to meet anyone's gaze. On the weekend, she clattered around town on a secondhand bicycle, gliding through intersections with her eyes closed. The bike riding was her escape, her way of clearing her head. She needed it. Edna was studious and serious.

women gasped in shock. Eliot began to laugh; he couldn't help it. This set Edna to giggling. Slowly, the others joined in. Everyone laughed a little too hard.

Eliot wasn't supposed to be a member of the special squad. He might have impressed the women in the office, but he didn't have the same effect on the supervisors. It was widely believed that he lacked the chops for high-level duty. He certainly didn't have the pedigree. The special agents, after all, had been handpicked and trained in the nation's capital. Many were Ivy League graduates, tops in their classes. Eliot had been just an ordinary Prohibition agent, a local boy.

The Special Agency Division stood apart from the rest of the Prohibition Bureau. The division oversaw ten "small, highly trained mobile forces of investigators," each led by a special agent in charge. Their mission: to handle large-scale liquor conspiracies beyond the scope and training of the average Prohibition office, and to clean out dishonest agents wherever they found them. George Golding, a cocky, barrel-chested former New York City cop, led the twenty-man team dispatched to Chicago. Another George — George E. Q. Johnson, the new U.S. attorney for the Northern District of Illinois — considered the team's assignment to the city a significant coup. Many in the Treasury Department, home to the Prohibition Bureau, believed Golding to be the best lawman in the federal government. He had plenty of fans in the Justice Department as well. Assistant Attorney General Mabel Willebrandt, who was in charge of Prohibition cases, said a hundred George Goldings could dry out the entire country.

Johnson was satisfied to get the one and only. The U.S. attorney had dedicated himself to bringing down the region's booze syndicate. But he realized that before he could take on the liquor gangs, he had to roust the criminals within the Prohibition Bureau itself — or at the very least bypass them. The Chicago Prohibition office had recently forced out most of the longtime temperance activists who had joined the agency through political patronage. But the crooks were proving harder to dislodge. The problem had been going on from the very beginning. In 1922, two years after the arrival of the constitutional amendment that banned the sale, manufacture, and transportation of alcohol, a local federal grand jury had declared that "almost without exception [Prohibition] agents are not men of the type of intelligence and character qualified to be charged with this difficult and important duty and Federal law." That was understating the matter. Dozens of dry agents in the office were on the Mob's payroll. Some were even full-fledged members of a gang. With Golding in place, Johnson believed this shameful state of affairs could finally change. He and Chicago's Prohibition administrator, E. C. Yellowley, announced that "no dry agents or other government employees violating the law will be dealt with leniently."

Landing in the city in the fall of 1927, Golding met with reporters on his first day on the job. The big, brash New Yorker charmed them right down to their toes, telling them eye-popping tales of derring-do and insisting that his tenure in the nation's second city was going to be "all action." The newspapers dubbed him "Hardboiled Golding" and announced that the war against the gangs finally was in good hands. Hardboiled wanted to have an immediate impact, before the glowing headlines about the team's arrival could molder in birdcages. He big-footed ongoing investigations into the booze syndicate and his agents started shouldering their way through locked doors, usually with reporters right behind them. "The agents swooped down on unsuspecting Chicago, their eyes blazing and their guns in hand," recalled Elmer Irey, head of the Internal Revenue Service's Intelligence Unit, which provided training to the Special Agency Division. "The chief of this new group led his men through miles of popping photographers' flash guns as he rounded up dozens of illicit backroom gin mills and bathroom alcohol stills. He even knocked off a few breweries."

But Hardboiled Golding's hero worship would be short-lived. In March 1928, one of Golding's men shot an off-duty municipal court bailiff in the back while the team was raiding a saloon on the South Side. Overnight, the glowing press notices ground to a halt. The newspapers, careful to stay with public opinion, responded to the shooting with outrage. They questioned the raiders' competence, forcing Johnson to defend the squad in a makeshift press conference. The U.S. attorney insisted the special agents were cracking down on the "Kensington–Chicago Heights alcohol ring, to whom this department attributes at least three murders." He added that the squad was seeking Chicago Heights gangster Lorenzo Juliano, along with evidence that the mobster was responsible for setting off a bomb at the home of U.S. senator Charles Deneen, a well-known foe of gang rule.

Johnson's defense wasn't good enough. Or it never had a chance to be, for Golding immediately undermined it. The special agent in charge announced that the bailiff, William Beatty, had fired two shots at his men. He said the wounded man, under guard in the hospital, would be charged with "obstructing justice and assaulting officers." But eyewitness testimony was unanimous that the bailiff had no gun on the night of the raid and posed no threat. Beatty, it turned out, was running away from the agents — he thought they were gangsters robbing the place. Reporters didn't doubt this version of events. Golding's men cultivated a black-ops image and rarely identified themselves when they crashed through doors. They had arrived at the saloon on South State Street in four unmarked cars and raced into the joint wielding shotguns, rifles, machine guns, and sledgehammers. When the police showed up fifteen minutes later, the special agents told them to turn right back around. "You get the hell out of here; we'll handle this," one of them told the officers. Added another, "It's none of your business."

Local law-enforcement officials took their cue from the newspapers. "I want to know whether a bunch of gun-toting roughnecks from the east side of New York can come into Chicago and shoot an unarmed man and then tell the police to go to hell," Police Commissioner Michael Hughes demanded. The state prosecutor issued an arrest warrant for Myron Caffey, the agent who shot Beatty. Newspaper headlines about the cocked-up raid continued to stretch across Chicago's front pages day after day, turning Caffey into the most reviled man in the city. Irey recalled that the special agent "had to go into hiding in the Federal Building, sleeping and eating in an Assistant United States Attorney's office until his victim disappointed the critical Chicago press and recovered from his wound." On April 5, Caffey surrendered to the police.

Assistant Attorney General Willebrandt, alarmed by the reports coming into her office, decided to make an emergency trip to Chicago for a day of meetings. On her way into the Transportation Building, the Printers Row tower where the Prohibition Bureau kept its offices, she waved off reporters who tried to determine the reason for her visit. "The situation here is so tense that I think it better for me to say nothing at all," she said. In the bureau's offices, rumors sprouted like mushrooms in the dark. Surely somebody was getting fired; surely there was going to be a shakeup. In his meeting with Willebrandt, Johnson "begged that the special crew be withdrawn before somebody got lynched." Golding scoffed at the U.S. attorney. He still refused to acknowledge that he or his men had done anything wrong. He made it clear that he had no plans to slink out of town, no matter how bad the situation looked. Retreating wasn't his style.

On May 31, 1928, two months after the Beatty shooting, Eliot Ness received orders to report to the special agency squad. He stared at the piece of paper, stunned. Most of the agents in the Chicago Prohibition office were desperate to distance themselves from Golding, whom the newspapers were now calling a rogue cop, a legal gangster. The papers reported that the Justice Department was investigating the special squad after dozens of barrels of confiscated beer had disappeared from a government warehouse on the West Side. Gossip circulated in the office about Golding attempting to get a traffic cop prosecuted for obstruction of justice for trying to give him a jaywalking ticket. But Eliot wasn't one of Golding's or the squad's critics. He had requested the transfer. He was twenty-six years old and had just a year and a half in the bureau, but he felt disillusioned. He often gazed out his fourth-floor office window at South Dearborn Street below, his melancholic blue-black eyes soft and unfocused, unable to get himself out the door to do his job. The fug of corruption permeated the office. He suspected that his own partner was taking money from the booze syndicate. He knew of agents who socialized with gangsters. It disgusted him. He didn't care what the newspapers or the police said about the special squad. He wanted to be a part of it. He believed in Golding and his hardboiled tactics. He believed that only ruthlessness could win the war against the bootleggers.

The question was, What kind of special agency squad was he joining? That George Golding took Eliot onto the team was a sure sign that the champagne had gone flat for the special agent in charge. From their initial interview, Golding pegged Eliot as an odd duck. The candidate, Hardboiled noted, seemed unsure of himself, too eager to please. Golding had a good eye. Eliot surely was trying too hard. The young agent couldn't believe he was being considered for the team. He'd put in the transfer request — weeks before — to make himself feel better, not because he thought he'd get it. He knew what his record was. He was a college boy — University of Chicago, class of '25 — but his grades were awful. He'd started his career at the consumer-reporting powerhouse Retail Credit Company, a definite plus, but he spent most of his year there doing clerical, not investigative, work. He hadn't done much since coming to the Prohibition Bureau, either. Eighteen months was enough time to make a mark in the dry service, and yet Eliot could boast of no significant arrests, nothing to set himself apart. He'd pretended to be a student down on the University of Illinois campus and busted a few coeds for drinking. And he was among the few agents in the office who actually managed to pass the civil service exam. That was about it. Golding put down that Eliot had landed at the bureau through family connections.

Nepotism certainly played a part in Eliot joining the bureau's ranks. His brother-in-law was Alexander Jamie, Edna Stahle's boss, a senior manager in the Chicago office. Eliot had always wanted to follow in Jamie's footsteps. The forty-five-year-old assistant Prohibition administrator, a former FBI agent, had been something of a father figure to Eliot over the years. Eliot's actual father, Peter Ness, rarely took a day off from the thriving wholesale bakery business he owned, so it was the tall, grim-faced Jamie who had taught Eliot how to drive a car and shoot a gun. It was Jamie who had taught him about the importance of honesty in all things. (Woe unto them that call evil good and good evil, he told him.)

Ever since adolescence, Eliot had sought to make Jamie proud of him. He wanted to be just like his brother-in-law: upright, tough, uncompromising. As an agent, Eliot hadn't scored many arrests so far, but he took the badge seriously — more seriously than most. He carried the Prohibition Bureau's rule book around in his jacket pocket every day. He trawled for speakeasies even on his own time. He was the kind of agent Jamie expected him to be. Crooked Prohibition agents had built-in radar for like-minded colleagues, and the meter never blipped when it settled on Eliot Ness. He fit all the do-gooder stereotypes. He still lived at home. He took his meals there and called his mother every day to let her know if he'd be late. He wore the same two suits over and over. As a junior agent, he earned $2,500 per year, which was enough for him. That was the problem. He couldn't find a friend in the office. No one wanted anything to do with him.[*]

Golding was an honest man, too, the questionable investigative tactics of his team notwithstanding, but he didn't want to be Eliot's friend any more than the crooked agents did. The special agent in charge was frustrated by his limited personnel options. When he and his team had arrived in Chicago eight months before, he could boast of having the bureau's crème de la crème. No more. This Ness kid clearly was not qualified for the special squad, but Golding took him because few others wanted to work for the team anymore. Golding had even been forced to bring on college interns to fill stakeout shifts. The transfer to the elite squad moved Eliot from Prohibition agent to special agent — skipping over the investigator grade entirely — but, in a telling bureaucratic decision, it came with no change in salary. (A memo from Washington the week before his reassignment stated that "it is not desired to

[*] $2,500 in 1927 is equivalent to about $32,000 in 2013.

promote him at this time.") On June 5, Golding personally gave him the oath of office. Eliot replaced Caffey, now under indictment for murder.

CHAPTER 2
MAMA'S BOY

It didn't take long for Eliot to get the action he craved, the kind that would impress a starry-eyed secretary during hushed, conspiratorial lunchtime conversations. Shortly before Eliot joined the team, Golding and his men had captured Juliano. Golding insisted the arrest justified the raid in which Beatty was shot, seeing as Juliano had been the target that night. Thus, the arrest justified Beatty's shooting. This was how Golding thought. "The way of the transgressor is hard, the Bible states, and it seems to me that the work of enforcing laws is no cinch," he announced to the press. The special agent in charge had recovered his verve.

One thing you could say about Hardboiled Golding, he was consistent. He never learned from his mistakes. By summer, the Beatty debacle had receded in the public's mind, which to Golding meant it never happened. He was ready for action again. On August 21, a few weeks after Edna and the other

44

secretaries had had their secret weekend holiday, Golding's special agents burst into rooms 803 and 804 of the City Hall Square office building downtown, seeking records for the Northside booze syndicate.[*] This was the first major raid by the squad in which Eliot played a key role; he was charged with securing the first room. Golding would praise a handful of agents in his official report (Eliot was among those he singled out), but no one outside of the special squad would view the mission as a success. That was because in the second room, room 804, a man named Merle Adams had responded to the intrusion by punching an agent in the jaw and fleeing, sliding out the door on freshly polished shoes and scrambling down the hall like an overeager puppy. One of the raiders, Arthur Franklin, gave chase, pulling out his revolver as he leapt into the hallway. Up until this point, office workers along the length of the floor had been watching from doorways, agape at what appeared to be an audacious robbery. Now screams echoed in the enclosed space, and men and women rushed inside their offices and underneath desks. A deafening pop resounded throughout the floor. This prompted more screams and gasps from the

[*] The building, at Randolph and Washington Streets, was torn down in 1965 and replaced by the iconic Richard J. Daley Center.

scattering peanut gallery. Franklin — a twenty-three-year-old "student dry agent," it would turn out — watched as the fleeing man issued a small "Ooopphhhh!" and dropped to his knees at the top of the stairwell. The student agent turned and strode back to room 804. He leaned his head in. "I got him," he announced.

That hardly was the end of it. While the intern boasted about his marksmanship, Adams slowly righted himself and continued his flight. He made it down to the seventh floor before Agent Edward Gill, following the trail of blood, caught up to him. More office workers watched as Gill whacked the wounded man in the head with a blackjack. Gill and another raider carried the suspected liquor-syndicate accountant back up to the eighth floor and ran the gauntlet of gapers down the hallway. "Get into your offices, we're government men," the agents barked as they alternated between hefting and dragging Adams, periodically thumping him with their clubs. "For God's sake," Adams finally wailed to no one in particular, "call Mrs. Adams at Longbeach 4800 and tell her I'm shot." Leaving the door to the office open, the agents dropped Adams into a chair and told him to open the cashbox or else. They put wet towels on his wound in a halfhearted attempt to stop the bleeding and continued to threaten him when he didn't respond. Then they took the

46

phone receivers off the hooks so they could concentrate on the safe without interruption. A woman from across the hall, after watching for half an hour as Adams bled through the clump of towels, decided she should call a doctor. Someone else had already called the newspapers, and the reporters beat the doctor to the scene. "Get out — we'll smash your cameras and your faces," a special agent bellowed when the hacks arrived in the doorway. This, they should have known by now, was not the best way to handle the press.

"Hardboiled George Golding's special prohibition squad shot a fleeing suspect yesterday in the City Hall Square building," the *Chicago Tribune* blared. The city's newspapers had plenty of eyewitnesses to feature, and none of them put the special agents in a positive light. Office workers had crowded around the hacks to tell about being violently shoved back into their offices "by a couple of boys who looked like college students and who dressed as such but who kept displaying gold badges and yelling, 'We're federal agents: get back.' " Miss Constance Bemis, a secretary, told reporters that Agent Franklin "acted as though he were in a frenzy" as he chased the suspect. She added: "I was standing in the hall when the men ran out, the agent with gun in hand . . . I nearly fainted when I saw the other man crumple to the floor as the bullet struck him."

The papers railed against Golding's "terrorist" tactics — first the Beatty shooting and now this — and called for his dismissal. Editorials and analysis about the raid dominated the city's front pages. The *Tribune* even used the City Hall Square incident to indict the entire Prohibition Bureau. "All previous records for brutality, depravity, and utter ruthlessness in prohibition enforcement were broken during the last 60 days, when dry sleuths in widely scattered sections of the country killed three citizens, maimed dozens more, and even seduced a schoolgirl — all 'in the line of duty.' " That proved to be the last straw. The killings and the ruined schoolgirl had nothing to do with Golding, but it was because of him that the news was now flying around the country on the wires. The special agent in charge wasn't going to be able to brazen this one out.

The state's attorney charged Agents Franklin and Gill with "assault with intent to commit murder," and neither U.S. Attorney Johnson nor the bureau publicly supported them, as they had Caffey. Willebrandt was so upset at Golding's recklessness that she supposedly never spoke to him again. The Treasury Department called Golding back to Washington, and he left without a word to the press or his men. Yellowley, Chicago's bureau administrator, abruptly disbanded Golding's squad, calling a press conference to make the announcement. The Prohibition Bureau dismissed a handful of the special agents from the service and reassigned the rest. Two weeks later, Yellowley named Jamie as the acting special agent in charge and told him to build an entirely new team.

Just a few years before, prohibitionists even in their worst nightmares wouldn't have been able to conjure up the need for someone like George Golding — or even Alexander Jamie. At first the federal prohibition force was primarily a PR outfit. Veteran temperance activist Georgia Hopley, hired by what was then the Prohibition Unit of the Bureau of Internal Revenue, spent the first two years of the dry era on the road, heralding the Eighteenth Amendment.[*] She loved the assignment. The stout, stern-faced woman, always in her signature birdcage dresses, found herself inspired by the transformation she was seeing everywhere: sober faces, healthy faces. America on the rise. At one stop in 1922 a

[*] The Bureau of Prohibition was promoted to independent status within the Treasury Department in April 1927, seven months after Eliot became an agent. The agency was undergoing long-overdue professionalization at the time, including the establishment of formal law-enforcement training for agents and the institution of the Special Agency Division.

reporter asked her if more women were drinking today than ever before. Hopley snorted, but with a smile, as if a child had said something funny. "A certain type, perhaps," she said. "But not the backbone of the nation."

Hopley saw what she wanted to see. She loved to quote "the highest authority of the Nation," President Warren G. Harding, a personal friend, on the glories of dry America: "In every community men and women have had an opportunity now to know what prohibition means. They know that debts are more promptly paid, families better fed and clothed, and more money finds its way into the savings banks. The liquor traffic was destructive of much that was most precious in American life. In another generation I believe that liquor will have disappeared not only from our politics but from our memories."

The president, of course, did not for a minute believe his own words. White House staff, if not President Harding's good friend Miss Hopley, had seen the great man casually drinking alcohol in the Oval Office on more than one occasion. But even such a sight could not possibly have swayed the dusty-dry sisters and brothers of the movement. It made sense in those early years that Georgia Hopley would serve as the public face of the dry force. The prohibition movement had been founded and largely driven by women — women who had seen husbands, brothers, and fathers destroyed by drink, their weekly paychecks washed away, their children gone hungry. In the second half of the nineteenth century, when the movement began to pick up momentum, the typical American adult knocked back ninety bottles of 80-proof liquor every year. The rise in the popularity of spirits, thanks in part to modern distilling innovations, had created a new class of drunks: addled, unrepentant, irredeemable. Something had to be done. Righteous members of the Woman's Christian Temperance Union, Hopley's predecessors, sought to change hearts and minds by gathering in front of saloons to pray and cry.

Yet even decades later, after years of the WCTU marching through the streets of major cities, of the Anti-Saloon League declaring (and proving) that its sole purpose was "administering political retribution" against politicians who opposed prohibition, few Americans seemed to believe a booze ban could ever actually happen. When the Volstead Act — the Eighteenth Amendment's enforcement arm — went into effect in January 1920, a full year after the constitutional amendment was adopted, the new reality caught many by surprise, emotionally if not intellectually. "The whole world is skew-jee, awry, distorted and altogether perverse,"

Secretary of the Interior Franklin K. Lane wrote in his diary the day before the liquor ban officially took hold. True enough, the world was now skew-jee, but prohibitionists, despite their astounding legislative success, proved to be deadly wrong about what would occur next. Most activists believed that removing the temptation — the brewery-owned saloons on almost every commercial corner of every decent-size town in the country — would cause the desire to fade away, like smoke from a dying fire. Never mind that the booze business was — or had been — the fifth largest in the country, or that to millions of Americans drinking was as culturally significant as marriage. Never mind that the timing was particularly poor. The World War, finally ended in 1919, had brought about a most unexpected lucidity. Millions of Americans suddenly seemed to accept that life was short and ugly, and that maybe there was nothing to come after it. The war had changed everything — art, music, politics, literature. The old world had been swept away completely, as if it never existed. Americans in the 1920s wanted to listen to jazz and to dance, and they did. They wanted to buy automobiles and drive them fast, and they did. Most of all, they wanted to drink. Prohibition — a strange remnant of that old world, somehow renewed — had to be defied. They might not have been able to articulate why, but legions of Americans felt a kind of moral imperative to defy it. No law had ever inspired such contempt across the country.

Instead of the tranquility and good will the prohibitionists had expected, the Eighteenth Amendment brought turmoil and violence. And, somehow, alcohol. It was everywhere, more so than ever before. The Volstead Act hardly worried anyone. Indeed, for the right kind of entrepreneur, the possibilities of Prohibition proved endless. A huge, long-established industry had been wiped off the books with the arrival of the constitutional amendment, but the trucks, equipment, supply chains, relationships, know-how, and other accoutrements of the liquor business were still there in the real world, waiting for a new breed of men who didn't mind taking new kinds of risks. The spoils would go to those who thought big — and showed no mercy. In Chicago, the country's second largest city, vice king Johnny Torrio was such a man. Torrio brought in a twenty-one-year-old hood from Brooklyn named Al Capone shortly before the Volstead Act went into effect. Torrio's gang took control of many of Chicago's breweries, whose owners at first saw the gangsters as saviors. Without the underworld's intervention, the brewers would have had to produce yogurt or soft drinks to stay in operation, and where was the self-respect in that?

Few members of Congress — or managers in Washington's Prohibition offices, for that matter — had anticipated this. Gangsters were now industrialists. The new economic landscape meant hoodlums suddenly did everything on a much bigger scale than they ever had before. Such was especially the case in Chicago, which overnight became the headquarters of Prohibition resistance. Once upon a time the city's hoods ducked into alleys when they saw a copper. Now they greeted him warmly and slipped him an envelope. They had no other choice; any half-competent patrolman with a functional nose could find beer being brewed in the city. Next came payoffs to judges and politicians. The notoriously corrupt William "Big Bill" Thompson, Chicago's mayor since 1915, had primed the city for the gangland takeover of its police department and judicial system. By 1923, as much as a million illicit dollars a month were going into the pockets of Chicago officialdom. A visit the following year showed Mabel Willebrandt just how bad things were. In the nation's second-largest city, she sneered, police suffered from "sleeping sickness" — her picturesque way of saying they were taking money to look the other way. When Prohibition agents conducted raids on speakeasies, they usually found cops happily drinking at the bar.

This scared Willebrandt. Trying to enforce the law, she said, was "like trying to dry up the Atlantic Ocean with a blotter." The assistant attorney general hadn't been a prohibitionist before she joined the Justice Department. She freely admitted that she'd "had liquor in my own home in California." But she and her allies believed that if the government allowed the Volstead Act to go unenforced, terror and violence would take over society. Criminal gangs would run the country. That was why, in the middle of the decade, she had helped run Hopley and other temperance veterans out of the bureau and replaced them with a force of professionally trained law-enforcement agents. Of course, by then it was too late. Gang control had already arrived — again, especially in Chicago. "The skies were black with smoke from 'alky' cooking plants, beer was as easy to get as water, and it was a foolhardy policeman who dared molest a citizen peddling whiskey that would eat a hole in a battleship," noted Elmer Irey. No place in America took to illicit drinking like Chicago. Songwriter Fred Fisher called it "that toddlin' town," and he meant it literally. Hundreds of men stumbled and twirled around the downtown Loop every evening, looking for a taxi or the steps to the elevated trains. The booze that inspired most of these late-night interpretive dances came from Torrio's so-called Outfit, which dominated the bootlegging scene from its headquarters in the western suburb of Cicero. "Chicago, the world's Fourth City, has fallen," a local reporter wrote of the Outfit's sudden and extreme rise to power. This news quickly spread far beyond the Chicago metropolitan area. When Torrio's forces, led by young Capone, took over Cicero's elections in 1924, the *New York Times* high-lighted the Chicago Problem on its front page, declaring that "bullets, bricks, blackjacks and fists were used generally instead of ballots to decide the issue." The election, wrote another paper, was the underworld "announcing that it realized its power."

Chicago had become the symbol of all that had gone so wrong in the war on liquor. Willebrandt understood that the federal government *had* to take a stand there. She had sent Golding because the city needed her best general. And when he flamed out, poisoning public opinion, she decided to keep the special agency squad in place, even with three of its members facing murder charges. The fight would go on. For Prohibition, it was Chicago or bust.

It really couldn't have worked out better for Eliot. He was one of the few special agents on Golding's team to be kept on in Chicago. He'd received valuable experience under a daring leader but not so much that he'd ended up in the dock. And now he would serve under his own brother-in-law, who was more careful and professional than Golding, and who took Eliot's best interests to heart.

It was far from certain, however, that Alexander Jamie would be able to remain in his new position for long. Before returning to Washington, Golding had done his best to destroy the man who was his logical successor. Jamie "is lazy and takes three hours to do that which another man would do in fifteen minutes," Golding wrote in a memo to Yellowley. "He is sort of Bolsheviki, all the time expressing to other agents statements relative to his political power . . . and how he could have the Administrator's post or mine whenever he desired." The attack almost worked. Yellowley fired Jamie, only to have Johnson intervene on the assistant administrator's behalf. Jamie was unemployed for twenty-four hours before he was returned to the bureau's ranks and given the promotion — albeit without additional pay — to acting special agent in charge. Though he probably never saw Golding's memo, Jamie knew Hardboiled had gone around the office slandering him. Already he was self-conscious about having only a grammar-school education and having gotten his start as an investigator by informing on union efforts for the Pullman Company, the Chicago maker of railroad cars and a notorious union buster.

(When Eliot was in college, Jamie helped him land second-shift work at the Pullman plant as a stacker, a dangerous and physically draining job.) Now that Jamie had the position he'd always wanted, albeit on an interim basis, he was determined to prove that he belonged in the corner office. The disastrous Beatty and Adams shootings notwithstanding, he intended to lead an active, aggressive special agency unit.

To that end, his first target as acting special agent in charge was a big one: Chicago Heights, the industrial town about thirty miles directly south of downtown Chicago that Lorenzo Juliano called home. Nearby Inland Steel, producing a million tons of ingots every year, promised the Heights economic stability, which helped bring one of the first major highways straight through town, giving the burg the nickname "The Crossroads of the Nation." The highway also made it a perfect place for bootleggers. Jamie and other bureau muckety-mucks believed the town was central to the syndicate's statewide operations. They had good reason to think so: a lot always seemed to be going down in this small workingman's city of twenty-two thousand. The dry law, the *Tribune* declared, had "transformed the peaceful industrial community with its happy homes into a haven for a great alcohol cooking ring, a terrain of contention, locale of alky wars and a battle ground of bootleggers." In 1926, the Heights's preeminent liquor boss, the Sicilian gangster Philip Piazza, had been ostentatiously murdered in front of his café in the middle of the day. Since then, more than twenty men had been killed in the town's "alky wars." Another Sicilian, Joe Martino, president of the local branch of the Unione Sicilione, stepped forward after Piazza fell, but others also were in the mix. The Torrio gang had been taken over by Al Capone after rival bootleggers seriously wounded Torrio in a 1925 attack. The Outfit's influence stretched across most of the metropolitan area, and that included the Heights. Still, much of the violence seemed to be spurred not by Martino or Capone but by the trigger- and bomb-happy Juliano, a dapper, chubby man with a sleek little mustache fit for a cinema comic. The police believed him to be responsible for at least eight murders, including the beating death of a paramour he suspected of being a double agent. But the blood continued to flow even after Juliano's capture. Earlier in the year, gangsters had shot to death South Chicago Heights police chief Lester Gilbert, who had resisted bribery attempts and even seized some of the bootleggers' trucks. No one had been arrested for the murder.

Jamie decided he would break the Chicago Heights syndicate by taking out Martino and infusing the town's bootlegging ranks with fears of turncoats. Of course, such a bold objective would require undercover work. It would require agents who knew the area, who understood the far South Side. His young brother-in-law, he recognized, fit the bill. The South Side was the city's — the region's — industrial heartland, its own world, cut off as if by an impassable moat from the glamorous bustle of downtown Chicago and the wild bohemia of the North Side. Instead of classical skyscrapers and elegant townhouses, the South Side offered "ungainly, picturesque outlines of steel mills with upturned rows of smoking stacks, of gas-holders and of packing-houses." The noise — "a mighty clattering and reverberating of . . . echoes" — was ceaseless.

This was Eliot Ness's world; he grew up on the far South Side and identified as a Southsider, not a Chicagoan. The difference from the rest of the city — in attitude, in outlook, in experience — was unmistakable. On the far South Side, men came home from work singed and defeated, a retreating army. Everyone drank, the men so they could face another day, the women so they could face their husbands. "I would not want to live there for anything in the world," the Italian playwright Giuseppe Giacosa wrote after visiting Chicago in 1898. He would not have thought differently four years later when Eliot was born, on April 19, 1902.[*] He would not have thought differently eighteen years after that, when Eliot, still with no experience of any other part of town, graduated from Christian Fenger High School. Giacosa hated most everything he saw in the city, with its "extraordinary number of sad and grieved persons," but he thought the South Side was by far the worst. Smoke hung from the air there like drapery. The neighborhood streets, hemmed in by steel plants and ironworks, "seemed to smolder a vast unyielding conflagration," the mammoth blast furnaces glowing orange and white throughout the night. Children on the way to school clumped through hard granules of soot that fell from the sky like hail, through a deadened landscape where not even "a ghost of the sun shines."

Eliot's neighborhood, Kensington, started out as a railroad stop called Calumet Junction. The Illinois Central and Michigan Central Railroads met there in 1852 during the track-building boom that settled the West and made Chicago a central player in the country's life. In the four decades that fol-

---

[*] Eliot's birth date would be entered incorrectly in his college records, listing him as being born in 1903. Many news reports and even his cemetery memorial would give an incorrect age for him in the years that followed.

61

lowed, immigrant Irish, Germans, Scandinavians, and Italians poured into the area. The nearby company town of Pullman, with its nine thousand worker-residents, banned saloons, so Kensington served the need, earning the nickname Bumtown. Eliot arrived on the scene in the wake of a catastrophic Pullman strike that had radicalized the area. Bumtown was where embittered unionists came to drink, shout about injustice, and fall down. (During his seven years with the railroad-car company, Jamie spent his evenings following these men from pub to pub.) During the World War, crowds in Kensington jeered as young men from the neighborhood marched off to boot camp, because the boys wore the same uniform as the federal soldiers who had beaten down strikers back in 1894. The kids of the far South Side were notoriously aggressive, innately mean. The area produced first-rate athletes in unusual numbers during the first half of the twentieth century, boys like Tony Zale (Gary, Indiana) and George Mikan (Joliet) and Dick Butkus (Roseland), boys who would do anything to win, to escape.

Eliot didn't seem to fit. He was a mama's boy, the youngest — by far — of five children. His mother, Emma, a Norwegian immigrant like her husband, missed her three grown daughters, who had married and left the house, and so she coddled young Eliot. Un-

signed Albert Nabers, Eliot's new partner, and Eliot to go with the more experienced agent to meet Giannini. The agents drove over the next day. Eliot knew the Heights well enough to have spent as little time there as possible while growing up. The town's small downtown had some class, especially the Hotel Victoria, designed by Louis Sullivan, but it was a thin facade. Three blocks in any direction and you felt like you might be set upon by wild dogs. The *woof-chunk* of heavy machinery could be heard everywhere, all the time; in many parts of town it could be felt, a perpetual mini-earthquake, rattling cups and nerves. For Eliot, it was the feel of home, the feel of the South Side. The three agents strode into the downtown Cozy Corners saloon in iconic Wild West style, screwing their expressions into the kind of hardened, cynical looks they figured dirty agents had. A uniformed policeman stood at the bar, shooting the breeze with the bartender. Kooken sidled over and showed his badge. Neither the barkeep nor the cop blanched: they were expecting him. The bartender poured drinks — real drinks, not colas or near beer — and the dry agents found a booth in the back.

Eliot had hit it off right away with Nabers, a war veteran and a fellow college man. Years later he would describe Albert as "the handsomest man I have ever seen. He was built like a Greek God, with natural, light wavy hair." The Georgia native, only recently assigned to Chicago, had a gregarious, open-faced personality, as alien to Southside Chicagoans as Swahili. Eliot began inviting Albert to dinner at the Ness home on South Park Avenue. They didn't talk much about their work while under the Nesses' roof. Emma disapproved of her youngest son's career choice. A devout Christian Scientist, she hated the idea of her sweet-tempered boy spending his days around all those dishonest men in the dry service. Eliot, who as a child had dutifully attended church with his parents, tried to bring his mother around. "If there's anything you taught me, mother, it's to be honest," he told her. Eliot's father apparently didn't have an opinion on the subject. The baby of the family was — and remained — an afterthought to Peter Ness, who now, in his old age, wanted only to concentrate on the bakery he had spent so many years making a success. He had been nearly fifty years old when Eliot was born, and he'd already raised a clutch of children while struggling to get his business going. Eliot had worked at the bakery throughout his adolescence, but he never felt like he really got his father's attention. Peter had more than twenty bakers to oversee, as well as "store girls" and drivers and a stable man. He paid attention to every detail. Later in life Eliot would try to put a positive spin on this monomania. "He never had a lot to say, but when he did speak, I knew it was something worth listening to," he said of his father. "I always took it to heart because I didn't see him all that much." With his singular focus, Peter didn't like anything to upset his equilibrium, at work or at home. Emotions were kept on an even keel around him, never too high or too low. Eliot learned early to hold back his feelings, to express himself only in reasonable tones. This could be stressful. While in grade school he began a lifelong habit of biting his fingernails, gnawing away whenever he faced a decision or a school exam.

Eliot's nervousness, his inclination to bottle up his feelings, no doubt made Albert Nabers attractive as a colleague and friend. Albert was loud. He was larger than life. Eliot viewed him as the brother he never had, one close to his own age and who shared his interests. (Eliot's brother, Charles, was more than a decade older than him, his three sisters older still.) They might not have talked about it over dinner at the Ness home, but the two young federal agents relished their work. It was no moral crusade for them, as it had been for the dry movement's founders; they weren't concerned with the rightness or wrongness of an after-work beer. But the call proved no less powerful. They had the sense they were doing something important. Neither man understood what exactly that something was — not yet, anyway — but for now, the objective was almost beside the point. What mattered was that *they* mattered.

At least they thought they did, and working an undercover operation with Don Kooken surely helped that perception. After a few minutes of sipping their drinks and pretending to chitchat at the Cozy Corners, the agents looked up to find Giannini coming toward them, a big smile thumbtacked to his face. Kooken took charge of the conversation, and he impressed Eliot with the way he charmed the Italian with his "slow, quiet, Indiana drawl." Soon enough, Giannini passed over $250. The four men clinked glasses, drank, laughed. The gangster seemed pleased with himself. He already had "things pretty well arranged with the police and Prohibition Department," Giannini said, but he admitted this was a real coup. Eliot couldn't help but swell with pride. "We, of course, were the Special Agents," he would report.

The dry agents left the saloon a bit tipsy and feeling good about themselves, but they knew this successful meeting was only the beginning. No one — certainly not Jamie — cared about nailing small fry like Johnny Giannini. The bureau wanted to build a conspiracy case, "which would include corrupt police, city officials, and perhaps Prohibition

68

agents." Which meant the three agents had to prove to the syndicate that they deserved to make *real* money, that they had ambition. A couple of nights after the bonhomie at the Cozy Corners, Kooken took Eliot and Albert on a tour of the Heights. Their chauffeur was Frank Basile, a smiley twenty-seven-year-old who had been a member of a "Kensington cooking gang" before getting busted on Volstead violations. Basile, who spoke fluent Italian, had turned government informer to stay out of jail, and now he worked for the Chicago Prohibition office for $5 a day and expenses. He and Eliot, both from Kensington and the same age, knew each other from the neighborhood. They quickly became close; Eliot considered him all but a fellow agent.

Basile drove the men up and down the Heights's outer streets, and it didn't take long before first one and then another car fell in behind them. The next night, the dry agents slowly toured another part of town, and again two sedans mimicked their pace and their every turn. Both nights they ended up at the Cozy Corners for some drinks. It was a fine place to be — a haven for bootleggers from all over the region who used the sparkling new highway that cut through the small city. "They would leave their cars with the bartender, and the cars would be driven away by members of the Chicago Heights alcohol mob," Eliot would relate later. "The drivers from out of town would stay at the bar, drinking, or avail themselves of what the brothel located on the second and third floors had to offer."

Eliot did not admit to availing himself of the offerings on the second and third floors, but he and his partners did do a fair amount of drinking on the ground level. While in college Eliot had discovered that he enjoyed booze, and becoming a Prohibition agent hadn't changed that. He had an illicit drink almost every evening — often more than one — before heading home to his parents' house. And now he was drinking as part of the job — and getting a bit loud about it, laughing and slapping backs. Even Basile joined in, pretending he didn't understand when anyone spoke Italian to him; he was posing as "just Mexican," just a boozer. It was an enjoyable way for the men to build up their bona fides.

That done, Kooken and his two junior agents returned to the Heights on another night, this time leaving their car on a back road outside of town and walking in through farm fields and empty lots, each taking a separate route. They met up in an alley after satisfying themselves that they'd avoided the "Mafia scouts" — fledgling gangsters at unofficial checkpoints, gas-station attendants on the edge of town, grandmothers peering out living-room windows. Now, keeping to the shadows, they followed their noses, for the stink of fermenting mash was almost impossible to hide. They put in miles during the night, staying low in the darkness as they came up on farmhouses and squat suburban homes, and then doubling back again for a second pass. The men found more than a dozen illegal brewing operations and took "careful notes," which they knew they'd need for search warrants. The next day, and for the rest of the week, they made sure to be back out in the open, especially at the Cozy Corners, laughing it up, drinking, being seen. Finally, they sought out Giannini again. They made plain they knew where most of the stills in the Heights were — and that they wanted to be real partners with the Martino crew. Giannini excused himself, leaving the three special agents and Basile to sit and worry. Albert slammed back a whiskey; Eliot chewed on his thumb. Soon, two large men loomed over the table.

"Come and talk to the boss," the twin statuary said.

The agents stepped through to a back room, where they found Giannini and a "big, swarthy," heavy-shouldered man — Joe Martino. They barely bothered with pleasantries. Eliot, assigned the role of eager beaver, laid it out for the don of Chicago Heights: a full partnership, all aspects of the business,

71

including gambling and the other rackets. They could provide protection for everyone in the organization — everyone they knew about. Martino gave the kid a hard-eyed appraisal, before sitting back and sweeping the lot of them with a half-lidded gaze.

"How do I know you can put in the fix?" he said.

The agents waved their badges like backup singers. "Money will do anything," one of them said.

"How much?"

Kooken smiled. "First we've got to see how much it's worth to you."

Eliot, "the hungry one," threw his knowledge of the syndicate's operations in Martino's face. The forty-five-year-old Mob boss had managed to stay out of jail — and the cemetery — for years while running a good-size bootlegging ring in a particularly violent corner of Chicagoland, but he apparently bought what this greenhorn agent was selling. He joked about owning Kooken, and local cops galore, and that he would own this pushy new kid, too. That made Eliot push harder still. The young agent loved the opportunity to assume a role, to take on a bigger and bolder personality than his own. He and Martino "had quite an argument about the amount to be paid," Eliot recounted later. Finally, they grudgingly agreed on a weekly payment amounting to a thousand dollars a month, and the special agents shoved away from the table. No one seemed especially happy with how they were leaving things.

Frank Basile, who'd been standing by the door like a servant, looked ashen as the agents turned toward him. He took Eliot's arm. "The silk-shirted Italian has just asked Johnny whether or not he should let you have the knife in the back," he whispered. The words penetrated slowly. Eliot stood there paralyzed. He noticed, for the first time, a lithe, stone-faced man in the background. He was indeed wearing a silk shirt. The other men in the room seemed to melt in place, Wicked Witch–like, leaving only this blank-eyed killer. "I felt young and alone at that minute," Eliot would admit years later. He felt like an amateur. Until Basile pointed him out, he hadn't even *noticed* this man who was proposing to kill him. Basile — his eyes locked on Eliot, searching for proof that he'd been heard — said the agent's name, snapping Eliot back into real time. Eliot knew now, if there'd ever been any doubt, that this was no game. He managed to leave without turning his back to the mystery man.

Eliot kept his paralyzing fear to himself. He didn't tell the other agents what the silk-shirted man had said. He was too ashamed. He couldn't accept that his fear was a normal and reasonable reaction. So the murderous query — spoken in Italian by the gangster, who assumed none of the federal men understood the language — did not get factored into the agents' next move. Even if Eliot hadn't been embarrassed by his terror, he wouldn't have dared hold back the operation. He believed they were close. A thousand dollars for the three of them — Basile was just the driver and got nothing — was a good start, but not exactly a partnership. They had more work to do to prove their worth to Martino, to prove their power. There was only one way to do that: show the Mob why they should be taken seriously.

Not long after the meeting, Eliot and Albert stood on the side of the highway outside of town, stamping their feet and clapping their hands to beat back the creeping numbness in their extremities. It was late and there wasn't much traffic, but eventually the cold night disgorged two sets of massive headlamps. The agents stepped into the road and brought the booze-laden trucks to a gurgling, sliding halt. Moving quickly, shouting over one another, they yanked the drivers out of their cabs, "squeezed their balls and beat the shit out of them, hit them with clubs," recalled a bootlegger who worked with Martino. "It looked as though the shipment would not be delivered, but then money changed hands, and the trucks got through," the bootlegger said, amazed at the audacity of the move. Martino's crew, he said, now understood that the agents "wanted to be a fifty percent partner in the stills and the whorehouses."

Eliot and Albert continued to hang around the Cozy Corners and collect their money, which they dutifully turned over to Jamie. Kooken moved on to another case, but the two younger agents made it clear to Giannini that they would take Kooken's share as well every week. They also began pocketing $100 for each independent "alky cooker" in the area they reported to the Martino gang. The weekly grind of taking bribes and getting drunk soon paled, though. Nothing ever came of it. Their hijacking gambit hadn't paid off. They had made a place for themselves in the crew, but while they were taking in good money week after week, they weren't being given more responsibility. They couldn't find out who else the gang was bribing or how exactly Martino's distribution network worked. "It was apparent," Eliot wrote, "that we were not going to be taken into the confidence of the gang any further."

As the calendar flipped to November, the head office told the agents they would have to make do with the evidence from their nocturnal treks around the Heights and their meetings with Giannini and Martino. Volstead violations and bribery were penny-ante stuff in the grand scheme of things, but better than nothing. Eliot and Albert obtained search warrants for eighteen stills. The stills were relatively small, but they were good enough to mobilize the special agency unit and garner the loan of a clutch of Prohibition agents.

However disappointed he must have been at being unable to put together a conspiracy case, Eliot decided to make the best of the situation. That meant hitting the Cozy Corners hard, at the height of business. Eliot found himself teamed up not with Albert but with another young special agent looking to make his mark, Marty Lahart, a sparkly-eyed Irish kid who'd been one of Golding's favorites. Accessorized with sawed-off shotguns and with a brood of Prohibition agents in tow, the two men stormed into the saloon. They planted their feet as if to release dueling jump shots and called out: "Everybody keep their places, this is a federal raid!" Stunned silence met the announcement, followed by the thump of weaponry hitting the floor. These were mostly customers and freelancers, not Martino's men; nobody wanted a shoot-out with federal agents, especially when the G-men clearly had the drop on them. The Prohibition agents herded the saloons' customers and staff to a wall and began to frisk them, while Lahart scooped up as many discarded guns as he could. He jammed four revolvers in his belt and slung a second shotgun over his shoulder. Eliot no doubt had told him about the delights on the second and third floors. Lahart took the stairs at a lope. "Everybody keep their places!" he yelled again as he bounded down the brothel's hallway and banged open doors to expose the prostitutes in their natural habitat. These girls were not prone to hysterics. They'd seen a lot of violence; they'd been on the receiving end of it and accepted it as normal. One girl, nonplussed at the sight of Lahart weighed down with guns, cracked: "Look who's here. Tom Mix."

The Cozy Corners raid was about sending a message — and nothing else. The eighteen stills, hidden in houses and industrial buildings around town, were the real target. Agents spent the night smashing through doors and carting away brewing equipment and ledgers. "Luckily, the raids were successful," Eliot recalled, "and in most places we captured prisoners, machinery and alcohol."

Not all the evidence made it into the evidence lockup. Late that night, Eliot showed up on the doorstep of Armand Bollaert, his University of Chicago fraternity brother. Bollaert followed his friend out to the curb, where he found the trunk of Eliot's car packed to the gunwales with liquor. "It was the most beautiful collection of booze in the city of Chicago," Bollaert would remember years later. Without a word between them, the two men hefted the alcohol into the house.

You never knew what you were going to find on the side of the road in Chicago Heights, but a dead body was never a bad guess. That winter, it became a great guess.

Martino, inevitably, started the trend. On Thursday, November 29, with news trickling through town that an indictment had come down as a result of the raids, Eliot and Albert arrived at Martino's home and politely knocked on the door. The gangster let them into the house, where the agents read him an arrest warrant. Martino had a revolver in his belt, and when the agents presented him with the warrant, he took out the gun and tossed it onto the floor. He stepped to the closet to retrieve his coat and hat, but he didn't make it. He broke down. "He became deathly sick and we had trouble getting him to the station," Eliot reported.

Martino understood what his arrest meant: he was now a liability to his fellow Chicago Heights gangsters — and to Capone. Everyone knew prosecutors would offer him a deal to talk, and no one could say for sure he wouldn't. He spent the night in jail, and in the morning he posted a $10,000 bond. Around midday, his driver dropped him in front of his "soft drink parlor" on East Sixteenth Street in the Heights, where he stood on the curb and considered the crisp afternoon. A black sedan turned the corner at Wallace Street and eased down the main drag. The windows were rolled down despite the cold. All at once, Martino toppled backward like a narcoleptic — the witnesses all said they heard nothing — and the car continued to glide along the street, slowly disappearing into the gray day. Martino sprawled on the sidewalk in his own gore, his hands still in his pockets. He'd been pierced by a profusion of bullets. Men, women, and children gathered around to gawk at the town's best-known citizen. "He apparently had not been [back] in the Heights for more than two minutes," Eliot would marvel after seeing the police report.

No one had any illusions about why the powerful Joe Martino now had to be swept up like a kicked Halloween pumpkin. Assistant District Attorney Dan Anderson told reporters that the new indictment clearly had served as the gangster's death warrant.

What was left of the Chicago Heights liquor ring began to unravel fast. A day after the murder, a massive explosion rocked Wellington Avenue on the West Side. Brewer Nick Guletto, noticeably nervous since being arrested along with Martino, had apparently gotten careless while operating a five-hundred-gallon still. He staggered from the building and collapsed. He died shortly after arriving at the county hospital. Ten days later, an unidentified man — police suspected it was Johnny Giannini, also named in the indictment — was found outside of town with two bullet holes in his head. He'd been thrown from a car.

After another three days, a fourth body turned up. At 7 a.m. on Wednesday, December 12, a man walking to work on 127th Street found a corpse lolling in a drainage ditch. The way the limbs were twisted, he obviously hadn't fallen where he lay. The dead man had been shot through the right eye four times.

The police at the scene didn't recognize the victim. Just another expendable junior goon, they figured. But shortly after the corpse arrived at a funeral home near the Kensington police station, someone identified him. The dead man wasn't a mobster. He was Frank Basile. The police placed a call to the Chicago Prohibition office. Within the hour, a clutch of federal agents arrived at the funeral home, rolling up in matching black sedans. They fished a calendar out of Basile's pocket. It had been filled out until 6:30 Monday evening.

U.S. Attorney Johnson, his mind on the bigger picture, made a bloodless public statement about the murder. "Basile was a government witness and was to have been one in the future," he said. "There is no doubt why he was killed. We will cooperate with the police to solve this murder." Eliot took the news much harder. Basile wasn't just a government witness to him; he was a colleague and a friend. When he saw Basile at the funeral home, laid out on a slab in a rubber body bag, he "felt hot tears stinging the corner of my eyes, a roaring in my ears." He barely held it together. Had he been responsible for Frank's death? Because he pushed so hard at that meeting with Martino that the man in the silk shirt felt compelled to offer his services? Because he couldn't understand Italian — or Neapolitan or whatever the hell it was — and needed his friend to tell him what was said? He would never know. He'd tell Edna — and many others over the years — about Frank Basile.

However unsettled he might have been, Eliot refused to be cowed by the murder of one of the bureau's own. He became even more determined to bring down the booze ring: it was now personal. He and Albert made a point of being seen going about their business in the Heights, even though their cover as corrupt agents had been blown with the raid. They kept at it even after the police arrested a suspect in Basile's murder: a small-time goombah named Tony Feltrin. They kept at it even after news got out that Feltrin had been found hanging by his necktie in a cell at the Kensington police station. Coasting around town in their government sedan, Eliot couldn't help but feel eyes on him at all times. Everyone seemed to understand that this was now war. He and Albert kept sawed-off shotguns in their coat pockets. At restaurants, Eliot recalled, "We always took a corner table as the danger of our undertaking was becoming more imminent." The jumpiness, the constant worry, became a habit. More than two decades later, long after leaving law enforcement, Eliot would still always sit at corner tables in restaurants, his back to the wall. He quietly, bashfully, smiled when friends ribbed him about it.

Which is not to say Eliot's worrying was pure paranoia. Chicago's Prohibition Bureau office, noticing the collection of bodies piling up in little Chicago Heights, decided there was a conspiracy case there after all. The bureau ratcheted up its investigation once again, focusing anew on tying the liquor ring's operations to city officials. Yellowley and Jamie pushed for more evidence, which meant more harassment at clubs and "soda parlors," more interviews with suspects, more eavesdropping on conversations — and more violence from increasingly harried and desperate bootleggers. Three days after Christmas, while on one of their cruising tours of the town, Eliot and Albert noticed "a flashy new car" with a lone occupant right behind them for block after block. Albert punched down on the accelerator of their Cadillac —

and so did the car behind. Next he slowed to a crawl, and so did their pursuer. Finally, following Eliot's direction, he swung into a residential neighborhood, found a narrow street, and slid the car "diagonally across the street . . . forming a block for the car behind us." Eliot leapt from the Caddy and grabbed the driver, pinning his arms to the wheel. Albert ran around the back of the car and pushed the barrel of his shotgun through the open passenger-side window. The man, who appeared to speak only Italian, was unfamiliar to them; they couldn't recall ever seeing him at the Cozy Corners or any of the other gang hangouts in the area. But they found a gun on him, the numbers filed off. It was loaded with dumdum bullets, the kind that expands on impact, spreading the damage. Eliot, still thinking about his friend Frank, still blaming himself, believed he was the target.

"This gun," he said, "was obviously meant for me."

CHAPTER 4
FLAUNTING THEIR BADNESS

At 5 a.m. on January 6, 1929, a dozen Chicago police cruisers arrived at an undeveloped lot on East Ninety-fifth Street. The cars carried officers three abreast in the front and back seats. None of them knew why they had been sent to this desolate spot early on a Sunday morning. Then a small army of federal agents climbed out of parked sedans, their collars pulled up high, hats squashed down low. The agents fanned out in the subfreezing morning air, providing instructions to the cops, handing out arrest warrants. When a policeman clapped his hands to ward off the cold, he was told to cut it out. Agents gave each car a specific assignment and a time frame within which to accomplish it. Police officers were traded out with Prohibition agents so that each automobile was mixed. The cars idled in the lot for no more than fifteen minutes, the mission hammered home emphatically. Then doors slammed, engines revved, and the cars pulled onto the street and ripped southward, heading for the Chicago Heights city limits.

This was the new world order. Republican Herbert Hoover, an unabashed dry, had just been elected president of the United States in a landslide over the Democrats' wet candidate, Al Smith. The president-elect publicly declared that the country faced a law-and-order crisis, and so the Chicago Prohibition office wanted to make clear to Washington that it was vigorously pursuing its mission. On Friday Jamie had told the press that Chicago Heights was "a Mafia nest and [bootlegging] ring operating in Chicago, St. Louis, Cincinnati and New York." The Chicago office made sure the newspapers knew about the arrest of the man who had been following Eliot and Albert, a hoodlum called Mike Picchi. "George E. Q. Johnson and State's Attorney John A. Swanson cooperated yesterday in the speedy indictment of an alleged Chicago Heights bootleg gangster, suspected of plotting the assassination of two prohibition agents," the Tribune reported. Jamie and Johnson were setting the scene for what was to come next.

Now, three days after that report, the papers were going to have a much bigger story. Someone arrested in the November raids clearly had talked, despite the best efforts of the area's Mob enforcers. The caravan of police and federal agents crossed into Chicago Heights shortly before dawn, crunching over the icy back roads where gangsters had been enthusiastically tossing bodies the past two months. The two lead cars, one of them carrying Chicago's deputy police commissioner, John Stege, split off from the rest and headed for city hall, where police headquarters was located. "It was felt that unless we took over the station," Eliot wrote, "hoodlums throughout the town would be given the alarm from the police station itself."

On days like this, Stege truly loved his life. He was a tubby little gray-haired man with round granny glasses and a double chin that swung like a hammock, but he carried himself with flair. He used to write a column for the *Chicago Herald and Examiner* headed by a photo of him holding a tommy gun. Somehow he pulled off the look. Now he told his men to wait on the front steps for a minute so he could enter the Chicago Heights police station alone. With daylight beginning to rub through the morning blackness, he turned and strut-waddled through the station's front doors. He held his badge above his head so the gold would catch the overhead lights.

"Where are the keys to this joint?" he bellowed, unable to suppress a smile.

Within moments, as Stege's men began to file through the door, he was unlocking the station's jail cells. They were empty except for one containing three women. Stege shooed them out.

"We'll need all the room we have in a few minutes," he said.

The desk sergeant huffed at this. "Who are you and what do you think you're doing?"

Stege's answer: "We're running the place for a while."

The outsiders placed everyone in the station house under arrest, except for those actually facing charges — the three women. They sent the women, all freelance prostitutes, out into the streets. Stege happily let news photographers take pictures as he put the Chicago Heights policemen into their own cells. He smiled proudly as the flashbulbs popped. He had been forced to resign from the Chicago Police Department eighteen months before when a newspaper revealed he had been convicted of murder when he was fifteen. He was a good cop, though, a reformed man, and everyone who worked with him knew it. So when the scandal subsided, the city had quietly brought him back into the department. This was his chance to prove to the public that he deserved the second chance.

The feds were happy to give Stege his moment. He was a longtime critic of gangster chic, decrying how smirking, well-dressed hoods "flaunt their badness, boast of their bloody conquests, jeer at the widows of their victims, scoff at the suggestion of retributive justice." He had shown contempt for the city's mobsters years before it became socially acceptable to do so.

With the police station under federal control, the hundred or so officers and agents out in the Heights could take their quarry by surprise. The raiders pulled up in front of small clapboard houses, two-story brick apartment buildings, and a warehouse that served as the syndicate's "distributing depot." They broke into twenty private residences, pulling men out of their beds, their wives screaming, children crying. Some of the hoodlums managed to take flight, with agents running them down in the street. Agents and officers reported in at the police station with their knees scraped up and hands bruised, their prisoners missing teeth. One bootlegger sat in a cell and sobbed into his hands. As a general rule, dry agents described mobsters strictly as dead-eyed murderers, nothing more. Eliot would do the same in his public comments, but he didn't actually have such a black-and-white view of them. He hated arresting men at their homes, in front of their wives and children. "It was astonishing what good family men some of them were," he would tell his wife two decades later. He added: "There would be a lot of emotion at the separation of the women and children from their men. In fact one of the hoodlums took it so hard he was sick all the way to the police station."

Agents brought twenty-five gangsters to the Chicago Heights police station that morning, along with dozens of guns and hundreds of boxes of ammunition. Over at the distribution depot on East Fourteenth Street, men with axes split open barrels and watched beer rush into the street. They also found four hundred slot machines, which they bashed up with ball-peen hammers. At his office in downtown Chicago, George E. Q. Johnson took responsibility for the town's takedown, declaring that Chicago Heights "had fallen into the hands of a syndicate which made millions of dollars through its monopoly of slot machines and booze." The *Tribune* triumphantly announced that "Chicago Heights, known as the most lawless town in Cook county, has been cleaned up."

By midday, paddy wagons ferried prisoners into the Loop, delivering them to the detectives' bureau for questioning. Later, the police brought Picchi into the county jail so all of the Heights goons could give the suspected assassin a good long look. No one admitted knowing him.

"None of the prisoners is talking," Jamie told the press. "Their silence smacks of the Mafia." He insisted they planned on charging Picchi with the murder of Joe Martino.

Standing around in the Prohibition Bureau office, Eliot watched Jamie grandstand for reporters. He watched agents laughing and roughhousing. He didn't want to join the celebration. He felt carved out, like he'd been kicked in the stomach. The exhilaration of the chase hadn't lasted long; now a black cloud was following along behind it. This was nothing new to Eliot. He had battled depression his whole life and never understood where it came from or what it meant. Deciding not to wait for his brother-in-law, he climbed into his car and drove home.

CHAPTER 5
THE CAPONE FANS

The Chicago Heights operation was an unmistakable success. The newspaper headlines said so, as did the memos the local Prohibition office sent to headquarters in Washington, DC. Unfortunately, the one valuable conclusion the Chicago bureau office could draw from the demise of the Chicago Heights bootleg syndicate was that Joe Martino had been a small fish. He was mostly just a traffic cop directing booze between Chicago and the southern reaches of the state. Al Capone had owned him, just as Capone owned almost every bootlegger in northern Illinois.

This should not have been a surprise to the Prohibition Bureau. By now Alphonse Capone was the best-known man in Chicago. He had arrived in the city only nine years before, just as the Volstead Act was going into effect. At the time, he had been barely old enough to vote — not that he did — and as round and amiable as a vaudeville comic.

Kids and mothers loved him. He set himself up as Al Brown, secondhand furniture dealer, with a storefront at 2220 South Wabash Avenue. His business card and dusty shop didn't fool anyone. The distinctive scars along the left side of his face suggested that Capone wasn't always as amiable as he appeared on first meeting. He glommed on to the notorious Johnny Torrio, becoming his right-hand man while running whores and providing muscle whenever and wherever needed. Capone had a soft spot for the prostitution game, but, no dummy, he quickly pivoted to where the real action was.

If Capone had simply wanted to make a nice, crooked living, he could have stuck with hookers, gambling, and shakedown rackets. These were tried-and-true businesses, mature businesses. But bootlegging, particularly in the big cities, was for men of ambition. Bootleggers wanted more than a big wad of cash at the end of each day. They wanted status, too. "We're big business without high hats," said Dean O'Banion, a flower-shop-owning gangster who controlled the North-side liquor trade — until he took a spray of bullets in 1924. Thugs finally could offer a service that respectable men wanted, and they were becoming wealthy beyond all conception by offering it. (Another local bootlegger, Terry Druggan, liked to show off his solid silver toilet seat.)

More than any of them, Capone became an object of fascination. The social worker Jane Addams despaired over how boys were "tremendously aroused" at the very sight of Capone and his cohorts. When his bulletproof black sedan rumbled through a neighborhood — any neighborhood — kids would crane their necks "as eagerly as for a circus parade," wrote the journalist Fred Pasley. "There goes Al," they'd say, and whistle in admiration. How could they react any other way? The man had style. The man had money and power. It wasn't as if kids — or anyone else — could look to the city's hard-hearted industrialists for inspiration. The economy was booming, but for average Chicagoans, the boom was the sound of an anvil coming down on their heads. "Morally," the writer Nelson Algren said of bootleggers, "they are sounder than the 'good' people who run Chicago by complicity." To young toughs around the city, the 1925 changing of the guard at the city's biggest gang — from the forty-three-year-old Torrio, heading off into semi-retirement, to the twenty-six-year-old Capone — represented something special, proof that merit could be rewarded, even in America. Twelve-year-old Louis Terkel, a student at John McLaren Elementary School on the West Side (he would later become known as "Studs"), listened raptly when two older classmates schemed for membership in the Forty-twos — "junior members of the Syndicate . . . What the Toldeo Mud Hens are to the New York Giants."

They dream of the Forty Two's as North Shore matrons dream of the Social Register. An older brother of one and a young uncle of the other, Forty Two alumni, are in the employ of Al Capone, one of our city's most highly regarded citizens. The uncle, a few years later, was seen floating down the drainage canal. And no water wings. It was a strange place for him to have gone swimming. The waters were polluted even then.

Such swimming jaunts had become rather commonplace. Capone — the Big Fella or Number One to his men, Scarface Al to the press — sought to lock down his new standing and expand his domain the only way he knew how: through terror. In 1926, seventy-six hoodlums were killed in Chicago as rival gangs fought it out over turf and hurt feelings. The following year, fifty-four more mobsters fell. Many of these killings happened in public, in drive-by machine-gun attacks. That meant civilians were falling, too — including an assistant state's attorney, William McSwiggin. Anyone walking in the Loop began to flinch, or outright panic, whenever they heard an automobile sliding around a corner at a decent clip. Many a man dived for cover only to have a taxicab scream past. The tension in the popular image of the bootlegger — glamorous modern-day prince, ugly cold-blooded killer — divided Chicagoans into two distinct classes: the romantic and the realistic, the stupid and the street-smart. One night at the Paramount Club downtown, the actress and vaudevillian Mildred Harris, Charlie Chaplin's ex, introduced a handsome young patron to fellow performer Sally Rand. "I want you to meet a sweet and lovely man," Harris purred. Rand, a dancer at the club, was impressed with the man's duds and manners — and flattered when he began hitting on her. But later, in the dressing room, one of the other dancers said, "You're certainly in high society tonight. Machine Gun Jack McGurn." Rand began to shake uncontrollably. She sneaked out the back door, forgetting her coat, and ran to her hotel, where she locked herself in her room.

Capone took offense at the suggestion there might be something wrong with the way he conducted business, whatever the reputation of McGurn, his chief hit man. This was the twentieth century. Laws were passé; the country had evolved beyond them. He told the *Chicago Tribune*'s Genevieve Forbes Herrick: "They talk to me about not being on the legitimate. Why, lady, *nobody's* on the legit. You know that and so do they." Capone needn't have worried so much about what delicate flowers like Sally Rand thought. Al couldn't please everybody, but he could please enough of them. Unlike Torrio before him, the Big Fella loved to talk to the press. He loved to have his picture taken, as long as the camera got his good side. " 'Public service' is my motto," he declared, flashing a pleasant, boyish smile that had become a front-page staple. By 1926, he was as recognizable in Chicago as Cubs pitching ace Grover Alexander, a regular Capone customer. He had become an honest-to-goodness hero to thousands, and not just to the kids on the street corner. Industrialists and bankers admired a good bootlegger, too.

The novelist Mary Borden, a native Chicagoan and an expatriate visiting her hometown for the first time in twelve years, was shocked to find herself one evening listening to a socialite "who spoke to me with tears in her eyes of Capone. I was already getting rather sick of the Scarface, but this suddenly made me feel quite ill; this sentimentality frightened me. I had heard, of course, of the Capone fans — he had more adorers, so I'd been told, than any movie star — but I had not expected the friends of my childhood to be numbered among them."

Even two years in, George E. Q. Johnson was still trying to figure out how to do his job.

The fifty-six-year-old Iowan's reputation

for unshakable honesty, along with a passing acquaintance with reformist U.S. senator Charles Deneen, had landed him the big office in Chicago's U.S. district attorney's office. His skills as a prosecutor, however, were suspect. During his thirty-year career in private practice, he had almost exclusively handled civil, not criminal, cases. For that entire time he remained little known outside his modest Swedish American community. But this inexperienced U.S. attorney did have the one characteristic that was absolutely essential for the job. When he came to Chicago from small-town Iowa as a young man, he began using the initial of his middle name so he would stand out from all the other George Johnsons in the big city. Not satisfied, he soon added a second, invented initial. You could say it was the E and the Q that would make him famous. Only a truly vain man would go after Al Capone.

Of course, even the vainest men in the city didn't covet the task Johnson had given himself, especially now. One month after the dry bureau's Chicago Heights raid, Chicago police sergeant Thomas Loftus answered a call reporting gunfire on the city's North Side. He arrived at 2122 North Clark Street at eleven in the morning and stepped inside the dank, smoke-filled industrial building. He smelled burnt gunpowder and heard a wet scraping sound. Then he spotted a man on

97

all fours crawling toward him. He recognized the man — Frank Gusenberg, a member of Bugs Moran's crew, one of the few remaining gangs that didn't answer to Capone. Gusenberg's clothing was shredded, blood streaked behind him like an airplane contrail. Only then did the policeman notice the horrors beyond — the herd of men bloodily arrayed against a brick wall, steam from their gore rising softly into the cold February air. An eyeball oozed on the slick concrete floor like a poached egg.

The newspapers ran with the story for weeks, until the horror lodged deep in the city's collective consciousness. "Can you imagine standing seven guys against the wall and running a machine gun and killing all of them?" said one Chicagoan, who, like millions of others, greedily read every word printed about the slayings. "You'd have to be crazy, right? Got to be doped up, no matter what kind of enemies they are." The St. Valentine's Day Massacre, as the killings came to be called, "was the worst thing that ever happened to Chicago as far as racketeering went." After years of winks and chuckles about the gang wars, public opinion had finally turned. Wives worried endlessly about their husbands' safety downtown during the day. Mothers kept their children from public playgrounds. Fear gripped every social stratum in the city. The violence, agreed the newspapers and politicians and everyone else, had to stop. Enough was enough. Even gangsters from other locales gaped at what was happening in the Second City. New York's Lucky Luciano, after a visit, called Chicago "a real goddam crazy place. Nobody's safe in the street."

The public's obsession with the Valentine's Day murders, which everyone assumed Capone had ordered, meant life became harder for George Johnson. Johnson had been pursuing a tax-fraud case against Capone from almost the day he took the oath as U.S. attorney for the Northern District of Illinois. Tax fraud wasn't an exciting course of action, but it looked like a promising one — at least to Johnson. U.S. Attorney General William Mitchell wasn't convinced. From Mitchell's vantage point in Washington, Johnson had been futzing around with tax statements for a couple of years now and had nothing meaningful to show for it, while Capone was lining people up against walls and mowing them down. So he sent backup to Chicago in the form of U.S. Assistant Attorney General William Froelich. Johnson suddenly realized his job might be on the line. He wrote a long, defensive reply to Mitchell, insisting "that I am quite able to do this." He knew income-tax charges worked against gangsters. He was convinced it was the best way to get Capone. After all, the tax laws had already been used to nail Al's brother Ralph and Al's bagman Jack "Greasy Thumb" Guzik, both convicted of tax evasion. But Johnson took Mitchell's hint: a tax case, no matter how promising, was no longer good enough. As the Internal Revenue agents working the case wrote: "Alphonse Capone is, without a doubt, the best advertised and most talked of gangster in the United States today. . . . [He] has been mentioned in connection with practically every major crime committed in Chicago within the last few years." Capone, in short, had become a PR problem. President Hoover, and so Attorney General Mitchell, wouldn't be satisfied with a mere conviction. They wanted to make an example of Capone.

CHAPTER 6
GOOD-HEARTED AL

Johnson understood the challenge he faced.

Golding had been a disaster, but Johnson, like Willebrandt, wasn't willing to walk away from the special agency squad. Willebrandt had once said she refused to believe that "out of our one hundred and twenty million population . . . it is impossible to find four thousand men in the United States who cannot be bought." Johnson wasn't sure about four thousand, but he knew there were indeed men out there who couldn't be bought: he was one of them. He became determined to find some of the others.

Johnson had listened to Willebrandt's discourses on Prohibition enforcement over the years. He had approved of many of her proposals, such as specialized training for dry agents and the transfer of the Prohibition Bureau from the Treasury Department to the Justice Department, both of which had eventually come to pass. By the fall of 1930, however, Willebrandt was gone. She had finally resigned in frustration and returned home to California to take up a private practice. But Johnson had not given up. With Mitchell providing pressure through Froelich, Johnson had pushed ahead in his fight against Capone, egged on by the gangster's continued consolidation of power in the months after the St. Valentine's Day Massacre. The U.S. attorney now decided he would adapt Willebrandt's dream of an incorruptible bureau — an impossibility — into an idea that *was* possible: a small, incorruptible team within Chicago's special agency squad. And this time he would create it himself, rather than send away to Washington for it. The Justice Department had been encouraging Johnson for months to make a "greater effort . . . to reach the sources of the bootleggers' supply and get at the revenue which finances the organized gangs." He would make this objective a priority, and turn it to his own aims. His special squad within the special squad, acting entirely on its own, would be limited to one goal only: squeezing Al Capone's income stream. Johnson figured there could be no better way to make the Big Fella buck and scream, to make him lose focus on what should matter most to him — being careful. You make a man angry, and he gets sloppy. The U.S. attorney's tax case needed Capone to get a little sloppy.

At the end of October 1930, Alexander

Jamie requested an indefinite unpaid leave from the Bureau of Prohibition so he could take over the Citizens' Committee for the Prevention and Punishment of Crime, popularly known as the Secret Six, a private, extralegal group dedicated to bringing crime under control in Chicago. The prominent local businessmen who bankrolled the committee had deemed it necessary because the police and the local Prohibition office were so corrupt and chronically underfunded. Jamie was taking Don Kooken with him as his deputy director. In a letter he included with his leave-request form, he made a bold recommendation. "As Mr. Kooken and myself are leaving the office, the question naturally arises as to someone to take the position of Special Agent in Charge," he wrote. "Insofar as I may be permitted to suggest, I would like to recommend to you for this position, Special Agent Eliot Ness who is the oldest Special Agent in this office in point of service and for approximately a year and a half has been considered my second assistant. Mr. Ness is known to you personally, as is also his reputation for honesty and ability to hold such a position."

The twenty-eight-year-old assistant to Jamie's assistant did not get the job. The older and far more experienced W. E. Bennett was named the special agent in charge in Chicago. But Jamie did not abandon his lobbying campaign on behalf of his brother-in-law. A short time later, on the recommendation of the new chief of the Secret Six, George Johnson opened up Eliot's federal personnel file. He noted that the agent had been commended for his "coolness, aggressiveness and fearlessness in raids." This was gravy: Johnson greatly respected Jamie's opinion and trusted that he would recommend the right man for the job. The Swedish American federal prosecutor took a good look at the photo clipped to the inside cover, at Eliot's stoic Scandinavian expression and perfectly coiffed blond hair. The young agent in the picture looked trustworthy and decent, just as Jamie had said. Johnson believed that honesty, loyalty, and reliability, not experience, would count above all else for the leader of his new operation. He sent for Eliot Ness.

Johnson's interview was perfunctory. After just a few minutes, he stood up and shook Eliot's hand. Everybody in the Chicago Prohibition office knew the U.S. attorney was putting together a special "Capone squad," and Eliot had hoped he would be chosen for the effort. When Johnson told him he not only was on the team but would be its operational leader — Froelich would serve as the unit's administrative supervisor — Eliot couldn't believe it. He would later recall that he "felt like leaping out of my chair and doing a jig right there in the office of the United

States District Attorney."

Legend has it that Eliot personally selected the men who would become known collectively as the Untouchables. "The success of the entire venture," he wrote in his memoir, "was predicated on there being no 'bad apples.' " To that end, he wrote, he went through mounds of personnel files delivered from Washington, picked out the agents with the best records, and put them "under the 'microscope.' " He weeded out any agent who had the slightest hitch in his background until he was left with only the most accomplished and upstanding men in the entire bureau.

In reality, Eliot, Johnson, and Froelich took pretty much anyone they could get. Good men were hard to come by in the Bureau of Prohibition, and so regional administrators resisted giving up their best agents, insisting the requested men were in the middle of cases or had subpoenas pending or specific skills the office could not do without.

In November and December 1930, after much bureaucratic wrangling, a handful of agents from around the country received orders to report to U.S. District Attorney Johnson for "temporary detail on special work." (Eliot himself wouldn't be officially put under Johnson's direction until December 8, which suggests he may not have had anything to do with selecting the team's original members.)* With a few exceptions, the agents assembled for the team were not the bureau's standouts. Some would qualify as misfits, a couple bordered on incompetent. Eliot, via his cowriter Oscar Fraley in *The Untouchables,* would write that he had specific, definitive qualities in mind for the team members: "single, no older than thirty, both the mental and physical stamina to work long hours and the courage and ability to use fist or gun. Nor would mere 'muscle men' do because each had to have special investigative techniques at his command." This checklist was straight out of George Golding's playbook; Golding liked to take young college men, blank slates he could mold into his own image. Eliot liked the idea of that, and it would become a famous part of Untouchables lore, but it's not what he ended up with. All of the agents in the squad were older than him, some by more than a decade. Most were married and had children. Thanks to Eliot's

* Twenty-five years later, in his memoir, Eliot would incorrectly remember the day he was given the job as September 28, 1929, a month before the stock market crash that hurtled the country into the worst economic tailspin in its history. He may have been remembering his return to school; the fall of 1929 was when he began a graduate-level police-administration course at his alma mater, taught by renowned criminologist August Vollmer.

memoir, ten men — plus Eliot, their boss — have been credited as the team's members, but in fact there never was a set lineup. Agents moved in and out of the unit during its brief existence for various official and nonofficial reasons; some worked on the operation for just a week or two before returning to their regular assignments. Only a few men stayed the course with Eliot from beginning to end.

George Golding's special agency unit had been the inspiration for the Capone squad, the operational and philosophical starting point. But though Eliot continued to admire the former special agent in charge, he would not run things like Golding had. Hardboiled Golding, for all his hail-fellow bonhomie, didn't like people. He didn't trust them, didn't think about their families or off-duty lives. He put their names in books, kept score, waited for them to turn on him or show they were fuck-ups. They usually proved him right, one way or another, and look where that had gotten him: bureaucratic oblivion in Washington. Eliot had learned a few things from Golding, tricks he would use for years to come, but he never took up his suspicious nature. He believed the best of people — until proven wrong. That would be his approach to the Capone squad, to the men who would help define his reputation.

From the start, three men were obvious

picks for the team. Joe Leeson, a celebrated agent in Detroit, was Don Kooken's brother-in-law and thus could be counted on to be a reliable man. Johnson had worked with Marty Lahart, the Golding veteran, and been duly impressed by the "tall, happy Irishman." Another former Golding man, Samuel Seager, was one of Jamie's favorites.*

Seager was just shy of forty when he joined the Capone squad. A former upholsterer and chiropractic student, his only law-enforcement experience before signing up for the Prohibition Bureau was as a prison guard in upstate New York. Despite this, he had proved himself an exceptionally capable agent, a natural-born cop. Jamie thought so highly of Seager that a couple of years earlier he had blocked the agent's request to transfer to another city. Seager had been shocked by the gung-ho amateurishness of the Golding operation and had wanted out. Jamie instead sent him on temporary assignment to southern Illinois, where, according to reports signed by Jamie, he single-handedly broke up

---

* Special Agent F. P. Neww and "special employee" E. A. Moore would be the first agents to join the team. They would stay with the squad for only a short period. That Albert Nabers didn't even make the short list for consideration is another indication that Eliot had little or nothing to do with choosing the unit's men.

a major bootlegging operation in East Saint Louis. Seager, known to friends as "Maurice," was one of the first men to report for duty with the Capone squad. Eliot, though not yet formally assigned to the operation, brought Seager up to speed on the plans for the team. Maurice would immediately see something special in Eliot: intelligence, determination, the capacity for loyalty. He would become Eliot's closest, most trusted colleague in the unit.

Joe Leeson's family connection to Kooken, now with the Secret Six, wasn't his only calling card for the special squad. He was known in the bureau as "the best 'tail car' man in the country," which Eliot figured would be a valuable skill in tracking Capone's men and shipments. And having worked for two years in the Detroit division, he knew the ins and outs of that city's Purple Gang, which supplied Canadian booze to Chicago's bootleggers. Leeson's boss in Detroit, Ernest Rowe, fought hard to keep him in Michigan's biggest city. After receiving Johnson's request for Leeson's services, Rowe sent a beseeching telex to Washington, listing a series of reasons why he couldn't spare the man. When he was instructed to send him anyway, Rowe wrote that Leeson would report to Chicago on December 22, and added that he "keenly feels the loss of this man. He is one of our best agents."[*]

Not everyone joining the team was accustomed to such high praise. On December 15, William Jennings Gardner reported to Johnson for assignment to the Capone squad. Eliot was thrilled. The forty-six-year-old Gardner also had been on Golding's team, before being transferred to Syracuse, New York. Better yet, he had been a college football hero. Eliot admired athletic prowess more than almost anything else; he believed that success on the field of play corresponded with strong moral fiber and was specifically predictive of success in law enforcement. His fandom, in fact, blinded him: Gardner's Prohibition Bureau personnel file couldn't have been put "under the microscope" without bursting into flames. In the fall of 1927, the rangy North Dakotan, then working in the New Jersey office, had been fired from the bureau for laziness and repeated insubordination. He was saved only through the sustained application of political pressure. "I am exceedingly interested in the case of W. J. Gardiner [sic], recently dismissed from the service in New Jersey," U.S. senator Gerald P. Nye of North Dakota wrote to Seymour

[*] Johnson also tapped another Detroit agent, Ulrich Berard, to join the squad, but Berard was soon returned to Michigan, perhaps in an effort to keep Rowe happy.

110

Lowman, U.S. assistant secretary of the Treasury for Prohibition. The senator, keen to exploit his prerogatives, even for the benefit of a dodgy Prohibition agent, continued awkwardly: "Since he is a North Dakota man, I have been more especially interested in his case and being quite well acquainted with him was rather dumbfounded when the word of his dismissal came through. . . . Is it possible that he was let out of the service through petty jealousies and the fact that he was a man of extraordinary ability who might be overshadowing some of the other officials just above him?"

Lowman did not flinch at the implied threat. The former lieutenant governor of New York was a dedicated and honest dry who fiercely opposed his state's wet governor, Al Smith. A week before receiving Nye's letter, Lowman told a reporter, "There are many incompetent and crooked men in the service. Bribery is rampant. There are many wolves in sheep's clothing. We are after them. . . . Some days my arm gets tired signing orders of dismissal." He did not rescind Gardner's firing.

But Gardner, who was half Chippewa and played politics with swinging elbows, did not leave it there. He turned to another powerful patron, U.S. senator Charles Curtis, one of the first men of known Native American descent to reach high public office. Curtis liked to proudly declaim that he was "one-eighth Kaw Indian and one hundred percent Republican." In just a few months, the Kansan would become Herbert Hoover's vice presidential running mate, but first he went to battle for one of his own. Curtis, it turned out, had more oomph than his colleague from North Dakota. Prohibition Bureau commissioner J. M. Doran wrote to Curtis in March 1928:

> The Administrator under whom Mr. Gardner was formerly employed reported that he was lazy and inefficient. In view of your interest in the matter, however, we will give him another opportunity to demonstrate his fitness for the service by appointing him as a Special Employee for a period of sixty days. At the end of that time, if his services are satisfactory to the Special Agent in Charge at Chicago, under whom he will be assigned to duty, steps will be taken to bring about his continuance in the service.

So Gardner was assigned to Chicago — the beating heart of Prohibition resistance — and to the squad specifically charged with cleaning up the Chicago office. For everyone else, assignment to Golding's prestigious team was a reward for exceptional work, or at the very least a sign of professional promise (e.g., young Harvard men willing to bypass banking careers in favor of busting heads for a mere $2,600 a year). For this politically connected troublemaker, by far the oldest man in the unit, it was a punishment, most likely with the expectation that he would wash out under the glare of publicity that followed Hardboiled Golding's operations. That didn't happen, but not because Gardner had reformed himself. He just happened to not be around when the special squad imploded. Indeed, it appears that he viewed the assignment as a no-show job, or perhaps that was how Golding, who had always picked his own men, had defined it for him. Gardner's personnel file offers not one word about his work during the five months he was a special agent in Chicago; it simply notes his report date and then his reassignment to upstate New York.

No one in Chicago sought out Gardner for the Capone squad, either. Instead, the agent had asked earlier in the year to be transferred back to the city and the special agency unit, now run by Jamie. He listed "twofold reason . . . one is to better my status, and the other is to be nearer to my family." (He had relatives in Michigan.) His supervisor in New York approved the transfer request without expressing regret. Jamie, who would soon move over to the Secret Six, was loath to turn down the transfer, under the theory that, in the aftermath of the Golding disaster, beggars couldn't be choosers.

Gardner wouldn't be the only misfit on the Capone squad. Johnson and Froelich realized the squad needed a "pencil detective" — that is, an agent with the kind of methodical, detail-oriented mind to take bits and pieces of seemingly disparate evidence and string them together to create a clear picture of organized intent. Forty-year-old Lyle Chapman, a Colgate University graduate and a Prohibition agent in Indianapolis, had that kind of mind; the problem was getting him to use it. "I remember my knees shook like jelly when I got the orders telling me what was up," he would later say of his assignment to the Capone squad. "Frankly, I pondered how to get out of it." This was the kind of reaction his superiors had grown to expect from him. Six months before Johnson requested Chapman for the team, agent B. F. Hargrove Jr. wrote to his supervisor that Chapman "just simply does not want to work or do things that we request him to do and on such occasion he puts up some excuse as to why he doesn't want to. . . . It has got to a point where none of the agents wants to work with him." Chapman had received hardly any satisfactory efficiency reports during his four years in the bureau, and none in the previous two years. That summer, the head of the Indianapolis division, Dwight Avis, reprimanded him in writing, closing: "I suggest that it would be very advisable for you to show a little more initiative in your work." It was the last entry in Chapman's file before his transfer to the Capone squad.

A friend of Chapman's, thirty-four-year-old Bernard Cloonan, also joined the operation. He was a former marine and a member of the prominent veterans organization the Forty and Eight. Eliot would describe him as "a barrel-chested giant who fitted the popular conception of the typical Irishman with his black hair, ruddy complexion and ready smile." Cloonan and Eliot had joined the Chicago office at the same time, and Eliot had been awed by his sheer physical presence. Cloonan, he figured, would provide the muscle as needed.

Rounding out what would become the core group were the "drawling" Virginia native Mike King, hard-boiled former private investigator Jim Seeley, and bashful former Pennsylvania state trooper Tom Friel, who was so shy he could barely speak in mixed company. The Capone squad was an eclectic group, there was no doubt about that. Eliot, the youngest member of the team and the boss, would struggle to figure out the best way to motivate them. But that difficulty had little to do with his youth and inexperience. In 1930, nowhere in America did one size fit all. Three decades later, pharmacist and World War I–era baseball player Davy Jones would point out just how diverse the country had been: "You know, we didn't have the mass communication and mass transportation that exist nowadays. We didn't have as much schooling, either. As a result, people were more unique then, more unusual, more different from each other. Now people are all more or less alike, company men, security-minded, conformity — that sort of stuff." Sure enough, there wasn't a company man to be found on the Capone squad — except perhaps for its young leader.

Eliot brought his team together for the first time in late December 1930. They all seemed to recognize just how big their new job was. The world outside the Transportation Building had turned especially cruel in the past year. Gang violence had spiked again, with Capone declaring that when it came to gang war, "the law of self-defense, the way God looks at it, is a little broader than the law books have it." When a football fan set off fireworks at Union Station while changing trains on his way east for the St. Mary's–Fordham game, a panic ensued. Homicide detectives and a morgue truck screamed to the station, expecting to find wounded thugs and civilians scattered about. Worse than the rise in gang violence was the reason behind it: the 1920s' economic boom had proved to be little more than drunken wishful thinking. The stock market had crashed late in 1929, throwing the country into depression. The federal government's response — most notably the Smoot-Hawley Tariff Act — only intensified the downward spiral. By now, a year after Wall Street's collapse, the depression had become the Depression. The unemployment rate approached a third of the available nonfarm work force and was still rising. On his way into the office every morning, Eliot picked his way around homeless men sleeping on the sidewalk and stutter-stepped around queues at soup kitchens. A friend remembered him frequently handing over loans of $5 and $10. He wasn't earning much as a special agent but he knew he was lucky to be earning anything at all. Now and again the unemployed would be marching down State Street when Eliot emerged from the Transportation Building. These parades included banging drums and chanting calls for government action. For months, the men worked themselves into a frenzied state over and over. But after a year of unrelieved misery, hope was slipping away. Eliot, hitting the street for lunch one day, found himself watching a straggly mockery of a march. The men passing by, operating on muscle memory, shuffled down the street like survivors after the end of the world. They made no noise at all. They had no demands left.

"The Depression was *so* real that it became unreal," recalled Julia Walther, a Chicagoan whose family company tottered but managed to survive. "There was a horror about it, with people jumping out of windows. I remember the first time motoring under the Michigan Avenue Bridge, under those streets, where the *Tribune* is, and seeing not hundreds, but thousands of men, rolled up in their overcoats, just on the pavement. I remember being so horrified, so overwhelmed." It was, she said, the searing "first experience of something, of realizing that life was not the way you had thought it. Until you actually saw someone dying, you can't know what war is like. Now I have an inkling of what the Depression was for some people, although I never slept under the bridge."

By the end of 1930, there was no escape from this unreality. Optimism about a recovery being right around the corner had curdled into bewildered acceptance that this terrible, ugly new world had settled in for good. Sally Rand, the performer who caught Jack McGurn's eye at the Paramount Club, was a ballerina in her early twenties when the economy collapsed. She hadn't made it big, but she'd made it, traveling across the country with a company run by the Russian choreographer Adolph Bolm, Anna Pavlova's onetime partner. The economic implosion put an end to that. "Suddenly, all the copybook maxims were turned backward," she would remember nearly four decades later. "How could it be that a man who had been at his job thirty years couldn't have a job? How could it be that a business that had been in business for a lifetime suddenly isn't any more? Friends of mine who had been to Harvard, Yale and Princeton jumped out of windows. With accuracy. The idea of the stock market quittin' was unbelievable."

Rand, the beloved daughter of a conservative West Point man, turned to nude fan dancing to survive. It was that or prostitution. "It was economically sound," she would later joke about her act, "because I didn't have any money to buy anything" to wear on stage. Even with this titillating routine, she managed to land work only because she knew someone who knew a couple of low-level gangsters. The hoods paid a visit to the owner of Chez Paree, one of Chicago's most popular nightclubs. "It'd be a terrible thing if this place got a stink in it," they said. The owner blanched: "Wha-wha-wha-*what*?" Rand went on that night, fans fluttering, to cheers and whistles.

Capone took advantage of the dire situation. He opened up a soup kitchen downtown, the largest in the city. A straightforward, elegant sign over the door declared, "Free Soup, Coffee, and Doughnuts for the Unemployed." Mary Borden, working on a magazine article about her wild native city, was not fooled. "The bread line outside of Al

Capone's soup kitchen," she wrote, "stretched down one of these bleak, windswept streets past Police Headquarters. I had been [inside the police offices], turning the leaves of what they call the Death Book, most dreadful of all souvenir albums in the world. And there was undoubtedly a connection between the two lots of men, those who stood shivering outside the soup kitchen and those who, enclosed in the covers of the police album, lay sprawled on the bare boards of matchbox rooms or crouched in the corners of taxis with their heads bashed in. For Al Capone is an ambidextrous giant, who kills with one hand and feeds with the other."

Borden was making a connection that those in Big Al's soup line didn't want to think about anymore. To them, the St. Valentine's Day Massacre seemed like a very long time ago. Men who still had jobs and homes could worry about Mob violence and how gangsters preyed on the weak and troubled. The down and out could worry only about themselves. "Good-Hearted Al," they mumbled when asked about the underworld boss. If Capone wanted to call himself a twentieth-century Robin Hood, that was fine with them, as long as his kitchen stayed open. On top of this new image of good-hearted Al, the economic immolation had brought back the see-no-evil, hear-no-evil crowd in local political circles. Borden feared the situation had produced "a creeping civic paralysis, the spread of some moral intoxication or fever that, like the effects of certain drugs, will produce in time a complete immunity from the sensation of horror or disgust or fear."

This much was certain: Johnson, Jamie's Secret Six, and the incipient Capone squad were truly on their own. After being booted out of office in the mid-1920s by a reformer, Big Bill Thompson had returned to city hall. The gangs were running Chicago's city government once again, including the police department. A socialite, trekking to a soirée on the roof of one of the city's best hotels late in 1930, would recall the odd feeling she had as "we walked through the seething, smoke-laden lobby of the hotel; I suppose that the crowd of men who eyed us over their large cigars, their hats pushed back onto the backs of their heads as we stepped past in satin slippers and ermine coats, represented as tough a crowd of crook politicians and crook business men as any you could find in the world." As she headed upstairs, along with her fellow "pretty, delicate girls, such nice, boyish men," to a party that would be awash in illegal liquor, she grew angry at the state of official Chicago:

Suppose that crowd downstairs hadn't chosen to let us have our party? Suppose they decided not to let these attractive

121

people have any parties any more? Suppose they told them to clear out of the town altogether? Weren't they helpless? Wouldn't they quickly disappear? What could they do about it? Fight? Well, why didn't they fight, then? Why wait? What actually were they doing in regard to the governing of this town of theirs? Nothing.

The socialite perfectly captured the conflicted angst of the city. Chicagoans high and low hated Prohibition, but their very own flouting of the dry law had helped make their lives — their entire world — scary, without order or reason. Increasingly, people wanted to be saved from themselves. The crook politicians and crook businessmen would continue to do nothing; no one expected otherwise. But that didn't mean no one was willing to step forward and fight. The perfect moment had arrived, at long last, for the hated Prohibition Bureau to produce a hero.

CHAPTER 7
THE FIRST STEP

The Capone operation was a hydra: bootlegging, extortion, union racketeering, prostitution, gambling. A dogged investigator had myriad entry points to exploit, as well as many blind alleys he could stumble down. But not the Capone squad. Their focus, Eliot told his men, was the breweries — and only the breweries. They were going to find them and knock them out, one by one. The brewery business made for a prime target, Eliot said, "having the most capital invested . . . the most complete organization, the quickest turnover and the greatest income." And it was especially vulnerable, he pointed out, because "their product was bulky and because they have the toughest transport problem."

This very specific objective sounded easy enough to achieve, but despite all the money poured into police payoffs, the Outfit actually went to considerable trouble to hide its brewing work. The Mob used decoy buildings, trompe l'oeil techniques to conceal entire rooms, lookouts, and advance and trailing cars to secure deliveries. The syndicate frequently moved its heavy equipment among dozens of buildings across the city, and its beer trucks regularly changed their routes. Counterintuitively, little family stills, many of them under Capone's control, were relatively easy to find; they were less professionally run, less secure, less mobile — and, more than ever, neighbors talked. The big breweries, the ones that pulled in the serious money and should have been difficult to hide, were much tougher to track down.

In its first weeks, the new special team focused on cultivating informants, surreptitiously following bootleggers, and figuring out where best to place phone wiretaps, a relatively new law-enforcement practice. Eliot's life was changing fast — again. In the year and a half between the end of the Chicago Heights operation and the creation of the Capone squad, he had settled into a routine at the bureau, mostly tracking down small-time brewers in the suburban and rural areas outside Chicago. He'd even had time for a real personal life. Being so much younger than his siblings, he'd essentially been an only child growing up. He'd always been uneasy about sharing his physical and emotional space. But that finally had begun to change. He was in love. When they were alone together, he and Edna became comfortable opening up about their feelings. They began to trust not just each other but themselves. After several months of exclusive dating, they had married on August 9, 1929, in suburban Oak Glen and moved into a small apartment near Palmer Park on Chicago's South Side. The rent was $65 a month. For the first time in his life Eliot was out from under his parents' roof. And he found that he loved married life; he loved being the man of the house. He and his new bride spent almost all of their free time at home together, reading or listening to music or working on jigsaw puzzles. It was the happiest he had ever been. But now, a year after their marriage vows and with an astonishing career opportunity before him, the honeymoon was over. No longer was he on the periphery of the action at the bureau. He was right back in the middle of it. Eliot once again moved into an all-encompassing work mode. He went out to the shooting range every day, until he became the best shot in the office. He diligently made a list of every known gangster in the region, along with each man's known haunts and associates. His address book filled up with killers. He worked late into the night and then got up early in the morning after just a couple hours of sleep. He discovered that the best way to find Capone's breweries was to keep it simple: he and his men hung around outside speakeasies, all hours of the day and night. "We knew that regularity was necessary in their operation, and it wasn't long before we learned of the special hauls on Fridays in preparation for Saturday speakeasy business," Eliot would later tell a reporter. For a while, the squad tried following the trucks after their delivery, but that led nowhere useful. A truck would deliver beer, and the next day it would deliver office furniture. Then it might sit on the street for days. It turned out to be a better bet to stay with the booze.

The squad noticed that, as a tavern filled up on a busy weekend night and the place started rocking, bartenders would regularly heft empty beer barrels into the alley. "The first observation we made was that the barrels had to be used over and over again, and that if we could successfully follow a beer barrel from a speakeasy, we would wind up locating a Capone brewery," Eliot noted. In February, Eliot assigned Leeson and Seeley to park outside one of the city's biggest speakeasies. The empty beer barrels stacked up in the alley as the night wore on. Hours went by, the bar emptied out, and the lights went off. Finally, shortly before dawn, a truck rolled up to the alley and a couple of men nonchalantly loaded the barrels into the back and drove on. Leeson and Seeley followed the barrel truck without detection — no small feat with the streets empty in the middle of the night — to a building near Comiskey Park, the Southside home of the White Sox baseball team. They had their first breakthrough. In the following days, the team rented rooms near the building and began watching it around the clock. They quickly discovered they hadn't found a brewery; it was a barrel-cleaning facility.

Now Leeson's expertise as a "tail man" really came into play. About twenty-five trucks filled with empty barrels rumbled into the building each day. A similar number left the facility, presumably bound for breweries. Eliot was determined to be careful. He knew they'd get only one shot at this; any hint that the dry cops were onto them and the Outfit would close up shop and disappear. So as trucks left the building with freshly cleaned barrels, Leeson and Seeley — or sometimes two other agents from the team — would follow them, but only for a few blocks before turning off. Each truck was at the center of a small convoy, with sedans cruising ahead and behind it, looking out for anything suspicious. Each morning, the agents picked up the chase where they had left off the previous day, swinging out behind the convoy and following for a handful of blocks before turning down a side street and letting the truck rumble on. Sometimes they would follow by driving ahead of the convoy and watching through the rear-view mirror, or they'd tail the beer truck by driving along parallel streets. Finally, Leeson and Seeley managed to track a truck to a garage on the West Side. "The garage was on Cicero Avenue near Western Electric Co.," Eliot remembered. "Across from the garage was a field with tall weeds." That's where the two agents crouched in the middle of the afternoon. They were still there at three in the morning, when at last the garage came to life. The truck, they realized, was only there to be "cooled off." Now two Ford coupes emerged from the building and set off down the street, one after the other. The men in the coupes slowly canvassed the neighborhood, peering into parked cars and down alleys "to detect any observers." Yet Leeson and Seeley managed to stay hidden. Once the all-clear was given, the truck exited the garage — with the agents hustling to get to their car undetected. The truck drove down South Cicero Avenue and pulled into a long, one-story brick building with a sloped roof. Leeson and Seeley drove on past. The Capone squad had found its first brewery.

The team's progress pleased Eliot, and for good reason. In a few short weeks, they had found Capone's barrel-cleaning plant and one of his major breweries, and they also were beginning to see results from the first batch of wiretaps they'd put in. They had bugged a hotel — possibly the Lexington, where Capone often stayed — as well as casinos and whorehouses in Cicero run by the Outfit.

These developments were highly encouraging, but personnel issues sucked some of the excitement out of Eliot's job. For much of January 1931, at the end of sixteen-hour days in the field, Eliot found himself sitting blurrily at his desk writing memos to Washington that didn't exactly put the fledgling Capone squad in the best light. The biggest problem was Gardner, the former football hero whom Eliot had been so excited to have join the team. Just days after reporting for his new assignment in December, Gardner had requested thirty days' leave for personal reasons. Eliot passed the request along to Froelich, who turned it down. They needed more men, not fewer, Froelich told him, so allowing a leave of absence at this time was "out of the question." But Gardner never took no for an answer. He began making his request anew to every supervisor in the vicinity, receiving a staccato burst of brush-offs in response, most referring him back to Froelich and Johnson. On January 18, a Sunday, Gardner called Seager at home and petulantly declared that if his leave wasn't approved immediately he'd resign. Seager raised no objection. That night, Gardner checked out of his hotel and disappeared.

From the very first day of the Capone

squad's existence, Eliot, in what would become a pattern throughout his career, embraced his men as brothers. He didn't allow himself to see anything but their best qualities, homing in on the good bits until those qualities alone defined their characters. The agents would have various complaints and requests over their months together, and Eliot sent off determined memos to Washington attempting to satisfy them. He sought promotions and pay raises for his men, even though the bureau's budget was being severely cut. He gave them glowing efficiency reports and recommendations. The one consistent exception was Gardner. It had taken less than a month for the football hero's act to wear thin. Eliot's memos about Gardner's conduct were brisk and factual, no more. He made no special effort on his behalf. When Gardner rematerialized a couple of weeks after walking away from the job, Eliot accepted him back on the team without comment. With the discovery of the brewery on South Cicero Avenue, he needed all the men he could get, and the bigger and stronger the agents the better. But he wasn't happy about it.

Unlike most of his men, Eliot had no military background, other than ROTC in school. He was not a man's man, as much as he wanted to be. Even at twenty-eight, he remained repressed and unnaturally shy, a stranger to himself as well as others. He'd spent his childhood playing with his older sisters and a small group of boys from the block. His Friday evenings had been taken up schlepping pans at his father's bakery instead of knocking heads on his high school's football team. His life had been insular, self-contained. One high school friend remembered him being "uneasy in social settings." During lunch break in the school cafeteria, Eliot preferred reading Sherlock Holmes stories to chatting with whoever might be sitting across from him. "Once you started talking to him," the friend said, "he loosened right up and was fine. He just didn't ever take the first step."

Now, as leader of his own special unit in the Prohibition forces, he had to take the first step. He had to be a leader. Eliot could be found sitting in his office at seven every morning, chewing on his fingernails. The anticipation of the team's first paramilitary action made him nauseous. Eliot was eager — probably overly so — to show results, to prove himself worthy of his new position. He might be bashful, but he wanted to win; he would do almost anything to win. His men picked up on their young boss's drive. They had been dubious of him because of his youth and self-consciousness, but now, whether he realized it or not, they were growing to respect him. They understood he was one of them, and that no one was going to outwork him. On January 20, just six weeks after being assigned to Johnson's special squad, Eliot sent a report to Dwight Avis, now the new chief of the Special Agency Division at the bureau's Washington, DC, headquarters. "At the present time several forces are brought into play in Chicago and the operations of the Capone syndicate have for the last few days been absolutely stopped," he wrote. "After experiencing great difficulty, we have been able to secure telephone taps covering the various headquarters' spots of the Capone gang and are in a favorable strategical [*sic*] position to obtain considerable information relative to their workings as soon as operations again begin."

The long, detailed memo impressed Avis, who would become one of Eliot's bureaucratic champions. He responded that he could "readily appreciate the difficulty that you are having in keeping men on the job in connection with this special work." He was referring to the fact that Leeson and Chapman had been called out of town to give testimony in trials. Willebrandt was gone, but the Justice Department had finally become serious about prosecuting Prohibition violations. Avis told Eliot he would reassign Special Agent W. Bruce Murray from Kansas City to Chicago to assist the squad for a couple of weeks and promised to push for the assignment of a Philadelphia-based agent named Paul Robsky, whom Eliot had requested. He also added that he was not surprised to hear about Gardner's "misconduct, as he has resigned three or four times from the service, I understand, under similar circumstances."

It's impossible to know what Eliot meant about the Capone syndicate being "absolutely stopped." The squad was just beginning to get stakeouts and other operations under way. Perhaps the squad's early, probing raids — Eliot admitted they hit a few "dry holes" in their first attempts — had made the gang briefly go into turtle mode. More likely the young agent was just trying to puff himself up.

Whatever he meant, Eliot was clear about one thing: he was just getting started.

CHAPTER 8
KID STUFF

"There it is," Joe Leeson said. He sounded relieved, as if the block-long building they had carefully staked out for a month might have been quietly lifted up and carried away in the night. The building, at 1632–1642 South Cicero Avenue, sat in a heap on the side of the road, like a fresh bear dropping. Leeson and Eliot watched from the cab of their idling truck as steam puffed from vents along the building's sides, nearly invisible in the snow-lashed landscape. The nation's freight rail loadings, a key indicator of Chicago's economic health, were down thirty-two thousand from the previous week, and 25 percent from the previous year. This was no surprise. Gross national product had fallen by more than a third since the beginning of the downturn — and was still falling. The pain was spreading far and going deep. Yet Al Capone's breweries blasted away, as hard and often as they dared. The agents had figured out that this brewery was producing at least a hundred barrels of product a day. Eliot wanted to take it down at the height of its production cycle.

The truck heaved and coughed in neutral as Eliot exchanged hand signals with agents in the car behind. They needed to be synchronized. The squad had spent weeks preparing for this moment. It was late March already. Their plans had been put on hold three weeks earlier by sixteen inches of fresh, fluffy snow, which buried parked cars and bleached city streets for miles. Even now, old piles of snow still choked alleys and clogged gutters, and a persistent gray mist cut visibility to a few feet. But the squad could wait no longer. The convoy had begun its slow trek up the main boulevard in Cicero shortly after dawn. The truck at the head of the pack had five men in it, including Eliot in the front passenger seat, wearing a leather football helmet. More men trailed in black sedans. Intent on the element of surprise, Eliot and his team — plus a handful of borrowed police officers — had planned the raid "as we would design a football play." Everyone knew what he was supposed to do.

The Prohibition Bureau had long before learned that Capone's breweries were kept behind reinforced steel doors and came equipped with escape hatches. Most brewery raids over the years had bogged down right at the start. There'd be dozens of men balled up in front of the building, as if in a huge rugby scrum, loudly banging on the doors with sledgehammers and crowbars. By the time they actually made it inside, the brewers and sometimes all of the equipment were long gone.

Eliot's raid would be different. The squad's small size and insular method of working lowered the risk of any wayward cop or dry agent tipping off the Outfit. The more pressing issue was how best to quickly get inside the brewery's walls and prevent escapes. To solve this problem the squad built a huge, snowplow-like battering ram, shaped almost like an arrowhead. The team worked on it in a government garage on the northwest side, usually late at night. They kept it hidden from other agents in the bureau; Eliot didn't even tell Johnson about it. The battering ram would be the team's secret weapon. For Eliot, the possibilities were electric. It was Arthur and Excalibur.

Eliot waved his hand, and Leeson put the heavy truck into low gear and jammed his foot down on the accelerator. Whiteness streaked past the windows. The battering ram vibrated against the grille as the truck slid and gained speed. There was a flash when it hit. Eliot blinked and peered through the windshield as the truck groaned. He could feel his heart bouncing around his ribcage; he could hear wood cracking. The truck lurched and then struck a second set of doors, this time solid steel. After a shaking, stuttering, endless moment, with Eliot holding onto the seat to keep from flying into Leeson's lap, the steel seam sprang with a thunderous clap. The truck's headlights shone into a dense, dark nothingness. Eliot could hear the tiny *thuck-thuck-thuck* of his men scaling ladders to the roof, the trailing sedans clumping to a stop behind the truck and officers jumping out. Everyone was doing his job. Things were happening, the plan was in motion, but Eliot saw only an empty building. No stills. No barrels of liquor. Nothing. "My heart sank," he remembered. He sat there, stunned. He had failed. It had all been an elaborate ruse; the real brewery was somewhere else. He was sure of it.

But then, one of the agents — probably Leeson, the most experienced brewery raider on the team — spotted a blip of light from an interior door swinging shut, and yelled out. Eliot realized all at once what he was looking at. The Mob wouldn't reinforce a dummy operation with solid-steel doors. It was just the front room that was a dummy, painted black to simulate a vast empty building. Eliot leapt from the truck and raced toward the invisible door. As he banged through it, the brewery — the vats, the burners, the pumps — came violently into focus, as if being squeezed from a tube. Eliot and his men kept running "and were on the necks of five operators in less time than it takes to tell it." The brewers, shocked and scared, gave up without a fight. The squad captured not only the clutch of men operating the brewery, but three trucks and all of the brewery's equipment. A huge haul, an unprecedented haul, for a raid on a Capone operation.

Years later, Eliot would call his mission to dry up Capone "an obsession." This was the moment it became one. In those excited, wild minutes after Leeson pounded down on the accelerator and the truck jumped forward, Eliot felt "a certain sense of exhilaration, maybe even exultation." He felt *alive.* It would ruin him for normal life for years. He had been so careful and deliberate through the years, a follower of rules, an inveterate worrier. Now he had found a new god. From here on out he would do almost anything to recapture the emotional high that came from crashing through Al Capone's doors.

Standing in the middle of the room, Eliot took it all in. There were nineteen vats, each capable of holding about fifteen hundred gallons. Some thirty thousand gallons were on site and ready to be shipped. He knew that nothing like this had ever been captured before. Not in Chicago. Chapman moved around the room like a quartermaster. He wrote down the number of each truck, examined every piece of brewing equipment. He couldn't stop smiling. A valuable piece of hard evidence connecting Capone to bootlegging would be found on this day, in this building: a truck the gangster had bought before he stopped putting his name to things. "Circumstances connected Al Capone with this purchase, with the activities of the racket and also with income from the fruit of the racket," Eliot wrote. It wasn't much, but it was something.

The truck seizure was meaningful, but the biggest catch of the day was a person, not a thing: Steve Svoboda, Capone's chief brewmaster. Stocky, cow-faced, with a wide, pessimistic mouth like a dried-up old nun, Svoboda stared at the floor as beer sluiced around his feet. Behind him, agents smashed barrels and opened up the spigots of the vats. Soon they would all be wading ankle-high through beery foam.

The Capone network shuddered only for a moment. The press praised the unprecedented assault (Eliot clipped and saved the news reports), but that didn't matter much to the Outfit. Svoboda made bail and returned to brewing, production shifted to other breweries, business went on as usual. Which was exactly what the Capone squad had hoped would happen. The team's agents continued tailing trucks coming out of the barrel-cleaning plant, which inevitably led to new discoveries: another cleaning facility, a sales office where clerks took orders from speakeasies. Wiretaps followed, leading the squad to more breweries and providing them with a nearly definitive list of Capone's customers.

On Saturday, April 11, the squad took down a second large brewery, this one at 3136 South Wabash Avenue in Chicago. The seizure of the two breweries — the one in Cicero and now this one — would cost the Capone syndicate about $10,000 a day in revenue, Eliot told reporters as his men packed prisoners into a paddy wagon. The raid had been an almost perfect replication of the Cicero assault, except this time with better weather. The squad once again used the battering ram and once again arrested Svoboda, who didn't even bother trying to run. "We were to arrest him again and again as we took subsequent breweries," Eliot wrote in the first draft of his memoir. Evidence gathered in these raids — along with Eliot's testimony — would be used to indict Svoboda on Prohibition charges, putting pressure on the brewer to testify against others. One more thing for Capone to worry about.

The raid may have been a carbon copy of the earlier brewery mugging, but the aftermath wasn't. After busting up dozens of barrels of beer, hauling away prisoners, and posing for newspaper photographers, Eliot and his agents shut the doors to the building — the large tanks and pumps still inside — and climbed into their cars. They drove off, leaving no one to keep an eye on the place. Darkness fell, and as the hours passed the street remained silent, with no police guard anywhere. A surprising oversight, but perhaps understandable considering all the excitement.

The Mob noticed. An eyewitness report captured the scene the next morning:

> At 11 o clock four sedans swept into the neighborhood. For twenty minutes they cruised about. Nothing was seen to arouse suspicion. Then the four cars took up strategic positions so that from four street corners they could sight a car approaching from any direction.
>
> With the sentinel cars posted, another car rolled into the neighborhood, up the street and in front of the brewery. The car halted and Bert Delaney . . . hopped out with two other men. He sauntered to the brewery door, took a key out and unlocked the door. He and his companions walked in and away went the car that had carried them there.
>
> A few minutes' wait and a five-ton truck appeared and rolled up and into the brewery.

Delaney was one of Capone's brewers,

second only to Svoboda. He was directing the two men as they loaded a 2,500-gallon tank onto the truck when a sudden, violent cacophony outside spun him around. The drivers of the sentinel cars were pounding on their horns. None of the men in the brewery had time to react: federal agents appeared out of the shadows, surrounding them. They had been hiding in and around the building all night, slapping themselves to stay awake, peeing quietly in dark corners. One of the lookout cars screamed past the building, the horn wailing. Delaney watched it disappear from sight. He sat on the truck's fender and put his head in his hands.

Two days later, jacked up on success, Eliot took his men out to the site of his first big bust as a Prohibition agent: Chicago Heights.

This was not one of the squad's carefully planned operations. The boys simply felt like knocking some heads, and so with nothing on the drawing board ready for action, their leader decided they'd do it the old-fashioned way. Once they reached the Heights's city limits, Eliot stopped his car, got out, and took a big whiff. The others did the same.

What do you know — it worked. Following their noses, the agents walked up to a quaint Victorian-style house on Sixth Avenue on the east side of town. It turned out it wasn't actually a house, just the frame of one. Inside was one large room where a group of men operated a distillery. Smaller stills chugged away in the basement and in the faux double garage behind the house. The agents dumped more than thirty thousand gallons of mash before they went on their way.

They drove down the street, around a few corners, and once again Eliot stopped his car, got out, and sniffed. Reporters caught up to the agents at their next port of call. This time they found beer rather than the hard stuff. Coming out of the makeshift brewery, Eliot beckoned the reporters over. "We secured convictions against fifty-six men in this neighborhood last year," he told them. "We were just checking up today." The squad ended the day with some sixty-five thousand gallons of alcohol mash and five Capone bootleggers to add to their ledgers.

The impromptu raids, not surprisingly, proved an embarrassment to the local police, who had no idea they were coming. Major Harry Stafford, installed as police chief after the dry bureau's temporary takeover of the town in January 1929, arrived at police headquarters as Eliot and his men were walking out. "I can't understand it," Stafford told Eliot. "These fellows must have just slipped in. We've been keeping an awfully close check on things out here."

Eliot was feeling confident after his run of success; he felt like a new man. He gave

Stafford a little smile, savoring the moment like a postcoital cigarette. "I'll be back," he said, and swept out the door.

Eliot's sense of smell may have been excellent, but Johnson and Froelich were more interested in his hearing. Back in 1928 the U.S. Supreme Court had knocked down Seattle bootlegger Roy Olmstead's contention that phone wiretaps violated the Fourth Amendment's protection against "unreasonable searches and seizures." Ever since, law enforcement had been sticking in wires on the flimsiest pretenses.[*] Johnson and Froelich were especially keen to put taps to use, approving them on phones for virtually every office and backroom lounge that might have some connection to the liquor network. That meant Eliot would get to make use of the newest addition to the team: Paul Robsky, who had arrived early in April. The short, pigeon-chested former marine was itching to get in on the action. He'd spent the past three months in Philadelphia after being transferred from the cotton-mill town of Greenville,

[*] In 1967, the Supreme Court would overturn the "Olmstead standard," deciding that Fourth Amendment protections extended to wherever a person had "a reasonable expectation of privacy," thus necessitating a judge's OK before police could put in a wire.

South Carolina. So far he hated big-city life, which as far as he could tell consisted of nothing but pointless stakeouts and even more pointless paperwork. He preferred the Southern style of bootleg enforcement. Almost every day in Greenville he had undertaken a high-speed car chase through the mountains, with gravel flying and squirrels exploding on his grille. Yeee-ha! He claimed to have run thirty cars off the road in one month. "Working with Ness was kid stuff compared with running down those moonshiners in South Carolina," he'd tell a reporter years later.

In the Capone squad, Leeson handled the car chases, such as they were. Eliot brought Robsky in for the more pressing need: raking phone terminals, still a relatively rare technical skill, which Robsky had picked up while in the military. The new guy's first assignment: Ralph Capone's headquarters at the Montmartre Café in Cicero. Al's brother, who'd already been convicted of income-tax evasion, headed up the Outfit's bottling operation. Ralph's piece of the pie was key to building a Volstead case against Al and other high-level members of the gang. Ralphie and his crew frequently took orders and dispatched deliveries from the phone at the end of the speakeasy's bar. That being the case, they guarded the establishment like a prison. The operation would be the first of many wiretapping assignments for Robsky, but it also would be the hairiest, which was exactly what he needed to realize the Capone squad was the right gig for him. It also helped him to bond with Eliot, no small thing since Robsky hated all authority figures as a matter of course.

The squad rented a basement apartment just off Cermak Road, not far from the Montmartre. Robsky's job was to climb up the telephone pole in the alley behind the club and connect the line going into the building with the one going into the apartment, thus allowing the agents to listen in on every phone conversation coming in or out of Ralph's inner sanctum. The problem was that Capone thugs prowled the alley around the clock. Ralph was notoriously dense, but he was probably aware that federal agents might try to tap his phone. Certainly he knew that assassins sent by his brother's rivals would prefer to enter from the back of the building rather than the front. Whatever the reason for the goons, the squad had to get them out of the alley.

Eliot came up with a plan: on a bright, warm afternoon, Leeson and a handful of his fellow agents set out on "bait detail." The men slowly cruised past the front of the Montmartre in a big black Cadillac, the top down, giving everyone and everything a good long look. They went around the block, and then chugged past the club again, this time at an even slower pace and with everyone in the car taking notes. The Outfit noticed the agents right off, and the unusual behavior made the boys nervous. A couple of hoods came out of the club to watch. After the agents spent about five more minutes circling the block, the flunkies had seen enough. They jumped into a car, pulled out into the street, and followed the Caddy. Now a second car full of dry agents came along, also with its top down, also with the agents giving everyone and everything the stink eye. While the first Cadillac took its pursuer on a leisurely tour of Cicero-area Mob hotspots — gambling dens, prostitution houses, speakeasies — the second Cadillac took over the job of slowly and suspiciously circling the Montmartre and the nearby Western Hotel, over and over.

As the second Cadillac got in on the action — with a third ready to go, if needed — Eliot and Robsky hoofed it over to the backside of the alley. The agents, both wearing workmen's coveralls, peered in. It was a long, narrow passageway. A tailor's shop had been stuffed into one of the corners like a finger in a dike. The alley's walls rose higher, indicating the back of the speakeasy. Eliot stepped past the tailor's hovel while Robsky, squatting in the shadows, put on his tool belt and spiked climbing shoes. Eliot spotted two gangsters midway down the alley: they were smoking cigarettes, the outlines of fat guns bunching up their coats. Finally, after yet another pass by the second Caddy, the back door to the speakeasy swung open, and the goons began nodding and yessing at someone. The door banged shut as the alley dwellers stubbed out their cigarettes, climbed into a sedan, and started it up. When the car turned out of the alley to join the convoy, Robsky hustled over to the telephone pole, with Eliot right behind him. Robsky looked up at the terminal box etched against a blinding blue infinity. "It seemed to be miles away," the squad's newest agent remembered thinking. "But, clamping my lips together and throwing one quick look at the unguarded back door of the Montmartre, I jammed my spikes into the pole and started my ascent. The higher I reached the more naked I felt, even though the figure of Ness standing tensely below me with drawn gun offered a certain amount of solace."

A certain amount, but not enough. Robsky moved rapidly at first, with the crablike shuffle of telephone men everywhere: hand, hand, foot, foot, push. Hand, hand, foot, foot, push. He'd made it about halfway up the pole before he got a funny feeling.

He looked down. He was certain he'd heard something. He found Eliot directly below him, heater at the ready. Robsky's eyes flicked over to the back of the club. He saw nothing.

But someone could come banging through that door at any moment. Someone was sure to. He felt a prickle along his temples, another at the base of his spine. He'd begun to sweat. Panicked sweat. He closed his eyes, willed it away. He forced himself to look up. The terminal box stretched into the heavens. A pinprick at the top of the world. Hand, hand, foot, foot, push. Hand, hand, foot, foot —

Robsky froze. Someone had come through that door. *Shit.*

He didn't look down. He listened, hugging the pole like it was a Teddy bear. It was nothing, he told himself. A passing car braking at a stop sign. A street vendor slamming open his drawer for a customer. It wasn't the back door of the Montmartre Café. No way. He'd have heard gunshots by now.

He crab-walked higher. Hand, hand, foot, foot, push. Now he could see the terminal box. It was a real thing, with real dimensions. It *existed.*

When he finally made it to the top, Robsky threw open the box and stared inside. There were at least a hundred and fifty terminals. He developed a headache. He glanced down — Eliot was still there, unmolested — and he turned back to the box. He quickly raked the lines. A secretary at the bureau was supposed to call the Montmartre at exactly four and flirt with the bartender so Robsky would recognize her voice. It was now about ten past.[*] Chapman had been assigned to the phone in the Cermak Road apartment, where he would be talking with Lahart at the office, two more recognizable voices in the babble. Robsky flipped down one row and across another. Nothing. He looked down at Eliot until he got his attention and shook his head. Eliot waved at him to keep trying. Robsky began flipping through the terminals again, his fingers cramping from the stress. His breathing became ragged. Hanging up there in plain sight, he felt like "a clay pigeon in a shooting gallery." At last he hit one — Chapman, his distinctive booming laugh — and a minute later he got the secretary. *Bingo.* He gave Eliot the OK sign, slammed the door to the box, and began to work his way down the pole. He hit the ground with a spine-jarring thud, huffing, his face red from exertion and excitement. He beamed at Eliot, and his boss returned a dreamy smile. They ran out of the alley, pausing at the side of the building to pull themselves together. Robsky shrugged off his equipment. "Phew," he said. "I still can't get over thinking what would have happened if those monkeys had come back while

---

[*] The secretary was probably Edna. Robsky remembered the name when relating the story years later, and it's unlikely Eliot would have trusted any other secretary for such an assignment.

I was up there at the top of the pole."

Eliot eased the brim of his hat back with the barrel of his gun. He offered up a Sam Spade smile. "Why, Paul, I had this little old .38 all ready."

Robsky couldn't help laughing. Remembering the moment many years later, he wondered if Eliot somehow believed that he, and not Robsky, had done the hard part. Not that it really mattered. Robsky's boss got the tough-guy talk out of his system there on the sidewalk, because he couldn't do it anywhere else. This wasn't something he could tell the press about. The two men hustled to their car. They began celebrating — banging the dashboard and whooping — as soon as they closed the doors behind them. They knew they'd just made a big score. Eliot wrote later: "This tap was kept alive for many, many months, and we learned a great deal about the operations and personnel of the gang through it."

With wiretaps in place at almost all known Capone offices, the late winter and spring of 1931 became a swirl of activity for the squad. They hit a brewery at 2271-2273 Lumber Street on the South Side, crashing through four steel doors at the rear of what appeared to be a garage. "The federal men found 140 barrels of beer, nineteen tanks of beer and wort and other equipment," wrote the *Chi-*

151

cago Daily News. The brewery, with a capacity of a hundred barrels a day, had been up and running for only a month. At a warehouse on Calumet Avenue, the special agents seized twelve thousand gallons of "iced beer ready for delivery for the weekend trade" and arrested James Calloway, Delaney's chief assistant. (Calloway was already under indictment for conspiracy for his role in trying to retake the equipment from the raided brewery on South Wabash Avenue.) The agents ran a car off the road on the West Side and came away with $25,000 worth of wine. On his own Eliot chased a truck through busy downtown Chicago until the fleeing vehicle crashed into a post on Clark Street. There were only eleven barrels of beer onboard, but the driver was a wanted man. A few weeks later, the team took down a large still in suburban McHenry, north of Chicago.

During this raiding frenzy, Eliot became a regular at the Northwestern University forensic crime lab bankrolled by the Secret Six and run by Colonel Calvin Goddard. The lab was a one-of-a-kind experiment, predating even the FBI laboratory. Here Eliot met Leonarde Keeler, a twenty-seven-year-old prodigy who was trying to gin up interest in his "Respondograph" — a lie-detector machine. Keeler was a disciple of police innovator August Vollmer, whose graduate-level police-administration course Eliot had recently taken at the University of Chicago. Eliot also became friendly with Clarence Muehlberger, the toxicologist for the Cook County coroner's office. Eliot would grill Muehlberger about his expertise and its application to crime solving, watching him closely as he went about his business. Chemist John R. Matchett remembered seeing Eliot time and again hanging around the offices late at night, a "rather handsome man about five feet ten inches" — people always seemed to think him shorter than he was — "always smiling, but very earnest about his work." Goddard and his pioneering research into ballistics especially fascinated Eliot. The special agent turned over to Goddard every gun his squad confiscated, with the hope of being able to tie a murder around the neck of Al Capone or one of his top men.

Eliot typically went to the laboratory alone. He worried about being seen as different, as the weird guy at the bureau, and he knew his interest in the crime lab wouldn't help his image. Most cops and dry agents viewed the new field of police science with deep skepticism. A few years later, with Capone behind bars and headlines hard to come by, Northwestern sold the crime lab to the Chicago Police Department. The transition did not go smoothly. The criminologist Fred E. Inbau, who worked at the lab, invited command officers to come in so he could walk them through this new resource they had. "I have never met such a hostile group in my life," he would recall. "I just about got on my knees and said, 'Gentlemen, this is *your* laboratory. We didn't ask you to come in here to instruct you. We just want to show you what you now have that you didn't before.' " Inbau made it through his presentation, showing off the ballistics-matching equipment, the microscopes for examining soil specimens, and Keeler's lie-detecting machine, but tension hung over the room. "The ones who had some feeling of understanding or sympathy about it were afraid to even ask questions," Inbau said. "They didn't know what image this would create among their colleagues who professed that they could do the job without all of this jazz."

The promise of modern science thrilled Eliot, but for the most part he filed away his burgeoning knowledge for later use. It was the future of law enforcement, a future he was determined to bring about, but it could not be the present. He recognized that success against the Outfit would depend on old-fashioned police methods. Throughout the team's first months, he and his agents spent almost every night sitting in cars in the bruising late winter cold, their muscles twitching, their hands and feet so icy they felt scalded. They would take turns, one trying to sleep as the others kept watch. Eliot took pages of notes every night, describing everything he saw. He seemed to love every minute of it. Growing up in a house filled with memories of older siblings who were grown and long gone, he had in some ways always felt separate, alone in the universe. Now he felt that he was a part of something. Something substantive, something he could lose himself in.

It was a family, of sorts. Leeson, a former navy man, the quietest of the group, became the unit's unofficial cook. Years later, in another life, he would always prepare the meal for dinner parties, then hand his wife the apron before the guests arrived and insist she take credit for it. He was less embarrassed about his culinary skill when around his fellow squad members. He would cook up simple, meat-heavy dishes and take them out to the men on stakeout duty. His wife, Dorothy, was a worrier. Almost as soon as he left the house, a pot of stew under his arm, she'd start calling around — to the office and the other agents' homes — looking for him. All of the agents and their wives got to know her well.

The Capone squad lived in a hermetic, hothouse world of its own, like scientists racing against the clock to find a cure for a pandemic. To others working in the Prohibition Bureau offices, the team seemed to go everywhere together, always whispering to one another, communicating with nods and smiles. By now Eliot had earned respect around the office. His kindly manner and easy smile made people comfortable. As he walked through the halls in the morning he would light up when someone — anyone — said hello, as if he wanted to see no one else in the world. Agents and support staff noticed how, despite the stress he was under, he "never raised his voice or dressed down his men in front of others." This didn't necessarily mean he handled stress better than anyone else. Like Dorothy Leeson, he was a congenital worrier. Stanley Slesick, one of the Prohibition agents Eliot would tap to provide backup for large operations, always knew when a raid was coming. Eliot, he said, was a "nervous" man, and it showed in his eyes, his pallor. "He'd always bite his fingernails," Slesick said.

Eliot had good reason to be nervous. He wanted to believe in every member of his team, but the fact was he couldn't be sure whom he could trust. Even reporters had begun to speculate among themselves about the squad's agents. "He and the six or seven other people that were called the Untouchables, I don't know whether they were untouchable," former *Chicago American* photographer Tony Berardi would recall. Berardi had made his reputation by snapping pictures of

gangsters; he came to know many of them —
and their business — well. He understood
how things worked. "I think they were touch-
able," he said of the Capone squad.

So did Eliot. He realized everyone potentially was. After the Cicero raid in March, an
envoy from the Outfit told Eliot they'd match
his annual salary every month if he played
along. Eliot threw the messenger out of his
office and immediately informed Johnson and
Froelich about the bribe attempt. The next
day, an informant who worked both sides told
Eliot that the gang had dug up incriminating
evidence on him. "They have information
that you got your job under false pretenses,"
the informant said. "Wouldn't that go pretty
hard against you on the witness stand?" Eliot
told the man he wouldn't need his services
anymore.

These ham-handed bribe attempts forced
Eliot to reevaluate his trusting nature once
and for all. He knew the Mob must be approaching his men, too — and what did it
mean if the guys didn't tell him about the
enticements? In the squad's first couple of
months, he and Seager periodically spied on
their own agents, using Chicago police officers they believed they could trust. They told
themselves it was just a fail-safe, to put their
minds at ease, but sure enough, the information that came in occasionally proved dis-
heartening. Leeson would later tell his second

wife that "there were certain Untouchables in the beginning that were let go because they took bribes."

Eliot and Seager had no choice but to stay vigilant, even after the squad had been pared down to a core group. The Outfit believed in the power of payoffs like it was a religion; they would never give up trying to force cash on agents. "Capone's men would pop up from nowhere on a street and offer us money to lay off," Chapman recalled years later. The offers weren't just enticing. They were astounding. The amounts kept getting bigger and bigger. So whenever one of the squad's raids turned up an empty warehouse, or a gangster disappeared right after a search warrant had been issued, Eliot would start to worry. And he and Seager would initiate a secret search for a new potential turncoat. By late spring, they had a couple of suspects — the usual suspects.

CHAPTER 9
HOW CLOSE IT HAD BEEN

William Gardner looked like a G-man. He was tall and broad-shouldered, with a cocky, loose-limbed walk and an emotionless stare. No one ever expressed surprise when he said he was a federal agent.

He never really felt like one. Gardner had been born on Indian land in North Dakota, his mother a teenage Chippewa girl, his father a white soldier he never knew. Gardner would be successfully assimilated into the wider society — he wore sharp Brooks Brothers suits and spoke the King's English — but, half Indian and half white, he was never comfortable in it. The only place he ever believed he belonged was the playing field. He played college football for the Carlisle Indian Industrial School, a Native American boarding school/indoctrination camp whose stated purpose was to "kill the Indian and save the man." The institution almost always failed on both counts.

Gardner's Carlisle team had been the best

in the country, a sensation. (It was so good that the legendary Jim Thorpe was a second-stringer on the squad.) Gardner wasn't the most talented guy out there, but he was the most reliable. He thrived on pressure. When the Indians found themselves up against it during their glorious 1907 season, they didn't pull out the tricks — even though their coach, Pop Warner, was a proud innovator. They put the ball in Gardner's hands. Who was going to stop this tall, fluid end who moved like a freight train? No one. When Carlisle played Harvard, disbelief among the Ivy League's best soon turned to anger as Gardner ground out the yards play after play. The flower of America's youth couldn't accept being beaten by a bunch of Indians. Finally, Harvard defensive tackle Waldo Pierce snapped. Getting up after a tackle, he sucker-punched Gardner with a left hook to the jaw. They had to carry the Carlisle star off the field. But he would be back — and mighty Harvard would fall. To close out the season, the Indians crushed the University of Chicago, the Big Ten champion, a victory Coach Warner would later say gave him "greater satisfaction" than any other in his long career. Much of the credit for the win, he said, belonged to Gardner, who "had his leg wrenched and his jaw broken . . . and played on to the finish without telling me a word about it, afraid I would send in a substitute."

This courage was one of the things Eliot liked about William Gardner. He was well aware of Gardner's football career and often brought it up in conversation. Eliot respected physical strength and quiet authority. He would later describe Gardner admiringly as "a full-blooded Indian who was a very handsome boy, and a fashion plate. Bill must have weighed about 240 pounds and he was all muscle."

That was certainly the man Eliot wanted to see, but it wasn't the one he actually knew. Gardner's upstanding courage and all-muscle physique were long gone by the time he joined the Capone squad. He was now middle-aged and alcoholic and angry at the world. Eliot was under no illusions about this. Along with his having been fired for laziness, Gardner's record with the Prohibition Bureau was dotted with disappearances that his supervisors officially chalked up to family problems but were almost certainly alcoholic benders. And there was still another explanation for the disappearances, one even less palatable. Not long after Gardner returned to work in 1928, thanks to Senator Curtis's intervention, an anonymous letter arrived at the New Jersey bureau office. It was from a man claiming to be a permit holder — someone, such as a pharmacist, who had a legal reason for obtaining alcohol. It was addressed to an agent who'd recently had a high-profile case.

You appear in the newspapers in the role of sleuth. You are to be commended for this work but you ought to start in your own of-fice. You had a man named Gardner who loved to handle matters concerning alcohol and inspections. We understood that he was dismissed but one of my permit friends just told me today that he had word from that man who told him that he was on his way back and would report for work again soon. He said he had too many strong political friends to be sidetracked by you are [*sic*] that fellow Hanlon.

Now just a good tip. Gardner is a hustler and while a piker in some cases he is always busy getting his. I am a permit holder myself and I know. Some agent I believed named Connelly was at my place once while I mixed some of my denatured alcohol. This man told me I did not have to spoil it, just call Gradner [*sic*] on the tele-phone. He would fix things all right. This man Gradner [*sic*] at one time worked with Carife and Palmer and now my friend tells me that Palmer says he was double crossed by this indian. Now I am going right myself with my permit and living up to all the government laws and I believe others ought to also. I could get along better if fellows like Gardner who is trying to holf [*sic*] up people were out of this work.

Eliot undoubtedly knew about this old corruption accusation against Gardner. Alexander Jamie, who signed off on Gardner's transfer back to Chicago, mentioned it in memos to Washington. Of course, the charge didn't necessarily mean anything. It came from an anonymous source, which suggested a bootlegger could be behind it. Still, taken with Gardner's well-documented disappearances and insubordination over the years, it was troubling. Eliot decided to keep him out of the wiretap work, which he believed would bring the most useful evidence for court. And for field assignments, he often teamed him up with Lyle Chapman, his other problem agent.

Chapman was a morale killer, too, though in a different way than Gardner. Gardner was surly, but at least he kept to himself. Chapman was expansive, funny — and annoying. His boss in Indianapolis had complained that Chapman needed to "get it out of his head that all the women in the country are crazy about him and . . . somebody is always abusing him." With his bland good looks and bouncy personality, Chapman, though newly married, prided himself on being a cocksman and loved to talk about his exploits. This impressed his shy, self-effacing new supervisor in Chicago, for Eliot, despite being newly married himself, also couldn't help being drawn to attractive young women out in the world. This shared eye for the ladies did not lead the two men into a close friendship, however. Chapman, unlike Eliot, seemed to view assignments that required long hours and late nights — the very definition of the Capone squad's work — as a conspiracy by priggish supervisors to make him celibate. This was a problem, to say the least. Eliot, Johnson, and Froelich needed Chapman to be on his game. For all his flights of fancy, the man had a mind like a calculator. It was his job to sift and organize evidence from raids, wiretaps, informants, and prisoner interviews. More than that, he had to make sense of it all, to provide the U.S. district attorney's office with a guidebook to Capone's Volstead Act violations. Not many agents in the bureau could do this work well.

Chapman's biggest problem seemed to be a desire for attention. Bureau administrators sent worried memos back and forth, especially after a report came in that at private parties Chapman "shows and reads . . . various official papers [from the Capone files] to any one that cares to listen, evidently for the purpose of making himself appear as a 'big shot.' " This obviously did not speak well of the agent's judgment. He could single-handedly blow the Volstead case against

Capone. He could ruin everything. Eliot would have to keep a close eye on him.

Eliot and Edna had never gotten around to taking a honeymoon. Eliot was too ambitious. He wanted to get ahead in the bureau, move up the ladder. In his five years with the Chicago office, he had never even considered taking a sick day. Now that he was leading his own unit, he worked even longer hours — through the night and every weekend. He stayed hyper-focused on the task at hand: Capone, always Capone. When it came right down to it, his only romance was with the Big Fella.

For this reason, Edna would be almost entirely overlooked in the Ness mythos that would rise up in the decades ahead. She was easily eclipsed by the high drama that happened night after night in the Capone brewery hunt. She appears nowhere in *The Untouchables,* Eliot's memoir, even though the book's action takes place when she ostensibly was the most important person in his life. (Her name was replaced with "Betty," the name of Eliot's wife at the time of the book's writing, a woman Eliot didn't meet until years after the Capone squad had disbanded.) Edna may not have minded being overlooked by history. She liked to keep a low profile. She would never use her famous married name for attention or profit. "Her greatest wish was not to be known," longtime friend Maxine Huntington would say years later. Maybe so, but Alexander Jamie's former secretary certainly was well known in the Chicago Prohibition office, in Eliot's world. She understood her husband's work life better than any other woman ever would. That made her the perfect companion for Eliot, at least at this moment in his life, when work was everything. She was a law-and-order true believer herself. After the excitement of a raid, Eliot would lay in bed in their little apartment, Edna next to him, and roll the night's events over in his mind — the cocked guns and the screaming and the running. He'd sometimes shudder at "how close it had been." He would break out in a cold sweat thinking about it. He never told Edna about these moments of panic. He feared she wouldn't understand. Nothing ever put her in a panic. She was tough. Eliot liked that about her.

Edna worried about her husband, but she also egged him on. Eliot worked twelve, sixteen, eighteen hours a day, for weeks at a time. Edna never complained. Her father, a factory worker, had regularly clocked double shifts to feed his family, so Eliot's dedication to work was normal to her. On top of that, she was a part of it all; she worked right there in the Prohibition office, handled important paperwork, read the telexes. She saw that Eliot's long hours were beginning to pay off. Thanks to the Capone squad's raids — and the new safeguards and payoffs undertaken by the Outfit as a result — costs had spiked for the gang. By late spring, saloon owners had noticed that the syndicate's thirty-two-gallon barrels — the very ones the squad continued to follow around the city and back to the cleaning facility near Comiskey Park — were now being delivered with just thirty gallons of beer in them. When called on it, the goons told the beer sellers they were mistaken. The saloons continued to pay for thirty-two gallons while receiving less.

Frustrated by the diminished profit margin, the Outfit turned to harassing Eliot and his men. The Mob stole their cars and abandoned them miles away. It spread rumors about them. It called the Prohibition Bureau office and threatened whoever answered the phone. Gangsters began tailing the agents and hanging around outside their homes. "I remember twice Ness and I drove fast to my apartment when [my wife] reported hoods were outside and she was scared," Chapman recalled. One night Eliot caught a junior gangster lurking outside the Stahle family home. The man wasn't carrying a weapon, and he left without putting up a fight. Eliot's car was stolen at least twice. After he got it back the second time, he came out of his apartment the next morning to find it on blocks, the front wheels missing. Agent Dan Vaccarelli had been on assignment with the Capone squad for only a few days when his car disappeared. Lahart and Seeley also reported their cars stolen. The bureau was able to confirm the harassment when Prohibition agents arrested a mobbed-up nimrod named Albert Richter in suburban Winnetka. Searching his pockets, they pulled out a piece of paper with a list of fifteen license-plate numbers and descriptions of makes and models. All of the cars on the list belonged to agents on or working with the Capone squad.

Sensing the federal authorities closing in on Big Al, Capone's remaining rivals tried to take advantage. They moved in on his turf, or at least nibbled around the edges. They sent flunkies to be government informants. They knocked off delivery trucks just like the Capone squad. Chicagoans opened up the paper every morning expecting to read about the next St. Valentine's Day Massacre. Everyone knew what was going to happen when Scarface Al and his thousand-strong army became desperate.

Chapter 10
The Untouchables

On June 5, 1931, the government alleged in a twenty-two-count indictment that Alphonse Capone had earned at least $1,038,654.84 between 1924 and 1929. This haul, needless to say, was entirely illicit. He hadn't paid any taxes on it, putting him well over one hundred thousand dollars in arrears. The tax case, acknowledged IRS special agent Frank Wilson, one of its chief architects, was "circumstantial in character," seeing as Capone had no bank accounts, nothing in his name, and dealt only in cash. But the government had already proven it could use tax cases to put mobsters behind bars and keep them there. George Johnson planned to rely on the testimony of Capone associates who had the threat of long prison sentences hanging over them. After more than two long years of work, the tax men finally had a swagger about them.

A week later, it was the Capone squad's turn. Their evidence brought another indictment of the Mob boss, along with sixty-eight other gangsters, for violation of Prohibition laws and conspiracy. This indictment alleged more than five thousand offenses, most involving the transportation of beer. Through various methods — such as the Capone squad staking out barrel-cleaning facilities and counting the average turnover — Johnson argued that the gross amount of beer the syndicate sold in a year "exceeded $13,000,000.00" in value. As with the tax case, the evidence here was chiefly circumstantial. They would have to strong-arm Capone's indicted associates — distribution chief Joe Fusco and brewmasters Steve Svoboda and Bert Delaney, among others — into admitting that the man referred to in wiretapped conversations as Snorky, the Big Fella, and Number One was Capone. They could sort of link to Capone a couple of trucks confiscated in brewery raids in March and April; the trucks had passed through the Big Fella's hands before he became the boss and started keeping everything at arm's length.

The tax case against Capone would come first, though the bootlegging indictment would serve as an important fallback plan in case the tax charges failed to stick. Johnson worried that the Capone moneymen he was counting on to sell out the big man on the witness stand were wavering. They were "fearful and reluctant," Johnson wrote to U.S.

Attorney General William Mitchell. The deciding factor for the tax case going first, despite the shaky witnesses, was that prosecutors believed it would be easier to work up a jury's outrage over tax cheating — especially during a depression, when the government needed every dime it could get — than over providing liquor to willing customers. But while the tax case offered the best shot at conviction, the press naturally found the Prohibition charges sexier. The *Chicago Tribune*'s report leaned hard on the confiscated trucks:

The sensational rise of Al Capone on a tidal wave of beer, ministering to a $20,000,000 a year thirst in a decade of Volsteadism, is told by the government's evidence in the conspiracy case which is expected to hasten the fall of the chief of gang chiefs.

The beginning of that evidence, federal investigators disclosed yesterday, goes back to the incorporation in 1921, under the laws of Illinois, of the World Motor Service company, ostensibly a commercial trucking concern. . . . The first step after the organization of the new company was the purchase of four trucks of five tons capacity each. Two of these, the government's evidence will show, were bought by Al Brown, the purchasing agent and general handy man for the company.

Al Brown was the name used by Al Capone after he was brought to Chicago from the Brooklyn Five Points gang in 1919 to serve as bodyguard for Big Jim Colosimo, and later for Johnny Torrio, who displaced Colosimo. . . .

To clinch all this evidence against the "big shots" of the gang — the small fry having been caught tending breweries — the federal men have the reports of conversations on tapped telephone wires. These reports, say the agents, link the alleged conspirators together.

The article ended with a hat tip to the Capone squad: "United States Attorney Johnson yesterday praised the work of the eight young men of the special prohibition detail, headed by Eliot Ness, who perfected the conspiracy case. They worked at the risk of death and resisted the temptation of bribes several times as high as their salaries for a year, Mr. Johnson said."

This brief mention was the beginning of the legend that in the decades ahead would reach America's TV screens and movie theaters. Subsequent news stories about the squad declared that all of the agents had graduated from college, which meant they were the country's elite. Fewer than 5 percent of American adults then had a college degree.

The reports also insisted that the squad's average age was just thirty. Both claims were untrue, but truth wasn't important. The Capone squad had a catchy new nickname: "the untouchables." The Associated Press announced:

The "untouchables," eight young prohibition agents whose zeal and incorruptibility defied danger and lavish temptation to pile up evidence for the conspiracy indictment against "Scarface" Al Capone and his booze syndicate, today received their reward.

It was a declaration by United States District Attorney George E. Q. Johnson, director of the Government's campaign against Capone cohorts, that all the praise heaped on him for the dogged pursuit of the gangsters should be shared with the eight members of the special unit. They were the men on the firing line.

The report added that seven of the eight agents "remain anonymous for various reasons." Eliot, quoted briefly in the article, was the lone exception. The decision to have Eliot and only Eliot speak for the group was probably made by Johnson, who wanted to control the flow of information about the Capone case. (Most of the agents currently with the team received recognition within the federal law-enforcement bureaucracy. The week after the indictments came down, an agencywide Prohibition Bureau newsletter heralded the Capone squad's role in the case. "The whole accomplishment represents splendid unity of action between agents of the Intelligence Unit of the Treasury and the Bureau of Prohibition under direction of U.S. Attorney Johnson of Chicago," the newsletter said. "Great credit is due to Asst. Special Agent in Charge Eliot Ness, Chicago, and to Agent Jos. D. Leeson, Cincinnati, Ohio, and Special Agent Lyle B. Chapman, Detroit, Div. Credit is also due to Special Agents: Saml. M. Seager, Warren E. Stutzman, Paul W. Robsky, Martin J. Lahart, Bernard V. Cloonan, all of Chicago; Special Agent Robert D. Sterling, Detroit, Mich., and Special Agent M. King, Richmond, Va.")

Despite the internal huzzahs, Eliot's appearance in the newspapers sparked resentments that some of the squad members would carry with them for years. After weeks of talking to the press, the twenty-eight-year-old special agent had become a local celebrity — and he clearly loved every minute of it. In one of his first interviews after the indictments, he showed off his fancy college education by saying he didn't approve of the nickname the press had given the team, because "untouchable" was the name for members of India's lowest caste. Colleagues noticed that Eliot seemed to walk a little taller, act a little cheerier, after being interviewed by a reporter. This was undoubtedly true (Eliot would bask in the media spotlight throughout his career), but he didn't seek out reporters *only* for his ego. Influenced by the noted criminologist August Vollmer, he also believed that talking to the press helped law enforcement; news coverage made police efforts appear bigger and better, their success inevitable. Openness with the press, Vollmer had said during the University of Chicago police-administration course Eliot took in 1929, made the public more likely to support the police and punctured the criminal class's confidence. Eliot now saw that Vollmer was right. Even mobsters believed the squad's press notices. A Capone goon recognized one of Eliot's men on the street one day and marched up to him. "Everyone here in Chicago gets along good with each other," he said. "Why not you?"

With such encouraging results, Eliot wasn't above giving reporters an incentive for providing good press. "The United States government had, still has, a large warehouse on Thirty-ninth between Halsted Street and Ashland Avenue," recalled Tony Berardi, the *Chicago American* photographer, in 1999. "Whenever they raided a place and took the booze, they'd take it there. Eliot Ness would call the newspaper office and say, 'Listen, send one of your cameramen out here without any cameras.' He did that to me a couple of times. We'd go out there without any cameras and he'd fill our camera cases full of booze, and we'd take it to the office and split it." The *American* was one of the papers read by Eliot's parents.

On the same day the short article about the "untouchables" went out on the Associated Press wire, the *Chicago Herald and Examiner,* the *American*'s sister paper, produced the first profile of Eliot. The young special agent puffed up when he talked about his decision to become a Prohibition agent. "It offered a lot of excitement . . . for there certainly is a thrill in pitting your wits against others'," he said. "Besides, I don't think that I could stand the monotony of an office." The reporter, Priscilla Higinbotham, wrote that while Eliot wasn't a rabid dry, he believed strongly "in wiping out the evils that the law has brought about. It is not only his desire to run Capone and his henchmen out of town, but he particularly wishes to destroy the corruptive influences in politics that have resulted from the Capone reign." This had become a pet subject of Eliot's, ever since he had tuned in to a conversation on one of the wiretapped lines and learned that Capone had both candidates for a Cicero office in his pocket, one of whom claimed to be a reform man. Eliot hated hypocrisy.

The profile's theme, however, was Eliot's

gung-ho boyishness. "It's funny, I think, when you back up a truck to a brewery door and smash it in," he told Higinbotham. "And then find some individuals inside that you hadn't expected." Asked about the dangers of his job, Eliot reached back to the meeting with Joe Martino in Chicago Heights. He didn't mention Frank Basile's murder and the guilt he felt over it. He kept it light. When he told the reporter about the dead-eyed Italian leaning into Martino and asking, "Shall I put a knife into him?" Eliot chuckled and said: "We had thought everything was going so well, too."

Such insouciance — with those sad blue eyes, and that sweet, boyish smile — won over the twenty-two-year-old "girl" reporter. She left him with an embarrassing flush painting her cheeks. Her article would describe him strictly in heroic terms. It closed with Eliot heading out for a "tennis engagement": "This, he explained, was just a 'workout' necessary to prepare him for more hours and hours of intensive work to insure Alphonse Capone's ultimate sojourn behind bars."

Eliot didn't mean to sound flip when talking about such serious matters. Part of it was bravado. Reporters allowed him to be someone else, someone *more* than he thought he was. His confidence had bloomed since becoming a special agent back in 1928, but

177

his insecurities couldn't be entirely banished. They were as much a part of him as his boyish face. He wanted to convince reporters — and himself — that he was up to any task.

However flippant he may have sounded, Americans loved it. Fan mail started to flow into the Prohibition Bureau offices in Chicago. A representative sampling captures a country that no longer had a taste for "anything goes," a country that wanted its freedom, but safety and respect, too. Wrote Darwin H. Clark, an advertising man from Los Angeles:

Dear Mr. Ness:

Just a note to express my hearty congratulations to you and your associates for the good work you have done in landing Al Capone, and we hope others of his gang, behind bars.

I feel, like thousands of others in this territory, utmost respect for men of your caliber that cannot be touched by the lawless in a city such as Chicago. Your intelligence, courage and integrity deserve a great deal of commendation, and I hope you will keep up the good work.

Another man in California, a former Chicagoan, wrote:

Dear Mr. Ness,

God bless you and the others for the good work you have done. . . . Keep up the good work, as those rats surely will bob up again when they think no one is watching.

Even many repeal activists jumped on the Untouchables' bandwagon. Halbert Louis Hoard, the editor of the *Jefferson County Union* in Wisconsin, understood that the gangsters hardly wanted to be rid of Volstead. He wrote to Eliot:

Dear Mr. Ness,

I am 100 percent wet, but I applaud you for your bravery. The sooner you put these bootlegger drys where they can't vote for Prohibition, the quicker we can get a repeal of the 18th amendment. I'm for you.

Newspaper editorialists picked up on the enthusiasm. The *Hollywood Daily Citizen* wrote that "the country owes to this young man and the other unnamed workers who assisted him a great debt of gratitude." The editorial continued:

There is an inspiration in that young fellow's work not only for other young men but for the older people who have grown discouraged in the battle for good government.

No soldier on the battle field ever performed more heroic work than has Eliot Ness performed. He should be honored as are the heroes of the battle field honored.

This country needs more of the heroism displayed by Eliot Ness — more of war heroism in peace time.

This being America, such amazing press meant there was money to be made. A publicity man, Raymond Schwartz, wrote to Eliot offering to put his story, in his own words, in magazines across the country. He proposed a series of five or ten articles, "short but very brisk," about the special agent's work chasing down Al Capone. He said "the proceeds should run well into the thousands," with Eliot splitting it with the magazine wire service.

Eliot didn't take Schwartz up on the offer; it's possible his superiors at the bureau considered it unseemly. For now he would have to ride the publicity wave without remuneration. He continued to give interviews in his office and at raid sites. He tipped off the papers about arrests. Reporters inevitably found their way to the Ness family home, too. Emma, intimately familiar with the press her son had received, gushed that Eliot had been the best-behaved, most honest boy ever. Eliot's father said nothing. Or at least nothing memorable — he was never quoted. Eliot noticed. In a moment of rare emotional candor, he admitted to a reporter that he wished he knew his father better.

A week after the Prohibition indictments, only sixteen of the sixty-eight men named with Capone had surrendered or been arrested. The Capone squad, along with a series of special police details, went in search of the rest, swooping down on the gang's usual haunts. They stormed the Lexington and Metropole hotels on South Michigan Avenue, marched into the Montmartre in Cicero, muscled their way into Joe Fusco's "cabaret and pay-off joint" near the University of Chicago. Empty. Deserts. They'd all gone "on the lam."

It was frustrating for the squad, but it also meant the world had fundamentally changed. Gangsters were no longer strutting around like they owned the town. Some of Capone's most trusted lieutenants, stuck in hiding, couldn't conduct business. (Eliot would spot dashing Mob associate George Howlett, indicted along with Capone, at the Northwestern-Indiana football game. Howlett rushed out of the stadium, hopped into a new sports car, and roared off. Eliot zoomed out of the parking lot right behind him. By the end of the third quarter, Howlett was in the county jail, one more coconspirator scratched from the list of the missing.)

The wiretaps continued to bring in information. They showed that Capone's captains had already begun talking about who should succeed the Big Fella. Wrote the *Tribune*, in a scoop straight from Johnson and Prohibition administrator E. C. Yellowley: "In disputing among themselves, federal dry agents say, the gang captains have eliminated as possible successors to Capone all those who have been hit by federal convictions or charges. This means, say the special agents, that names little known are due to loom up as the result of the gang's reorganization. Four gangsters were mentioned by the federal men as heirs presumptive. They are Llewellyn Humphries, Rocco De Grasse, Frank Rio and Teddy Newberry."

In other words, nobodies. Second-raters. Johnson was declaring victory. The Chicago Mob would go on — everyone knew there was no way to eliminate organized crime entirely — but it would be with a haggard expression and a noticeable limp. The U.S. district attorney pressed Eliot to keep up the pressure. Already, the Mob was in lockdown mode; men were jumpy and exhausted. They increasingly avoided their regular places of business. No one was willing to take a risk. That meant customers went thirsty and market share began to shrink. This new reality for the gang was unmistakable in many of Eliot's handwritten wiretap transcripts

("In" represents the speaker on the phone being tapped):

> *Out:* Is Johnny there?
> *In:* No, he isn't.
> *Out:* Well, listen, I got a truck down here at the [undecipherable] and I haven't any more.
> *In:* How much do you need?
> *Out:* Around ten dollars.
> *In:* I can let you have it if you come after it.
> *Out:* I am not coming up there.

Another call complained about a delivery not arriving.

> *In:* You know we had a big place knocked off last night.
> *Out:* No, I didn't know it.
> *In:* Yes, a big place at 51st and Halsted.
> *Out:* That is too bad.
> *In:* I am going down there now. You better meet me there and we will have a drink.
> *Out:* No, I can't. There is nobody else here now.

To be sure, the Outfit wasn't about to just roll over. Gangsters had mortgages to pay; they had children and gambling habits to feed. And they still had some tricks. On a steamy day in July, after staking out the building for days, the Capone squad and some borrowed Prohibition agents hit a garage in the 3400 block of North Clark Street, rushing in from both sides with spirited whoops and hollers. When the men met up in the middle of the darkened interior, the only sound was their breathing and the odd cricket clicking away in the rafters. The place was empty except for them.

"Well, boys, it looks like we're dished again," Eliot said, no doubt wondering if someone from his own team had tipped off the gang. One of the men pulled a handkerchief out of his pocket to wipe his dripping brow — the squat building really packed in the heat — and out popped a fifty-cent piece. The coin bounced on the cement floor, spun, and rolled. And kept on rolling — until it dropped through a sewer grate. Everyone froze. No one wanted to lose even a dime these days, but that wasn't it. The coin had made an odd little thunk when it landed inside the grate. The men gathered around the opening in the floor. Eliot kneeled down, wrenched open the grating, and peered in. He saw the edge of a crate. They had discovered a twelve-foot-square underground chamber. Over the next hour, they hauled out a hundred and nine crates, each one packed with the "finest imported liquors." Eliot would estimate the value of the cache at $15,000. Plus fifty cents. They never found the dropped coin.

By now, with the press watching and Johnson preparing to bring Capone to trial, the Capone squad had become increasingly adventurous, its actions taking on a Three Musketeers quality. The battering ram wasn't enough anymore. It was old hat, boring. On the night of September 21, 1931, Eliot and three of his men crouched in the dark near the entrance to an industrial building at 222 East Twenty-fifth Street. When a truck pulled up to the entrance and tapped its horn for admittance, the agents slipped out of their hiding places and grabbed on to the back. They rode into the building, past the series of barricades, jumped off the truck's bumper, and locked the doors. The warehouse's four workers stood there gaping at them. None of them attempted to run. The agents looked around; the floor was covered with ice, forcing everyone to step gingerly or take a pratfall. The building was in the process of being turned into a full-scale brewery; the ice served as makeshift refrigeration. The agents kept everyone quiet until a second truck drove up to the entrance and the driver knocked. The agents opened the doors, guns drawn, hard smiles punched into their faces like puzzle pieces. The driver gave up without protest. His partner bounded out of the passenger seat and sprinted down the street. An agent took off after him. After a block, he rode the man to the ground.

Eliot found a phone and called the newspapers. Once the hacks showed up, the four Untouchables lapped the building with axes swinging. They dumped three hundred gallons of beer and took into custody fifty-six cases of hard liquor. The reporters went home with their coat pockets clinking.

The Outfit, its strong-arm tactics and bribes largely ineffective, realized it had to do something different. So it began to adopt the Capone squad's own methods. No agent noticed when men in coveralls scaled telephone poles along Dearborn Street outside the Transportation Building. In the weeks that followed, the phone company received dozens of complaints from downtown customers about disconnections and strange clicks. When it investigated, the utility discovered that several lines into the Prohibition Bureau's offices had been tapped. An anonymous agent told a reporter that the Mob had been listening to Eliot's calls for three months, but the young leader of the Capone squad denied it. Eliot would be embarrassed about it even years later; he would claim in *The Untouchables* that he discovered the tap himself.

The tapped phones surely helped the Outfit sidestep a fair number of raids, and it probably also allowed some indicted mobsters on the lam to stay on the lam. But it wasn't enough to hold back the tide. The following March, with the squad locking down evidence for a possible Capone trial on Prohibition violations, Eliot turned in a report detailing the team's major work. He wrote:

From the inception of the organization of the special group . . . six breweries with total equipment valued at $140,000 were seized. Observation of the workings of these breweries indicated that the total income based upon the wholesale [price] of beer manufactured would have totaled $9,154,200 annually. Five large beer distributing plants were seized in addition to the breweries. The total amount of beer seized in the breweries and plants was approximately 200,000 gallons having a wholesale value to the Capone organization of $343,750. Twenty-five trucks and two cars were seized, the value of which totaled approximately $30,950. Many of these trucks were large trucks exceeding ten tons and some of them were specifically constructed. Four stills were seized with an approximate value of $12,000. 403,500 gallons of alcohol mash were seized in connection with these stills, value of said mash approximating $4,000.

As Eliot's memo makes clear, the Untouchables did not shut down the Capone booze operation. Far from it. Soon after a brewery or cleaning plant or distribution facility would get knocked out, another would pop up somewhere else. Few saloons ever saw a break in their deliveries. That said, the raiders were undeniably having an impact. Costs were up, consistent revenue harder to come by. There was also the psychological effect, the siege mentality that now infected the syndicate. The *Chicago Daily News* wrote that Eliot Ness was "the especial thorn in the side of the Capone mob," estimating that the young agents' team had stopped output that would have totaled $2 million. "In addition to their steady drain on Capone's war chest," the newspaper continued, "the special agents have kept the Capone legal staff busy defending thirty-one men arrested in these raids. Capone's high-priced lawyers have had to prepare for the defense of Capone and sixty-eight others indicted for conspiracy."

What made all of this particularly bad news for the Outfit: it couldn't raise prices. For the first time since Prohibition began, the cost of a glass of "real beer" in Chicago had dropped, from 25 cents to 15 cents. The Outfit was getting hit with a double whammy: the Untouchables and the Depression. So far, the syndicate had refused to lower prices, keeping them at $55 per barrel, but saloon-keepers cut their prices anyway. They didn't have a choice. Customers increasingly went elsewhere and paid less for near beer. Some club owners took their lives in their hands by driving to Joliet or farther downstate to buy beer outside of Capone's purview for $35 a barrel. Their saloons often received warnings: rocks tossed through windows, customers harassed on the way into the bars. The warnings sometimes worked, sometimes not. The fact was, the gang's makeshift leadership didn't inspire the same fear as Capone, who was preoccupied with his coming tax trial. On a Sunday in July, truck drivers even dared to go on strike after the syndicate announced pay cuts, forcing Joe Fusco and Bert Delaney to make deliveries themselves.

"Why cut us?" one driver reportedly told Fusco. "You still charge $55 a barrel for the beer. We take all the chances and do all the work in this hot weather."

"All the saloonkeepers owe us money," Fusco told the men. "They're hard up and we can't make them pay. You've got to take a wage cut."

The drivers didn't buy that argument. On Monday, they again stayed home. Barrels of beer piled up at warehouses. The next day, Fusco brought out his enforcers, and after a few beatings and threats, everyone went back to work.

CHAPTER 11
A REAL AND LASTING IMPRESSION

On October 5, 1931, Al Capone went on trial for tax evasion. He tried to maintain his dignity, his above-it-all swagger, during this unsettling new phase of his bossdom, but it wasn't easy. Stepping out of his bulletproof sedan on the trial's first day and looking around — at the photographers standing atop their cars along Clark Street, the gawkers shoving and pushing to get close to the courthouse entrance — he understood that Chicago no longer viewed him as Good-Hearted Al. This mob of reporters and store clerks and housewives wanted to see him humiliated.

Eliot was already sitting in Judge James Wilkerson's sixth-floor courtroom when Capone came through the heavy, magnificently arched doors. The special agent craned his neck like everyone else. At last, the man he had been harassing for months became real to him. Not a bogeyman, just a man. A balding, fat, moon-faced young man in a shiny blue suit. An expensively dressed schlub. Eliot stared at the mobster with unrelieved fascination, his jaw clenched. "That's the first [time] that Eliot Ness ever saw Al Capone," insisted Berardi, whose colleagues furiously blasted away with their cameras as Capone strode into the courtroom, their flashbulbs disgorging thick puffs of smoke in the Mob boss's face. Berardi, with a miniature camera hidden in his hat, had found a seat in the front row, where he patiently waited for his opportunity to snap a page-one photo.

Despite the turnabout in Capone's popularity, no one could confidently predict the trial's outcome. George Johnson had been nervous enough about the case's strength that he negotiated a plea deal with Capone's lawyers back in July that would have put the gangster in prison for two and a half years. The attorney general signed off on it, but then the newspapers weighed in. Two and a half years for *Capone*? That was some sweet deal, they said. Papers across the country expressed their outrage at the leniency. A few editorials actually suggested that Judge Wilkerson had been bought off. That changed everything. At the eleventh hour the judge unexpectedly declared that he alone would decide the punishment, regardless of the plea deal, forcing Capone's attorneys to call the whole thing off.

Johnson, it turned out, had dodged a bullet. He had a winning hand — and the right judge to carry it through. On the first day of the trial, having received information that Capone's men had a list of the prospective jurors, Wilkerson switched jury pools with another judge. For the first time the Big Fella began to sweat the outcome. Sitting at the defendant's table throughout the first week, he stewed as men he employed — and in some cases had made wealthy — stepped up to the witness stand for the prosecution: mousy little Leslie Shumway, who kept the books at various Capone gambling joints; suave Edward "Easy Eddie" O'Hare, a lawyer and racetrack owner; oily Parker Henderson Jr., Capone's lackey in Miami; Fred Ries, a Capone gambling-house flunky. Capone's lawyer, Michael Ahern, preened and bellowed, accusing the prosecutors of this and that, and that and this, but it didn't help. Frank Wilson had broken the code for Capone's confiscated ledgers, allowing the prosecution to unravel the Mob boss's business finances and pinpoint his "salary." Johnson, taking over for assistant prosecutor Dwight Green for the closing arguments, easily swatted away Ahern's depiction of Capone as a latter-day Robin Hood.

"Did this Robin Hood buy $8,000 worth of belt buckles for the unemployed?" he drawled. "Was his $6,000 meat bill in a few weeks for the hungry? Did he buy $27 shirts for the shivering men who sleep under Wacker Drive?"

The *Tribune* marveled at the performance: "Mr. Johnson was earnest, so much so that he was almost evangelical at times, clenching his fist, shaking his gray head, clamping his lean jaws together as he bit into evidence and tore into the defense theories."

It worked — all of it. The trial lasted all of two weeks, and on October 17, after eight hours and ten minutes of deliberation, the jury reached a verdict. Al Capone was guilty on five counts. Women in the courtroom gasped. Reporters dashed into the hallway. The defendant sat stone-faced, his heavy shoulders rolled forward. By now, he had expected the guilty verdict.

The following week, Capone returned to court. Before another packed room, Judge Wilkerson sentenced him to eleven years in the clink, plus $50,000 in fines. Once again, gasps popped around the room. Court officers hustled Capone into the hall and toward the elevator for transporting prisoners.

"What do you say, Al?" a reporter yelled out.

The greatest and most-feared gang boss in American history stopped and turned. "It was a blow to the belt, but what can you expect when the whole community is prejudiced against you?" he whined. "I've never heard of anyone getting more than five years for income-tax evasion."

In May 1932, federal agents put Alphonse Capone on a train to Atlanta, where a prison cell waited. Chicago was done with him. The Mob boss, who was beginning to shows signs of mental degradation from untreated syphilis, would never return to the Second City. But the Prohibition Bureau's war against Capone's organization didn't end with its leader heading off to the pen. Now there would be a succession battle. In June, a machine-gun volley eviscerated one of the chief candidates for the big chair, George "Red" Barker. Six months later, another potential boss, Ted Newberry, would be murdered. Police considered Joe Fusco and one of Capone's brothers the chief suspects.

Despite the continuation of Mob violence, Eliot experienced a letdown. The cause of prohibition had never appealed to him. He wanted to do a good job for its own sake, for the principle of law and order, and because he saw how organized crime destroyed civic life. But with Capone gone, he now struggled with motivation. He always had difficulty finding emotional highs; only the lows came naturally to him. Shortly after Capone's conviction, he said to Robsky: "Did you ever think you wanted something more than anything else in the world and then, after you got it, it wasn't half as good as you expected? Has that ever happened to you?" For Eliot, this feeling of emptiness would recur time and again throughout his life. Periods of intense productivity would be followed by melancholy and feelings of inadequacy.

After the trial, the Capone squad as a separate unit was officially disbanded. Eliot tried to keep as many of his agents — his band of brothers — as he could. Seager, Chapman, Cloonan, Leeson, and Robsky all would stay on in Chicago and continue to work under Eliot in the special agency unit, where he was now the assistant special agent in charge. In January 1932, Eliot derailed an attempt to reassign Robsky to another city. M. L. Harney, Chicago's new Prohibition administrator, wrote to Washington that Robsky "has acquired a wide knowledge of the activities and personnel of Chicago beer and alcohol gangs, which would make him particularly valuable to Mr. Ness in his new assignment." Harney added: "I do not need to elaborate on the situation which confronts me in Chicago. I have an ambition to make a real and lasting impression on the hoodlums who have monopolized the illicit liquor industry in this vicinity, and I need the assistance of every capable Investigator that I can acquire."

Looking to reignite his own spark, Eliot didn't let his Untouchables bask in their accomplishments: he put them right back to work. On January 21, with Capone still sitting in the Cook County Jail, Eliot and a dozen agents raided a brewery at 2024 South State Street. They arrested five men and confiscated $75,000 worth of booze and brewing equipment. In May, Eliot launched a series of coordinated raids that shut down thirty-three saloons. His team also raided farms up in Lake County, where the Bugs Moran and Roger Touhy gangs ran stills. The press speculated that a new push was on to dry up the city before the summer political conventions. Both the Republicans and the Democrats were coming to the Second City to nominate their presidential candidates.

The agents' success was readily apparent. The syndicate no longer made deliveries in mammoth trucks that even civilians could tell were filled with beer. Now runners used ordinary automobiles that were tricked out to conceal their loads. After nabbing two men as they unloaded beer from a car outside a State Street nightclub, Eliot crowed to reporters:

The automobile was a Ford coach. It was fixed up for the specific purpose of delivering barrels of beer. All seats were taken out except the driver's. When the door on the side is opened, skids are automatically lowered to the ground. Then the barrels are rolled out on these skids. This is a radical departure from the old Capone method of making deliveries in huge and expensive trucks. We have seized so many of their trucks that the syndicate is running short on finances. Also, they probably thought they could fool the agents with these small automobiles.

By now, he had become blasé — even mindless — about the danger inherent in his work. The sharp hunger he had felt during the Capone squad days had dissipated, leading to a casual recklessness as he adjusted to what he viewed as a less important assignment. One night he was headed home to change for a black-tie event downtown — his appearance in newspaper columns led to occasional invitations to society parties — when he somehow ended up finding and smashing up a still in an empty private residence. The home invasion, undertaken single-handedly, made him late for the ball. So he called Armand Bollaert, his old fraternity pal, and asked him to swing by his apartment for his tuxedo and bring it over. Bollaert pulled up to the house and handed over the tux, but reinforcements hadn't shown up yet to cart away the brewing equipment. Eliot asked Bollaert to guard the home until his agents arrived while he went to a nearby police station to shower and change. His friend agreed, but, once Eliot roared off in his car, Bollaert became terrified. He realized gangsters could show up at any moment to discover their still smashed, with him waiting out front like an idiot. "I sat there what seemed like five hours," he remembered. "I wasn't very happy. I could envision all sorts of things."

Eliot could take some comfort from the fact that Al Capone wasn't completely gone from his life. In the spring, while the raids continued on Capone's successors, Eliot and his men increasingly spent their time organizing and cross-referencing evidence for a "new booze conspiracy indictment" against the convicted Mob boss. The previous fall, Eliot had sent Chapman on a tour of Midwest Prohibition offices to gather up evidence related to the Capone syndicate. The assignment took Eliot's "pencil detective" to Detroit; Springfield, Ohio; and a trio of small towns in Indiana — Michigan City, South Bend, and Hammond. Evidence gained through Chapman's travels — as well as through recent raids in the Chicago area — would be tallied up and put to use against the sixty-eight other men who'd been indicted along with Capone the previous June. Johnson told the press that the Volstead case against Capone was "airtight," but he added that he did not have any plans to take it to trial. The objective was to keep the indictment current, and so make Capone ineligible for parole. Even more important, it would be kept ready in case Capone managed to win an appeal on his income-tax conviction.

Back in Chicago, Chapman shut himself in a small office in the Transportation Building and buckled down to work, transcribing testimony, linking it up with specific seizures, and figuring out how the money went up the chain to Capone. On September 7, 1932, he reported to Harney that "I think I am going ahead in good shape. I have completed all evidence in the case for the years 1930, 1929, and 1928. This includes the Cotton Club and the Montmartre cases, which were both large and held me back quite a bit, because they were new to me, and I had to familiarize myself with these two angles before I could analyze the evidence. I have found a big wooden box full of the evidence in these cases and have gone over it thoroughly. However, before I am satisfied with my write-up of the evidence in these cases, I would like to have Goddard, Lahart, or one of the agents participating go over it and see if I have missed any vital points. There is an awful mass of evidence in all these various events in Case 122-B, and while it is slow work, I think that, with the ideas in mind that you gave me, I am on the right track, and will bring out a thorough and fine report."

Chapman was now the star, the man who could make connections in a chaotic mess of material. But a month after that upbeat memo to his bosses, things took a bad turn for him, though he didn't know it. The agent had been spotted at Vanity Fair on the North Side, a nightclub that Prohibition Bureau managers considered "a questionable place for Government officers to be." The bureau secretly opened an investigation and discovered that he was "frequenting places where liquor is sold and . . . consuming liquor not in the line of duty." In the early years of Prohibition, the bureau didn't pay much mind to what agents did during their off hours. They didn't have to, seeing as many agents were temperance veterans or had come highly recommended by prohibition activists. They figured agents would be self-policing. But with the professionalization of the bureau in the middle 1920s, and with repeal forces gaining strength, administrators now made an effort to see that agents met the standards they enforced. At least they did so until it potentially got in the way of high-profile work. Everett H. Kubler, the chief of the bureau's Special Inspection Division, recommended that the investigation of Chapman be held in abeyance. "Chapman is now, and has for some time, been engaged in writing the report of the Capone investigation, and [the Chicago office] believes it would be to the best interests of the Government if this investigation was not begun until that report is practically completed."

So the bureau let Chapman finish his work unmolested. The agent spent the entire autumn and early winter organizing and cross-referencing "all the testimony of witnesses in a certain event or seizure, then drawing off, from that testimony, the particular points which incriminate the defendants." The final case file was the size of the phone book, and his superiors judged the work excellent. But once that work had been tidily done up with a new bow, undercover agents spread out around Chicago searching for a different kind of testimony: evidence that Chapman wasn't fit to remain in the dry agency. The investigation, taken up in earnest in April 1933, ultimately would charge that Chapman and his wife frequented notorious speakeasies. Worse, the Chapmans often brought along a teenage girl, Viola Bourke, who investigators suspected had been "sexually corrupted" by the couple. Chapman's seduction method, Miss Bourke said in an interview with agents, included his taking her to the Transportation Building after hours, where he showed her evidence from the Capone case file, including "some photostatic copies of checks which he said had been signed by Al Capone himself, under another name."

The final investigation report described how the Chapmans encouraged the girl to knock back highballs until stinking drunk, and how they sometimes kept her out until dawn. The investigators also learned that the agent was deep in debt, including owing $300 to Alexander Jamie. Agents in the Capone squad had each been receiving $150 a month in hazardous-duty pay, and Chapman needed every cent of it. When the extra pay ended in June 1931, the month Capone was indicted, Chapman's spending did not see a similar drop-off. The investigation report alleged that "Mr. Eliot Ness knew of his financial struggle and stated that Mr. Jamie had some money at that time, which belonged to the Secret Six organization, but which was in a fund that was quite flexible, and that Mr. Ness arranged with Mr. Jamie for him [Chapman] to borrow the $300.00 for which he signed a note." Chapman's debts, the investigators noted, could make him susceptible to bribe offers, although in Jamie's case the loan appeared to be more of a gift. The Secret Six head never asked for repayment or any interest payments (and never received either). Chapman, confronted by agents wielding this damning report, launched a desperate defense of his behavior, insisting that his nighttime escapades were an effort to satisfy his wife's love of dancing and that he never took note of whether the "various clubs, hotels and ballrooms" they frequented served liquor. He declared that he was "opposed to the use of intoxicants and denies having consumed liquor on any of the occasions referred to . . ." He also insisted he had made good-faith payments on some of his bills and planned to pay off all of his debts.

It wasn't much of a defense, but it was enough. Sort of. No charges would be brought against him. He didn't even receive a letter of admonition. But in July he was furloughed, ending his government career.

The investigation into Chapman's conduct surely embarrassed Eliot. It reflected poorly on him as a supervisor, bringing his judgment into question. But it was only the latest embarrassment. Eliot had already dealt with a far worse problem on his team. In February 1932, according to a personnel memo,

Special Agents E. A. Doyle and Elliot [*sic*] Ness supervised telephones at the New Wabash Hotel, and at the Coliseum Garage in Chicago, Illinois, for the purpose of obtaining evidence against violators in that city. (Case Jacket 122-B) Among the conversations intercepted and recorded by Special Agents Doyle and Ness were four that seemed to indicate that Special Agent Bernard V. (Barney) Cloonan was in collusion with certain violators in Chicago.

This discovery must have rocked Eliot.

Until this time, he had given Cloonan glowing efficiency reports. He had come to rely on him as a dedicated agent, fearless and ready for any challenge. From the squad's beginnings, Cloonan had been knee-deep in every raid and regularly served time on the wiretapped phones.

The phone conversations that cast suspicion on Cloonan were recorded over the course of two weeks. In a phone conversation on February 4, a known bootlegger — identified as "Hymie" — told Cloonan he'd left something for him at the usual place. The agents listening in were certain Hymie and Cloonan were talking about money. Three days later, Eliot and Doyle recorded Hymie and another bootlegger talking about an unnamed agent "who had helped us before." One of the men said the agent had new information to pass along, presumably about impending raids. A week after that, on February 15, Hymie confirmed with an associate that "Barney" had been paid $100. After an investigation, the bureau determined that the conversations and other circumstantial evidence, when added up, "constituted collusion of a very reprehensible nature." An internal report stated,

The "Barney" referred to in [the February 15] conversation was identified as being "the guy who used to be downstairs and is upstairs now." This remark seems to constitute rather conclusive evidence that the man under discussion by these two violators, was Investigator Cloonan. There are two reasons for this assumption: The first is that Investigator Cloonan is generally known and referred to, even by members of his own family, as "Barney." The second is that just a short time prior to the date of this conversation, Cloonan had been promoted from Agent to Special Agent; and had moved from the quarters of the Administrator, on the 4th floor of the Transportation Building, to the office of the Special Agent in Charge, which was located on the 12th floor of the same building. It is submitted that this seems conclusive evidence that the person referred to was Investigator Bernard V. (Barney) Cloonan.

And that wasn't all. Eliot, surely hopeful that he might discover exculpatory evidence, dug deeper. He found only more bad news. A Chicago police officer told him that Cloonan and a police officer named Tom Coen "shook down" speakeasies in 1931, when the Capone squad was tailing beer trucks every day and compiling a list of clubs that bought booze from the Outfit. Eliot slipped the charge into Cloonan's file without comment.

Yet after an initial inquiry, the Prohibition

Bureau did not undertake an official investigation. A personnel memo from two years later noted, simply: "These allegations were not gone into, for the reason that it was deemed inadvisable to do so at this time." Why? We can only speculate. Maybe bureau overseers thought the evidence was too opaque, too open to interpretation. Maybe the U.S. district attorney's office, worried about Capone's pending appeal and its renewed Volstead case against the Mob boss, wanted to avoid any public revelations that might undercut evidence gathered by the "untouchables" squad. Cloonan was not questioned about any of the allegations; he never knew that his direct supervisor and bureau managers believed him to be crooked.

Eliot seemed happy to drop the matter. He blamed himself for Cloonan's apparent perfidy, or at least he blamed himself for not recognizing that his agent was susceptible to corruption. He also blamed larger forces at work. The rules of society had changed over the course of Prohibition. Eliot could never take a bribe — *never* — but he understood how another man, even a good man, could. He didn't hold it against Cloonan. In the end, he didn't seem to care that the higher-ups had squelched the investigation.

Within a couple of weeks, the bureau transferred Cloonan to the special agency unit in Denver. The Capone squad now truly was a thing of the past. A month later, Eliot was promoted to chief investigator of the Chicago regional office.

The promotion did not mean a great deal to Eliot. Repeal was marching toward its own special spot in the Constitution, and everyone in the bureau recognized what that meant. Pink slips started wafting through Prohibition offices in the spring of 1933. William Gardner, well known in the bureau for being a drunk and a troublemaker, joined Chapman on the chopping block. No political pressure could help him this time. A few months later, the bureau also booted Paul Robsky to the curb. The Chicago office saw its numbers drop by almost half, reducing what once had been the largest regional dry office to fewer than two hundred souls. The new president, Franklin D. Roosevelt, issued an executive order on consolidating government agencies. He needed money for the ambitious relief programs he had in mind, and so every department in the federal government would have to tighten its belt. Soon rumors began to swirl that the Chicago Prohibition office would take another 50 percent hit. Every dry agent in the city, the *Tribune* reported, was "on the anxious seat."

Bureau managers spent much of the summer fending off congressmen and their staff. In June, with the demise of Prohibition unmistakably on the horizon, a Chicago agent named Al Wolff exemplified politics' power to trump reality. When Wolff was one of hundreds of men furloughed in anticipation of repeal, Illinois congressman Adolph J. Sabath fired off a threatening telegram to the dry force's director. "It is most peculiar that of all the men selected to be released from the service one of them should be Albert H. Wolff Prohibition Inspector in Chicago who is a real active Democrat and in whom the National Committeeman of Illinois is greatly interested. Someone else should be let go in his place." Wolff was rehired. Fifty years later Wolff would insist — like dozens of former federal agents before him, some of whom had never set foot in Chicago — that he had been a part of the famous "flying squad" that took down the most famous gangster in the world. He called himself "the last Untouchable."

Wolff and the other remaining Prohibition agents did little work during the hot, draggy summer. What was the point? The sale of 3.2 percent beer had been legalized in March, making enforcement a real pain. A sip didn't tell you much; you had to get the chemist involved. Raids slowed to a trickle as state conventions began to take up repeal resolutions. There was no suspense; everyone knew the Twenty-first Amendment would be adopted, freeing up the taps and dooming the Bureau of Prohibition. Agents sat around the office, fretting over their bank balances and searching the want ads; secretaries ratcheted up their eye-batting in hopes of landing a husband while there was still time.

Another cull came in the fall, and Eliot survived that one, too. Like Wolff, he would be there until the bitter end.

CHAPTER 12
IT'S JUST TUESDAY NIGHT

At 4:29 p.m., on December 5, 1933, the news reached Chicago that the federal ban on alcohol was history. The announcement proved anticlimactic. The wettest city of the dry years remained quiet.

"Crowds were gathered in a few of the loop bars, but what cheers were heard were sporadic, and there was no general hilarity, although the real celebration was expected to come later in the evening," reported the *Herald and Examiner*. The paper added that "little groups of four and five girls, homeward bound from loop offices and shops, were frequently seen at the bar ordering 'sidecars' and 'manhattans' and other mixed drinks in a manner that indicated they were not novices." No one could mistake the implication. The saloon would not become the husband's refuge once again. Women were publicly in the sauce and were staying there, which bar owners thought was just fine. Downtown, the longest queue could be found not at a flashy drinking spot but at the Federal Building, where dealers — including many longtime bootleggers — rushed to pay newly adopted federal liquor license fees.

At about seven o' clock, a reporter named Warren Brown walked over to a popular downtown hotel and asked the maître d' what the younger generation was drinking on the first night in fourteen years that anyone could legally buy and consume liquor. "What else do they know, but gin and what they call 'hootch'?" replied the maître d'. "Wine? They don't know anything about wine. They don't order wine with their dinners. They wouldn't know how to drink wine with their dinners if they did."

Later, his notebook full, Brown stepped into the hotel's elevator. A fellow passenger was already in the box, rubbing his hands together, his cheeks flushed. "I suppose you're getting ready for a big night?" the man asked the elevator operator.

"Me?" said the operator. He smirked, and turned back to the controls. "I have been getting it all the time, as much as I want, whenever I wanted it. It's just Tuesday night to me."

The best of the bunch from the Capone squad continued in liquor enforcement after the end of the Prohibition Bureau. Repeal, after all, did not put an end to bootlegging.

The legalization of alcohol meant real revenue, desperately needed revenue, for the federal government. Men were needed to make sure everybody was paying up. Longstanding bootleg operations, the *Chicago Tribune* pointed out, "continue to operate wildcat and compete unfairly with the legitimate concerns by evading the $5 a barrel tax, and by using gang tactics to force saloonkeepers to buy their products."

Joe Leeson moved over to the Treasury Department's Alcohol Tax Unit (ATU), the Prohibition Bureau's bureaucratic successor. He was quickly identified as a rising star in the agency. Sam Seager became a special agent in the Internal Revenue Service's Intelligence Unit, working under Elmer Irey. He became an expert at fingerprint and handwriting identification and was soon tapped to head up the Buffalo division. Marty Lahart stayed with the Chicago Prohibition office until the arrival of repeal, when he moved to the Alcohol Tax Unit and transferred to Saint Paul, Minnesota. Two months after the Prohibition Bureau discharged Paul Robsky, the government brought him back on a temporary basis. By the end of the year, the Justice Department had hired him full-time and sent him back to Greenville, South Carolina.

Cloonan remained in the Denver Prohibition office until July 1933, when, lacking strong references from Chicago, he was furloughed in anticipation of Prohibition's repeal. But since no official investigation had been opened against him, the Alcohol Tax Unit rehired him in February 1934. Some weeks later, the agency assigned him to Chicago, and that's when red flags popped up. This time the agency launched a thorough investigation. His faltering marriage was laid out in bureaucratic detail, including that he "had not provided food and clothes" for his estranged wife and their adopted son, and that "Cloonan had struck [his wife] with his fists and had otherwise abused her, on three separate occasions." He also owed money to his mother and sister. In the end, though, the evidence wasn't enough to fire him. His domestic troubles ultimately were his own business. And too much time had passed to reach a definitive conclusion about the bribery allegations, though the report determined there was "considerable evidence tending to show that in February, 1932, Cloonan was in collusion with certain violators, and was accepting money from them." Cloonan was not disciplined and, again, was not informed that he'd been investigated. He would continue to work for the ATU, though with few opportunities for advancement.

As for Eliot, in September 1933 he joined the Justice Department's Alcohol Beverage Unit, a transition agency for Prohibition

Bureau agents during the march to repeal. (It would later evolve into the Treasury's Alcohol Tax Unit.) He'd gained some nice publicity as the public face of the "Untouchables," but ultimately it didn't mean much. Al Capone's fame would continue to grow after he disappeared into the federal prison system. His gangster credentials transcended Prohibition. He hadn't just trafficked in illegal liquor; he was the highest-profile, most successful, and most vicious gangster in American history. Eliot's celebrity, however, would fade away almost as quickly as it had arrived, like a fever breaking. His fame was inextricably linked to the dry years, an era everyone wanted to forget even before it was officially over. But at least the government was happy with him. The unit's Midwest administrator gave Eliot an impressive raise, to $3,800 a year, and assigned him to Cincinnati.* The raise took some of the sting out of having to move away from his hometown, but only some of it. When he arrived at his new posting he found he was completely unknown in the office; no one had heard of the Untouchables. He felt like he was starting over.

Eliot had a secure career as a liquor cop, which was no small thing during the Great Depression. But what he really wanted was to join the Federal Bureau of Investigation,

* $3,800 in 1933 is about $65,000 in 2013 dollars.

then called the Division of Investigation. He wanted a broader purview than alcohol. He submitted an application, and on October 30, George E. Q. Johnson wrote a letter of recommendation to the head of the division, a young administrator named J. Edgar Hoover.

Dear Mr. Hoover:

Mr. Elliot [*sic*] Ness, who is at the present time an assistant investigator in charge in the office at Cincinnati, Ohio, (prohibition department) informed me today that he has pending an application for appointment with the Bureau as a regular agent.

I saw a great deal of Mr. Ness while I was United States Attorney. He is a graduate of University of Chicago, is intelligent and has a fine experience.

During the Government's investigation of the Capone gang and their ramifications he had a special division working which reported to the United States Attorney; under his direction these men did a splendid piece of work. His integrity was never questioned and I recommend him to you without reservations.

Yours very truly,
GEORGE E. Q. JOHNSON

Eliot thanked Johnson in a letter from

Cincinnati, dated November 6, 1933. "Throughout my connection with the Government," he wrote, "I have been constantly benefited by action taken in my behalf by you, and I know that this again will prove very beneficial." He was wrong about that last part. His record with the Prohibition Bureau, backed up by Johnson's recommendation, should have made him an excellent candidate for the Division of Investigation, but that turned out to be the problem. Unlike the liquor agents in Cincinnati, Hoover *had* read the accounts of the Untouchables that had gone out on the national wires. And he would not allow anybody into his agency who might possibly upstage him. He squelched the application. Unsatisfied with that, he began a low-level interagency smear campaign against him. Even ten years later, with Eliot out of federal service, Hoover would still warn his agents to "beware of Ness."

PART II
CENTER OF
THE UNIVERSE

The Cleveland Police Department's first batch of sharpshooters receives a congratulatory audience at city hall with Ness and Mayor Harold Burton (to Ness's left).

CHAPTER 13
CHASING MOONSHINE

In late August 1934, on the hottest day since a record-breaking string of hundred-degree scorchers the month before, a fourteen-year-old girl was paddling around in Lake Erie when she noticed someone below the surface waving at her. She pushed her head under for a better look. No, it wasn't someone. Not quite. The girl screamed and rushed out of the water, heaving and spitting.

She'd seen a hand. A ragged stump of a hand.

Other disturbing reports followed. A fisherman snagged a clump of blond hair on his line. A ferryboat worker swore he glimpsed a human head rolling around in his boat's wake. Two men swimming in the lake saw strange blobs bobbing in the water. One of the swimmers jabbed at it with a stick. "It was flesh of some kind. It wasn't a fish," he insisted.

Finally, proof: On the morning of September 5, Frank LaGassie, a thirty-four-year-old

Photostat operator, was walking along the shore on Cleveland's East Side when he came upon what appeared to be a waterlogged chunk of tree trunk. It was actually the lower torso of a woman, the legs amputated at the knees.

Police arrived to stare at the gruesome find along with LaGassie. After searching unsuccessfully for the rest of the woman, they delivered the torso to the morgue. The next day, the Cuyahoga County coroner, Arthur J. Pearce, determined that the woman had been dead for about six months and had been in the water for at least half that time. He calculated that she had been about five and a half feet tall, one hundred fifteen pounds, and somewhere in her thirties. He noted that the skin was rough and reddened from the use of some kind of preservative, which explained why the torso remained largely intact after so much time in the water.

No one knew what to make of it. The coroner couldn't even say for sure that the woman had been murdered. The police called the victim the Lady of the Lake.

Stories about the Lady of the Lake appeared on the front pages of Cleveland's newspapers for more than a week. Eliot read all three of the city's dailies, but he probably didn't pay much attention to the grisly mystery. Murder and missing persons weren't part of his domain. It was still just alcohol. He and Edna had moved to Cleveland in August so Eliot could become the chief investigator for the Alcohol Tax Unit's Northern District of Ohio. After just a year in Cincinnati, where he'd been assistant investigator in charge, it was a nice promotion for him. His salary remained at $3,800, but he felt he was back in the big time.

Cleveland, after all, was a great city — or at least it had been very close to greatness. This gray, densely packed burg of nine hundred thousand had boomed throughout the first three decades of the twentieth century on the strength of its heavy manufacturing. Sixty-five percent of the population was "foreign-blooded" — Italians and Russians, Poles and Slovaks and Mexicans — and there were jobs for every one of them. The city's central location on the banks of Lake Erie made it ideally suited for a leadership position in railroads and shipping, steel and automobiles. It was first in the nation in producing iron castings, plumbing fixtures, paints, and printing presses.

The city had also become the center of modern art — truly modern art: mechanistic, mass-produced, forward-looking. Clevelanders were reinventing industrial design. Outfits like the art-deco furniture maker Rorimer and Brooks and ceramics pioneer Cowan Pottery introduced the burgeoning Cleveland

221

School to the rest of the world. More traditional artistic endeavors came running along behind. The Cleveland Museum of Art, housed in a $1.25 million neoclassical pile on the East Side, opened in 1916. Three years later, the museum debuted the Annual Exhibition of Cleveland Artists and Craftsmen, which soon would become the foremost art competition in the Great Lakes region. Locals called it the May Show. The Cleveland Orchestra launched two years after the art museum and quickly challenged it for local acclaim. Artur Rodziński became music director in 1933 and, with a single-minded dedication to structure and a clean sound, pushed the orchestra toward international prestige.

Of course, none of this high-art pretentiousness made the slightest bit of difference now. In 1929, a hefty 41 percent of Cleveland's workers had been employed in manufacturing-related jobs, helping to build America into the greatest economic force in the world. The city, the sixth largest in the country, had almost no unemployment. But following the stock market crash that began in October, businesses suddenly began to shut down. Fear spread quickly. In February 1930, some two thousand men tried to storm a city council meeting, sparking a small riot. One man ended up with a broken back, another a fractured skull. The violent protest didn't help the situation. The council could do nothing to stop the economic slide. By the end of the year, a hundred thousand of the metropolitan area's manufacturing jobs were gone.

It only got worse. The Standard Bank collapsed in 1931, setting off a panic. The same year, the president of Cleveland Trust Company, one of the Midwest's biggest banks, had to carry bags of cash into the lobby to calm hundreds of depositors and stop a run. By 1933, a third of Cuyahoga County's work force had no work. Cleveland drastically cut its budget to address falling revenue and dialed back basic services to help fund relief efforts.

The city was falling apart. Streets and sidewalks pitted by freezing weather remained unfixed. Blocks of apartments, vacant save for squatters, devolved into kindling. The downtown lakefront, which should have been the city's pride, became "Tin Can Plaza." Broke, out-of-work Clevelanders — "the lowest and loneliest of the down-and-out" — set up a "Hoover City" there just weeks after the stock market shocks. Hoover City residents lived in huts made from wooden crates and soiled sheets. Well-to-do businessmen occasionally walked over from downtown towers and paid residents a few pennies for permission to crawl inside the hovels for a look around. Some of these mindless thrill seekers would be building their own ram-shackle huts in Tin Can Plaza soon enough.

One industry, inevitably, remained immune to the Great Depression.

"Cleveland's bootleg output today — despite state monopoly — is greater than the city's consumption of legal liquor," wrote the *Cleveland News* in January 1935, citing Alcohol Tax Unit studies. The reason: the tax on alcohol was significant. That meant anyone who could put out spirits without the federal and state taxes would find a large, willing customer base — and stood to make a huge profit. Counterfeiting brand labels and bottles became a big business itself. The ATU believed there were "eight or nine big illicit liquor syndicates operating in Cleveland," pulling down profits that rivaled what the bootleggers of the Prohibition years had made. Pretty much every tavern in the city sold bootleg booze, some without even realizing it.

W. K. Bruner, the head of Cleveland's Alcohol Tax Unit office and a tough ex-marine, brought in the former Untouchables chief in hopes of improving morale and sparking a new urgency in the ranks. Eliot, at thirty-two, still looked like a college senior, but unlike in Cincinnati, he wouldn't have to face skepticism from his troops. Bruner knew all about the Capone squad, and he made sure his forty-five men did, too. He even called local reporters and told them he had the famous Chicago gangbuster on his team. The new chief investigator helped his cause by getting right to work, taking charge of a raid during his first day on the job. Eliot would set a scorching raid-a-day pace for more than a month. Having become adept at interrogation while in Chicago, he time and again forced low-level still operators to give up work routines and the names of superiors. Arrests for liquor violations immediately jumped. He had hit his stride as a federal agent. He was confident and eager to show off his chops.

"He was a very great person," said Mary Louise Gosney, Eliot's administrative assistant in both Cincinnati and Cleveland. "He really had wing — that is, inspiration and vision."

George Mulvanity, a Georgetown University graduate who went on to become one of the ATU's most decorated agents over a forty-year career, would insist that Eliot was the best boss he ever had. "He was rather quiet, considerate of the other men," he said in 1972. "He wasn't pushy. I enjoyed working with him."

The two men had similar personalities: modest, reserved, a dry sense of humor, obsessively dedicated to hard work. Mulvanity became Eliot's agent of choice for stakeouts and long nights trailing trucks they suspected of carrying sugar or molasses. Eliot "was a real eagle eye," Mulvanity said. One time, when they were driving back to Cleveland after a day of meetings at the Toledo office, the chief investigator told Mulvanity to follow an automobile he'd spotted up ahead. The younger agent didn't see anything suspicious about the sedan or its occupants, but he did as he was told. "When we stopped and searched the car, we found a hundred gallons of whisky in the trunk," he marveled.

Eliot's skills proved a boon for the office: the team made eighty-two arrests and seized fifty-four stills in less than six months. Bruner crowed to his superiors in Washington that his agents "worked day and night" and had the gangs on the run. Moonshiners around the state, afraid that liquor agents could come barreling through the door at any moment, increasingly cranked out "scared whiskey," so-called because the cook sped up the fermentation process by adding battery acid or other toxic — or simply disgusting — components to the mash.

Mulvanity paid close attention to how Eliot went about his job. "I learned a lot from him," he would say years later. He often drank with Eliot at a neighborhood tavern. The two men drove to work together, dropping Mulvanity's son Francis at school on the way. With saloongoers becoming violently ill and sometimes dying from scared whiskey, Eliot and Mulvanity talked about whether the ATU was actually making things better. In the years immediately after Prohibition, the moral high ground had dribbled away to almost nothing. It was just about the tax revenue now. That was all the government cared about. How did that make the ATU any different from the Mob? Mulvanity recalled that Eliot struggled with this. The chief investigator sometimes wondered aloud if he should get into another line of work. But then a tip would come in, and Eliot would clap his hands, jump to his feet, and head out the door. Years later Mulvanity told his son that Eliot "liked to imbibe and he liked women." Young Francis took that to mean that Eliot wasn't a faithful husband, and that he had "demons." This view into his supervisor's personal life didn't alter George Mulvanity's opinion of Eliot as an agent.

"Ness worked hard, took every risk he asked his men to take," said Francis Mulvanity. "He was honest and likable. My father respected him."

All of those risks, taken week in and week out, ultimately led here, a block-long brick building in south-central Ohio.

Eliot had been in the building nearly an hour before he spotted anyone. As he looked up from inspecting a grate in the floor, he saw a man casually pass through the hallway about fifty feet away. Springing to his feet, Eliot hefted his ax and ran after him. One long, dark corridor turned into another, and he blundered down them, his feet thudding, the ax jumping on his shoulder. The only unlocked door was at the end. He shouldered through it and skidded into a locker room. A stopped clock glowered from a wall, as if he'd stepped into Miss Havisham's parlor. Waxwork-like clothes hung on hooks across from a shower. Dust covered everything. Eliot poked his head into each bathroom stall, opened every locker. The man who had ghosted past him wasn't here — and yet there was no other door he could have gone through. Eliot rapped on the walls, one by one. His curiosity piqued by a hollow sound, he attacked the plaster behind a toilet.

The noise attracted other agents. They found Eliot standing in the middle of a chalky mess. "I believe you're seeing things," one told him.

Eliot tried to catch his breath. "I thought I saw a man, but I guess I didn't."

It was dawning on the agents that they might have tapped a dry hole. Frustrated, they decided to step out for a smoke. Climbing the stairs to the roof, the men listened to the building's emptiness echo in their ears. Eliot's charge as chief investigator was to bring down what his boss called "the main bootleg gang" in Ohio, a ruthless group comprising remnants of Detroit's Purple Gang and various local outfits. So far he hadn't had much luck. They'd arrested plenty of independent moonshiners in Eliot's first nine months on the job, but they'd only nibbled around the edges of the more organized gangs. This operation was supposed to be the breakthrough. Months of interrogations, wiretaps, and surveillance had led them to this former industrial pottery kiln in Zanesville, about 150 miles south of Cleveland. Two dozen agents had surrounded the three-story building at dawn. They surprised the three watchmen on duty, but they hadn't been able to find anyone else on the premises.

Eliot had learned over the years to pay attention to details. One time, after raiding a small distillery and finding no one home, he noticed perspiration droplets on the floor and followed them upstairs and into an attic, where he discovered a bootlegger folded up in a corner. Another time, he stopped to chat with kids playing stickball in the street, and they told him about a "haunted house" in the neighborhood where they said a woman had been murdered. The boys insisted they heard "strange noises" and "smelled funny smells" outside the house, which raised Eliot's antennae. The boys took him to the house, and sure enough, Eliot smelled funny smells and heard strange noises, too. Inside, he discovered a large still churning away.

As the agents stood smoking on the roof of the Zanesville building, Eliot noticed one of those important details: a vent emitting a steady stream of mist. The agents went over for a closer look. Quieting one another, they realized they could hear something — maybe engines humming inside the building. Their spirits lifted: they were in the right place after all. They pulled apart a skylight next to the vent and dropped a fire hose into the darkness. "Down we go," Eliot said.

Reaching the end of the hose, the agents fell into a small, black chamber. They climbed down farther, hand over hand, into nothingness. Reaching the bottom, they scrabbled around until they managed to set off a buzzer, freezing them in their places. A trapdoor opened and a man appeared through the floor. He climbed up a ladder and opened a secret door — leading into the toilet stall next to the one Eliot had smashed with his ax. Finding no one, the man disappeared back through the trapdoor. The agents smiled at one another in the dark and, after a moment, quietly opened the trapdoor and climbed through it.

They were not disappointed by what they found on the other side. Hidden behind false walls and floors and buried beneath surface level were eight twenty-thousand-gallon vats, each of which could produce ten thousand gallons of mash every twenty-four hours. The gangsters had built a tunnel so they could use large quantities of city water, tapping into the water main under pressure, a significant engineering feat. The operation stole so much water that the Zanesville water department, unaware of what was going on, had installed an extra pump at its main facility.

Cocooned inside their illegal factory, the alcohol cookers had no idea the building had been taken over by federal agents. Eleven men, hard at work, looked up quizzically when the agents stepped into their large underground workspace. An escape tunnel led to the sewers, but, taken by surprise, none of the men even tried for it.

Eliot and a handful of his agents stayed in the building for hours, poking into every crevice, taking notes and samples, labeling equipment. Eliot exulted as he went about his labors. He'd finally made a big bust — a really big bust. This might effectively put the gang out of business. Among those who'd soon be arrested for their connection to the operation: a former Prohibition agent and a Zanesville city councilman. After the agents finished up, they decided to walk over to the town's little commercial district to get something to eat. Sitting in a diner on the muggy June afternoon, Eliot greedily devoured a plate of poached eggs. Then he spent fifteen minutes deciding what he wanted for dessert: an ice cream cone or a bottle of beer. After paying the check — he ultimately decided on the beer — he pushed away from the table with a satisfied grunt. His work here, he announced, was done.

That was even truer than he suspected.

CHAPTER 14
REAL WORK

Harold H. Burton, Cleveland's newly elected Republican mayor, wanted a strong, independent-minded G-man to be his director of public safety. After all, it was a big job, the most important appointment the mayor made. The director oversaw the police, fire, and building departments for the sixth-largest city in the country. More than two thousand employees reported to him — 1,500 policemen, 1,200 firefighters and about 50 men in the building department. So in November 1935, just after his election, Burton went to Washington.

The mayor had just one candidate in his sights: U.S. Assistant Attorney General Joseph B. Keenan. Burton spent hours wheedling and cajoling the federal prosecutor, first at lunch and then again at dinner. The forty-seven-year-old Keenan had secured a sterling reputation by convicting kidnappers, the scourge of wealthy men and their families during the Depression. He was known as

233

tough and fearless. The second meeting between the mayor and the prosecutor broke up at midnight, with Keenan on the verge of saying yes. The next day, Burton visited the White House, where he met President Roosevelt. The president admitted he'd "hate to lose" Keenan. Burton nodded and said, "I think I'm going to get him."

Cleveland's newspapers plumped for the well-regarded federal prosecutor, with the *Plain Dealer* writing that "a Burton-Keenan combination . . . will restore respect for the law in this community and make the Cleveland underworld run to cover." The challenge of taking on the city's Mob appealed to Keenan, but he had trouble with the final hurdle, the one Burton knew would be a problem. Keenan feared getting bogged down in the city's dirty politics and police corruption. Cleveland was notorious. The mayor himself admitted that the city "had a reputation which was damaging us all over the United States. We were beginning to be tagged as a city unable to enforce the law."

Indeed, the tag had already stuck. Keenan woke up in the morning with a queasy feeling in his stomach. He called Burton and turned him down. The new mayor, sighed a *Plain Dealer* reporter traveling with him, would have to settle for "some man of the Keenan type for the vacant directorship."

■ ■ ■ ■

Burton returned to Cleveland in a bad mood. Stepping out of the plane at Municipal Airport, he climbed down to the tarmac in darkness, even though it was lunchtime. The winds off the lake had died away in the middle of the month, and with the lake frozen, the industrial city could only stew in its own effluent. For the second week running, midday looked like midnight. The mayor could hardly blame Keenan for not wanting the job. Even when you put aside the problem of corruption, the assignment wasn't all that appealing to someone who liked to get things done. The police and fire departments were underfunded and demoralized. Under Mayor Harry L. Davis, whose administration would be recalled as "a classic example of boodling and incompetence," the city couldn't pay its bills and had been forced to issue scrip. Just days after becoming mayor, Burton had to pink-slip sixteen hundred city employees as "an economy measure." He would have to concentrate on digging the city out from its financial mess rather than increasing funding for any department, no matter how great the need.

Still, the mayor was determined to find a new face for the safety director's office, someone far removed from the gang of entrenched political crooks and hacks who usually vied for it. The most recent director, Martin I. Lavelle, had been consumed by scandal over the summer when a speedboat party he was hosting ended with a young woman, a city hall clerk, falling overboard and drowning. The party was cohosted by a well-known gangster named Marty O'Boyle, whose brother Anthony soon would be indicted for his role in the Zanesville bootlegging operation that Eliot's ATU crew had taken down. In spite of public outrage over the incident, Mayor Davis had refused to fire his safety director.

The mayor had his priorities. Davis wanted the city to run wide open, and you needed a compliant safety director for that. Lavelle didn't cause waves, except out on the lake. A week after the funeral for the drowned clerk, a city hall reporter, wanting to move on from the endless speedboat-party coverage, asked the safety director if he would "launch a drive on the numerous gambling establishments" in the city, seeing as two prominent gambling-hall bosses had just been convicted of federal tax evasion. Lavelle's only response: "That's up to the chief of police."

The chief, of course, did nothing. George J. Matowitz was an honest cop, but he knew his survival at police headquarters depended on his knowing when to look the other way.

■ ■ ■ ■

Burton hadn't been the Republican establishment's choice for mayor — the incumbent, Davis, held that honor — but he ran anyway as an independent-minded reformer. Now, after winning, he was told he could be accepted back into the fold by picking loyal party men and palm greasers for his administration's key posts. He never considered doing so.

Wes Lawrence, the *Plain Dealer*'s federal reporter, happened to be at the paper's city desk when Keenan's decision to stay in Washington reached the newsroom. Editors began bandying about possible candidates for the safety director job.

"Ness would be just the kind of guy Burton needs," Lawrence said. When he received surprised looks, he added: "But it seems impossible that Burton would offer him the job. He's strictly nonpolitical. Harold tries to be independent, but he's still a Republican. I don't think Ness has any politics."

Lawrence wasn't the only reporter in town who thought Eliot might be a good man for the job. On December 8, even though the mayor's office had said nothing about Eliot being a candidate, the *Cleveland Press* presented him as the front-runner for the position — and Eliot embraced the idea.

He is Eliot Ness, University of Chicago graduate who headed the small band of young men known as the "untouchables" because they spurned offers of lucrative bribes from the Al Capone interests and wrecked the Capone breweries.

His blue eyes twinkling good-naturedly, Mr. Ness said he was reluctant to comment on reports that he has the "inside track" with Mayor Harold H. Burton for the safety directorship.

"I would like to get the job," he said. "I would like to see what I could do. But, whoever does get that job will have his hands full."

The *Press* went on to state, incorrectly, that Eliot had spent two years in Chicago as a private investigator before joining the Prohibition Bureau. It leaned hard on the Capone angle, and Eliot obliged. "Yes," he said in response to a question, "the same tactics we used against Capone and others could be used in combating crime in Cleveland. All crime is alike. The main thing is to get the evidence and submit it fully."

After the newspaper article appeared, colleagues with longtime experience in Cleveland warned Eliot that he would be taking on "an impossible mission" with the safety director job, that the corruption and racketeering went too deep in the city. Eliot listened carefully, and then ignored their advice. He viewed the safety director position as key to turning Cleveland around, and he frankly said so. He relished the challenge. The liquor beat certainly wasn't what it used to be. He was now arresting people simply for possessing empty liquor bottles; new federal regulations required "purchasers of liquor" to destroy empties. He was ready for a new and bigger mission.

At first, the Ness boomlet annoyed Mayor Burton. He had never heard of Eliot Ness until just a couple of months before, when the Zanesville operation hit the newspapers. But now, with editorials praising the federal agent and positive recommendations coming in from Cleveland ATU chief Bruner and others, he decided to give Eliot an interview. As their meeting approached, Eliot bubbled with nervous enthusiasm. He'd never been so excited about a job possibility. "I will accept the position if it is offered," he told reporters. "It would be an opportunity to do some real work, but it would be a tough assignment."

Working for Burton seemed like a natural next step to him. The new mayor had pledged there would be "no political pressure or influence on the police" in his administration. He said he would "not tolerate the playing of politics or the extending of special privileges." To everyone's shock, the former city law director actually meant it. Burton, at forty-seven, was a small, balding, nondescript man with deep bags under his eyes. The son of a college professor, he had gone to Harvard Law School and served as an infantry officer in the World War, earning a Purple Heart. He began his political career on the East Cleveland Board of Education. Formal, precise, and religious, he prided himself on being a man of his word. Already, city hall veterans were calling him "The Boy Scout," which was the same moniker Eliot had carried in Chicago. The two Boy Scouts spent well over an hour together for the official job interview. Each walked away impressed with the other. They spoke again later in the day.

Reporters weren't the only ones pushing for Eliot. Keith Wilson, Eliot's right-hand man at the ATU office, had called editors at the Cleveland newspapers on November 11, the day of Burton's inauguration. He pointed out that, as chief investigator of the local federal liquor squad, Eliot already knew how the city's Mob operated and was well aware of the situation in the police department. Tom Clothey, another agent in the ATU office, talked Eliot up among his contacts in the city government. And Joe Keenan, after turning Burton down, told the mayor he should consider Eliot. Keenan suggested Burton call Dwight Green, one of Johnson's assistant prosecutors during the Capone case (and later a governor of Illinois).

Eliot's partisans didn't just raise his profile; they played hardball. Rumors suddenly spread that U.S. Secret Service agent William Harper had been seen around town with various underworld figures. Harper was Eliot's chief competition for the job.

The mayor took the search for a safety director far more seriously than anyone had expected. He knew something had to be done about the city's institutionalized crime, and he knew it wouldn't be easy. Early in his administration, he frequently wore a police inspector's badge to reinforce his commitment. Some said he also carried a police revolver tucked into his pocket.

By the middle of December, after a week of excited newspaper coverage, Eliot's candidacy had become a symbol — and a test — of the mayor's reform credentials. Sure, Burton could talk a good game, and yes, he'd taken some encouraging first steps. But would he have the courage to put someone like Eliot Ness into high city office? In a column published just hours before the mayor made his decision, the *Plain Dealer*'s Philip Porter dared to believe:

Harold Burton's brief administration has been full of surprises, but none was more pleasant to the insiders who admire ability than his sudden serious consideration of

Eliot Ness for safety director. If Burton actually makes the appointment, the strictly political boys will be gibbering incoherently.

Porter marveled at how Ness, this man "without the slightest trace of political connection," could be a serious candidate for safety director of the city of Cleveland. It was almost inconceivable. The columnist threw aside any pretense of journalistic objectivity, admitting that reporters who had covered Ness "admire his courage and his skill, and they like him personally. Few government officials have won them in such a short time as he has. . . . It's a pretty safe rule that when reporters respect and admire an official, he's the goods. They see so many phonies that they can smell them out like bird dogs."

By now Eliot had won over Burton, too. Shortly before noon on Wednesday, December 11, the mayor called the ATU's offices at the Standard Building downtown. He offered Eliot the job, and Eliot immediately accepted. Burton told him to come right over to city hall to take the oath of office.

Eliot, nattily dressed in a double-breasted, gray-striped suit and red tie, walked over to city hall, skipped up the wide concrete front steps and ambled down to the mayor's office. As always in the first months of a new administration, the place was mobbed by men hoping for a nod. Eliot slipped into the back of the reception area. "For some time," wrote a reporter who didn't recognize him at first, Eliot "stood patiently with a horde of job-seekers in the mayor's outer office." Finally, someone recognized him and insisted he come through. Safely ensconced in the inner sanctum, he vigorously shook the mayor's hand and sat, keeping his overcoat on.

Joseph Crowley, the city's assistant law director, arrived to give the oath of office. The picture of the oath-taking that ran in the afternoon papers shows a grim-faced Eliot with his hand held high above his head, like a boy who's concerned the teacher will over-look him during attendance. When the new public safety director shook Crowley's hand at the end of the ceremony, his annual salary had just doubled, to $7,500. (This would be a nice surprise for Eliot; he hadn't even asked about the pay during the interview process.) At thirty-three, he was by far the youngest safety directory in the city's history. Within an hour, Crowley put out a statement declar-ing that Eliot would have "complete freedom in developing the law-enforcement policies of the city."

Eliot's arrival at the mayor's office, and the reason for it, quickly washed through city hall. When he, Burton, and Crowley came out of the office, they found city employees jamming the corridor, craning their necks to catch a glimpse of the new safety director. They noted the "heavy layer of pomade" in his hair, the well-tailored suit, the shy smile. "He did not present the formidable, bellicose appearance that Americans expect in their law enforcement officers," wrote George Condon, a longtime Cleveland reporter. Not that it mattered; his youth and his reputation as the man who busted Capone were enough to impress people. As Eliot came through the gauntlet, men shook his hand, slapped his back, and offered congratulations. A few whistled and whooped. The mayor told him he shouldn't expect this kind of welcome every day.

Eliot recognized a few reporters in the crowd, and he stopped to give the obligatory statement.

"Of course, I am greatly honored by the appointment," he said. "I have a keen sense of feeling of the responsibility that the office entails. I will bend every effort to fill the duties of the office creditably."

Reporters weren't willing to leave it at that. They trailed Eliot back to the Standard Building, throwing questions at him with every step. Eliot kept his head down as he walked, but he also answered the questions. He understood the importance of a strong first impression.

Asked about corruption on the police force and poor morale in the fire department, the new safety director said he hoped "to devise some method of properly rewarding policemen and firemen for efficient and honest work." He admitted he had a lot of "homework" to do.

Eliot's Untouchables experience inevitably came up during that walk back to the ATU offices, and reporters filled up their notebooks. In the next day's papers, the story of Eliot and Albert Nabers's Chicago Heights arrest of Mike Picchi would be retold, this time with Eliot creeping alone down a dark alley, noticing "the flash of light on metal" and throwing himself at his startled would-be assassin. The gun Eliot wrestled from him, the *Press* wrote, "now is one of Mr. Ness' prized possessions." (Eliot did not have Picchi's gun.)

The pack of reporters followed Eliot up to his office in the Alcohol Tax Unit's suite and continued to fire questions at him as he cleaned out his desk. "I am going to be a working safety director," he said. "I will do undercover work to obtain my own evidence and acquaint myself personally with conditions."

That engendered some double takes. He was going to do his own undercover work? No one knew what to make of such a statement. The directorship was a management job. A payroll-padding, speech-giving, hit-the-links-at-two job. Yet this new kid wasn't

245

even going to take the day to celebrate — he was getting right to work. When Eliot showed up at police headquarters for a look around, officers blanched. "I've served under five safety directors and this is the first time I ever saw the face of one of them," said one sergeant. City hall hangers-on received a similar shock when they heard about the mayor's choice.

"What did that guy ever do to help elect Burton?" one befuddled Republican lifer bleated. A *Press* columnist gleefully responded in print.

Well, nothing is the answer. Mr. Ness didn't even know Rees Davis, the Republican chairman who managed the political aspects of the Burton campaign, until Thursday, when the mayor introduced them.

Some political hacks and fixers refused to believe the newspaper reports. They'd seen goo-goos (good-government men) before, and most of them only gooed when a reporter was around. The next day, party men began showing up in the safety director's office. One by one they sat before Eliot, hats on knees, overcoats slung over the back of a chair. They explained how things worked in the city, offered advice, and coolly asked for the expected consideration. Eliot listened, expressionless, head down. He drew "doodlegrams" on a pad of paper until each caller finally was talked out, put his hat back on his head, and angrily walked out of the office.

Despite the quiet confidence he showed to the press and his new colleagues, Eliot knew he was taking a significant risk by accepting the safety director job. He'd never worked for or supervised a municipal police or fire department. He'd never overseen *any* big organization. And there would be no ordinary learning curve here. Now that Capone was gone from Chicago, Cleveland was arguably the most mobbed-up large city in the country, with the most corrupt police department. Recognizing the challenge, he turned for help to his former teacher, August Vollmer. Eliot had become a passionate acolyte of Vollmer's after taking the former chief's police-administration course at the University of Chicago. He'd made a point of staying in touch with "the old man" ever since.

Eliot chose his mentor well. Vollmer was widely viewed as the "father of modern law enforcement." In 1909, Vollmer became the police chief in Berkeley, California, where he remade the small department through an intractable belief in the moral power of professionalism. He eliminated the political patronage system through which policemen had always been hired and promoted in the town, put cops on wheels — first bicycle, later motorcycle and automobile — and instituted formal training for new recruits, a rarity at the time. Perhaps most revolutionary of all, he sought recruits with college degrees, even advanced degrees. His police department may have been the first in the country to use blood, fiber, and soil analysis in criminal investigations, the first to use intelligence tests in hiring, the first to equip squad cars with two-way radios. The definitive proof that he was an iconoclast: he believed in crime-prevention measures. Indeed, he considered them more valuable than crime-solving skills. In the same vein, he aggressively argued against vice laws, insisting that sexual deviancy and drug and alcohol addiction were "first and last a medical problem," not a police problem. Vollmer's views were downright radical. Critics dubbed him soft on crime.

Vollmer went on to become police chief of booming Los Angeles in 1923, declaring that he would clean up the department through scientific management. "I am going to strip all the mystery and hokum from police work and place it on the basis of efficiency," he said. Despite some notable successes — he created a police academy and reorganized the two-thousand-man department into discrete disciplines — his tenure ended abruptly after just a year. The city's power players turned against him after they realized he really meant to run crooked cops out of the department and shut down the city's gambling dens. When his opponents ginned up a sex scandal — a doe-eyed divorcée brought a breach-of-promise suit against him, insisting that he made love to her like a "cave man" — he decided he'd had enough of the big city. He would spend most of the rest of his life in academia, teaching his "Berkeley system" to criminology students across the country.

Eliot, unaware of the vehemence of the opposition his mentor's methods had kicked up in LA, planned to be the first man to fully install Vollmer's system in a major American city. The goal thrilled him. He would come up with few truly original ideas during his police career, but he would prove to be the foremost pioneer in adapting Vollmer's ideas to a large department. Sitting down to his typewriter a day after taking the oath of office as safety director, Eliot informed the fifty-nine-year-old éminence grise of American police work that he had a new job and "am facing problems which, because of your many years of experience, would seem minor." He then asked for advice on how best to revamp the way Cleveland's police department handled promotions. He said he planned to remake the city's force based on Vollmer's tenets of professionalization. He closed the letter: "I feel, and for many years have felt, that my connection with you at the

University of Chicago was one of the most beneficial things in my life."

During that first full day on the job, Eliot, Police Chief Matowitz, and Fire Chief Joseph Granger had posed for newspaper photographers at city hall. When one of the photogs requested a shot of just Eliot and the police chief, Matowitz lost his temper. A reporter had asked the chief earlier in the day if he feared he might be fired. The challenging query, along with an initial meeting with Eliot, had gotten to the chief. Matowitz believed the photographer wanted the picture for a story about him getting the ax. He refused to pose alone with Eliot, berated the photographer "in sulfurous language," and stormed off. Mayor Burton, witnessing the hissy fit, stewed at Matowitz's "ripe and incoherent remarks."

Eliot was unfazed by the outburst. He had no intention of firing the fifty-three-year-old police chief. And he figured it worked to his advantage to have Matowitz feeling insecure in his position. He expected the chief to do his bidding, and sure enough, the chief would do it.

The next night, determined to prove himself to the rank and file as well as to the brass, Eliot tagged along with two patrolmen on their rounds in the "Roaring Third," the city's notorious vice district. A sergeant loaned him a gun, a Smith & Wesson .38-caliber service revolver with a five-inch barrel. He would keep it throughout his tenure as safety director.* The two patrolmen took Eliot on a tour of the neighborhood, from East 105th Street and Euclid Avenue to East Fifty-fifth Street and Woodland Avenue. They pointed out gambling parlors that superiors had ordered patrolmen to leave alone and the hangouts of gangsters who were also beyond the law. At 2 a.m., they came upon a brothel on Orange Avenue where nearly naked girls wiggled suggestively in the windows, inviting men to come inside for a better look. Eliot decided it was time for action. Using a corner call box, Eliot called the nearest precinct station and told them to send over a paddy wagon and a patrol car.

A few minutes later, the patrolmen stepped up to the brothel's front door while Eliot covered the back. When he came around the side of the house, Eliot saw the back door wide open. Inside, the dank rooms were empty, except for the two patrolmen who'd just banged through the front entrance. "That was a quick getaway," Eliot said, laughing. He knew what had happened: the place had been tipped off.

By early January Eliot had begun to settle in.

* He noted the serial number — 678872 — in official police files.

He rented an apartment at 10017 Lake Avenue on the West Side, just over the Cuyahoga River from downtown, to comply with the requirement that city employees live within the city limits. (Edna, at least for now, mostly remained at the cottage in suburban Bay Village that they'd been renting since moving to the area.) Eliot wrote again to Vollmer, who had sent him some sample training materials. The letter started out with gossipy news about other Vollmer acolytes, including Alexander Jamie's son, a childhood friend who the year before had offered Eliot a job in Minnesota. "I guess you knew that Wallace Jamie was Assistant Safety Director at St. Paul and conducted a very thorough investigation of the police force and racketeers in that city," Eliot wrote. "He is now working on a special job at considerable remuneration in Boston and has resigned from his post at St. Paul."

The pleasantries done, Eliot turned to the task he had before him. He insisted he was "appointed here absolutely non-political," and that he had the support and trust of the mayor. He laid out his objectives: First, clean out corruption in the police department, and then modernize it. Next, attack the Mob. He admitted that reforming the police force would be no small task. "The department here is exactly as it was about forty years ago as far as selection, promotion, training, etc., is concerned," he wrote. He added that civil service was a problem, because "absolutely no recognition is given for anything except the ability to pass a written examination, which you can appreciate is extremely detrimental to the morale of the department as a whole." He said he already was working with the civil-service examiner on a new examination for chief of detectives.

Eliot had a plan for ridding the police department of crooks, he told Vollmer. "The situation here is in a sense similar to that of Chicago in the early thirties when the business men organized the Secret Six for the purpose of coping with the situation," he wrote. "I am going to receive some help along a similar line here but am proceeding cautiously on it in order that I do not become associated with any movement which may prove embarrassing or binding upon the work I hope to do as a whole."

Eliot was being modest — or careful, in case the plan didn't go well. Bringing the Secret Six model to Cleveland had been his idea. In fact, he had insisted on it. During his job interview with Burton, he said he would take the position only if he could hire secret investigators who reported solely to him. He saw this as the only effective way to ferret out policemen on the Mob's payroll. He told the mayor that he, Burton, would have to find a way to pay for them "out of unofficial funds."

The demand stunned the mayor. Such a thing had never crossed his mind. To Burton, it smacked of vigilantism — or even fascism. But Eliot, undaunted, told the mayor about the precedent in Chicago, and suggested he hit up friends in the business community who'd had enough of Mob rule in the city. Burton called around to acquaintances in Chicago to find out what this Secret Six thing was all about. He liked what he heard. A few days later, when he offered Eliot the job, the mayor said he would do his best to get him his unofficial investigators. That brought Eliot into his new position on a wave of confidence. He expected to have the police force cleaned up enough to begin an all-out attack on the Mob by the end of his first year in office. He couldn't wait. He wrote to Vollmer:

Racketeering here is rampant and the racketeers have virtual control of business and industry, much more so than is apparent on the surface. Almost every business association in the city is paying some sort of tribute to a well-organized Sicilian gang here. This angle, of course, is old stuff to me and will probably be one of the simplest.

That was the kind of bluster that had made Eliot's name in Chicago. But he'd discover that attacking Cleveland's gangs wouldn't be quite as simple as he thought.

254

Chapter 15
Tough Babies

On January 10, Charles McNamee walked up to the Harvard Club's front door at about 5 p.m. Pulling out a search warrant, he informed the doorman that he had come to raid the club.

"Oh, no, you don't," the doorman roared, sweeping the assistant prosecutor aside with a burly forearm. McNamee crashed into the side of the building and fell to his knees.

The half-dozen men behind McNamee, many of them brandishing truncheons, pressed forward — but they couldn't get past the guard. The doorman was a massive creature. He stood on the front step, punching and kicking like a hockey goalie in sudden-death overtime. The rumpus brought one of the club's owners, James "Shimmy" Patton, to the door.

McNamee, a professional and proud of it, was back on his feet by now. Reflexively, he shot his cuffs, straightened his tie. "I've got a search and seizure warrant for this place," he announced. He'd been joined on the doorstep by fellow assistant prosecutor Frank Celebrezze, who nodded tentatively.

Patton stared at the men. "The hell you do," he snarled. The squat, pug-like gangster hadn't been tipped off about a raid, so clearly McNamee and Celebrezze were here by mistake. "Where's that goddam Cullitan?" he barked. He looked out into the beige winter evening, trying to locate Cuyahoga County prosecutor Frank T. Cullitan. He wanted to go straight to the top to register his complaint.

"He's closing down the Thomas Club," McNamee said.

Patton's mind whirled. None of this made sense. The men McNamee and Celebrezze had brought with them clearly weren't deputies. Cuyahoga County sheriff John Sulzmann worked closely with the suburban casinos. Sulzmann believed absolutely in what he called "home rule" — meaning the sheriff didn't do anything about crime in a particular town unless the mayor specifically asked him to. Patton glared at the men stacked up in front of his doorman. He definitely didn't see any badges.

The gangster snickered — it was a pathetic display of humanity arrayed before him — but he held himself in check. He understood the value of violence. He also understood that you didn't start throwing haymakers at high-profile public officials unless you had to. "You fellows are prosecutors," he told McNamee and Celebrezze. "You just step aside and let those other fellows you've got with you try to get in here. We'll mow 'em down."

By now the club's security detail had arrived. Wielding Thompson submachine guns, they fanned out behind Patton like Ziegfeld girls.

"Anyone that goes in there gets their goddam head knocked off," Patton declared, loud enough for everyone to hear.

The gangster's "hard-boiled attitude" shocked McNamee and Celebrezze. They — and Cullitan — had figured even gangsters would stand aside when representatives of the county prosecutor, search warrant in hand, came calling. A wave of panic gripped the badgeless "special constables" behind the assistant prosecutors. They had been hired from the John J. McGrath Detective Agency for the night. They hadn't expected this kind of trouble either. The private dicks yelled at Patton's men to put down their weapons, to go back inside. The calls quickly grew high-pitched and shrill. Patton's minions stood their ground.

The standoff continued for about half an hour, until a line of cars rolled up, blasting their horns. It was County Prosecutor Cullitan and more McGrath men, flush with victory. They'd met no resistance at the Thomas

Club in Maple Heights. Cullitan climbed out of the lead car and buttoned up his coat. Looking around, he realized things hadn't gone so smoothly here. After a brief consultation with McNamee, he approached Patton.

"Mr. Patton," he said, "I've tried every decent way I could —"

The gangster stopped him with a raised hand. "No, you haven't." He meant Cullitan hadn't tried pocketing bribes. He hadn't tried looking the other way.

"This is my job to close this place," the prosecutor said.

"Why don't you quit your job?" Patton answered. He threw back his shoulders and smiled, pleased with himself.

At the gaming tables inside, gamblers slowly realized the standoff out front was serious. Some of them recognized the county prosecutor from his campaign signs. Shopkeepers and insurance agents and doctors started to stream out the back door. The notorious bank robber Alvin Karpis, one of J. Edgar Hoover's foremost "public enemies," coolly retrieved his coat from the money-counting room and sauntered into the night along with the panicked regulars. Employees began to load everything — the roulette wheels and slot machines and blackjack tables — into vans parked behind the building.

By this time, the private detectives in the

front had put away their clubs and hunched in on themselves. They'd seen enough of those machine-gun barrels. They had wives and children they wanted to go home to. Arthur Hebebrand, Patton's business partner, stepped outside to judge the situation. To make sure Cullitan understood their resolve, he told the prosecutor: "If an arrest is made, you won't go out of here alive." Cullitan believed him. He walked to a gas station, followed by a clutch of Patton and Hebebrand's men. Finding a telephone box, he called the county sheriff's office and pleaded for assistance. As expected, he was rebuffed. The message from Sulzmann: "Mr. Cullitan should call the mayor of Newburgh Heights and let him ask for assistance if he thinks he needs it. That is in accord with my home rule policy." Cullitan slammed down the phone. He had already tried and failed to reach Newburgh Heights mayor Jerry Sticha.

He fished in his pocket for more change, picked up the receiver again.

Cleveland had plenty of gambling parlors. They were hidden behind storefronts and jammed into the back rooms of laundries. Anyone stepping into one of these rooms would not be impressed. They typically looked abandoned — except for the fact that they were filled with people. The Mob made millions of dollars every year on these ram-

259

shackle places.

In the suburbs, however, Cleveland's gangs may have pocketed even more money from gambling than they did in the city, and they didn't have to make much of an effort to disguise their operations. No one in the 'burbs seemed to know that gambling was illegal. That was because gangsters owned a handful of local governments in the towns surrounding Cleveland, especially to the southeast of the city. At the huge casinos in these burgs, you had to ring a buzzer at the front door, and you had to stare down a beady eye that peered at you through the sliding slot. But this was mostly just for show, for the fizz of illegitimacy that heightened the excitement of the experience.[*]

"Long before there was a Las Vegas, there was Cleveland, and its place on the gambling map was most prominent," recalled reporter George Condon. The Thomas Club in Maple Heights and the Harvard Club in Newburgh Heights were the two best-known casinos in the region. The Harvard had grand pretensions. It was located in a former industrial building, but it had a fancy plantation-house facade stuck on the front. The club's opera-

[*] Until the Supreme Court decided in 1987 that Indian tribes could build casinos on reservations, the places in America where people could legally gamble were few and far between.

tors, Patton and Hebebrand, had recently taken over from the original owner, Billy Fergus. The police found Fergus buried in a limestone quarry, his head split open by three bullets. The Harvard's staff wore crisp uniforms and showed off the latest games and equipment, most of which were fixed. The club had limousines on call to pick up gamblers in downtown Cleveland at any time of the day or night.

The Harvard Club boasted some eighteen hundred "members." The Thomas had about two thousand. Forty years later, one member would recall the Thomas as "a clean-cut place. You never had any riff-raff out there. No stabbings, no crime and no bombings like you see all the time these days. They were very good to the people in the area. They employed people, helped the needy with coal in the winter and baskets of food, things like that. It was a really nice place to go to."

Not everyone agreed with this assessment of the casino. The club had a "special window" for strapped gamblers to cash relief checks. One man tried to kill himself after a particularly disastrous night at the gaming tables. "Have my body cremated and give my ashes to the Thomas Club. They have everything else," he wrote in a suicide note.

Decent people recognized that gambling was an evil, and they had facts on their side. No matter what the clubs' members believed, the plain truth was that the areas where gambling thrived had more robberies, assaults, and prostitutes than anywhere else. Cullitan certainly didn't have to be convinced. He considered gambling a plague on civilized society. He believed he was doing God's work when he set off for the suburbs that January afternoon, search warrant in his pocket.

The Cuyahoga County prosecutor tracked Eliot down at a city council meeting. An aide summoned the safety director to a nearby office to take the call.

"They're threatening to open fire," Cullitan heaved into the phone, his voice cracking with fear and stress. He told Eliot that the sheriff had refused to come to his assistance, that he was in a desperate situation. "We need help," he said.

The first time Eliot had laid eyes on Frank T. Cullitan, a couple of weeks before, he couldn't have been too impressed. The county prosecutor looked like a political hack at fifty paces. He had the fat red face and squinty pinprick eyes of the quintessential city hall hanger-on. He'd slap you on the back for no reason, his pendulous chin swinging, his laugh echoing down the long hall of the county courthouse, a laugh directed at nothing.

But first impressions could fool you. Eliot

had heard good things about Cullitan. He'd heard he was honest. He'd heard he wanted to do the right thing. Burton said he admired the man, even though Cullitan was a Democrat. Eliot decided to give the prosecutor the benefit of the doubt.

"Hold everything," he said into the phone. "I'm on my way."

The new public safety director's priorities were clear. When a reporter had asked him whether Cleveland would follow New York's lead in cracking down on women wearing shorts in public, he had snorted derisively. "They may wear all the shorts they want to on the street," he said. Eliot was a leg man — Edna had a great pair of stems — but that wasn't the reason for his attitude. He was sending a bigger message: he didn't care about the penny-ante stuff. New York officials could waste their time on things like public dress codes for women. He was Captain Ahab hunting his big fish. Cleveland, like Chicago before it, was overrun with gangsters. And gangsters undermined society and degraded their fellow man. The Mob and public corruption would be his focus.

Eliot called the county jail. He couldn't believe the sheriff had refused Cullitan's appeal for help. There must have been some sort of misunderstanding. "The prosecutor informs me he is in danger of his life," he said. "Will you send him assistance?" The man on the line said Sulzmann was home with the flu and couldn't be reached. Eliot didn't know what to make of that response. "Will you go out or won't you?" he demanded. Finally, he received a definitive answer: no.

Furious, Eliot drove over to Cleveland's Central Police Station, where he rounded up men coming off duty. He asked for volunteers. This would be unofficial duty, he said. There would be no extra pay, and there might be danger. To his surprise, the men liked the sound of that. Forty-two officers agreed to go. Eliot clapped his hands. They would head out to Newburgh Heights in a convoy, he said. The mayor had already given his safety director the go-ahead, but only as backup to Cullitan's men. Eliot and his officers were not to serve warrants or make arrests. They were acting as private citizens.

Even after that panicked call from Cullitan, Eliot was surprised at what he found along Harvard Avenue: a tense, crowded standoff that stretched into the street, blocking traffic. Prostitutes wearing little more than negligees and high heels lingered around the property's periphery, wary of going back inside the club, unwilling to go home without a payday. At a nearby gas station, the county prosecutor stood against a wall, helpless, surrounded by "many tough-looking 'birds.'"

"While the prosecutor's deputies were laying siege to the Harvard Club, the prosecutor himself was besieged," Eliot recalled later. "I would be unable to exaggerate the gravity of the situation. Even my fullest powers of description could not give you the picture as it was. I told our driver to open up his siren and split a way through the crowd."

Eliot stepped out of the lead car and shook hands with Cullitan. The safety director was wearing a tan fedora and a long, camel's-hair topcoat. He'd put on a crisp new shirt before heading out. "We are here to protect you, and to do that we must go where you go," Eliot told him. He nodded toward the Harvard Club.

The two men crossed the street, followed by Eliot's off-duty police officers. Eliot, to his surprise, realized that all of Cullitan's private eyes were clumped in front of the building. When he'd told the prosecutor to hold everything, he meant to keep people from leaving the building. He'd assumed Cullitan's hired guns had surrounded the place.

It was 10:30 by now; the standoff had been going on for five hours. The county prosecutor's detectives had clearly lost their taste for battle. Eliot noticed newspapermen standing around, notepads in hand. Despite Mayor Burton's orders, he decided to take charge.

He addressed his men: "Let's have a fight here. All right? Let's go."

Eliot strode up to the club's front door. He was unarmed, but the forty-two cops — "private citizens" — behind him wielded shotguns, pistols, truncheons, and tear-gas guns. Eliot hammered on the door and called out for the occupants to open up. The slider in the door flew back. "It's Ness. It's that goddam Eliot Ness," someone inside the club said. Everyone had heard about the new safety director's raids on Capone back in the day. The lock turned and the door swung open. Eliot disappeared inside. A moment later, he reappeared.

"All right," he said to Cullitan, "let your men go in there and serve their warrants. We'll back them up."

Cullitan's temporary constables, followed by newspapermen, marched into the room. The "Harvard men," as Eliot would call them, fell back, but not very far. They wouldn't let the McGrath detectives make their way beyond the front room. Eliot worried about keeping everyone cool. Looking outside, he saw that his officers were "just aching for something to happen."

By this time the gangsters had locked themselves into the main gambling room. "I looked through a hole [in the door] and saw one big fellow with a revolver," Eliot recalled. "I told Cullitan I thought gas was what we ought to use." He must have said it rather loudly, because the Harvard men began heading for an exit at the back of the gambling room. Eliot kicked in the door, but by then the long, wide room was empty.

Back in the entryway, Cullitan's men pulled a ladder down from a trapdoor in the ceiling. They climbed up, muscled aside a bulletproof glass shield, and found themselves in a low-ceilinged room with sniper slits cut into the floor. The openings allowed for machine guns to be trained on the gambling room and the money room.

Cullitan and his men pushed into the money room next. They had found $52,000 at the Thomas Club earlier in the evening. "And that was after [only] morning business," a reporter noted. "Imagine the money that must have passed from the public to this one gambling house in a full day." At the Harvard, they came away with nothing. Not a dime. They didn't even have the proprietors. Hebebrand and Patton had stepped into the money room a few minutes earlier — ostensibly to retrieve their hats and coats for the ride downtown — but they didn't come back out. They climbed through a hidden window near the ceiling and dropped ten feet to the ground behind the building. The McGrath detectives did a double take when they went in after them. The good guys just couldn't do anything right tonight.

Cullitan no doubt was embarrassed that the hours-long standoff at the Harvard Club resulted in no arrests. He had what little was left in the building hauled away — chairs, tables, phones, adding machines. The next day he had phone service to the club shut down.

"We have achieved our purpose — to put the Harvard and Thomas clubs out of business," he declared to reporters.

The next morning, Eliot woke up a hero.

"Eliot Ness last night showed the county of Cuyahoga in general and Sheriff John M. Sulzmann in particular that his reputation as a zealous, courageous law enforcement officer is no publicity build-up," wrote one reporter.

Eliot, faced with a scrum of reporters when he arrived at the office, praised the officers who had joined him on the raid — and puffed himself up as well. "It was a highly credible thing they did. . . . I went over to the station and found the boys just coming off duty and preparing to take off their uniforms and go home," he said. "I told them the circumstances and informed them I was going out there if I had to go alone. I explained that I'd like to have some of them go along, but they didn't have to volunteer. I told them I wouldn't hold it against them if they didn't go. Without an exception, they all agreed to go." He then provided the newspapers with the names of the forty-two men.

Of course, he couldn't leave it at that. The papers declared that he had proved something at the Harvard Club. That he had proved he had the right stuff for this job, that the Cleveland Mob was going to have a serious fight on its hands. Eliot liked the feel of all that praise. Speaking before a fawning audience at the Odovene Club a few days later, the safety director bragged shamelessly. "About the time we got there, a newspaper man came bounding out and told us the tough babies were ready for trouble," he said. "That was a welcome sound, because we were afraid we were missing something."

He insisted he never before "saw such a situation, not even when, in the government service, I lived with the Mafia or raided repeatedly the Capone outfit. Those fellows at the Harvard Club are called gamblers, but they certainly have learned the technique of gangsters. I am confident that if Cullitan had gone in there he would be dead today. They were not bluffing, but meant business."

The subject of Sheriff Sulzmann inevitably came up, and Eliot gripped the podium. He now knew that Cuyahoga County's sheriff was a crook, and he didn't mind saying so, especially to make a broader point. Before he and his officers had headed for the Harvard that night, he'd sent his executive assistant, John Flynn, to the county jail to check on the situation there. Flynn "found six deputies just sitting — perhaps waiting for the millennium," Eliot told his audience at the Odovene Club. He said the sheriff's actions added up to dereliction of duty — and worse.

"In any city where corruption continues, it follows that some officials are playing with the underworld," he said. "If town officials are committed to a program of protection, police work becomes exceedingly difficult, and the officer on the beat, being discouraged from his duty, decides it is best to see as little crime as possible.

"Now what about it?" he continued. "We hear the man on the street asking what harm there is in gambling. Now, I'm not a reformer, but let me tell you one or two things. Those gamblers said they had a gold mine out there. I am told that for $60,000 to $70,000 to change hands in one evening was not unusual. Is there any effect from that on legitimate business, do you think?"

After the reception he received at the Odovene Club, Eliot decided he wanted to keep the glowing headlines coming. He had planned on attacking the Cleveland Mob after reforming the police department; it was pointless to do so beforehand. But now he chose to go ahead and launch a hasty, very public assault on Mob-run gambling in the city. It would be an initial, probing thrust in anticipation of a much bigger push down the road; he was putting the gangs on notice. He told Lieutenant Michael Blackwell, a rising star in the department, to throw a scare into gamblers across the city, to get them twitching every time they heard the click of a shoe in the stairwell outside.

Blackwell could do that. The ambitious, honest young officer loved to kick in doors and yell, "This is the police!" In the weeks ahead, he and his men would charge into gambling rooms across the city, swinging sledge-hammers and waving guns. They pounded furniture into kindling, ripped out telephone wires, blew open safes full of money. A later addition to the raiding team described how he became swept up by the fervor of the squad's work:

> The excitement generated in these raids was contagious, and I quickly found myself wading in alongside my fellow raiders, breaking a sturdy leg off of a heavy oak table or swinging a metal chair to demolish vulnerable gambling room equipment. The enormous exertion expended would leave me sweating and exhausted, but also exhilarated. I had struck a blow at the gambling gang owners whose activities and bribes were corrupting the police and other city officials.

Along with Blackwell's actions, detectives began a sweep of the Third and Fourth

Precincts to disrupt the Mob's rotation of girls into its whorehouses, which often operated near gambling dens. The police moved out every girl in the district who couldn't prove she had an established residence.

The push appeared to have an immediate effect. A local manufacturer of negligees and women's silk underwear sent Eliot a letter declaring that, because of the crackdown, he had been "obliged to lay off almost half my factory help." Eliot put the letter in a frame. The *Plain Dealer* exulted that "now the gamblers never know when the police will arrive or where and that uncertainty is no small factor in cutting down the evil here." Letters to the editor poured into the newspapers in support of the safety director. "It is not only refreshing in thought but encouraging in civic spirit to find that we now have a director of public safety as independent in thought, fearless in action and supremely indifferent to the demands of the politicians as Eliot Ness has proved himself to be," read a typical one.

Yet the gambling racket proved much more difficult to hurt than Eliot expected. Too often gambling operators *did* know when to expect a raid. Gambling was deeply entrenched in the community; police officers in every precinct protected it. Most of the places Blackwell and his men smashed to bits would reopen in another back room a few days later. The joints began to move around every day, making it impossible for the special unit to stay on top of them.

Even the Harvard Club was up and running again a couple of weeks after Eliot's now-famous raid. Asked by a reporter about a rollicking new casino on Harvard Avenue, just down the street from the building Cullitan had shuttered, Newburgh Heights police marshal Frank Ptak offered a predictable response.

"I know nothing about it."

Chapter 16
This Guy Ness Is Crazy

January was wreathed in darkness. A thick blanket of smoke had smothered the city for a month, squeezing out everything but a collective mood of gloom and anxiety. Cleveland "was well on its way toward winning the dubious honor of being known as 'The Dark City,' " the *Press* wrote. The lack of sunshine wasn't the only problem. A cold spell gripped the region, the worst in more than a year. In the early morning blackness of Sunday, January 26, the watchman at the Hart Manufacturing plant on East Twentieth Street periodically stopped during his foot patrols to stamp and shimmy in place. It didn't help. The cold hit like a fast-acting poison. The watchman didn't see anything suspicious during his shift. He didn't see anything at all save for the dirty snow underfoot, the breath fogging the air in front of him.

It wasn't until midmorning that anyone noticed the two baskets on the ground behind the factory. At about 11 a.m., a woman bent

274

down and peeked under the burlap sacks that covered them. She continued on through an alley and around the corner to the White Front Meat Market on Central Avenue. She announced there was a basket of hams sitting against a wall behind the Hart building. The butcher, concerned that someone had broken into his shop overnight, went out to take a look. When he returned, shaken, he called the police.

Inside the baskets, detectives discovered two human thighs, an arm, a hand, and the lower part of a woman's torso, all neatly wrapped in newspaper. The basket and its contents were coated in coal dust, suggesting an initial hiding place for the remains. Patrolmen began to scour the area. They found two pairs of white women's underwear, also wrapped in newspaper.

Police identified the remains through fingerprints as those of a local barmaid, Florence Polillo, aka Florence Martin, Florence Sawdey, and Clara Dunn. The autopsy determined that "before her death, her entire reproductive system had been removed along with half her appendix." The report indicated that "all the cut surfaces had clean edges," meaning the dismemberment had been done with a surgeon's skill.

The newspapers jumped on the gruesome discovery. They competed for the biggest, most startling headline — "Woman Slain,

Head Sought in Coal Bins" — and offered up every lurid detail about the find. They catalogued the body parts, piece by piece, as if this could help readers solve the case. Only rarely — and incidentally — did they provide a glimpse of the victim as a real person. "She usually ironed on Saturday, and when I found she wasn't there, I was worried," her landlady told the *Press*. "She never gave us any trouble, and the only bad habit I noticed was that she would go out occasionally and get a quart of liquor — bad liquor, too — and drink it all by her lonesome in her room." The city's smallest paper, the *Cleveland News*, made a connection between the "hams" left behind the Hart building and the dismembered Lady of the Lake from more than a year before. The paper pointed out that police still didn't have an ID for the victim of that now-forgotten 1934 case.

The Lady of the Lake wasn't the only connection to be made. Four months before, in September 1935, a grisly double murder had baffled police. Two boys found a headless, emasculated man along a slope of Jackass Hill in Kingsbury Run, an industrial ghetto on the east side of the city. The corpse lolled on its side, as if the man had just drifted into a midday nap when something horrific happened. Drained of blood, he was naked except for cotton socks. Later in the day, another headless, emasculated corpse, older and stockier, was found nearby. A reddish-black discoloration to the bodies, like with the Lady of the Lake, led investigators to believe the killer had tried to burn the corpses. Sweeping the area, patrolmen stumbled over the heads and genitals in the underbrush.

The younger headless man was identified through fingerprints as Edward Andrassy, a twenty-nine-year-old knockabout and former psych-ward orderly. (The police weren't able to identify the older man.) Investigators learned that Andrassy was an occasional marijuana dealer, and that a few weeks before his murder he had gotten into a bar fight with someone associated with the Mayfield Road Mob, the city's most powerful gang. His father said that "Edward lived in continual fear of his life." The idea that his murder was a gang hit made some sense. This recent spate of bizarre killings might all be about the Mob sending some kind of message. Florence Polillo was a part-time prostitute, another racket run by the underworld. Middle-aged, chubby, and depressive, she wasn't *their* kind of prostitute, but still, the Mob didn't like freelancers. It was a long shot, but it was as good a guess as any.

Police worked the gangster angle of the Andrassy case hard. Tips poured into Central Station, overwhelming the secretarial staff, but not all the calls came from cranks. Dudley McDowell, a security officer for the New York Central Railroad, had spotted a swank green coupe in Kingsbury Run on numerous occasions before the double murder. Clean, expensive cars were a rarity in the Run. The coupe's driver always scanned the area with binoculars from the top of Jackass Hill before climbing into the car and blasting away. McDowell, a professional, had taken down the car's license-plate number as a matter of routine.

Through the plate number, police identified the car's owner as Philip Russo. Detectives went to the man's house on East 140th Street, but the place had been abandoned. Russo had disappeared.

Eliot took little interest in the gruesome case of the prostitute in the picnic baskets. It was one isolated murder, he figured. No doubt the work of a lunatic, someone who'd inevitably be caught soon. Besides, he was too wrapped up in the mundane details of his new job, the kind of details no reporter or headline writer could possibly find interesting. He was fascinated by the science of traffic safety, for example. Cleveland was one of the most dangerous cities in the country for motorists, and Eliot decided he would change that. He declared that the traffic division no longer would be "the Siberia of the police department." Also the city's police stations

278

and firehouses were in terrible condition —
vermin-ridden, moldering, filled with useless,
antiquated equipment. He wanted to fix that,
too.

The fire department was not one of Eliot's
top priorities during his first months in office, but that didn't mean he neglected it.
Though he had no experience with firefighting, he immediately reimagined the typical
fire official's typical day. He believed firemen
should feel the same sense of urgency in their
work, day in and day out, as police officers.
He declared that when they weren't fighting
fires or taking care of their equipment, firemen should be focused on fire prevention,
"instead of just hanging around in their fire
stations waiting to respond to fire alarms."
He sent out orders that officials in each battalion would conduct daily — not weekly or
monthly but *daily* — inspections of commercial and industrial buildings within their
area. Faced with concerns about men being
taken out of their firehouses, he announced
that he would equip battalion cars with two-
way radios, allowing inspectors to react just
as quickly to a call as if they were in the station. Eliot ignored complaints from the
department brass that he didn't know what
he was talking about. "People resent change,"
he said with a shrug. "There are folks who
start out: 'This guy Ness is crazy.' That's part
of the job."

The city's lawmakers, so far, were not among the resentful. With cheers for the Harvard Club takedown still rolling through the newspapers, Eliot convinced the council to pony up precious funding for the city's first-ever police training school. He considered this a game-changing victory. Some big-city police departments offered formalized training to recruits — this was mostly started during Prohibition in response to the rapid rise in organized crime — but these continued to be the exceptions. Many departments, including Cleveland's, simply handed new officers a badge and a gun on their first day and sent them out on the streets. They were expected to learn the job entirely by doing it, at best with tips and mentoring from veteran policemen.

Throughout the winter and spring, Eliot would oversee every aspect of the training school's establishment and launch. He found classroom space, designed the curriculum, and selected the instructors. The instructors included local jiujitsu expert Dewey Mitchell, the police laboratory's majordomo David Cowles, and various senior officers in the department. He selected trainees, too, personally recruiting student leaders at local colleges. (He also quietly recruited African Americans, believing they would do a better job policing their own neighborhoods than white officers.)

Eliot made it clear to the academy's first class that they would be a new breed of police officer in Cleveland. "If people have been accustomed to giving you things for nothing prior to your becoming a policeman, I suppose it's all right for you to continue to accept those things," he told the group of cadets. "However, if people who never gave you anything for free before now want to give you something without charge, you can conclude they are buying your badge and uniform."

Along with giving advice, Eliot served as an instructor, too. He especially enjoyed helping out with the self-defense courses. The *Press* ran a series of photos of the young, good-looking safety director showing off holds and escape moves. "Suppose you were a bandit and told Safety Director Eliot Ness to 'stick 'em up,' " the paper offered. "He might surprise you in any one of 30 different ways. And the next thing you'd know, you'd be on the ground. You might have a broken leg, a broken arm or 'just be stunned.' "

"He has become as quick as a cat," Dewey Mitchell said proudly.

By now, a legend had been born. Everyone, it seemed, wanted to be Eliot Ness. Mayor Burton's son, a college student, asked his father if he could spend the summer working for the safety director. By the end of Billy Burton's first week, Eliot had him staking out a bookie joint. Before school let out, Eliot spoke to hundreds of elementary-school boys who sported their official Dick Tracy badges. "You have a badge just like mine," Eliot said, prompting a wave of cheers and whistles. At about the same time, an unshaven man in a dirty overcoat walked into the mayor's office and told the secretary he was there for his meeting with the mayor. When asked for his name, he said "Eliot Ness." He disappeared before security arrived. A few days later, the same man walked into the safety director's office, sat down at Eliot's desk and got to work. This time, one of Eliot's men grabbed him. He was turned over to police for a psychiatric evaluation.

CHAPTER 17
THE BOY WONDER

Frank Cullitan turned in his chair and looked up. The county prosecutor's face — "as Irish as the keeper of the Blarney Stone," in one colleague's phrase — broke into a warm smile. Despite Cullitan's welcoming countenance, Neil McGill hesitated at the door. The fifty-two-year-old chief assistant prosecutor had been a farm kid; you could still see it in the sidelong way he entered a room, in the wary squint of his eyes when he met someone new. He always looked ready to take a heavy blow.

"Want you to meet Eliot Ness, our new safety director," Cullitan said, waving McGill in.

Eliot, sitting across from Cullitan, leapt to his feet. "Glad to know you, McGill," he said, grasping the lawyer's hand.

McGill, a formal man of the old school, "felt a slight twinge of resentment at this free-and-easy use of my surname on first meeting." He was *Mister* McGill even to longtime associates. He indicated his displeasure by offering a testy greeting in return, calling Eliot simply "Ness" — *that* would show him.

McGill wasn't sure what to make of the man standing before him. The safety director had managed to get himself in the papers quite a lot during his first two months on the job, and he'd come off looking a whole lot better than McGill's boss, Cullitan, with the raid on the Harvard Club. Looking him over, the assistant chief prosecutor could reach only one conclusion: he sure was young. McGill examined Eliot's "boyish face and disconcerting and disarming boyish smile." He decided he "just did not appear mature enough to cope with the Mayfield Mob, the policy and other rackets, the payoffs to the corrupt police and the racketeering in labor circles."

Eliot would get a lot of that in the weeks and months ahead.

The three men sat down in the large, cluttered office. The flagpoles outside thrummed in the wind. The lake, visible in the distance, shifted like a sour stomach. "Your move, Mr. Ness," Cullitan said.

Eliot got right to it. He was going to move aggressively, he told the two men. He wanted full cooperation in his investigations. And he wanted that cooperation no matter how much political pressure came with it — and there would be political pressure. It was an impressive, forceful call to arms, offered up in plain language. This young man who seemed so insubstantial at first glance now showed McGill that "behind that boyish smile was grim determination and the will to do a thorough job."

Cullitan answered Eliot, but he addressed himself to McGill. "Needless to say, Mr. Ness will get the full cooperation of this office. You, as chief assistant county prosecutor, will be playing an important role, along with Mr. Ness, in cleaning up the city."

McGill nodded, his enthusiasm for the conversation building. "I'll do my best," he said. "Where do we start?"

"At the logical place. We start at the source," Eliot said. "This thing called 'vice and corruption' is a many-headed serpent. We're going to start by lopping off those heads, one at a time, and let the chips fall where they may. Both of you know, as well as I do, that crime cannot flourish in any city without protection, police protection, and I have reason to believe that the crooks and gangsters are getting plenty of it in Cleveland. So we start with the police."

McGill turned to Cullitan. The county prosecutor grinned in reply. *Yes, you're hearing what you think you're hearing,* the grin said.

McGill had figured Eliot Ness would ratchet up his move against the gambling rackets, for that would allow him to lead late-night raids — and heroically kick down doors — with the press watching. Everyone understood that to effectively pursue organized crime in Cleveland, you had to address police corruption, but for years honest safety directors and police chiefs had ignored the rot in the police department while doing the best they could against the Mob. (The dishonest ones sat on their hands entirely, or worse.) If a safety director actually went after the *real* problem, he knew that one wrong step — firing a politically connected cop, for example — could end his tenure. But the new safety director wasn't one of the boys and didn't seem to care about his political future in the city.

"It's going to be hard getting evidence against the police," Cullitan said. Police corruption hadn't been tackled in Cleveland partly because previous city administrations had been partners in the dirty game. But another reason, the prosecutor pointed out, was that even the honest cops were loath to rat out their colleagues. That brought Eliot to his feet.

They would have to depend on "unconventional witnesses," the safety director said.

"Any offender that will come forth and testify against the police will be granted immunity from prosecution, as well as protection against retaliation," he continued. "We're going to promise them both. We're going to contact every known offender in this city, if we have to go all the way back to 1920. Any offender who will come forth and testify will get both immunity and protection. In fact, my men are already at work."

McGill told Eliot he was ready to get started. He actually had a lump in his throat. He would vividly remember this meeting for the rest of his life. It was risky to go after dirty cops in this city, and it was a risky strategy to use known criminals against them in court. They had never tried it in Cleveland — certainly not on the scale and with the seriousness Eliot was proposing.

The young safety director broke out that disarming smile. He stood and shook McGill's hand and then Cullitan's, seemingly well pleased with himself. "Well," he said, "I must be about my master's work." He promised to be in touch, turned, and strode from the room.

Cullitan closed the door behind Eliot, swiveled to look at his chief assistant, and let out a long, jaunty whistle.

Cullitan and McGill might have wondered what Eliot meant when he said his men were already at work. The safety director's office didn't come with much of a staff, and police departments didn't yet have internal-affairs divisions. But with the success of the Harvard raid, the world had opened up for Eliot.

Now that his director was being celebrated around the city, Mayor Burton had no trouble coming up with the funds to hire a handful of secret investigators, answerable only to Eliot (and the mayor). Burton's chamber of commerce supporters had indeed had enough of the padded costs that came from the Mob's protection rackets, which affected everything from truck deliveries to janitorial services. And now, quite suddenly, they believed something could be done about them. So the money came in, and Eliot quickly made the hires. Having built up a bulky dossier on the area's bootleggers and their accomplices while at the Alcohol Tax Unit, Eliot had excellent leads to get them started. His key hires, in fact, came from the ATU along with his files — including Keith Wilson and Tom Clothey, who had helped raise Eliot's profile when the new mayor was looking for a director.

The team became known around the city's newsrooms by a catchy nickname, the Unknowns, a sly nod toward Eliot's famous Capone squad in Chicago. Which, of course, meant that this new team wasn't exactly, well, unknown. Reporters who had sat through a boring budget meeting one night had learned that Flynn, Eliot's executive assistant, officially would be in charge of a small group of "civilian investigators who will visit precinct stations and inspect the work of policemen on beats and in cruising squads." Flynn, a thirty-seven-year-old lawyer and former Notre Dame football player, seemed ideally suited for such a role. He was six feet four inches tall, with broad shoulders, slicked-back hair, and the kind of abbreviated lip rug that Germany's new fascist leader was making fashionable. He looked more like a gung-ho safety director than his boss. Flynn told the city's financial officers that the new men under his charge would not be "spies."

It hardly mattered that the team's cover had been blown. By the end of the Unknowns' very first week, *everyone* in the Roaring Third and other corruption hot spots was aware that new cops were poking around, even if they didn't know whom exactly the men worked for. Wilson and Clothey were the lead investigators on the "secret" squad, but, as he made clear when he was hired, Eliot wasn't going to sit around and let others have all the fun. He gave Flynn authority to make bureaucratic decisions in his absence, and he began disappearing from the office for days at a time. "No fox hound ever hit the trail quicker than Ness hit the trail of the corrupt police," said McGill.

Eliot pushed himself hard, starting work early every morning and staying at it deep into the night. "Time meant nothing to him when he was on the job," said Cleveland police deputy inspector Frank Story, who would sometimes cross paths with Eliot late at night. For days at a time, just like during the Untouchables' period, Edna saw her husband only in passing. Flynn saw him little more than that. Eliot's undercover investigators followed their boss's example. Most of them were young and single, and so they didn't have anyone at home to miss them.

Eliot knew the police force was in bad shape, but what he found truly shocked him. Officers weren't just taking bribes to look the other way. Well-organized cliques in almost every precinct operated as miniature crime families, with patrolmen kicking up to sergeants, lieutenants, and captains. Some officers acted as actual enforcers for racketeers; other cops ran their underworld bosses' competition out of business through repeated raids that earned the officers promotions and public praise. Honest policemen were bullied into silence or slowly reeled into the malfeasance.

The Unknowns began following leads to restaurants and bars, to fruit carts and newsstands and laundries, promising immunity for cooperation. They met wary shop owners who offered up stony silence; no one wanted to put their business and possibly their life at risk to testify against something that had long been normal operating procedure in the city. "Patrolman *Who*?" they'd say. "Pay tribute — what's *that*?" You couldn't blame them for the dumb act. New administrations always promised to act against corruption, but none ever did, not really. It wasn't going to be easy to convince people that this time was different.

Eliot made his objective clear to the public, stating baldly: "We have no place for traitors in the police department. We want to know on which team every man is playing, Cleveland's or the underworld's." Then the safety director himself scored the investigation's first significant witness when he convinced a fifty-six-year-old widow, the owner of an East Side social club, to end years of silence. The woman believed that harassment by police officers demanding bribes had helped lead her husband to an early grave, but she'd never dared say it out loud — until Eliot showed up on her door. Eliot excelled at getting people to disgorge information they had no intention of ever telling anyone. There was something about his boyish seriousness that could be hypnotizing. It was a hair's breath from being ridiculous — it seemed so self-conscious, so careful, like little Oliver Twist asking for more. Sitting down with the widow, the safety director used his earnestness to devastating effect. He quietly cajoled her into admitting she'd been a party to public corruption — and then agreed with her that officers who'd sworn to uphold the law had taken advantage of her. Sure enough, the dam broke, and long-repressed emotions poured out. The woman swung from tears to anger as Eliot listened. "Line them up, director," she finally told him. "Line up the police department and I'll show you every crook."

Eliot was prepared to do exactly that. This woman told him that during the Prohibition years she and her husband had paid Cleveland police officers $10,000 in protection money, not including $150 she forked over at Central Station one night to have a liquor arrest "fixed." Better yet, he didn't just have to take her word for it. The couple had carefully put down every payoff in a ledger book.

"My husband was forced to buy all kinds of tickets from the police," she would tell a grand jury. "Generally, they cost $3 and $5 a piece and he always took at least two. Once when I asked Pa if he was going to a police clambake he had just bought a ticket for, he said: 'No. That was held last week.' My husband always paid. He never argued with them. I used to get mad when police would come in from other precincts, but my husband would say: 'Keep quiet, now. This is all right.' "

What particularly infuriated her was that the police didn't play by the rules they had made up. They'd arrest the couple whenever they needed a bust or just to show them who was boss. "About seven years ago Sergeant _____ came in with two cops," she said.

(The officers' names were redacted from grand jury documents.) "They arrested me, put me in the squad car and took me to central station. There I waited in the courtroom for a long time while the police went into the judge's office. Finally I told them I had to go home, that my husband was sick and the children would be home for lunch. They went into the judge's office again and came out and said I had been discharged. They put me in the squad car and on the way they told me the 'fix' would cost $150. When I got home I got the money from my husband and handed it over to the Sergeant."

The woman insisted that for seven years three patrolmen came into the club twice every week and she gave them $10 each. "I bought off everyone except the feds. . . . I had to pay police protection before I could pay my rent." She said she also had to give officers free liquor, chickens, and other food. She ultimately identified thirty-seven police officers who'd "badgered" her for money.

Not to be outdone by their boss, the Unknowns soon collected reams of testimony from dozens of their own witnesses. The investigators mostly focused on the Prohibition years, 1920 to 1933, for bar owners and former bootleggers no longer had to worry about prosecution for Volstead violations. Said one saloonkeeper: "I didn't mind paying the $25 a month or more, but after work the police would come to my bar and drink free and eat all my free lunch. Sometimes there wasn't room at the bar for paying customers."

CHAPTER 18
RIGHT TO THE HEART OF THINGS

When Clayton Fritchey arrived at his desk in the *Cleveland Press*'s newsroom one early January morning in 1936, he found an imposing man in work clothes waiting for him. Gus Korach had come to see Fritchey because the Slovenian immigrant was worried he'd made a big mistake. He was right — and it was a mistake that would have profound repercussions for the Cleveland Police Department.

Korach had put $2,000 — his entire savings — into cemetery lots. The salesman, who'd shown up at Korach's door unannounced, had convinced him it was an easy, no-risk investment. The man didn't mention it was illegal in Ohio to resell cemetery lots for a profit. Korach knew that many of his neighbors had already invested in lots. He'd heard some of them crowing about all the money they were going to make. So he bought eighty of them. But the more the laborer thought about it, the more he wondered if he'd gotten himself into something shady. And now he couldn't find the salesman.

Korach came to Fritchey because the reporter, with his plainspoken prose and working-class sympathies, wrote for men like Korach. This was not a writerly pose. There was nothing slick about Fritchey. He had heavy brown hair that rolled back across his scalp in placid waves. His thick forehead, backlit by small, lively blue eyes, suggested a gritty kind of worldliness. He'd grown up in Baltimore, where his father worked for the Baltimore and Ohio Railroad. At fourteen, Fritchey dropped out of school. He worked as a seaman, on the railroads, and at various menial jobs before ending up, at nineteen, as a rookie reporter for the *Baltimore American*. In 1934, at thirty, he moved to Cleveland, where he quickly made a name for himself as a hard-hitting city reporter for the *Press.*

Fritchey told Korach he would look into the situation, and later that day he began interviewing other Clevelanders who had received visits from cemetery-lot salesmen. Within days he would report on the *Press*'s front page that a group of charlatans was preying on recent immigrants. The outfit had sold more cemetery lots than Cleveland would need for five hundred years. Once Fritchey's story hit print, and prosecutors jumped in, the racket unraveled quickly, leading the cemetery salesmen to scatter and their boss to commit suicide.

That appeared to be the end of it — except for one loose end that bothered the reporter. The name John L. Dacek, one of the scam's operators, had come up repeatedly in Fritchey's investigation, but neither Fritchey nor prosecutors had been able to track the man down. The name sounded familiar to Fritchey, but he couldn't place it — and he couldn't leave it alone. Finally, after he'd spent hours one night staring at evidence he'd collected, the letters of Dacek's name reordered themselves into one he knew well: Cadek.

Louis Cadek was a well-known police captain, and police reporters had long suspected he was as dirty as an oil slick. The lumbering cop, weighing in at three hundred pounds, had been booted from the department in 1933 for dereliction of duty, but he managed to gain reinstatement shortly after Harry Davis's election the following year, Davis's second term in the mayor's office after an absence of fifteen years. When Davis became mayor the first time, in 1915, Cadek's rank suddenly jumped to sergeant, then lieutenant, and then captain in rapid succession. And he began to move around; ultimately he would be transferred twenty-eight times in thirty years. But this constant movement from one assignment to the next wasn't because no one wanted him around. He was on a Cleveland cop's version of the grand tour. He followed the money: from the Eleventh Precinct, home turf of the Mayfield Road Gang, to the Fourth, ground zero of the prostitution trade, to the Third, where illicit gambling and drinking clubs thrived. The big man was one of the most powerful cops on the street. Fritchey thrilled at the possibility of bringing him down.

It didn't take long to find the stink. Fritchey learned that Cadek owned two "de luxe automobiles" that typically would be beyond a police officer's price range. The reporter dug deeper — and discovered that Cadek had $139,000 stashed away in accounts in a handful of out-of-the-way banks, most of them under false names.[*] Canvassing Cadek's recent precincts, he made a list of storeowners, bootleggers, bookies, and small-time crooks who paid the captain for protection. Then he did something strange. Instead of going to his editor with his discoveries, he went to the safety director's office.

Eliot's wariness quickly fell away as Fritchey described what he'd found out about Captain Louis Cadek. The reporter explained to Eliot that he considered journalism a public ser-

* $139,000 in 1936 is equivalent to about $2 million in 2013.

vice. That meant he was willing to work with law enforcement when he deemed it appropriate — as long as he got first crack at putting the story into print. Eliot took him up on the offer. After a two-hour private meeting about Cadek, he pulled Fritchey into his police-corruption investigation, essentially making him one of the Unknowns. The next day, the *Press* reporter opened up his notebook for the team. He quickly bonded with the investigators in the office, as well as with the safety director himself. Wilson and Clothey admired Fritchey's smarts and drive. The three of them began to go out in the field together to conduct interviews. "Clayton was the best investigative reporter in Cleveland. He was able to get information of great value to Eliot," said Arnold Sagalyn, who was one of Eliot's Unknowns and would become a friend of Fritchey's. "He knew how to get right to the heart of things."

Fritchey's reporting was so solid that little more than a month after the newspaperman came on board, Eliot was ready to move on Cadek. The safety director wanted the captain to be the test case that would show him — and Cullitan and Burton — whether Cleveland was ready to get serious about ending police corruption. In April, Eliot suspended Cadek from duty and ordered him to appear in his office for questioning on "a departmental matter." Cadek refused the order. His attorney, Gerard J. Pilliod, showed up in his stead and handed the safety director a statement that denied wrongdoing and accused "political enemies" of plotting his downfall. Eliot accepted the statement with a smile; he now could add insubordination to his list of charges against the captain. The next day, with the Unknowns pushing forward in their broad-ranging investigation of the police department, Cullitan began presenting evidence to a grand jury, pointing out that Captain Cadek had somehow accumulated more than one hundred thousand dollars in savings even though his total salary over thirty years as a policeman came to only $67,966. Cullitan's case would have nothing to do with the cemetery scam that had first brought Cadek to Fritchey's attention. Eliot was determined to convict Cadek for being a corrupt cop, not for being a run-of-the-mill shyster. Nine former bootleggers appeared before the grand jury to admit they had given the police captain bribes for years. Some said they had paid him every month thinking he was collecting for his whole precinct. On the last day of testimony, a dim-bulb mobster wannabe came to the courthouse looking for his brother, one of the witnesses on call. "Where's my brother?" he asked a reporter in the hallway. "The gang told me to tell him to keep his mouth shut. He might be put on the spot for what he told." The hack shared the exchange with Eliot, who dragooned the reporter onto the witness list.

The case moved with lightning speed. Cadek was indicted on five counts of bribery, and in May he went on trial. On the first day, dozens of men and women crowded the courtroom, keen to get a look at the big cop they'd been reading about in the papers. Wrote the Cleveland *Plain Dealer* the next morning:

> Two and two make four, the earth circles about the sun, and a bootlegger will never talk, they said.
>
> Yesterday in a courtroom the prohibition era was referred to as some almost unbelievable period in history. In the same courtroom a bootlegger began to talk.

Not just one — a dozen of them. John Brodzinski, known as Johnny Brodie, testified that Cadek had told him one rainy October day during Prohibition that he wished he had "a little car." Brodie responded, "That ought to be easy enough, captain; I'll see what can be done." The next day, after passing the collection plate among his fellow bootleggers, Brodie delivered a brand-new Hudson. Other former bootleggers told of being raided out of business when they balked at the captain's shakedowns. Former speakeasy proprietors testified that their customer base suddenly dried up when they refused to pay protection money. Cullitan presented evidence, carefully prepared by Eliot and Fritchey, that in the late 1920s Cadek had made large deposits at local banks for the wife of bootlegger Joseph Antoszewski, and that he had presented $5,000 worth of Pyramid Savings & Loan passbooks to the bootlegger's daughter. The prosecutor even suggested that Cadek and Mrs. Antoszewski were having an affair while her husband was in prison.

The trial ran on the front page of the city's newspapers day after day. Readers couldn't get enough. After all, this was unprecedented. Cadek, pointed out the *Plain Dealer,* was the first policeman "ever to face trial here for bribery." Everyone knew that bootleggers had corrupted police officers by the trainload during Prohibition, but now, for the first time, Clevelanders were hearing the bootleggers themselves admit they had "made allies of those whose business it was to enforce the law." Police reporters saw it as a turning point, a come-to-Jesus moment for a department that had been corrupted at every level.

On May 26, a jury convicted the fifty-two-year-old police captain on four counts of accepting and soliciting bribes from bootleggers. The five men and seven women deliberated for just an hour before reaching a verdict. Cadek didn't take the witness stand during the trial, but in the hallway afterward, waiting to be transported to the county jail, he spoke up. "A good guy always gets kicked around," he told a deputy. The deputy agreed.

Reporters caught up to Cadek when he was being booked. The police captain stared straight ahead at some distant nothingness as the hacks threw questions at him. When he was led from the room, he finally turned to the reporters and smiled. "I'll see you later," he said.

By the time he arrived at the jail half an hour later, his bravura had deflated. He felt sick to his stomach. Still wearing the white straw hat and light-colored suit he'd picked out for court, Cadek sat on his cot for hours, staring at the floor, barely moving. He refused dinner. At seven that evening, jailers removed him from his cell and took him to the hospital ward. He was having a panic attack.

"Captain Louis J. Cadek, the man who commanded bootleggers to 'pay up or go to jail,' today himself awoke in County Jail to contemplate the price he will have to pay as a convicted bribetaker," Fritchey triumphantly wrote for the front page of the *Press*, finally getting to tell the story he'd had in his hip pocket for more than a month.[*]

[*] Cadek, sentenced to two to twenty years in the Ohio Penitentiary, would take his case all the way to the U.S. Supreme Court. The appeal failed. The court refused to accept Cadek's contention that "he

The reporter didn't know it yet, but he and Eliot were just getting started.

could not be convicted of receiving bribes from bootleggers after state prohibition laws had been repealed."

CHAPTER 19
VICTIM NO. 4

A little after midnight on Saturday, June 6, a wave of excitement snapped through the crowd. Finally, the line was moving forward again.

The first group had walked through the morgue's ornate, Egyptian Revival halls early in the evening. News of the horrors they'd seen spread quickly. Now the line swung around the outside of the massive concrete building on Ninth Street, made a sharp turn, and stretched past the Cuyahoga County Courthouse two long blocks away.

They had all come out to see the latest victim. The head, which the coroner had determined had been neatly severed while the man was still alive, lay on a gray metal gurney outside the morgue's freezer room, waiting patiently for a passerby to recognize it. The head had been swaddled in white towels in hopes of giving the impression of an intact corpse. Police officials, deeply divided over the macabre exhibit, feared women would scream or pass out when they realized just what they were looking at.

Of course, most of the people in the queue wanted the grotesque shock. They knew they weren't going to be able to identify the man or provide the police with a valuable clue. They just wanted to see the poor soul for themselves. Inside the morgue's front doors, the sharp odor of preservatives and bleach swept over visitors, sticking to the nasal cavities like peanut butter, making sensitive stomachs twist and loop. The women in particular must have felt regret at the sight of the head, which had been found the previous morning in Kingsbury Run. Like Edward Andrassy, he was young and good-looking, with straight black hair swept back from his forehead. It was the face of a rogue, an adventurer — the kind of face no young woman could possibly resist. So far, more than a thousand men, women, and children had filed past the dead man's head. Many more would follow over the next few hours, before morgue workers shooed away the remaining lookie-loos and slipped the head into a freezer.

He would become known as Victim No. 4. (The Lady of the Lake would not officially be put on the bloody ledger.) The police were desperate for an identification — the faster the better. By now, they felt sure that the four

306

macabre killings were not coincidences. Cleveland had a serial killer.

CHAPTER 20
THE ORIGINAL MYSTERY MAN

The constant stream of news about Eliot's police-corruption investigation — and even the more recent blaring headlines about a "maniac killer" on the loose — couldn't bring Clevelanders down. Big things were afoot, exciting things. In the first sign that the economy finally might be improving, the city had lined up more than a hundred and fifty conventions and trade shows for 1936, ranging from the Loyal Ladies of the Royal Arcanum Supreme Council to the biggest catch out there, the Republican National Convention, which promised drama and excitement as the highly motivated opposition sought a candidate to defeat President Roosevelt.

But best of all would be something even grander than the Grand Old Party: the homegrown Great Lakes Exposition. Boosters had come up with the idea of a huge, summer-long bash. They billed it as a celebration of the city's centennial, but its real purpose was to lift Cleveland's reputation around the country and thus help pull it out of the Depression. The organizers sought to make it bigger and better than Chicago's Century of Progress International Exposition of 1933. They were determined to outshine even the Nazi Olympics, scheduled to kick off in Berlin a month after the Cleveland Expo's launch. Headed by philanthropist and former city welfare director Dudley S. Blossom, the civic committee had quickly drummed up $1.5 million, including sizable donations from Standard Oil of Ohio, Republic Steel, Bell Telephone, Sherwin-Williams, The Plain Dealer Publishing Company, and U.S. Steel.

Early in the year, police cleared out Tin Can Plaza for the exposition grounds. The campus would stretch from West Third Street to about East Twentieth Street, including the lakefront, the downtown Mall, the Public Hall auditorium, and Municipal Stadium, where Major League Baseball's Indians played. All told, the exposition would take up 125 acres, a fair amount of it reclaimed from decrepitude. After years with virtually no new construction, a series of impressive new buildings suddenly rose into the sky downtown, along with a huge bandshell and a temporary "International Village." To connect downtown with the lakefront, the Expo built a 350-foot bridge over the railroad tracks. The city laid down fifteen miles of new asphalt roads and installed new water and sewer lines. Expo construction put nearly three thousand men to work.

The plumped-up work rolls were great, but no one forgot that the point was to bring out-of-towners — and their money — to Cleveland. This exposition would not be highbrow. Scheduled to open on June 27 for a hundred-day run, there would be bathing-beauty contests, fan dancers, and three dozen showgirls "5 feet 6 inches and upward." There would be boxers, prestidigitators, comedians, midgets, circus animals, dueling orchestras, and a rotation of celebrities such as Xavier Cugat and Ted Weems. Let Adolf Hitler top that.

Officially, the Expo was a family-friendly extravaganza, but city officials decided to be liberal in their definition. Sex, after all, was what the public wanted. "They have forced it on us," insisted Almon Shaffer, who was in charge of concessions. "The pressure has been so great no man could stand against it. . . . You have no notion how popular sex is with a lot of people." The triumphant French Casino nightclub exhibit, one of the biggest buildings in the International Village, promised "Callipygian Beauties Treading Pavanes and Rigadoons in Diaphanous Garments that Will Be the Talk of All America!" Mayor Burton ordered bras painted on the nude posters outside the nightclub, but he offered no comment on the braless ladies inside. He didn't need to. The women spoke up for themselves. "I feel wicked as hell — I've never appeared this nude before, and my family don't know what to think," admitted Trudye Mae Davidson, who, as Toto Leverne, was the French Casino's headliner. A nearby stall called the Little French Nudist Colony went further still. For twenty-five cents, customers received a four-minute peep through special windows at live naked girls lounging around a bath. What saved the show from the censors: "trick lighting and reflecting processes" that reduced the girls to four inches in size and gave thousands of squinting men headaches.[*]

Beauty came in many forms at this exposition — including huge. The heroic figure *Beauty* — along with its male counterpart, *Protection* — rose above the campus like the Second Coming, nude save for a slash of plaster cloth across her privates. Eliot surely noticed the mammoth sculpture when he walked through the exposition grounds dur-

[*] At the Expo's revival the following summer, Eliot, by now fully briefed on the attractions, would attend the Aquafemme tryouts at the Allerton Hotel. Aquacade producer Billy Rose insisted the pool be maintained at a near-frigid temperature during the auditions to encourage tumescent nipples. When asked, an assistant in the safety department said the director was there in an "unofficial capacity."

ing a safety inspection at the beginning of June. He also must have noticed the artwork's creator. Everyone else did. The contrast between artist and art was extreme, so much so that a reporter couldn't help but comment on it in print. "The enormous statues that will greet visitors to the Great Lakes Exposition this summer measure 12 feet from toe to top, but the sculptress responsible for them is not much more than 5 feet tall . . . in high heeled shoes," the reporter wrote.

Elisabeth Andersen Seaver, with her bulbous cheekbones and petite figure, could fire a man's imagination more than any statue ever could. No one was ever surprised to learn she was taken. The beautiful thirty-year-old sculptress was the wife of architect and watercolorist Hugh Seaver. Hugh had a solid reputation in the city, but Elisabeth was making a name for herself entirely separate from her husband. Her talent had brought her into the spotlight against her better nature. Throughout her life, teachers, clerks, and friends would misspell her name — with a "z" instead of an "s" for the first name, and an "o" instead of an "e" for her maiden name. The placidly acquiescent Elisabeth — Betty to her friends — sometimes spelled it wrong, too, rather than correct someone else's mistake. When she came out of the Cleveland School of Art in 1927, adjunct instructor Guy Cowan tapped her to work at his influential pottery, an impressive first job for any new art-school graduate. The Cowan Pottery produced arguably the finest, most distinctive commercial pottery in the country, helping define the city's art movement. Her signature work for Cowan was *Spanish Dancers,* a seductive, nine-inch-tall decorative piece that one critic called "spirited . . . very modern in treatment, simple and stylized without being in the least extreme." Following a brief tenure at the pottery, she won repeated first-place honors at the May Show, the city's popular annual art competition. Her success became a source of discord in her marriage, for Hugh could be petulant and insecure. Elisabeth nevertheless graduated to more ambitious work, including stone-relief panels at the city hall of her hometown of Sioux Falls, South Dakota, and a public fountain in Bloomfield Hills, Michigan. Now, back in Cleveland, she was embracing epic statuary. Hugh didn't like it, which made Elisabeth feel guilty, but she kept working. She wanted to have her own life.

Elisabeth spent long days on the exposition grounds, high up on scaffolding, the fragile rack of her shoulders tilted into the lake's snapping wind. The commission from Sherwin-Williams had come in at the last possible moment — less than a month before the statues needed to be finished and in place on the Mall, where they would bookend the performance space occupied nightly by the Great Lakes Symphony Orchestra. She had cast the pieces with two tons of clay and was now lacquering them to survive a hundred days in the sun. "It's a twelve-hour-a-day job," she said a week before the Expo's official launch. "I start in at 7:30 a.m. and am lucky to leave by 7:30 in the evening."

Elisabeth's dedication to her work was impressive, but it was not monomaniacal. From her perch near the top of ten-foot-high scaffolding, she noticed Cleveland's director of public safety moving about the grounds on his inspection tour, his hat pulled low on his head, topcoat flapping behind him. *That's a very attractive man,* she thought when she caught her first live glimpse of Eliot Ness. Below her, the city's celebrated safety director had to stop every few strides to shake hands with Expo workers who stepped into his path. Elisabeth didn't climb down to join the crowd on the director's trail. She didn't like to be pushy. But she made a mental note to secure an introduction.

Focused as always on work, Eliot decided there should be a police exhibit at the Expo featuring a fingerprint service. He believed this simple booth would help solve crimes in the region for years to come by bulking up the department's noncriminal fingerprint files. Officers manning the stall would take one hundred thousand prints during the Expo's one hundred days. Eliot also prominently displayed Victim No. 4's plaster death mask in hopes of identifying the man. Just as it had at the morgue, the man's striking face was an irresistible draw, with many Expo-goers lingering in front of the display for long minutes. Alas, no one came forward with the man's name.

Preparations for the Expo were a distraction from the police-corruption investigation, but by the time the extravaganza opened to the public, the safety director had identified his next target: Captain Michael J. Harwood of the Fourteenth Precinct. For months, a city councilman named Anton Vehovec had been insisting that Harwood and his men looked the other way on organized vice in his district. Harwood dismissed the councilman's claims. "Vehovec has made a mountain out of a molehill," he said. "This vice stuff is greatly exaggerated." The councilman, the police captain suggested, was a buffoon who just wanted attention.

Incensed by Harwood's insult, Vehovec asked Eliot to take a walk with him through the district. He said he would show him a booking joint run by Harwood's son. Eliot didn't know what to think of the accusation — Harwood was right that Vehovec was a blowhard — but he took the councilman up on the offer. Late on the morning of June 6, at about the same time that Victim No. 4 was being put on public display at the city morgue, Eliot, Vehovec, Detective Walter Walker, and a couple of reporters came up to 1775 Ivanhoe Road NE. The front of the building housed a restaurant, but it was obvious something else was going on. There were men in the corner booths on each side who clearly weren't patrons; Eliot and Walker pegged them as lookouts. The men in the booths froze when they realized it was the city's safety director staring them down. Over just a few minutes, more than two dozen men entered the restaurant — and went straight through to the back. Eliot and Walker followed them and discovered a buzzer for entering a room behind the kitchen. Even though he didn't have a search warrant, the safety director decided it was "imperative to enter."

Eliot tried the buzzer, but he couldn't gain access. So Detective Walker began pounding on the door with a brick. When they finally made it into the room, they found the back door wide open. There were twelve men remaining in the room, the floor littered with gambling receipts. Eliot and the detective grilled the men, most of whom were drunk. Three admitted they had been playing blackjack. Some of the others said they were listening to race results when people began piling out the back.

As Eliot and Walker were gathering up signed statements, a young, heavyset man walked through the door. He stopped abruptly, surprised at what he was seeing. Eliot asked him who he was. Harwood, the man said, in a tone that suggested he believed he should be asking the questions. Edward Harwood, Captain Harwood's son. He said he owned the building.

"What are you doing here?" Eliot asked.

Harwood chewed his cud for a moment, his eyes darting around the room. The ball finally dropped: these were cops. Harwood said he had been at his family's restaurant, a few blocks down the street, when he heard "something funny was going on down here."

Eliot sat him down and began peppering him with questions. Harwood said he rented the back room to someone named Joe. He said he didn't know the man's last name. He admitted he had been in the room many times in recent weeks but insisted he had no idea that Joe was running a gambling parlor. In a report, Eliot would call Harwood's claim of ignorance a "thin denial which warrants careful investigation." He added: "His whole story is contradictory, is hesitantly told and leaves many things to be explained, particularly how such an establishment could run in a precinct commanded by his father." Indeed, Eliot would later learn that Harwood had been in the betting room all morning, but, luckily for the raiders, he had made a trip to the drugstore just moments before Eliot and his group arrived. The younger Harwood was an expert at turning a room quickly. He could empty it of all evidence of betting and have gamblers playing Ping-Pong and pool within three minutes. He'd later tell an associate that if he had been in the room when the safety director and his men started banging on the door, they "wouldn't have gotten anything at all."

But he wasn't in the room when the raid started. He had walked in fifteen minutes later, so now he was in trouble. Harwood asked to make a phone call. A few minutes later, another man arrived in the back room. The man said his name was Joe McCarthy and that he was the proprietor. He admitted it was a gambling joint and said "Eddie" knew nothing about it.

"Didn't Harwood telephone you to come down here or he would have to take the rap?" Eliot asked.

"I'm the guy," McCarthy said.

"You're quite sure you want to take the rap on this?"

McCarthy was sure — but Eliot wasn't going to let him. The safety director found keys on Harwood that worked the locks in the gambling room. The keys found on McCarthy did not.

Now it was Eliot's turn to make a phone

call. He reached Chief Matowitz at Central Police Station and told him to immediately relieve Edward Harwood's father of his command of the Fourteenth Precinct. The younger Harwood barked at Eliot that he couldn't do that. Eliot asked Matowitz to hold the line, turned to Harwood and told him to pipe down.

Outside, a clutch of reporters had gathered. Vehovec was giving an interview when Eliot stepped into the street. The hacks nearly knocked the councilman over to get to the safety director. "The matter has now gone far beyond the operation of a single bookmaking establishment," Eliot told them. "It is a question of police efficiency, discipline and honesty in the Fourteenth Precinct, and every officer in it is going to be called on for a recital of everything that is known."

Later that night, Captain Harwood met with his son at the family's restaurant on Euclid Avenue and "bawled Eddie out."

"You were a damn fool to go back in and let them get just the man they wanted," the police captain hissed. He told his son he had "a good mind to take a belt to you now."

Early in July, Tom Clothey and Keith Wilson began waiting around outside the police academy. They picked off their targets one by one over a couple of days, tapping them on the shoulder on the busy sidewalk or introducing themselves on the streetcar. Eliot had identified five men as the best recruits in the department. Now he needed them for temporary undercover duty. He simply could not trust anyone who already wore a badge.

The assignment: to take down a large bookie joint in the Eighth Precinct. Police officers protected the place, acted as its bagmen and muscle. The Unknowns had watched it for a couple of weeks, but they kept their distance. By now, the city's gangsters could recognize many of the safety director's investigators on sight. So on Friday, July 17, Eliot began sending his new conscripts up to the third floor of the building at 2077 West Twenty-fifth Street. The public safety department had issued each of the men a small amount of cash for placing bets and buying drinks. Over the weekend the fledgling officers lost all of it. The gambling equipment, they believed, was rigged.

On Monday evening, while some of the undercover men lounged in the bustling gambling room, a secretary in the safety director's office called the Eighth Precinct. Her voice cracking, she told the patrolman at the desk that her husband had lost all of his money in the place on Twenty-fifth. The patrolman said, "Oh, you mean that bookie joint down the street." Yes, she said, that bookie joint down the street.

Everyone in the neighborhood knew about

the place; it was run by Tommy McGinty, a high-profile hood and boxing promoter. The secretary said she wanted the gambling den shut down. The patrolman was sympathetic to the woman's plight, but he also was suspicious. After hanging up, he called the safety director's office and asked if they knew anything about the call. The secretary claimed ignorance, and the cop didn't realize he was talking to the same woman who'd just called. Ringing off, he then phoned the Ninth Precinct and asked if they could pop their heads in at 2077, because the Eighth didn't have men available. The Ninth sent two patrolmen to the address, but before they arrived, the lights in the gambling den flashed off and on, which sent everyone into frenzied action. When the patrolmen stepped into the room, there was nothing to see. The officers tipped their hats, left the building, and reported to the Eighth that they found no evidence of gambling. Twenty minutes later, the place was packed with gamblers again.

The next day, Matowitz ordered the Eighth Precinct's commander, Adolph Lenahan, to report to Central Police Station. When Lenahan arrived at the chief's office, Matowitz handed him a resignation letter and told him to sign it. Lenahan, stunned, refused. The chief suspended him on the spot — for being drunk on the job. Lenahan demanded that he be taken to the hospital for a professional medical opinion on his condition, but Matowitz waved him off. Instead, he brought in two officers and told them to take Lenahan home.

A few hours later, Eliot and a raiding party rolled into the Eighth Precinct and turned onto West Twenty-fifth Street. Again the lights blinked at the gambling den and the joint's employees launched into action. Except this time the five undercover men also came to life. They grabbed the operators. One tackled a cashier who was trying to dump receipts and recording books out a window. Gamblers headed for the exit, but Eliot, his assistant John Flynn, and a clutch of officers met them on the stairs. A paddy wagon arrived to take away suspects. For the next hour, the officers carried gambling equipment piece by piece down the narrow staircase to a police truck waiting at the curb. Men and women on the street, who had been living with raucous gambling parlors in their neighborhood for years, couldn't believe what they were seeing. By the time the place had been emptied out, several hundred people ringed the building, agape at the sight.

"The suspension by the chief brought the matter of the bookie joint to issue at once," Eliot told reporters. "I have had it watched for a week, and Captain Lenahan will now be asked to answer why this establishment was allowed to run as openly as it was running."

The next day, Eliot grilled the precinct's deputy inspector, Timothy J. Costello, who admitted that his three sons worked for McGinty at a dog-racing track. Costello would survive the investigation, but the upward trajectory of his career abruptly ended. He soon would be reassigned to the police radio room. Lenahan, the precinct's commander, told reporters he planned to fight the intoxication charge against him, but after a few days of thrashing, he quieted down. At the end of the month, he resigned from the force.

The safety director kept the pressure on. In the days that followed the raid, police barged into a dozen more gambling rooms around the city. A reporter caught up to Eliot one evening as the safety director was leaving city hall. He asked what was going on. "I am interested in whether the precincts are meeting their responsibility," Eliot said. "A certain philosophy has grown up in the police department in the last ten years, and it takes some time to overcome it. I don't want periodic activity. I want continued activity."

Late in the summer, Eliot disappeared from public view. Reporters learned that he had given Flynn and Chief Matowitz the authority to handle "routine matters" while he was gone. They quizzed safety department staff and Mayor Burton's assistants about his whereabouts but got nowhere. "He is the original mystery man, and none of his associates is ever completely in his confidence," one reporter wrote about the safety director. "His speech sounds candid, but it rarely is." When another hack happened to come upon the safety director on the street one day, Eliot refused to say what he was doing. "Mr. Cullitan will know how to get in touch with me," he said, mysteriously.

The reporter didn't know how lucky he was to score a Ness sighting. In August and September, Eliot quietly left the state time and again to track down witnesses and take statements. On one weekend he made a "sudden dash" to New York to interview a former bootlegger. Later in the year, federal agents would help him find two fugitives in northern Michigan who had been seen marching off into the woods. They came upon the potential witnesses near an icy lake, huddled under a tent, wearing business suits and polished shoes, trying to clap circulation into their extremities. Eliot and the agents probably saved the men from freezing to death. On the drive back to Cleveland, one of the men admitted he had been a "payoff collector" for Harwood. The other stayed silent, save for his chattering teeth.

The old guard, scared by the headlines and the incessant speculation about the safety director's activities, began to play furious defense. When Eliot heard that patrolmen from the Fourteenth and Fifteenth Precincts put the word out that no one who talked to the director or his investigators would be safe, he acted immediately. Like Judge Wilkerson swapping out the entire jury for the Capone case, Eliot ordered the Fifteenth Precinct to be completely turned over. Matowitz transferred twenty-two officers out of the precinct in a single day. He admitted to reporters that the safety director had handpicked their replacements. The move was so unusual that Eliot issued a written statement about it:

My investigation shows that there has been police collusion in the Fifteenth Precinct over a number of years and that condition has resulted in residents losing all confidence in police generally. My order should not be construed as a reflection on the men transferred today. I have not gone into their individual integrity. I have faith in most of them, but, as matters stand now, they are working in a shadow of suspicion that is detrimental to both themselves and the community in question.

Fenton E. Barrett, the captain of the Fifteenth Precinct until being transferred, insisted he would fight the stain on his reputation. A month later, like Lenahan before him, he resigned.

With the press cheering him on — "the community waited long for a safety director like Eliot Ness," wrote the *Plain Dealer* — the housecleaning took on an irresistible momentum. Tipsters called the safety department with the addresses of police-protected gambling joints. Surveillance on one suspected officer would lead to others coming under scrutiny. The Ness mystique continued to grow and deepen. At city hall functions, suburban house parties, and inner-city bars, people talked about how the safety director had "spent one hundred consecutive summer nights following the trail of police crookedness through some of the city's worst dives and some of the metropolitan area's nicest suburbs." He would be just as busy through the fall and winter.

"As a federal investigator for 9 years he crashed into gang hide-outs with steel-nosed trucks, shot it out with gunmen, and tapped the wires of wire tappers. His tamer sports are handball, badminton, and tennis." American *magazine* *embraces the Ness myth in 1937.*

*Eliot Ness, University of Chicago, class of
'25*

*Ness and his fraternity brothers, grim-faced in the midst of
Jazz Age prosperity*

Left to right: "Untouchables" Sam Seager, Lyle Chapman, Paul Robsky

Al Capone, aka the Big Fella

Eliot Ness, leader of the Capone squad

Chicago's Prohibition administrator, E. C. Yellowley (left), and Assistant Administrator Alexander Jamie (right) pose with Frank White and Eliot Ness after the young agents break up an illegal liquor-importing operation carried out by Pullman passenger-train porters.

With tear gas wafting through the air, strikers at the Fisher Body plant hurl stones at police.

The most popular man in Cleveland

"Suppose you were a bandit and told Safety Director Eliot Ness to 'stick 'em up.' He might surprise you in any one of 30 different ways." Ness shows police recruits how to fight for their lives.

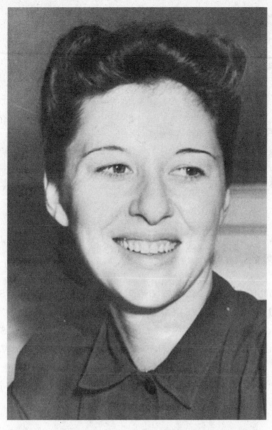

Sexy, troubled Evaline McAndrew Ness

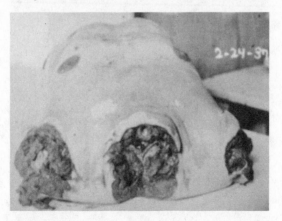

The torso of a young woman, victim number seven of Kingsbury Run's "Mad Butcher." Her head and limbs are never found, making identification impossible.

CLEVELAND POLICE DEPARTMENT

Precinct:

Date: 19

Picked by: Rank

Date & time picked up: 19

Cal of:

Turned over by: Rank

Received: Rank

LABORATORY NO.

PROPERTY ROOM NO.

FOR BULLETS OR OTHER VALUABLE EVIDENCE

"He certainly doesn't leave many, if any, clues," Ness says in frustration as public pressure builds to stop the torso murders. Over five years, Cleveland police collect hundreds of items from the crime scenes in hope of piecing together the killer's identity.

Mrs. Hugh Seaver, stylish and headed for divorce

Eliot Ness for mayor. Not even his dutiful new wife believes he has a chance at winning.

The lion in winter

CHAPTER 21
THE SADISTIC TYPE

Kingsbury Run stretched out in a large parabola along the East Side. With its natural watershed, this once had been an idyllic spot, before heavy industry and then the Depression moved in. Now it was Cleveland's colostomy bag. The city's detritus emptied day after day into the sprawling urban ravine. A constant haze of industrial smoke provided natural cover for the toxic runoff that oozed in from the Flats district along the banks of the Cuyahoga River. Homeless men set up camp along the high ground. The city's railroad system — with crisscrossing tracks carrying freight to Chicago and commuters to the suburbs — seemed to be the only thing keeping the area from collapsing in on itself like a dying star.

On the morning of September 10, 1936, a twenty-five-year-old hobo looking to jump a freight train for the East Coast noticed a headless and limbless human torso drifting in an expanse of dirty water along a bend near

East Thirty-seventh Street. By early afternoon, word had spread. Hundreds of men and women in the Run walked over to the area to watch policemen drag what quickly would become known as "the torso pool." They whispered nervously to one another as they watched the operation.

The bodies were adding up fast: six total over the past year, four in Kingsbury Run. There were the two men on Jackass Hill, their heads and genitals expertly removed. Then the prostitute, cut into pieces, the thigh, pelvis, and right arm placed in the picnic basket and left near the meat shop. Next came the victim whose head officials had displayed at the morgue. Two boys had discovered it; the dead man's body was ultimately unearthed two hundred feet away. Another headless, naked body was found July 22 just outside the city limits, in Brooklyn Township, the head not far away, wrapped in the victim's clothing. And now this latest victim, the torso halved and plopped into the Run's rancid waters like hot dogs. The pace of killings was quickening — everyone knew that much.

When the coroner, Arthur Pearce, emerged from the morgue that evening, he found himself in demand. Reporters surrounded him and fired questions, but he didn't know what he should say. The six murders, with their true, forceful amputations of heads and limbs, unnerved him, just like everyone else. He believed it was likely the work of a surgeon, someone with talent. "The killer is apparently a sex maniac of the sadistic type," he said. "This is indicated by the condition of his victims. He is probably a muscular man. The slayer definitely has expert knowledge of human anatomy. The incisions of his knife are clean and were made in each case without guesswork. He may have gathered his knowledge of anatomy as a medical student. Or it is possible that he is a butcher." This kind of statement did not help the situation. Headlines in seventy-two-point type featuring the words "sex maniac," "sadist," and "butcher" reached newsstands within hours. Those were followed, at long last, by public panic.

Eliot had mostly steered clear of the investigations into the bizarre murders. Only in the last couple of months had police decided they were all connected and thus deserved special attention. But that wasn't why the safety director had stayed away: after all, a couple of months was not an insignificant amount of time when there's a serial killer on the loose. The better reason for his reluctance to get involved was that he recognized the killings as the work of a psychopath. Such crimes defied logic. They required luck to solve, and Eliot didn't like to rely on luck. He also didn't like to delve into the dark recesses of men's motivations. He didn't have that kind of curiosity — not even about his own motivations. He wanted only to act, to strike out against the enemy.

Now, however, the degree of his involvement was taken out of his hands. The torso pool — coming on the heels of the death mask at the Expo — finally would make the case priority number one for Mayor Burton and his administration. The so-called torso murderer had become big news in the city, relentless news. The *Plain Dealer* called the killer a "New Insane Type." The *News* wrote, "Of all horrible nightmares come to life, the most shuddering is the fiend who decapitates his victims in the dark, dank recesses of Kingsbury Run." Offered the *Press:* "He kills for the thrill of killing. He kills to satisfy a bestial, sadistic lust for blood. He kills to prove himself strong. He kills to feed his sex-perverted brain the sight of a beheaded human. He must kill." The editorials and headlines became a drumbeat, pounding down Cleveland's reputation just as the Great Lakes Exposition came to a close. The news had gone out on the national wires and even spread overseas. *Pravda,* the Communist Party newspaper in the Soviet Union, cited the murders as evidence of America's moral degradation. Cleveland's business leaders had begun screaming for the case to be solved. Everyone in the city was screaming. Chief

Matowitz had just assigned the case — all of the murders — to the police department's best detective, Peter Merylo. But that meant little to Burton. The mayor didn't know Merylo. He knew Eliot. Burton called Eliot into his office and told him to take charge of the investigation.

On September 12, Eliot began interviewing the various officers who had investigated one or more of the murders. He sent a wave of patrolmen into Kingsbury Run to roust and question every hobo who might have seen or heard something. He ordered police cruisers to make regular circuits of the Run, twenty-four hours a day, and to stop any car driving near the area in the wee hours. All of that done, he called up Merylo's captain and told him to send the case's new detective over.

The forty-one-year-old Merylo, an army veteran born in the Ukraine, was a tough bird. He didn't play politics. He'd earned his detective's badge in the most unusual of ways: through long hours and hard work. Matowitz knew what he was doing in putting him on the case. The detective arrived at Eliot's office within an hour of the summons. Though Merylo had been on the case for just twenty-four hours and was still reading through the police reports on the six murders, Eliot pressed him for details. The safety director was known for his soft touch, but Merylo, a prickly man, took offense at the questioning. The stocky, balding detective offered up half answers, clearly impatient. He had never met the safety director before but he knew he didn't like him. He'd seen the headlines, read the articles. Eliot was slick; Merylo hated slick.

Merylo told the director he thought the killer was a "sex pervert" but couldn't yet offer much more than that. Eliot nodded. He asked a few more perfunctory questions, then told the detective to pursue the investigation as he saw fit and to keep him informed. Merylo rose and marched out of the office, fuming. He felt he was being called to account, that he was being criticized. He never got over it. "You can't bring up Eliot Ness to Peter," Merylo's wife, Sophie, would say years later, after Merylo had retired. "He starts to get nasty. He did not like the man."

Merylo's belief that the killer was a pervert would underpin his every move as he and his partner, Martin Zalewski, set off into the Run. Indeed, that belief would only deepen and harden in the months that followed. In one report, he wrote: "I am of the opinion that the murderer is a Sex Degenerate, suffering from necrophilia, aphrodisia or erotomania. . . . This may be a case of infatuation for statues, the kind with head and limbs broken off, such as the torso of Hercules or of Satyr." Merylo's theories about the killer — along with the coroner's insistence that "if

332

he is ever caught, it will most certainly be by accident" — unnerved the police brass. Chief Matowitz freed Merylo and Zalewski of all other obligations. The torso-killer investigation would be their only case.

The detectives committed themselves to the hunt completely. They scoured Kingsbury Run's shantytowns and the broken-down neighborhoods of the Roaring Third. Merylo dressed as a hobo and slept overnight in the Run. He hopped on and off train boxcars. On a few occasions he even dressed in what he considered homosexual garb and paraded ostentatiously around the Flats late at night. Merylo would write that "we received thousands of tips and examined as many suspects. We were compelled to work many hours over time, checking on every tip regardless of any significance. We spent from one hour to five or six weeks to check on a single suspect before we were able to check him out to our satisfaction that this individual could not have had any connection with these crimes." They followed hundreds of doctors, butchers, and "known perverts," searched through their mail and garbage. He and Zalewski got charged up over rumors about well-to-do men who trawled the Roaring Third for homosexual sex. A bartender at a grimy dive told of a tall, elegantly dressed regular who claimed to be a doctor. The man "seemed to be very accommodating and if anyone wanted to go anywhere he would take them in his car." But Merylo wasn't convinced the killer was a doctor. Perhaps it was someone who reached "sexual gratification while watching the blood flow after cutting the jugular vein of his victim," he wrote. For a while, he zeroed in on a "chicken freak" who every week brought a live chicken to a whorehouse and paid a prostitute to cut its head off while he masturbated to climax. Puzzling over the few disparate facts at hand, he constructed a profile of the killer. He thought the man may have "only finished grammer [*sic*] school. He reads newspapers and detective story magazines, especially murder mysteries." One thing Merylo was absolutely sure about: "This man would not stop killing as long as he is at large and alive."

The investigation quickly traveled far and wide. Hearing of seven similar murders over the past ten years in New Castle, Pennsylvania, an industrial outpost near Youngstown, Ohio, Eliot sent Flynn to the town to check out their evidence. Flynn didn't find a lot of substantive similarities, but seeing as he was Eliot's man, his opinion didn't matter to the case's lead detective. Merylo would write in an unpublished memoir that "Flynn returned to Cleveland a little dubious about the New Castle torsos. He wasn't sure those murders had been committed by the man responsible for those here. I was sure."

■ ■ ■ ■

Eliot wished Merylo would go ahead and find the pervert already.

He didn't want to spend any more of his time on this serial killer. The whole case made his skin crawl, everything about it. Disease was inherent in man; Eliot the rationalist understood this, but his childhood in Christian Science — the one true faith — rebelled at such conclusions. "All is infinite Mind and its infinite manifestation, for God is All-in-all," wrote Mary Baker Eddy, Christian Science's founder. Eliot took up a career that in many ways stood at odds with his — with his beloved mother's — optimistic beliefs. Now, with the torso case, he found himself in a horrible house of mirrors, everything distorted and ugly. He much preferred ordinary human corruption, the kind that could be cured through a shifting in consciousness.

Eliot was not a religious man. He had struggled with Mrs. Eddy's ideas throughout his adolescence, but still there was something about them he couldn't deny. There was a force out there, a leveler of history and time and ego. All things were one thing.

He refused to dial back his police-corruption investigations to suit the mayor's preoccupation with the torso murders. Putting the serial-killer case to the side, he pushed forward, day after day, until on October 5 he showed up in Cullitan's office with hundreds of pages of testimony and "documentary evidence and exhibits," all carefully organized and vetted. Eliot had targeted as witnesses not only men who'd been shaken down by cops, but also retired police officers and police widows. The report named nearly twenty current officers as being involved in bribery, bootlegging, and protection rackets.

The grand jury went into action three days later. Eliot paced in the county courthouse corridor each day until bribery charges came down against eight officers. He punched a fist into his hand and headed back to city hall.

Michael Harwood, as expected, topped the list of indicted men. The others were Deputy Inspector Edwin C. Burns, Lieutenant John H. Nebe, Lieutenant Thomas J. Brady, Sergeant James Price, Patrolman Clarence H. Alberts, Patrolman John W. Shoemaker, and Patrolman Gaylord Stotts. The indictments charged that during Prohibition and beyond the officers "put protection payments on a systematic monthly basis," that they "knocked off bootleggers and then 'cleaned up' by agreeing to 'fix' the case," and that "when bootleggers refused to pay protection, some officers framed them by planting liquor on their premises and raiding them." The indictment also asserted that some of the officers went into the bootleg business themselves. The grand jury's forewoman, Mrs. Lucia McBride, said the testimony of a large number of witnesses shocked the jury members to their cores. The evidence presented to them, she said, "displays a callous brutality and studied intimidation by police officers" in the city.

Reporters rushed to Harwood's home, where they found his wife sobbing uncontrollably. "Isn't it terrible? Isn't it terrible?" she wailed. "All our lives we've worked so hard, and all they do is torture you." Later that day, a hack found Harwood and a business associate at the police captain's new hobby: a nightclub called the Green Derby he had just opened at Euclid Avenue and East 172nd Street. The place had been the family's restaurant, the Checkerboard, until just a few weeks before. "Can't you see I'm talking business with this man?" Harwood snapped when the reporter approached.

The other policemen facing charges affected stunned disbelief. Burns, found at his home, told reporters: "To my knowledge I haven't violated any of the rules of the department. I don't know what this is all about." Nebe, coming out of the Tenth Precinct station, said the same thing: "I haven't the slightest idea what this is all about. I don't know who would give me anything." Offered Patrolman Stotts: "I never took a dime from anybody. When I was on the liquor squad we knocked off anybody and everybody. Of course, there's a lot of them sore at us and glad to have a chance to sock us. Well, my word is as good as any of theirs."

Eliot — and, more important, Cullitan — was willing to test Stotts's theory.

Captain Harwood went on trial in December, the first of the eight indicted officers to have his day in court. Every day, men and women packed the gallery. Housewives plunked down on the benches in the second and third rows, tutting at the testimony and offering up their opinions, oblivious to Harwood's family sitting near them. Men stood in the back, craning their necks for unobstructed views of the bootleggers on the witness stand, men they once bought pints from and shared jokes with. Harwood was the man on trial, but most of the attention focused on Eliot, who sat in the courtroom every day. Spectators wondered about the notes he constantly jotted down on large yellow pads. They thrilled when he whispered to his "undercover men," who flagrantly carried their guns on their hips for everyone to see. Reporters began what would become a years-long habit of speculating about the safety director's courtroom demeanor, how he seemed "neither at work nor at play, neither bored nor excited."

Just as with the Cadek trial, the bootleggers, saloon owners and bartenders who took the witness stand told of Harwood and his men brutalizing them during Prohibition, usually with the harassment ending with Harwood telling them they should pay up "in order not to be bothered." One former bootlegger said that when he refused to pay, Harwood insisted he "would be sorry." In the weeks that followed, he said, a series of raids forced him to get out of the business. Still another man, who ran a saloon without a liquor license after repeal, maintained that Harwood encouraged bootlegging right up into this very year.

James C. Connell, attorney for the defense, refused to concede the high ground. A bulky, energetic man with an actorly flourish in court, he contended that Harwood was the victim of a revenge plot by bootleggers, instigated by Councilman Anton Vehovec. The thirty-eight-year-old lawyer blasted the safety director for bringing forward tainted evidence. Unlike Cadek, Harwood took the stand to profess his innocence. He testified that as captain of the Fourteenth Precinct, he did not undertake any gambling raids "because there were written orders that Captain [Emmett] Potts would take care of all gambling and slot machine complaints." Potts was well known to have been the corrupt Mayor Davis's street enforcer. The testimony didn't help: Connell didn't have those orders to present to the court, nor did he have any witnesses to back up the claim. Cullitan then subjected the captain to eight hours of cross-examination, tripping him up on numerous points, including his son's business activities.

Worse yet for the defense, the reporters covering the trial reacted to Harwood's testimony with unconcealed disgust. The *Plain Dealer*'s Philip Porter, who had followed Harwood's career for more than a decade, found the defense outrageous. "Harwood's ludicrous story of being a kindly law enforcer, victim of a foul plot by bootleggers and reporters, was a good laugh to those who knew him," he wrote. "He has never been anything but a tough, ruthless conniver, using his blue suit to cover his phenagling [*sic*]." Newspapermen knew all about the police force's worst offenders and always had, but they'd mostly kept quiet over the years for fear of being shut out of police stations and even courtrooms. Eliot now gave them license to let loose.

Cullitan rode the public outrage. "The defense largely has been muddying the waters, claiming that we are trying to destroy Harwood," he said in his closing argument. "He is the one who dirtied himself, by lining his dirty purse with bootleggers' money." The prosecutor, well aware of the attention being paid to Eliot throughout the trial, also vigorously defended the safety director.

"Mr. Ness is of a different political faith than I am," the Democratic prosecutor said. "I do not know him socially or move in the same circles. But I do want to say to you that I have nothing but admiration for the determination he has shown in his efforts to rid the city of gangsters, mobsters, racketeers, and to clean the police department of crooks. I want you to remember that he is doing this work for every decent citizen — for you, for me and for us all."[*]

On the evening of December 16, the seven women and five men on the jury announced they had reached a verdict. Harwood entered the room with a small smile on his face. Word had come down the previous night that one jury member — an elderly woman — was holding out for acquittal. It sometimes took just one person with passionate conviction to turn the tide. With Harwood standing stiffly next to his lawyer, the bailiff opened the verdict and read it out in a clear, deep voice. A collective gasp rolled through the courtroom, and Harwood put his face in his hands. Behind him, his wife fell off her chair, passed out cold. He had been convicted on six of

[*] It was assumed that Eliot was a Republican, since he worked for a Republican administration, but he had never publicly laid claim to a political affiliation.

seven bribery counts. One of the police captain's two daughters, Helen, began to sob uncontrollably. Harwood himself struggled to control his emotions. "Harwood's face was ashen," Fritchey wrote. "Then, as the blood returned to it, he became livid. He parted his lips as if to speak — and words would not come." Judge Frank Day asked Harwood to comment on the verdict, but the defendant didn't seem to hear. Tears came to his eyes. He walked out of the courtroom without saying a word. Harwood's wife and daughters, all weeping, followed him out. His other daughter, Mrs. Marie Kohl, turned to Eliot. "Thank you for this, Mr. Ness," she said. As she passed by, she spat on him. Eliot said nothing. He waited until she had disappeared out the doors before wiping the spittle from his face.

Many of the attorneys for the other seven indicted officers sat in the back of the room. The looks on their faces — disbelief, discouragement, maybe fear — would be duplicated across the city's police precincts when newspapers arrived in the morning. The Cadek conviction hadn't been an aberration, a one-off thanks to a weird subplot involving cemetery plots and hoodwinked immigrants. No, the world had changed. The impossible was now possible. Director Ness actually was cleaning up the police force, one crooked cop at a time.

Once he'd pulled himself together, Harwood turned his attention to winning on appeal. Just days after the conviction, he hired private investigators and technical experts. He wanted to show that Cleveland's safety director had framed him and the other seven officers.

Without informing his lawyer, the newly convicted former policeman offered two women $100 each to lure the prosecution's most damning witnesses into a trap. The women, Mrs. Marie Murray and Mrs. May Green, agreed to the plan — and decided not to tell their husbands, who worked for Harwood at the Green Derby. Murray and Green were young and sexy, with pointy breasts and fat, bloodred lips, but they were new to femme fatale duty. Only one of the witnesses, Casper Korce, took the bait. The former bootlegger, who had testified against Harwood at trial and against others during grand-jury proceedings, followed the ladies to a swank West Side apartment that had been wired for sound. Murray and Green got Korce liquored up and unbuttoned, and began to press him about how much he "got out of the cases." Korce thought he was getting the celebrity treatment, seeing as his name had been in all the papers, but the good times abruptly ended when his dirty talk proved a turnoff. "I was offered $2,500 to testify for Harwood instead of against him," Korce said. The mood ruined, the women handed him his hat and sent him on his way.

Harwood tried again, paying the women another $100 each to invite Korce around a second time and press him harder to "open up" about the safety director. Korce again gave in to the women's winks and smiles; once in the apartment, he yammered on about his bootlegging days and how Ness and Fritchey had interviewed him for hours about his relationships with police officers. But the women couldn't get him to cough up anything incriminating on Eliot or the reporter. Korce, no doubt turning blue from frustration, found himself pushed out the door again. Harwood was even more frustrated. He told Murray she would have to testify that she'd heard Korce say that Ness had paid him $3,200. The woman, though afraid Harwood would tell her husband about her participation in the seduction plot, refused. She would rather have her husband mad at her than Eliot Ness.

After Harwood's conviction, it was Deputy Inspector Burns's turn in March. The trial was a carbon copy of Harwood's, including a handful of repeat witnesses. The bootleggers assigned the same litany of abuses to Burns that they had to Harwood; some of Burns's colleagues on the police force, meanwhile, took the stand to insist the defendant was a stand-up guy, as honest as they come. As the jury filed out of the room to begin deliberations, the fifty-five-year-old Burns, a "tall, husky, handsome man" and a popular officer in the department, approached Eliot and stuck out his hand. "I just want you to know that, no matter what happens, there are no hard feelings," he said. "I know there was nothing personal in your activities."

Eliot was surprised — and visibly moved — by the gesture. He was sensitive about how the rank and file in the department viewed him. The emotional outburst that Harwood's daughter directed at him at the end of her father's trial had hit him hard. He shook Burns's hand. "Nothing personal at all," he said.

Five hours later, the jury returned and pronounced Burns guilty on all five counts. The deputy inspector smiled for press photographers and did not look at Eliot as court officers led him from the room.

The police-graft investigation did not always offer up clear-cut cases. Neil McGill prided himself on being a hard man, but he admitted he felt sorry for John Nebe, who came to trial three weeks after Burns. During Prohibition, the young patrolman had pocketed five bucks here and five bucks there, mostly to be somewhere else when men unloaded trucks full of liquor. "This was chicken feed compared to most of the bribes given (to the other indicted officers)," McGill noted. He pointed out that Nebe's lawyers would focus on how poorly Cleveland police officers were paid. And that they could argue that Nebe wasn't trying to get rich; he was just trying to keep a roof over his children's heads and bread on the table. The policeman had a big, attractive family that surely would be sitting in the front row every day of the trial. That kind of thing could sway a jury.

"Eliot, we may have trouble in getting the jury to convict Nebe," McGill told the safety director during a planning meeting. "You know that the difference between a bribe and a tip is that a bribe is given before the service is rendered, and a tip is given after a service is rendered. These amounts of five dollars and ten dollars are not in the bribe class."

Eliot nodded. "That's true, but you and I know, and Lieutenant Nebe knew, that a bribe, even disguised as a tip, is given to influence the conduct of a public officer or public official. We will let the jury have the facts."

The jury hung on Nebe, just as McGill had feared, but Eliot would not let it go. Right was right, wrong was wrong. He convinced Cullitan to try the officer again. The second time around, Eliot brought in three "surprise witnesses." The trial judge agreed to put them on the stand even though the witnesses hadn't mentioned Nebe in their grand-jury testimony.

Former bootlegger Louis Gregorcic, who had testified against Harwood and Burns in their trials, now said that he paid Nebe $50 a month for eight months during the later years of Prohibition. John Mozina, a butcher, told of being arrested by Nebe for having two gallons of sour wine in his home. Mozina said he paid Nebe $50 and that the case was subsequently dismissed. "He did not ask me for it; I just gave it to him," he said. And finally, Mrs. Mary Anslovar insisted Nebe once forced his way into her home and took away a small amount of illegal booze she had. She said she paid him "$200 or $300" to stay out of the dock. All of these new bribery allegations involved much larger sums than what the witnesses in the first trial had claimed they'd paid the policeman. Eliot did not like to lose.

Nebe was convicted.

McGill worried that Eliot might be overdoing it with the investigation, that he might be pushing too hard. John Flynn, the assistant safety director, felt sure of it. Flynn admitted privately to a friend that he thought the police-corruption investigation was "worthless." His reason for concern, however, was very different than McGill's.

347

Flynn was a Republican precinct committeeman in Shaker Heights, a well-to-do enclave on the eastern edge of the city. He had electoral aspirations, and during the summer of 1936 he had started making moves that smacked of political positioning. As acting safety director while Eliot was in the field, he appointed Louis Cadek's nephew to the police force, jumping him over seven recruits who were ahead of him on the civil-service list. When Eliot returned to the office, he revoked the appointment, calling it "ill-advised." A reporter asked who exactly had advised Flynn, and the safety director snapped: "That's what I intend to find out."

He soon did, and he didn't like what he found. He discovered that his assistant was, if not corrupt, then disturbingly malleable. In just a few short months in the job Flynn had become known around city hall as the man to see for "politicians who want little favors done." With the assistant safety director exposed, a group of local power brokers had approached Eliot directly in July. They offered to secure the resignations of most of the policemen in his sights if he wouldn't oppose pensions for the officers and would "call off the dogs" — that is, end his corruption investigation, which some political players in the city worried would eventually reach them. Eliot threw the emissaries out of his office. At about the same time, Flynn tried to push through a retirement request with full pension for Captain Harwood before formal charges could be brought against the officer. Eliot went before the civil-service board and put a stop to it.

The end came in December when Flynn popped off to a reporter as the jury in the Harwood trial was meeting. "I don't believe they ever will convict him," he told the hack. "It would have saved thousands of dollars to have accepted his resignation." The next day, the verdict on Harwood came down. The above-the-fold headline on the front page of the *Cleveland Press* — "Police Captain Convicted on Six Counts He Took Graft from Bootleggers" — stood in stark contrast to Flynn's comment, which the paper also highlighted. The assistant safety director submitted his resignation before the end of the week. He told reporters he would be returning to his private law practice.

The imbroglio must have been disillusioning for Eliot, who liked Flynn and had respected him. He moved quickly on a replacement. Robert W. Chamberlin was another lawyer and another former football hero (though in his case only a high school star, not college). More important: Chamberlin, who met Eliot and Edna when he rented his Bay Village guest cottage to the couple, was a close friend. Eliot felt confident he wouldn't have to worry about his new assistant's loyalties.

The successes in court, stretched out over
eighteen months, were impressive. Juries
convicted Cadek, Harwood, Burns, Nebe,
and Sergeant James Price. Lieutenant
Thomas J. Brady pleaded guilty. The string of
trials raised Eliot's profile, already high, into
the stratosphere. Unlike Flynn, average
Clevelanders didn't consider the safety
department's myriad investigations of the
police worthless. In Eliot they saw a white
knight galloping forth to save them from an
entrenched corruption that had paralyzed the
city for years. The safety director's name
dominated headlines week after week. Reporters surrounded him when he went to lunch
every day, asking question after question as
he tried to quickly eat a sandwich at his
favorite diner.

The newsmen weren't the only ones who
trailed around after the safety director. The
same faces could be found outside court during every police-officer trial, desperate to
catch a glimpse of the most popular man in
Cleveland. The fans gathered three and four
deep beside the front steps, as if waiting for a
parade. A small, bald man, as blissful and
anxious in his excitement as a penned-up col-
lie, hopped in place whenever Eliot stepped
out of the courthouse. A tall, middle-aged
woman waved cheerfully at Eliot, her arms

high above her head, only to fall back into the jostling crowd whenever he looked her way. Mayor Burton, just like everyone else, recognized how popular his safety director was. When he began to gear up for his reelection campaign early in 1937, he made a note to himself in the margin of a memo: "Need Ness."[*] Eliot, though he had never been involved in any political campaign before, would accede to the mayor's requests and go out on the stump for him, always attracting huge crowds. Calling Burton "my boss" and "a great man," he urged Clevelanders to vote for him. The mayor breezed to reelection.

With Burton safely ensconced in office, and the corruption convictions piling up, more than twenty senior police officers hurried into retirement before the graft investigation could turn their way. Many others decided to keep their heads down. They stopped taking gangsters' money, stopped collecting protection dues from shop owners and other small businessmen. "By now the entire department knew that the kid, Ness, was for real, and plenty tough," recalled Porter, the *Plain Dealer* columnist. Even the Ohio Supreme Court, after rejecting Harwood's appeal, credited the professionalism of the man the

[*] Cleveland held mayoral elections every two years until 1981, when the term was extended to four years.

newspapers were calling Cleveland's "Boy Wonder."

"Other [police corruption] cases are on their way up and there will be others to come," said Chief Justice Carl V. Weygandt, responding to a question about the safety director after giving a speech at a businessmen's association luncheon. "I want to comment on the ones we have decided. May I tell you that the members of the Supreme Court have commented repeatedly on the outstanding completeness and care with which this group of cases was prepared. It would greatly relieve the reviewing courts if they were to get more cases prepared with the same care and thoroughness as the group to which I am alluding."

A few weeks after that statement, another Cleveland policeman went to trial, with Eliot, as always, observing the proceedings every day. Following a week of testimony and arguments, a jury found thirty-nine-year-old patrolman Gaylord Stotts not guilty of strong-arming $240 in bribes from a bootlegger in 1927, the first acquittal in the corruption push. When the judge read the verdict, an eerie quiet fell over the courtroom. Stotts, confused, leaned over to his attorney. "Did he say not guilty?"

CHAPTER 22
SOCIAL WORKERS

With the corruption prosecutions heading down the home stretch, Eliot began to change the debate. The city should support its police force, he argued. Police officers deserved respect — and better pay and equipment.

"Please remember," he told a group of businessmen at the Hotel Cleveland, "that, although some of the dirt has been coming to the surface here lately, there are 1,500 members of the police department, with only a few splotched by the dirt." He added that funding for the police force was "completely inadequate," that Cleveland had the "smallest force, proportionately, of any of the ten largest cities in the country, with the safety problems here more complex than in most of those cities." Because of pay delays, many officers had been forced to move in with relatives, to "stave off grocers and resort to other distasteful means in keeping body and soul together."

Eliot made a compelling case, but it didn't

work. The city was still broke. When the safety director went before the city council to lobby for an additional tax to raise $240,000 a year for the police and fire departments, he received a cold reception. The departments would remain underfunded, and they would continue to have too few officers and fire-fighters.

The situation frustrated him, but, once the gloom lifted, Eliot realized it also gave him a license to experiment. The only way to solve the funding problem for the police was to dramatically reorganize the department and rethink its methods. Staring him in the face was the opportunity that August Vollmer had been dreaming about for decades. Eliot had to create an entirely new, entirely modern police force: he had no other choice. He would change what it meant to be a big-city policeman.

From Cleveland's founding, policing had been built around the patrolman walking a beat. That no longer could be the case. The department didn't have enough bodies any-more to use foot power to cover a sprawling city with nearly a million people in it. Cleve-land had boomed for decades before the Depression began to reverse its fortunes. The police force's ranks had never kept up with population and geographic growth. To ad-dress the manpower problem, Eliot aban-doned the precinct system and reorganized the department into districts. He closed seven police stations. Officers increasingly would spend their shifts in cars. (Eliot would rent a fleet of new cars because the city didn't have the money for capital investments.) Each patrol car would be equipped with a novelty: a two-way radio, hooked up to a centralized radio bureau — what Eliot insisted would become "the very nerve center of the Police Department." No longer would beat cops have to hustle to the nearest Murphy call box, sometimes blocks from a crime scene. Thirty-two new cars, Eliot announced, would "constitute the basic patrol, and they patrol 24 hours a day in three 8-hour shifts," each guided by the radio bureau. The cars were painted bright colors to make them more visible. Some officers thought the tricolor scheme made the cars look ridiculous, but it worked. They were so distinctive that people noticed and remembered them, giving the impression that the cars were everywhere, all the time. Eliot also started a motorcycle unit and a mounted unit, both of which were partially funded through private sources. Indeed, he pursued every possible innovation that might save on personnel and overall costs: specially designated pursuit cars, high-powered binoculars to spot "thieves preying on parked autos," Teletype updates sent regularly between station houses, motion-picture cameras "triggered automatically to catch bank robbers." Eliot also directed David Cowles, the head of the scientific bureau, to buy the latest equipment for his lab and to ramp up ballistics work.

One of the most ambitious innovations — and the only one that was actually manpower-intensive — was Eliot's crime-prevention campaign, which focused on young gang members. He didn't care that most of his senior officers thought the idea foolish. Policemen tended to mock the new-wave academics who defined crime as a disease caused by an unhealthy environment, but Eliot took the social scientists seriously. He thought policemen should be intimately involved in their community — "the policeman as social worker," as August Vollmer put it. More than that, Eliot believed in redemption. People and lives could change, especially if they were young. He empathized with troubled kids from poor and broken homes. He wanted to save them. As an experiment, he sent plainclothed officers, mostly new recruits, into the Tremont neighborhood south of downtown. Tremont was one of the worst pits in Cleveland: brutally ugly and rundown, with a juvenile delinquency rate three times higher than the rest of the city. In short order, the officers identified forty-five youth gangs in the area.

One of the most fearsome gangs set up its headquarters in an alley. "The leader is 24 years old, 5 ft. 5 in. tall, weighs 150 lbs., has blue eyes and chestnut hair and the upper part of his face is scarred from a knife wound," a report to the safety director stated. "The gang's principal infractions of law include car stealing, box car breaking, shop lifting, house and store breaking, at one time dope peddling, and a tendency to interfere with and to prostitute women and young girls."

Another of the gangs called itself the Jefferson Club or Moxie's Gang. "They meet in a pool room," a Tremont undercover officer reported. "They work in unison. They go out ten or fifteen in a group, expecting to eliminate opposition by force of their numbers. Their deeds are performed with precision. They are smart and when property is obtained it is quickly disposed of. Nothing is left on their hands for the Police to identify. . . . The leader is 6 feet 2 inches tall, has dark hair, dark eyes, says little and is very handy with a knife. Practically all members carry black jacks."

For years, the police had more or less left these youth gangs alone, pursuing individuals for specific crimes but rarely focusing on the gangs themselves. (The Mob mostly left them alone, too, deciding they were too volatile to co-opt or use for recruiting purposes.) Eliot decided he would break this pattern, but not in the way anyone expected. He toured Tremont, dodging debris thrown from upper-floor windows and shouldering through the rotted doors of buildings that were abandoned or should have been. He cornered gang members and invited them to a local church for a meeting and a free dinner. On the designated night, dozens of boys showed up. It didn't go well: the leaders of two rival gangs fell into an argument, and one pulled out a gun and shot the other in the hip right in front of the safety director.

Eliot didn't give up. He held more meetings with the gangs, where he told war stories straight from police files, getting the kids laughing and nodding. In his talks, he gave special attention to the story of Joe Filkowski, a legend among the Tremont crews. A tough kid from the Flats, Filkowski's criminal career spanned fifteen years, until he was convicted in 1932 of murdering a man during a payroll robbery on the West Side. Eliot, the scientific policeman, brought out a ledger. He showed the young gangsters that, taking into account the amount of money Filkowski was known to have stolen (and then doubling it) and the amount of time he'd spent in prison, he had "earned" seventeen cents an hour for his criminal career.

The presentation worked. Eliot was constitutionally shy, but somehow he could project a swaggering confidence — and irresistible charm — when he needed to. This was especially the case with kids. "He had an instinct about children and an understanding of their needs," Elisabeth Seaver would attest years later. He didn't see himself in these hardened, rebellious boys: he'd never been poor and desperate. What he saw was lost potential, paths never to be taken. They broke his heart.

During his time as Berkeley's police chief, Vollmer had kept a city map on his office wall on which he stuck a pin for each juvenile delinquent in the small town. The pin would be removed when the "problem child" was placed in an institution or graduated from school. Eliot now did the same for the gangs of Tremont. He knew his map would be much harder to clear than his mentor's, so he started by offering the gangs a "deal." He wanted to establish boys' clubs and Boy Scout troops for the younger gang members and other boys in the neighborhood. If the older boys got behind the effort — meaning they didn't harass kids for joining the Scouts or for going to the clubs — he'd help them find jobs and promised that the city would build baseball diamonds and basketball courts in the area. When Chief Matowitz heard about this offer, he let out a string of expletives. He thought it was crazy to go into business with gang members.

Tremont's youth gangs weren't Eliot's only passion project. Along with its high crime rate, Cleveland was the second deadliest city in the country for motorists. Automobile accidents were a mundane, unsexy urban problem, but a serious one, and Eliot took it up with enthusiasm. He established an accident-prevention bureau and put in charge a veteran, respected officer, Edward Donohue. The bureau immediately launched an ambitious program: "The Three E's of Safety — Enforcement, Engineering and Education." As with everything he undertook, Eliot committed himself completely to the task. He hired a traffic engineer from the Northwestern University Traffic Safety Institute and went with him to the city's most dangerous traffic spots to take notes. As a result, curbs were rounded, safety islands built, traffic signals installed. The bureau equipped "manslaughter squads" with cameras and other gear, such as instruments to measure skid marks at crash scenes. Conviction rates in traffic-accident cases quickly doubled, reaching 96 percent. The bureau launched a public-relations campaign to educate Clevelanders on safe driving, an effort that went above and beyond that of any other city. Donohue started special programs in schools and civic clubs. He and Eliot urged churches to give safety sermons. And everywhere on the roads drivers saw signs: "Cleveland Values Your Life — Protect It" and "100 Are Alive Today." Eliot probably went a bit far when he ordered patrols to randomly stop cars to test their brakes and lights, but few drivers protested.

The animating force behind all of this activity — the safety campaign, the youth-gang outreach, the binoculars and two-way radios — was one clear idea: that law enforcement should be put on a "scientific" footing in Cleveland, not just in the lab but in every aspect of the police department's work. "At the end of the month or at a designated time, statistical records of crime, indicating the volume, the nature, the location, the time of happening, and the particular kind of crime, will be analyzed by the Captain in charge of a district, the lieutenant who may be in general supervisory command of several zones, and the officers comprising the zone and adjacent zones," Eliot wrote in a typical directive. The idea was to flood trouble spots with officers and to use lonely patrol cars to cover larger, quieter areas. Reporters who covered the police were uniformly impressed with the changes in the department — and they were quick to credit the safety director. Philip Porter wrote that Eliot "looked less like a detective or private eye than anyone could imagine. He had a baby face, a soft voice, a disarming youthful ingenuousness. But he had a brilliant mind." Command officers in the department, though they mostly liked the safety director personally, tended to be a little less enthusiastic about the upheaval. "He was not too opinionated and had some good ideas for the police department, although some of them were naïve," recalled Frank Story, who would go on to become Cleveland's police chief in the 1950s.

However naïve some of the ideas were, the effects of Eliot's efforts proved striking. An internal history of the Cleveland Police Department from the 1960s described the reorganization under Eliot as "the most significant in the history of the City of Cleveland. Nothing like this had ever been done before." It added: "To Cleveland belongs the credit of being the first large city in the country to substitute a full motorized radio-controlled patrol system for the old foot-patrol method of policing. . . . Cleveland's experience has proved that the substitution of the zone car for foot patrol not only reduced enormously the cost of police protection but it reduced crime to limits not considered possible back in the 1920s."* But Eliot didn't need to wait for the judgment of history. Just eighteen months after he began instituting his changes, crime in the city fell more than anyone could have hoped for —

* Years later, the foot patrol would come back into vogue, and "community policing" would be held up as a way to make officers once again a part of the neighborhoods they served.

25 percent — while arrests and convictions rose 20 percent. And in 1938, the National Safety Council would name Cleveland the "safest big city in America," after the city cut its traffic deaths nearly in half. Requests for the safety director to give talks about his successes came in from towns and cities across the country. Eliot would turn down almost all of them. He already had too much to do.

Chapter 23
The Virtues of Courage

On a piercing June day in 1937 Evaline McAndrew boarded a train at Chicago's Illinois Central Depot. She walked with her usual dreamy sway. The floor hummed under her feet, a marvelous feeling, like she was inside something living, something that owned her. Evaline loved trains. They were portals to her fantasies. When life wasn't going well — and it was never really going all that well — she could hop aboard a train, any train, and start all over again.

Right now, Evaline especially liked the idea of starting over. She wanted to be a commercial artist, but so far the dark-haired twenty-five-year-old had mostly paid the bills in Chicago by posing for department-store ads. She had kind of a funny face for a model — heavy cheekbones topped by a wide prairie nose and a gummy smile — but that hardly mattered. "She wasn't beautiful, but she was wonderful-looking," recalled Ann Durell, a longtime friend and colleague. Durell got it exactly right. Tall and fluid, Evaline exuded an idealized Great Depression sexiness: elegant, self-reliant, satisfyingly cool to the touch.

Eliot noticed her right off. On his way to Minneapolis to lure that city's assistant traffic engineer to Cleveland, he was sitting in the club car when her long legs scissored past. The legs folded into a nearby seat, dropping her torso — and her arresting profile — into view. He liked what he saw. Everything about Evaline — her makeup, her clothes, the expression on her face — was exactly how it should be. Eliot appreciated the effort she put in. He introduced himself. She reciprocated, polite but unwelcoming, as was to be expected. Eliot did not give up.

The timing was perfect. Evaline had bought a train ticket because she needed something more from her life. It wasn't just her career prospects that frustrated her. She needed a spark. A thrill. A shock. She didn't know what. She hadn't been able to find it in big, bustling Chicago, to her surprise. She didn't think she'd find it in Canada, her destination, but a visit to another country sounded like a good substitute until something better came along.

As the train got under way, Eliot and Evaline started talking. He wasn't very good at intimacy in marriage, but with perfect strangers he excelled at it. He loved to drink in the contours of an interesting new face — and Evaline's offered an intriguing mix of abrupt angles and soft curves. He loved discovering an active mind — and Evaline's was so active she seemed on the verge of levitating. At the same time, this brash young woman found Eliot funny and suave, with crinkly, forlorn eyes that were somehow comforting rather than mournful. Mile after clacking mile the two good-looking infatuates leaned into each other, shoulder to shoulder, whispering and smiling. Evaline, smothered for months by an indefinable unhappiness, felt the angst lift and float away.

"Eliot and I talked a lot . . . looked at each other at the same time a lot . . . laughed a lot and kissed a lot when I got off the train," she remembered.

That last part — the kissing — was cause for shame. Eliot Ness was married. And so was Evaline Michelow McAndrew.

Edna wouldn't have been surprised to learn about her husband's tête-à-tête on the train. She had long suspected he was fooling around. Beginning more than a year before with Eliot's famous one hundred straight nights tracking down leads for the police-corruption investigation, the marriage had all but ceased to exist. He loved his work, and only his work. That was clear to Edna now. The job communicated something to Eliot that his wife simply couldn't. Something about beauty in the world, how we created it but most often ignored it or turned it inside out. It was his responsibility to keep the world from getting too ugly. How could marriage — how could one woman — compete with that? Eliot's dedication to his work was so complete that, early in his tenure as safety director, the *Cleveland Press* assumed he was single, mistakenly calling him the most eligible bachelor in the city. The newspaper's error was at worst a technicality. Eliot worked long, hard hours every day, but he always had time for a smile and a compliment for the prettiest secretaries at city hall. By the time he returned home each night after another sixteen hours of intense work and flirting, he had wound down like a pull toy. On good nights, he would stretch out on the floor and read Arthur Conan Doyle or Shakespeare while listening to opera. More often, he poured himself a drink, or many drinks, settled into a chair, and zoned out. He always looked so lonesome sitting there, with his hair slightly mussed and his tie undone, but no matter how much Edna cajoled, she couldn't get him to open up to her. She was heartbroken by her inability to connect with him anymore, her inability to be a true partner. She'd been heartbroken for years.

On top of the daily frustrations and disappointments of her married life, there was still personal danger for Edna to deal with, too, all these years after Capone. The investigations into police corruption had kicked up threats against the troublesome safety director. Someone even took a shot at Eliot with a rifle as he drove home one night. Just as he did in Chicago, Eliot refused to admit that the threats and close calls bothered him, but Edna could no longer match his stoicism. She worried for her husband's safety, and for her own as well, stuck all alone every day in their little rented apartment. When Matowitz assigned Eliot a bodyguard for a time, Edna told a friend she didn't know if she could take it much longer.

Eliot's obsessive commitment to work — and his increasing interest in seducing other women — was broken in November when his brother Charles called from Chicago. Their mother had died of a heart attack. She was seventy-three. The next morning, Eliot and Edna packed up the car and set out for Illinois. It would be the first time in a long time that the couple had spent a significant amount of time together.

The trip would remind Edna how much she missed Chicago and her own family. The long drive back to Cleveland after the funeral must have been torture for her, and not just because she was leaving her native city again after little more than a day. It was because Emma Ness was a saint. Everyone had said so at the funeral, over and over. Now Eliot wouldn't be able to think of his mother any other way. This was not a new problem. Emma had always had high expectations for her youngest son. In her eyes Eliot could do no wrong. He was the golden child. Edna, plain and socially awkward and far from golden, never could measure up. When Edna and Eliot arrived back in Cleveland, they learned that the city council had issued an official resolution of condolence for its public safety director. "WHEREAS, it is at a mother's knee that the virtues of courage, honesty and straightforwardness are inculcated," it began. The platitudes rolled on, paragraph after paragraph. Eliot was deeply moved. He pasted a copy of the resolution into his scrapbook, along with condolence letters from friends and relatives, pages of them. The letters and cards were sober proof that the woman who gave him more than anyone else, who gave him life and life lessons — the very moral code he lived by — truly was gone. The scrapbook, which he'd started keeping in college, offered no mention of his father's death five years before.

CHAPTER 24
GUN, BLACKJACK, AND
BRASS KNUCKLES

Philip Porter could feel it coming, like an ache in the bones before a nor'easter. Big news was about to pop. In his column in the *Plain Dealer,* he noted that no one had seen Eliot around city hall for a while.

> In the old days, it was nothing particularly unexpected for a director at City Hall to be absent from his office most of a day, or most of several days. Former Mayor Davis was absent most of the time after the first few months.
>
> When Eliot Ness is absent, however, it means something entirely different. He has been absent from City Hall (but not from town) for most of the last week. You can look for something almost any minute now.

Porter was right. Eliot had been safety director for more than a year, and his police-corruption trials were wrapping up. In recent weeks, he had turned his staff's attention to the citywide tire-theft ring and to the marijuana trade. He had zeroed in on the illegal distribution of "filthy" magazines. He personally took up a kidnapping case. But it was finally time to go after a much bigger goal. Eliot was ready to launch an all-out war on the underworld.

The Mayfield Road Mob, also known as the Hill gang, was Ohio's leading crime outfit. They did business however they pleased, without fear of police interference. Cleveland mobsters didn't shoot police officers, but unlike the Capone gang back in Prohibition days, it wasn't because the boss forbade the practice. It was simply so much easier to pay them off. Some of the cops, the dumbest saps, would look the other way for a dollar a week. But now the gangsters were increasingly coming into contact with young, idealistic police officers who had bought into the Cult of Ness. You couldn't grease these guys. You couldn't bully them. And now even the old-guard officers were willing to make arrests, if only to keep up appearances.

The city's mobsters couldn't decide on the best course of action, which led to an unusual temporary paralysis. Herman Pirchner, who would go on to become one of Cleveland's best-known restaurateurs, had just opened a place in the city center. A couple of years before, he'd walked away from his first eatery when the Mob demanded a stake in the business. "We had never heard of the Mafia before then, but we did not want to get involved with guns, so we gave it up," he would say some forty years later. But with the promised protection of Eliot Ness — "the legendary safety director," the restaurateur liked to call him — he decided he would fight for his new establishment. When the gang's muscle came calling, he told them he wasn't paying, and he dropped Eliot's name. He refused to back down even when the toughs warned him of the possible consequences. He braced himself in the days ahead for a bombing or a fire or a rap on the head as he closed up at night, but nothing happened. This time, it was the gangsters who walked away. "The Mafia decided to leave us alone," Pirchner said. "From that time until now, they never bothered me again."

What was a self-respecting gang to do? George Mulvanity, still over at the ATU and working undercover, warned Eliot that discussions about knocking him off were flitting around the gang's outer edges. The mobsters had watched closely as the safety director brought down senior police officers, men they relied on. They knew they had to act, to assert themselves.

Eliot was fully aware of the kind of fight he was wading into. The gangster Angelo Lonardo, looking back on more than five decades in crime, would tell a U.S. Senate subcommittee in 1988 that when he was coming up, "you would have to have killed someone and stood up to the pressure of police scrutiny" to become a member of Cleveland's La Cosa Nostra. Even Chicago's Outfit didn't have such stringent membership requirements. And while the membership rolls remained secret, the members' viciousness didn't, which meant Cleveland's gangsters could impose themselves on almost any business in the area.

For starters, everyone was paying protection money — or "union dues," as it was often called. The Mob set the retail price of whatever the product was, with their cut factored in, and if anyone — even one little cigarette hawker — tried to sell at a discount, he'd be fined a hefty amount. If that didn't bring the renegade into line, Mr. Muscles would show up. The Mob — and the dirty cops who made the racket possible — extorted money from bars, restaurants, butchers, dry cleaners, massage girls, window washers, fruit sellers, deliverymen, even real estate agents. The protection racket, inevitably, led to other crimes, including robbery (often of the businesses the robbers were "protecting") and murder (hey, things happen). And the cops who had been bought off for one crime now found themselves being forced to help out with other, more serious ones.

The protection game provided steady, reliable income to the Cleveland Mob, and they were loath to let even a single business owner — like Pirchner — get out from under it. That stuff traveled. But it was a secondary stream of income for the gang, a baseline. By the mid-1930s, with Prohibition gone, the most profitable racket of them all — the one to protect above all others — was a highly efficient gambling operation called "policy and clearing house." The most basic policy game involved individuals placing bets on numbered balls in a bag. You could bet a penny or your entire paycheck, with odds up to 400 to 1 on nailing all three numbers, in order, being pulled from the bag. With clearing house, players bet on published figures, such as the last three digits of the clearing-house balance released by the Cleveland banks or the last three digits of the day's total closing number for the New York Stock Exchange. Runners would dash around the city to bars and shops and diners, informing players when and where the results would be announced.

Policy and clearing house had started out as a small-time diversion in the city's black neighborhoods. By the 1920s, however, it had become a big business, if largely under the radar. The major operators — Rufus "The Emperor" Jones, J. B. "Hot Stuff" Johnson, and Willie Richardson — brought some flash to a rather straightforward racket, sporting tilted derbies and fat cigars and tooling around town in brightly colored sedans. Stolid, butcher-shop owner Frank Hoge was the only white member of what became known as the "Big Four," and he kept a low profile. These policy and clearing-house kings operated a respected racket, known for paying out promptly and without retribution on the rare occasion of a big score. During Prohibition, policy and clearing house mostly wasn't worth the Mob's time — nothing could compare to the profits bootlegging brought in. But once the repeal movement began to pick up momentum, lottery games suddenly looked like a very appealing business.

On March 4, 1933, four men paid a visit to Clarence Murphy, who operated a game in the heart of the black section of town. They informed the policy operator that they expected him to start kicking up 50 percent of his take to them. Murphy refused. Two days later, as Murphy was leaving his home in the morning, three men with shotguns appeared. They started firing before Murphy could say anything. He fell backward, cracking his head on the pavement. The men kept firing until the body began to break apart and smoke had wafted halfway down the block.

The rout was on.

Soon, Rufus Jones was packed away to prison for income-tax evasion, where he promptly died, with conspiracy theories abounding. J. B. Johnson took a bullet, and after recovering he signed on with the Mob. Longtime operator Benny Mason tried to retire from the business, but the gang wouldn't let him — he was too popular with his game's players. Willie Richardson and Frank Hoge also stayed on after the muscle men moved in, with Hoge becoming one of the gang's key men in the racket. None of this was a secret. The Mayfield Road Gang "conquered with gun, blackjack and brass knuckles and today are blackmailing a 40 percent cut from a racket that yields riches of $5,000,000 to $10,000,000 a year," the *Press* reported.

The Mob didn't just take over the big games. Jacob Collins, a thirty-one-year-old East Side man who ran an independent policy game that barely paid the rent, was yanked into an alley one day and told to report to "Little Angelo" Scerria at Hoge's butcher shop on Central Avenue. This was not a directive anyone wanted to receive. "Big Angelo" Lonardo and "Little Angelo" Scerria ran the gang's policy and clearing-house operations. The *Press* labeled them the "co-king of the 'numbers' racket." The one-eyed Scerria, who'd beaten two murder raps, served as the enforcer. He had "the dread reputation of always carrying out a threat."

When Collins arrived at the butcher shop,

he found Scerria waiting for him. Little Angelo didn't like to be kept waiting. He flapped his one good eye at the small-time policyman.

"Who gave you permission to book?" he said. "Don't you know you have to get a commission?"

Collins, his hands shaking, apologized profusely and backed out of the butcher shop. "I then got out of the racket," he later testified.

Other operators fell into line or, like Collins, abandoned the business. The gang "set up a franchise system," collecting varying percentages off the top each week — usually in the 40 percent to 60 percent range — regardless of the operator's profit or loss. As Clayton Fritchey put it: "There were no Sherman or Clayton anti-trust laws for these mobsters to worry about."

With the Mayfield Road Gang now firmly in charge, the games lost some of their ring-a-ding-ding fun, but profits soared. The reason: cheating. For years, policy and clearing house were believed to be reasonably fair games of chance, though an individual gambler's odds were never good. But now, the games were fixed. This could be done in various ways. For the policy game, they would heat the balls bearing the numbers most heavily played, so that the guy rifling through the bag would grab and draw out only balls cool to the touch. The *Plain Dealer,* tipped off by Eliot, pointed out a less subtle tactic for clearing-house games: "When the house is hit hard, a police raid before the bets are paid also comes in handy."

Angelo Lonardo's father, Joe Lonardo, had been Cleveland's dominant crime boss in the 1920s. Unlike Capone in Chicago, he kept a low profile, fostering a mystique in the city's underworld as all-knowing and all-powerful. But during the later years of Prohibition, an offshoot led by Joe and Vincenzo Porello made a bold play for regional control of the production of corn syrup, often a key ingredient in moonshine. "Killings were followed by retaliatory killings, gangsters were gunned down by machinegun fire from fast-moving limousines, or shot to death in barber shops and restaurants," remembered Neil McGill. Joe Lonardo was murdered in 1927. The Porello brothers fell three years later.

The ultimate survivor of this war was a third faction, the Mayfield Road Gang, led by Frank Milano. Soon this operation had absorbed much of the remaining Lonardo and Porello gangs, including young Angelo Lonardo. In 1928, the nineteen-year-old Angelo, known as "Baby Face," made his bones by taking revenge on the Porello associate responsible for his father's death. The "thick-necked, thick-fingered, and pasty-faced" young hood almost went away for the murder, but witnesses and evidence disappeared. This double whammy — the murder and the efficient avoidance of judicial consequences — led to Angelo being put up for membership, an arcane affair complete with burning candles and incantations. In the 1930s, initiations usually took place at the Statler Hotel in downtown Cleveland. The gangsters would roll through the lobby doors in tailored black suits, their pants bulging from guns and the excitement of it all. They'd swagger past the ballrooms where Cleveland's frivolous swinging set spent their evenings drinking and dancing. The black-suited men would disappear into rooms specially set aside for them, their bulkiest guards at the door.

The men conducting the initiation — usually an underboss and a "captain" — always carefully explained the rules of membership to the initiates. You weren't allowed to take drugs or run prostitutes. You couldn't sleep with the wife of another "made" man. And "whatever illegal activity you engage in, you have to report to the boss and receive permission to engage in that activity." These were the official rules, the rules you had to promise to live by or else, but of course it was understood that they could be bent or broken. The whole organization, after all, was built on contempt for rules and laws. You just had to be smart about the way you did it.

"Once you accept the rules of membership, they lift a cloth off a table; underneath is a gun and a dagger," Lonardo explained. "You are told that you now live and die with the dagger and the gun. You die that way, and you live that way. You are then given a card with a picture of a saint on it. This card is placed in the palms of your hands and lit. You shake the burning card back and forth until it is burned down to ashes. They then pinch your finger to draw blood, and then everyone gives you a kiss on the cheek and says, 'You are now a member.' "

There was a purpose to this ritual. Loyalty and discipline mattered. Angelo's father and his successors were killers, but they weren't mindless killers. They considered themselves businessmen — smart businessmen. By the early 1930s, in fact, the city's Mob bosses had frozen membership because, in the wake of convictions in Chicago and New York fueled by gangsters ratting out other gangsters, they saw that bad things happened when you "were not making the 'right' kind of people."

Eliot declared his intention to bust the Mob in a speech at the same downtown hotel where the gangsters liked to congregate. Success or failure, he told a businessmen's group at the Statler, would turn on his ability to attack one key racket: that old bugaboo, gambling.

"It is debatable whether gambling is morally wrong," he said. "But from the policing standpoint you have an entirely different picture. I am inclined to be liberal in my views of amusements and I do not want to intrude my opinions on others, but as a safety director I must recognize everything which contributes to a lawless situation. By that, I mean major crime. Gambling brings into financial power citizens recognized as law violators."

Eliot would make this case time and again throughout 1937. As he prepared to directly tackle the Mob, he knew he would need the public's support. That meant getting even people who liked to gamble to back a gambling crackdown.

"Two hundred thousand dollars a week is poured into the coffers of racket bosses in Cleveland as their 'cut' from gambling alone," he told the Advertising Club in another speech on the subject. He informed the ad executives that the policy and clearing-house racket had "grown one hundred percent since relief payments began," that gangsters sucked money out of the economy by taking "from the poor boys, from persons on relief," and that the government saw none of that money in tax revenue. He made a point of differentiating between a card game among friends and Mob-controlled gambling. "The mild, unorganized and personal forms of gambling," he said, were generally harmless, but "when organized crime outfits run gambling, it's anything but harmless. Organized gambling activity is always controlled by racketeers and supplies them with heavy revenue with which to carry on their sinister, anti-social operations."

The Mob used the cash it pulled down from gambling to muscle into legitimate enterprises, he pointed out. It laundered money by strong-arming businesses into putting hoodlums and prostitutes on the payroll. It took over unions, collecting dues from members and controlling prices for services and products. The corruption moved like a diseased fish from the gutting line to the finest restaurant, reaching all the way to the city's highest public officials. Eliot had seen in Chicago what happened when the Mob took effective control of a city's government and economy. Whatever your personal views of gambling, he told the city's business leaders and opinion makers, you had to put them aside in the effort to stop the gangs.

Eliot planned to conduct a methodical investigation, as always, but not against one gangster at a time, as he had with corrupt police officers. He wanted to bring a massive single indictment against every leader in the sprawling organization, to sever the Mob's head with one great swing of the ax. And he was determined to do this despite the inconvenient fact that Ohio did not have a conspiracy statute like the federal law the FBI used for such cases.

Eliot knew he would have to infiltrate the Mob to really get anywhere, but he also understood that insinuating one of his own men into the gang would be dangerous and time-consuming. So instead, he sought out double agents — gangsters he had something on and could manipulate. His decision to rely on these criminals led to spirited debate between his team and the county prosecutors. "He got information from informers," one former assistant prosecutor said years later. "He was a great believer in them. But you can get a paid spy to tell you anything." An investigator on Eliot's team would insist: "Those informers were very important. They risked their lives to do the right thing."

One of those paid spies was a former numbers runner named Oscar Williams. To get Williams to talk, Eliot promised to hide him out of town for as long as necessary, and to pay him $35 a week for living expenses. Justice didn't come cheap in Cleveland. In one interview session, Williams told Eliot about a time three thugs — Lonardo, Alex "Shondor" Birns, and Joe Artwell — kicked their way into a backroom game, wielding

383

revolvers and sawed-off shotguns. They thumped Williams's partner in the face and, as he lay bleeding on the floor, threatened to kill him on the spot. "I ought to smash your head," Birns snarled when Williams tried to talk his way out of the situation. The smiling, slightly delirious look on Birns's face would stick with Williams for the rest of his life.

Shondor Birns, Eliot was discovering, was unique in Cleveland. Like the most popular kid in school, Birns seemed to have immunity from the group loyalty expected of everyone else. He somehow managed to successfully cross between various rival factions in the city's underworld. Everyone wanted the guy around.

He was even popular with the average Clevelander. Birns cultivated a pleasant, roguish public image and often gave interviews to reporters. The press labeled him "Cleveland's Public Nuisance No. 1" and "Cleveland's number one racketeer," but most people tossed around the appellations with a smile. Birns's own smile frequently lit up his bland, Slavic face. He was a "dapper extrovert" known for wearing a beautiful woman on each arm and firing off a hyena-like cackle at popular nightclubs. Though only in his midthirties, he was hailed as the most arrested man in Cleveland. Over the years he'd been pinched for robbery, assault, bribery, and attempted murder, among other crimes, but there hadn't been a conviction since he was a teenager. One anti-Burton politician cracked that he was "untouchable."

Eliot decided to harass Birns at every opportunity. When he found out that Cleveland's most arrested man spent winters in Florida, he contrived to get him booted from the Sunshine State for failing to register as a felon. As soon as Birns arrived back in Cleveland, police came calling. "Boy, I hardly had a chance to take my clothes out of the car before they picked me up," he said at Central Police Station. Reporters, notified by the safety director, were waiting for him as he came out of the building.

"Where's the sun tan," one hack asked him.

"Sun tan?" Birns said. "You can't get any sun tan when you have to run around behind palm trees all day to keep the police away from you."

"Say, we'll quote you like that," another reporter said. "That's the nuts."

"Yeah, the coconuts," Birns joked.

The gangster knew the Cleveland authorities had tipped off police in Miami, and he wasn't happy about it.

"Why can't they leave a guy alone?" he said. "I can't go anywhere without being picked up. They don't give you any break. Oh, well, it was getting cold in Florida, anyway."

Eliot surely enjoyed seeing Birns's whiny complaints in the papers the next day. It wasn't as good as a conviction, but it would do for now.

In the second half of 1937, Eliot began to increase the frequency of police raids on gambling halls and bookie joints. Poker, off-track betting, bingo, policy, slot machines: raiders found every variety of gambling in back rooms and basements across Cleveland. Gambling appeared to be the city's favorite pastime.

The new year brought a breakthrough. On January 6, 1938, police took over the central office of five big policy and clearing-house games in a building on Euclid Avenue. The hero of the day was Lieutenant Ernest Molnar, one of the department's rising stars. He stormed the room with two young officers, but he didn't just arrest the men inside and confiscate the "top sheets" and accounting books. He sat down at the phone bank and, for more than an hour, answered calls, leaving the Cleveland Mob in the dark about its own rackets.

It was a smart move, costing gangsters many thousands of dollars more than if Molnar had simply shut the room down. Information, after all, was power. Even with telephones and telegrams, the straight dope remained hard to come by; communication could be slow and unreliable, and facts difficult to verify. This made the criminal network that linked outfits in various cities extremely valuable. The interval between, say, the end of a horse race in New York and the public dissemination of results in Cleveland offered myriad possibilities for making money. One key call that Molnar took came in from Pittsburgh, with the caller asking for Frank Hoge.

"I told the man in Pittsburgh that I would take the number, and he said, 'The stock number today is 098 and the exchange number is 152,' " Molnar told reporters. Today, the lieutenant boasted, gangsters who took advantage of information would lose big.

The everyday gambler, of course, also lost. Those who had already put down bets weren't getting their money back just because the results went missing. Eliot could make something of this, too, in the public-relations war against the gambling syndicate. Few of the city's thousands of gamblers had much cash to spare for bets. Jobs remained difficult to find, and government relief had dried up. The state of Ohio, like the city of Cleveland, was effectively broke. The legislature in Columbus bickered over what to do about it, while in Cleveland some sixty-five thousand families on relief listened to their stomachs gurgle and grind. On the same day that Lieutenant Molnar made his big bust, Bishop Joseph Schrembs of the Cleveland Catholic diocese sent thumping telegrams to Governor

Martin L. Davey and the state Senate committee on taxes and relief. "Cleveland situation very critical," it read. "Rural districts may smugly smile but day of retribution sure to come. French royalists at Versailles said to have laughed at the Paris population, saying, 'Feed them cake.' Paid with their heads for their ribaldry. Remember, empty stomachs and frozen bodies and evicted families do not reason. I beg of you stop bandying words and vote sufficient relief."

In the days that followed, the legislature managed to pass a makeshift relief bill that put the burden on local governments and a hoped-for sale of bonds, and the Cleveland City Council pledged the city's payroll as security for food orders. When Clevelanders received their belated relief checks, however, not everyone rushed to the grocer. Queues also formed for neighborhood policy and clearing-house games. Gamblers refused to be shamed into giving up their hobby. They needed the distraction from their lives. A few even went public with their dismay at the safety director's crackdown, including one anonymous reader of the *Cleveland Press*.

To the Editor of the *Press*:
   I play the horses. Sucker? You play the stock market. Sucker? Well, maybe and maybe not.
   The stock market is in the same cat-

388

egory with horse racing investments. They're both gambling to some people. I envy the market investor. He doesn't have to mingle with a bunch of rats and slink around like a rat himself. I'm tired of it. And so are the other two out of every five adults in this city. We are all tired of the stigma under which we must play the ponies.

And I don't have to tell you that Mr. Ness is badly mistaken if he thinks for one minute that he or anyone else can stop booking in this or any other city. Where one is stopped two start.

The state and city governments are passing up a sweet revenue. I don't think I'll ever see the day when they license bookmakers, but if they do then, and then only, will bookmaking racketeers be wiped out. Why? Because now if you make a sizable bet you're never sure the bookmaker will be around when time comes to collect. Licensed bookies couldn't do that because of the large bond they would be required to post. The horse players assured of honest dealing would go to the licensed bookie (of which there would be a limited number) and illegal booking will die of its own accord. The state and city would have another source of revenue and everybody will be happy. So help me.

Pony Boy

Eliot liked this letter. He had long believed that gambling should be legalized — as long as it was tightly regulated, like the stock market now was. He snipped Pony Boy's letter out of the paper and saved it.

CHAPTER 25
AGAINST RACKETEERS

At the same time that Eliot's drive against the Mob was picking up steam, he also took on another challenge: union racketeering. He decided to target two of the most powerful men in the city: Donald A. Campbell, president of the Painters District Council, and Campbell's partner John E. McGee, president of the Laborers District Council.

His interest in labor corruption wasn't new. Back in September 1936, Eliot submitted an eighty-one-page report to the county prosecutor on a "shakedown racket" at the Northern Ohio Food Terminal, where "a gang in the guise of a labor union" extracted bribes to unload trucks. Those who refused to pay — or dared to unload their own trucks — faced severe beatings. Eliot soon learned that the labor shenanigans went far beyond the Food Terminal. Many of the city's labor leaders, including Campbell and McGee, had gained their positions "through sluggings, shootings and intimidation," and they ran rackets that

391

rivaled any that the Mayfield Road Mob controlled.

Eliot had met Campbell shortly after becoming safety director, running into him by chance on a downtown street. At the time, he was investigating the attempted murder of the labor leader Frank Converse. New in the job and fishing around for potential allies, he asked Campbell if he knew who did it. The thirty-eight-year-old painters' union boss reacted as if he'd been slapped. He told Eliot that he should know the answer to his own question and walked away from him. Eliot, his antenna raised, returned to the office and opened a file on Campbell.

"Being union officials gives Campbell and McDonnell a nice 'in,' " Eliot told Neil McGill after beginning an investigation of Campbell and painters-union business agent James McDonnell. "They can put 'stop work' orders on the builders, or make things otherwise pretty damn nasty for them. Their approach is always the same — pay . . . or else!" He believed Campbell, McDonnell, and McGee had extorted millions of dollars from businessmen and kept hundreds of their union members from working during the very worst of the economic depression.

McGill didn't need to be told about Campbell and McGee. Cleveland was a union town. That meant nothing got built, torn down, repaired, moved, installed, painted, or unloaded without organized labor having its say about it. The county prosecutor's office had targeted Campbell and McGee back in 1933 and '34, when Campbell was head of the glaziers' union and the city was enduring an endless wave of window smashings. Cullitan talked Chief Matowitz into putting six officers, working in two-man shifts twenty-four hours a day, on the union leaders. Campbell and McGee mocked the move. One morning, the swaggering labor bosses hired a five-piece orchestra and put them in an open touring sedan. Like the musicians, the union men dressed in formal wear, including top hats and silk gloves. They climbed into a second open sedan. Off the two cars went, with the sure knowledge that the policemen on their tail would follow dutifully along. The orchestra played "Me and My Shadow," over and over, as the three cars — Campbell and McGee's, the musicians', and the policemen's — slowly lapped downtown Cleveland, with a guffawing Campbell and McGee waving and tossing candy to people who stopped to watch. The police soon ended the round-the-clock surveillance. Cullitan never brought charges.

But that was then. Eliot would not be so easily scared off. As with the police-corruption investigation, he went after the victims. Over several months, the safety director and investigators Keith Wilson, Tom

Clothey, and Dick Jones followed the trail around the country: to Toledo, Columbus, Detroit, Pittsburgh, New York, Chicago, Boston, and Saint Louis. They garnered testimony from dozens of businessmen who had left Cleveland because of the constant shakedowns. They learned that the state-of-the-art, nine-thousand-seat arena that businessman A. C. Sutphin built for his American Hockey League team, the Cleveland Barons, had been held up for ransom. "These people had us just where they wanted us," admitted Carl Lezeus, the arena's general manager. When the arena's grand opening was imminent, with only the painting and installation of seats left to do, the union workers suddenly went missing. They wouldn't show up to finish the job until Campbell received a $1,000 bribe. "A postponement would have cost us a lot of money," Lezeus told Eliot. "We did the only thing we could do — paid the $1,000."

Eliot loved this part of the job. A critic once described Arthur Conan Doyle's Sherlock Holmes, one of Eliot's heroes since childhood, as "a tracker, a hunter-down, a combination of bloodhound, pointer, and bulldog." That description fit Eliot, too. And as with the fictional Holmes, there could be no personal life, no interior life, so long as the game was afoot. Night after night Edna ate dinner alone as Eliot tracked down one more witness or followed the money through one more pair of hands. Eliot personally convinced Vernon Stouffer of the popular Stouffer's restaurant to cooperate, even though the restaurateur, worried about the impact on his business, had refused to help Cullitan four years earlier. Campbell and McGee had made Stouffer cough up $1,200 before they would allow union glaziers and painters to finish work they'd begun at Stouffer's restaurant. Campbell later came back for an extra ten bucks. Stouffer asked for a receipt for the sawbuck so he could put it on the company expense account. Campbell snarled, "Go to hell. I don't give receipts." Once Stouffer stepped forward, several other signature Cleveland retailers — the owners of the Samuel stores, Lerner stores, and the Avon Shop — followed his lead and sat down with the safety director. "When I approached them they could hardly believe that a cleanup was going on," Eliot later said.

When Cullitan convened a grand jury to sift through Eliot's evidence, the labor leaders realized they faced a serious threat this time. On December 1, 1937, McGee stood up at a packed Cleveland Federation of Labor meeting and declared that the union's members had nothing to worry about. No one could convict him of anything, because he hadn't done anything wrong, he insisted.

"The grand jury has been there three weeks and nothing has come out," he said. "And I don't think anything is going to come out."

Then McGee changed the subject, bringing up a recent steel strike in the city. Workers had violently struck Republic Steel Corporation over the summer, and Eliot, by following Mayor Burton's policy of "strict neutrality," became a union villain during the fight. It had been an ugly face-off during long, brutally hot days. Early on, Eliot had taken Burton with him to shut down an airfield the company was using to resupply "scab" workers. He expected to be hailed as a labor hero, but instead, strikers staking out the field set upon the safety director's car, rocking it and banging on it so furiously that Eliot had to wave his service revolver to get the men to back off. The union could never trust a Republican administration. After Eliot sent in policemen to stop strikers from beating replacement workers on their way into the mills, hundreds of union men marched on city hall. Standing below Eliot's office window, they chanted "Traitor! Traitor!" and unfurled a huge banner that read, "The Police and Militia Can't Beat This Strike." Eliot stepped out on his balcony to see what was going on and was met by a thunderclap of boos that grew and grew until he disappeared back into his office. Now, four months later, McGee understood that attacking the most popular man in Cleveland could work — at least with a union audience. He told of a recent meeting in which the sniveling, two-faced safety director tried to curry favor with McGee and turn him against Campbell. "McGee, I like you. I've always liked you," Eliot supposedly said. At which point the heroic labor leader cut him off. "I don't like you, and you don't like me," he sneered. "Let's cut that stuff out." Done with his reenactment, McGee threw back his head and held up a fist. He declared that Eliot Ness was trying to destroy the union for daring to have "aggressive leadership." The hall roared to its feet.

Campbell, perhaps trying to reel in the expectations his partner was building up, followed with his own speech. He said there would be indictments, because "you can't find a grand jury that would have guts enough to return a no-bill. We'll be indicted on general principles, and the prosecutor won't need any evidence in court. All he'll have to do is bring in copies of the newspapers. If we go into that jug in Columbus [the state penitentiary], we'll go in with a smile because we have put thousands to work." The hall again erupted in cheers, and the celebration carried out into the street after the meeting broke up.

Eliot had spies in the hall taking notes on what was said. He realized that attacking

Campbell and McGee personally would only build up their credibility among union men. When asked about the charge that he was against unions, he said, simply, "I am against racketeers in labor. I am against racketeers in the police department. I am against racketeers."

Campbell was right: the grand jury didn't have the guts to return a no-bill. He and McGee were indicted later in December. The grand jury charged them with "exacting tribute" from builders and business owners by threatening to withhold union labor. (McDonnell was also indicted but would be tried separately.)

Campbell and McGee came to trial in February 1938. The two men, staring straight ahead from the defendants' table, seemed stunned by the amount of evidence rolled out against them. Eliot's team had tracked down just about everyone the labor leaders had ever come into contact with. With Eliot sitting with the prosecutors, Cullitan and assistant prosecutor Charles McNamee showed that contractors and business owners often had to pay thousands of dollars beyond the honest cost of the work to get their projects done. As a result, the number of building permits in Cleveland had plummeted far below that of similar-size cities around the country. McNamee told the jury that before

Campbell had schemed his way into a leadership position of the glaziers' union, he'd been arrested repeatedly for picking pockets and stealing cars. McGee, for his part, had been arrested more than twenty times.

Vernon Stouffer dominated the trial's second day. The respected restaurateur, with his low, resonant voice, told of the defendants shaking him down for hundreds of dollars and then coming back time and again for more. Jurors watched the witness with rapt attention as he laid out how Campbell and McGee held his business hostage. McGee's attorney, William Corrigan, realized his client was in deep trouble. After Stouffer stepped down, Corrigan rose, straightened his suit jacket, and dramatically asked for a mistrial. Eliot Ness, he declared, was putting his client in a "precarious position." Judge Alva R. Corlett sent the jury out of the room. The safety director's celebrity, Corrigan continued, made his presence at the prosecutors' table prejudicial. "This is not an ordinary trial," Corrigan said. "This —"

Corlett cut him off. "These defendants are getting the same kind of trial, as far as this court is concerned, as any humble defendant," he said. "It is just an ordinary trial to the court."

"But for the city it is not," Corrigan insisted. "Here's the safety director sitting right here. Never in my thirty years' experience have I ever seen —"

"He doesn't impress the court," the judge insisted.

"But how about the jury?" Corrigan asked.

Eliot unconsciously turned to look at the empty jury box, a small smile inching across his face. Judge Corlett followed the safety director's gaze, but he quickly snapped back to Corrigan and waved for him to sit down. He would allow Ness to remain in the court-room and to sit wherever he wanted, he said. But in a sop to the defense, he told the jurors when they returned that he hoped they would be "no more impressed by Eliot Ness than by anyone else in this courtroom." The directive caused a wave of laughter to roll through the room. No more impressed by Director Ness than anyone else? The idea was ridiculous. Flustered by the response, the judge banged his gavel. He had bailiffs remove those specta-tors he deemed to be laughing the hardest.

The court proceedings dragged on, but they didn't get any better for the defendants. In March, after a twenty-four-day trial, the jury of six men and six women convicted Camp-bell and McGee of extortion. Cutting off requests for bail pending appeal, Corlett im-mediately sentenced the pair to serve one to five years. Officers hustled the union leaders, dazed by the verdict, out of the courtroom and into a car for the drive to the Ohio

Penitentiary in Columbus. Eliot saw the men to the waiting sedan, and gave the roof a satisfied tap as it pulled away from the curb. Three deputies accompanied Campbell and McGee on the ride down to the state pen. They refused the new convicts' appeals to stop for something to eat or even to relieve themselves. Arriving at the prison at 7:30, the union bosses stepped out of the car amid a flurry of popping flashbulbs, their eyes betraying the unease of men coming to terms with a terrible new reality. They spent the night in a holding cell, awaiting their prison clothes and numbers. Neither managed to sleep.

The next day in the *Cleveland News,* a reader cheekily wrote in a letter to the editor: "I was one of the spectators when McGee and Campbell made their famous auto parade through the downtown streets, and I recall that each one of them wore a brand-new plug hat. Can you tell me if either gentleman wore his plug hat on the recent trip through the streets of Columbus to the penitentiary?" The same edition of the paper brought news that the Miller United Shoe Company would remodel its fourteen Cleveland-area stores. The company, wary of having to deal with Campbell and McGee, had held off on doing the work for years.

Three days after the convictions, Mayor Burton wrote to Eliot. It was as effusive as the reserved, buttoned-up mayor got.

Dear Eliot:

Confirming and developing my oral statement immediately following my receipt of the news of the conviction of Campbell and McGee, this letter is to express to you my official and personal appreciation of the exceptional public service which you rendered in this case.

This case and the long investigation leading up to it has dealt with one of the worst conditions in Cleveland. From the first day that you joined us, you have in a quiet and modest way led the attack on this evil. The conviction of Campbell and McGee marks a major victory in the battle and I believe marks the turning point in our campaign to drive out the rackets. . . .

I hope that you enjoy your well earned vacation and will return to your duties here ready to continue the drive with your usual vigor and with increased assurance of success.

With personal regards to Mrs. Ness and yourself,

> Yours sincerely,
> Harold H. Burton
> Mayor

Frank Cullitan, talking to Eliot after the verdict, had offered a more succinct response to the victory. "Campbell and McGee asked for it," he said.

The convictions, coming on top of the police housecleaning and the gambling-racket assault, made Eliot a national figure once again, even more so than during the Untouchables' heyday. This time not just newspapers but the glossy national magazines jumped on the Ness bandwagon.

Newsweek wrote that Eliot had "lifted fear from the hearts of honest men." *Cosmopolitan,* then a literary and opinion magazine, wrote: "Next time anybody tells you that individual opportunity is as dead as the dodo in this corporate age, and the chance for adventure along with it, please introduce him to Eliot Ness, Director of Public Safety for Cleveland — the remarkable young man who found a dramatic challenge in an ordinary job and who represents a brand-new school of crime smashers."

Reader's Digest noted that Eliot earned $7,500 a year as Cleveland's safety director and had been offered many times that by private companies to make the leap into the business world. "Someday I may take one of those jobs," it quoted Eliot as saying. "Right now, however, I want to prove what an honest police force with intelligence and civic pride can do."

CHAPTER 26
THE DOCTOR

Cleveland's serial killer kept interrupting Eliot's good work.

Back in February 1937, the torso of a young woman had swirled out of Lake Erie and thumped ashore near the end of 156th Street. This latest corpse — officially victim number seven — reignited public fascination with the murders, even though the county's new coroner, Samuel Gerber, couldn't say for sure it was the work of the same "maniac butcher" who had been scattering body parts around the area for more than two years. Inevitably, the investigation became a political issue. Martin L. Sweeney was a Democratic congressman from Cleveland and a determined Burton antagonist, for the Republican mayor looked to be headed for higher office. That meant Eliot also was on the ambitious congressman's hit list. (Sweeney called him Burton's "alter ego.") Even though the campaign season hadn't begun yet, the congressman told Clevelanders that if they rid themselves of Burton, "we can send back to Washington the Prohibition agent who now is safety director." That line of attack fell flat — no one minded that the city's hard-charging safety director had once been a liquor cop — but Sweeney kept up his criticism. A couple of weeks after the discovery of victim number seven, the congressman, playing on Clevelanders' fears, declared that Eliot was wasting precious time on police-corruption cases when he should be focused on catching the city's serial killer. "There's a killer out there," he would declare time and again.

Eliot never highlighted the torso investigation when talking with reporters, but he spent large parts of every week on the case, monitoring Merylo and Zalewski's progress and at the same running his own counterinvestigation that he kept from them. He decided to let the cocky Merylo be the public face of the case. The detective liked to talk and beat his chest. Eliot figured that he and his Unknowns could pursue their own leads unnoticed behind Merylo's gruff razzle-dazzle. Separate from Merylo and Zalewski's work, the Unknowns broke down each murder fact by fact and reinvestigated it. Slowly, they tied up loose ends, though this never seemed to lead anywhere useful. One example: in September 1935, after the discovery of Andrassy and the still unidentified second man on Jackass Hill, detectives had tried to find a Philip Russo. His car had been seen numerous times at the top of the hill, with a man — presumably Russo — surveying the area with binoculars. Police considered it a promising lead, even more so when they couldn't find him. Now, almost two years later, investigators tracked Russo down, only to quickly strike him from the list of suspects. It turned out that a woman who lived in an apartment facing Jackass Hill had carefully planned out her marital indiscretions. She would sometimes tell Russo, her inamorata at the time, to wait at the top of the hill with binoculars. When her husband left the apartment, she would flap a tablecloth out the window, the sign for her lover to hop in his car and zip over to the building.

When the weather turned nice that summer of 1937, the killer picked up his pace again. On June 6, the neatly severed head of an African American woman was found underneath the Lorain-Carnegie Bridge. Her torso had been stuffed into a burlap sack and left nearby. Gerber would be able to identify this latest victim — her name was Rose Wallace — based on distinctive dental work. Like Flo Polillo, she had been a part-time prostitute. A month after the discovery of Wallace's remains, the torso of a white man — along with other pieces of him — turned up in the Cuyahoga River, victim number nine. That was three new bodies in less than six months.

Eliot and his team finally got a break in the case eight long months later. On a warm, breezy day in March 1938, with the Campbell-McGee trial heading toward a verdict, a dog bounded out of the woods near the town of Sandusky with a human leg in its mouth. The dog's owner, horrified, called the county sheriff's office. The local coroner, E. J. Meckstroth, would determine that the appendage belonged to a young woman. "The leg shows as neat a job of amputation as I ever saw," he remarked. This raised a red flag sixty miles away in Cleveland. David Cowles, the police department's superintendent of criminal identification, drove out to Sandusky to inspect the mystery leg.

Cowles's work in the lab had earned Eliot's respect over the past two years. The feeling wasn't mutual. Like Merylo, the short, round Cowles resisted Eliot's natural friendliness. After all, Eliot was everything — good-looking, charming, intrepid — that Cowles wanted to be but never could manage. But if Eliot recognized the antipathy, he ignored it. Cowles, a self-taught chemist, was a strong advocate for ballistics and lie-detector technology, two much-derided scientific innovations that also fascinated Eliot. Their agreement on the value of scientific policing led Eliot to begin giving Cowles fieldwork. Most notably, he had put him in charge of running informants for the safety department's under-the-radar torso investigation.

Cowles believed this severed limb found far from the city represented a major breakthrough. He had cultivated a source at the Osborn State Prison Honor Farm who was providing him with tantalizing information about a disgraced forty-four-year-old doctor, Francis Sweeney, who periodically checked himself into the veterans' hospital at the Ohio Soldiers' and Sailors' Home. The six-hundred-bed hospital stood near the prison work farm in Sandusky. Now, on Cowles's recommendation, Eliot and his Unknowns turned their attention to Sweeney.

Dr. Sweeney was a big man, certainly strong enough to subdue and hack up prostitutes and even young, fit men. The investigators dug into his background. They learned he had been gassed during the World War and never really recovered. He spiraled into mental illness in the years that followed — "going down and down and down with the booze," in Cowles's description. Sweeney's wife, a nurse, sued for divorce and full custody of their two children in 1934, after twice trying to have him committed to an institution. Sweeney's medical career had collapsed by then, and with his wife gone, he fell off the map, slipping into the netherworld where no one keeps records or asks for your name. The only official sign of him came from his stays at the Soldiers' and Sailors' Home, where, as a voluntary patient, he could come and go as he pleased. The investigators obtained an old psychiatric evaluation that stated Sweeney had a "frustrated desire to operate." Excitement swept the group. This looked like their man. They also discovered something else, something that could complicate their pursuit of the suspect. Francis Sweeney was a cousin of Martin Sweeney, the congressman who frequently criticized Eliot's handling of the torso investigation.

Eliot and his investigators watched Francis Sweeney for a month. They wanted to have some solid evidence before hauling him in for questioning, but they couldn't come up with anything. When he was in their sights, he did nothing much of interest; and when he wasn't, he seemed to drop into a void. Some of the safety department's investigators believed the doctor to be a harmless nut, not up to the task of murdering several men and women and expertly covering his tracks. But in April, pieces from a tenth victim bubbled up in the Cuyahoga River, nine months after the last body had been found. Gerber determined that the death had been recent, within days. That prompted Eliot to act. His team grabbed Sweeney off a street corner and took him downtown to the Cleveland Hotel, where they had a suite waiting. They shut the curtains, dropped him into a chair, and began the interrogation.

"We played on him for a long time," Cowles said in an interview years later. He remembered the suspect being drunk when they brought him in. Cowles and a detective, Louis Oldag, grilled him eight hours a day, day after day. It couldn't have been pretty: the two policemen didn't mind securing a confession through sheer brutality. But Sweeney didn't break. The doctor kept feeding them gibberish and taunts and riddles. He seemed to be enjoying himself. At some point during the weeklong interrogation, Eliot took his turn with the suspect. The safety director believed harsh tactics led to false confessions — a minority opinion in law enforcement at the time. He preferred to throw his subjects off balance, to wear them down with repetitive, rhythmic questioning until they got tangled up in their own lies and began to see the truth as the only way to make it to the finish line. It had worked time and again for him over the years.

Not this time. Sweeney didn't confess to the murders. He apparently didn't deny committing them, either. Eliot couldn't nail him down on anything. The doctor patiently demanded his release. It was the only thing he said that wasn't open to interpretation. His frustration growing, Eliot stopped the examination. He left the room and placed a call to Leonarde Keeler, who he'd met at the Northwestern crime lab back in 1931. Keeler was the foremost developer of the lie detector, now called the polygraph.

In Chicago, Keeler had met significant resistance to his machine. The police refused to give up the third degree in favor of the "electric detective." As one cop put it, holding up a meaty fist: "Here's the best lie detector." But the polygraph, with its promise of honest, dispassionate justice, long had fascinated Eliot, and he wanted to bring it to Cleveland. Now he had a reason to do so. He knew Keeler had spent years perfecting his apparatus and his technique. Keeler had tested friends, college students, and mental patients, carefully noting the changes in their blood pressure and breathing and sweat production. He was absolutely convinced he could tell when someone was lying.

Keeler came to the safety department's hotel suite straight from the airport. After a brief consultation with Eliot, he got right to work. Sweeney didn't object to being tested. To him, it was just one more phase of this interesting, drawn-out game they were playing. He showed no sign of concern as Keeler hooked him up to the machine; he exuded confidence and answered questions with authority. He seemed to think he and Keeler had a nice rapport. The results were unmistakable. Packing up his equipment after multiple tests, Keeler told Eliot that this big, bemused man definitely was the torso killer. "When Keeler got through, he said he was the man, no question about it. 'I may as well throw my machine out the window if I say anything else,'" Cowles later said. He recalled that Eliot, just to be sure, brought in another expert as well, someone from Detroit, who "gave us the same opinion."

Eliot and his team believed they had solved the case. But the polygraph remained a controversial, disputed technology, so they had no hard evidence they could take to court. They still couldn't get Sweeney to confess. With the lack of actionable evidence, and the inconvenient fact that the suspect was related to a congressman who had criticized the safety director's handling of the torso investigation, Eliot had no choice but to let the doctor go.

After releasing Sweeney back into the world, Eliot returned home to discover that Edna wanted to be let go, too. Back in March, after the Campbell-McGee trial and with the mayor's best wishes, Eliot and his wife had headed out of town. But it wasn't for a vacation, as Burton had assumed. The couple drove down to Florida to set up an apartment for Edna so she could establish residency and, when the time was right, return and file for divorce. Now, just a few weeks later, she told him the time was right. His week at the Cleveland Hotel had been the final insult. She didn't care why he was there; she packed her bags and called ahead to the train station before telling him of her decision.

Once they worked out the divorce settlement, she would never speak to Eliot again.

Eliot worried about his future. He was a public man. His political opponents — like Congressman Sweeney — surely would feast on news of a divorce. In Catholic, working-class Cleveland, good men didn't get divorced. Eliot was not a religious man, but he nevertheless believed in such religious dictates. He believed he had failed a moral test. He even considered stepping down as safety director, before anyone found out about his and Edna's separation. For weeks, he skirted the edges of depression; he felt alone and adrift. He was touchy, on edge, unsure what to do.

One evening, he settled into a seat at a city council meeting hoping to keep a low profile. Councilman Clarence L. Young noticed him right away. Young brought up a council resolution to hire an additional building inspector. Eliot, as he had done in private conferences with the council, told Young he would be happy to hire more building inspectors if the council provided money for their salaries.

"The director says he'll do this if we find the money for him," Young declaimed in full oratorical mode. "Well, then, I'd like to find out right now what he has done with that extra $17,000 in his department for common labor this year. It's going to pay all those secretaries in his department. I'd like to find out what all those secretaries are doing."

Eliot leapt to his feet. He feared rumors were circulating about his wife leaving him. He'd been seen at a nightclub recently with one of the city hall pool secretaries, a small, pretty girl who sometimes worked late into the evening with him. He simply could not allow this kind of insinuation to go unchallenged.

"Mr. Young has been sharpshooting at my department for a long time," Eliot barked. "Principally because we indicted and convicted officials of a union he was thrown out of the other night."

"That's a lie!" Young responded, pounding the table. "That's a lie, and don't go saying those things around here. I was never thrown out of any union."

Council watchers hadn't expected this. Most of those in attendance didn't realize the screaming match wasn't actually about building inspectors. Nor was it about Eliot's personal life, it turned out. Young was poking the safety director not about his marriage or any rumored infidelity but about his "secret" budget for special investigators. A longtime member of Campbell's painters' union, he resented Eliot and his Unknowns for making union racketeering front-page news with the trial of Campbell and McGee.

Chamberlin took his boss aside. "Don't let 'em get your goat," his assistant said. Eliot, embarrassed, quickly calmed himself. But he refused to back down on the importance of the Unknowns. "I apologize for engaging in personalities," he told the council. "But I can tell what those 'secretaries' are doing. They're helping in the many things we've been doing to right wrongs in this town. We've saved the citizens a lot of money in our safety work. We're engaging in a complete reorganization of the police department. All that requires extra help. The job would cost the city $100,000 if you brought outsiders in to do it." He added that he didn't mean to say Young had been booted out of the painters' union, only that he'd been removed from a recent meeting.

That got Young worked up all over again. He hadn't been removed, he declared. He had walked out of the union meeting in question. Fine, Eliot said, you walked out. Then the safety director got up and walked out himself.

The next day, coincidence or not, news

broke that the Nesses had been separated for the past three months and that Mrs. Ness had left Cleveland. "We have sort of agreed to disagree," Eliot stammered when asked about the state of his marriage. "We have, however, visited one another several times during the summer. We are parting as friends."

Recognizing that they had caught the safety director off guard, reporters pushed for more. "We just agreed a mistake had been made and set about in a sensible way to correct it," Eliot said. He would be no more forthcoming than that.

Eliot nervously waited to see what Burton would have to say about it. To his surprise, the mayor never publicly addressed the issue. He offered only praise for his safety director's job performance and waved away all other questions.

That summer, word began to leak out that Al Capone, "the personification of gangster power," couldn't handle prison life. He refused to leave his cell for meals and often unexpectedly burst out in song. He'd developed a mania for making and remaking his cot, spending hours at the task. A consulting psychiatrist at Alcatraz Island, where Capone was held, diagnosed him with paresis, or motor-nerve damage. That actually sounded much better than it was. Advanced, untreated syphilis was eating away at his brain.

The man who'd helped bring down Capone had sex on the brain as well. In the aftermath of his and Edna's separation, Eliot began going out late at night, trawling for female company. The divorce deeply embarrassed him, but once he realized Mayor Burton wasn't going to ask him to resign, he decided to put it behind him and restart his life. Eliot hadn't had much fun since arriving in Cleveland more than three years before. Work had been satisfying but stressful, and his marriage had been quiet but tense. He needed an outlet, and now he had found it. The well-known local artist Viktor Schreckengost remembered being introduced to Eliot at a nightclub. "I was looking for a big fellow," he said. "And here's this quiet guy who never likes to brag but would just sit back and listen. Not the kind of fellow you expected to be a gangbuster at all. In fact, he was the last person you'd think would ever have anything to do with Al Capone."

Eliot began showing up at downtown ballrooms and nightclubs most weeknights, walking over from the office at 10 or 11 at night. Sometimes he'd arrive with a city hall secretary, and they'd quietly knock back drinks. Other times he would join a group of already well-lubricated friends, and he'd hit the dance floor. He was an excellent dancer. One night he took Betty Seaver out of her husband's arms for an energetic spin around the floor. The young sculptress had finagled an introduction through friends sometime before; now she laughed high and loud, flying in his arms. She liked to wear half a dozen or so silver bracelets on each wrist, and they clinked and shimmered, causing heads to turn. Hugh Seaver took her home as soon as the dance ended.

"Women were attracted to him," recalled Philip Porter, "and during his bachelor period, he never lacked for gals who were charmed by his boyishness." Eliot knew how to make the most of that natural charm. Unlike most men, he remembered things — details — about the women in his professional and social circle. All the girls around city hall noticed it. He would tell a secretary or telephone operator, a woman he saw day after day, "I'll never forget the first time that I saw you. You were wearing a red dress." He had a soft, confiding voice when he said such things, flattering in its sudden intimacy and endearing for its apparent schoolboy earnestness. Eliot took advantage of the swooning he caused, but strictly on a short-term basis. A few nights of dancing and drinking, maybe a trip back to his apartment in the city, and that was that. "Few people really knew him," Porter believed. "To me, he often seemed lonely."

Women didn't reach the same conclusion.

He appeared to be the happiest, most popular man around. "He was handsome and charming, very quiet and witty, just as nice as anyone could possibly be," said Marjorie Mutersbaugh, a local socialite. His flirtatiousness became legendary. He seemed to need the response — the blush and giggle of feminine interest — to prove he was all right. The attention would pull him up from depression or anxiety, as if to a high diving platform, where he would stand on the edge of a knife-like drop into pleasure. But could he make the leap? One woman confided to a friend that Eliot "didn't have the essentials to keep [a relationship] going," surely a polite way of admitting he gave her cab fare and showed her the door when the night had run its course. Another danced with him a couple of times and became convinced he was falling for her. He never called for a date, but she would spend years telling friends she once was engaged to Eliot Ness.

The truth was, Eliot needed to be in a relationship. He wanted to be married. He was a traditional man who couldn't stand going home to an empty house. And he knew exactly who he wanted to fill that space. He just had to work up the courage to go get her.

CHAPTER 27
AN UNWELCOME SURPRISE

When Eliot Ness left her on a train platform on that warm summer afternoon in 1937, Evaline McAndrew figured she would never see him again. He was just a sweet tourist fling, a romantic day trip, nothing more. And so the encounter ruined her Canadian getaway. She didn't even bother making her connecting train — or, more likely, she simply forgot all about it. She'd decided, in the heat of her first and only embrace with this perfect stranger, that she had met her "second True Love." (The first True Love was not her artist husband, but a young Iowa medical student she'd rejected when she was a coed. She had feared a conventional marriage would turn her into her mother.)

Evaline believed in True Love. She believed in Romance. Or at least she thought she did. She hadn't seen any of it while growing up. Her father, Albert Michelow, a Swedish émigré, had once been a dashing freelance photographer, but that was before he married and started a family. Evaline grew up in sooty Pontiac, Michigan, the youngest of four — "an unwelcome surprise," she was certain. From as far back as Evaline could remember, the house was tense, full of resentments and strangled fury. By the time she could walk, her father was an assembly-line worker at Ford Motor Company, his shoulders irretrievably slumped, his eyes watery and unfocused. He slept in his own bed, in a different room than his wife. Evaline's mother, Myrtle, a former Southern belle, had been beaten down by this life, too. "Too many children. Too much cleaning, cooking, washing, ironing for six people," Evaline recalled. Most of all, "too little money." The result was predictable: "My father's and mother's romance was over and never revived." Evaline decided at a young age she wouldn't let that happen to her.

She was wrong about never seeing Eliot again. His face periodically showed up in national magazines. He always looked so grim in these photos, at least compared to the relaxed, open-faced man who had spent hundreds of miles smiling at her from across the club car's armrest. (On one occasion, the face peering out from the page looked like it had aged twenty years since their encounter a few months before. *Newsweek* magazine had accidentally identified Czechoslovakia's president, Edward Beneš, as Eliot Ness.) His high profile only made Evaline certain that Eliot, this important and impressive man, had forgotten all about her.

Soon after her aborted train trip, she and her husband realized they needed a change and so left Chicago for the teeming anonymity of New York City. She had expected to be revitalized by the country's biggest, brashest city, but, just as in Chicago, she instead felt empty. Her husband, Mac, immediately found work as a commercial artist, but the less experienced Evaline couldn't get an assignment, not even to draw a pair of shoes for an advertisement. She tried to work on personal projects, but she began to realize that her work was derivative, uninspired. She returned to modeling for other artists. She hated every moment of it, the being on display, turning her hip when requested, smoothing out her dress just so. She and Mac started to drink — and fight — every night. She had married him to get out of the house, to try something new. She hadn't thought it out. By now, just the sight of this kind, eager-to-please young man made her sick to her stomach. She began to have dreams of dying, her body breaking apart like an ice floe, her life force crushed into powdery white flakes and swept off by the wind. Evaline realized what was happening but felt powerless to arrest it. "Shades of my father's dark Swedish despondency," she worried. "Day by day, my low spirits slumped lower. I bickered with Mac. I refused to laugh. . . . I was tired of living. And I was twenty-five years old."

Evaline left her husband and moved into a run-down little one-room walkup with the bathroom at the end of the hall. It was all she could afford. She sank deeper into blackness. She walked through her days in a kind of fugue state, the outside world helpless against her gloom. When she wasn't working — turning her hip, smoothing out the fabric — she was drinking. Or sleeping. After draining a bottle, she could sleep through an entire day. She worshipped the slow, numbing slide into alcoholic unconsciousness, her arms and legs feeling rubbery and alien. She needed another shock, another jolt, something to get her back among the living.

Out of nowhere, she got it. One Sunday afternoon, the phone rang.

"Eliot!" she exclaimed when she recognized the quiet, calm voice she was hearing — for the first time in more than a year. The lifeline she needed most. He was in New York, he said. "Would you have dinner with me?"

"Yes!" she enthusiastically answered.

"Would you meet me at the Sherry-Netherland Hotel?"

Again — "Yes!" In her shock and surprise, she seemed capable only of this single syllable.

Evaline barely had the patience to climb

into a dress — the slinkiest, sexiest one she had — before rushing out the door. Even some three decades later she would recall their reunion with the vividness of a perfect dream:

When I saw him in the hotel lobby, he stood still and opened his arms wide. I walked into them and smothered my face against his chest. It was the most comforting feeling that I could remember.

Over dinner, Eliot told Evaline his marriage had come to an end. Evaline said that hers, too, was over; she just had to get a divorce. They smiled at each other across the table like giddy children. "Why don't you move to Cleveland?" he said. "Where I can see you, touch you, talk to you in the process?"

"I will," she responded without hesitation.

For Evaline, it was the most natural decision in the world, even though she barely knew this man and had never been to Cleveland. That their intimacy was unearned seemed only to make it more powerful. From the moment she heard his voice on the phone, the fledgling relationship consumed her. Within days she was alone again — Eliot couldn't wait for her to wrap up her New York life; he had to get back to Ohio — but now she had hope again. And a definitive plan. She was going to be with her True Love, in some place called Cleveland. She lounged in her single bed at night and let her brain roll through what had happened, over and over. She couldn't believe Eliot Ness had found her. That he'd *wanted* to find her. "Eliot had many talents," she decided, "but his 'detective' skill was the one I liked best."

Eliot believed his detective skill had served him well in the hunt for the torso killer. He'd had to let Francis Sweeney go, but he was convinced he had the right man. Eliot ordered his team to keep a close watch on the doctor, and so they did — for months. Day after day an investigator fell in behind him as he came out of a restaurant or the latest flophouse he was staying in. Sweeney, crazy but clever, soon figured out what was going on. He would saunter along the street, walking for blocks, pretending to window-shop, until he identified his pursuer. Then he'd start the game. He'd walk into a store, and exit out the back. He'd put down his fork at a diner, step into the restroom — and squeeze out the window.

One rookie investigator attached to the safety department lost track of his quarry when Sweeney, feigning sleep on a streetcar, suddenly jerked to his feet, leapt through the closing doors, and sprinted to catch a cross-town trolley. The investigator wrenched the streetcar's doors open and jumped out into the road, but he couldn't make it to the other car before it clacked away. Embarrassed, he returned to city hall to admit he'd screwed up, but Sweeney had beaten him to the punch. The chief torso suspect had called police headquarters a few minutes before. "That kid you had following me wasn't very good," Sweeney told a befuddled sergeant. "If he wants to try again tomorrow, tell him I'll be in the men's department at Higbee's Department Store at 2 p.m." Eliot couldn't help chuckling when he received the news. He told the rookie to be at Higbee's the next afternoon and to tip his hat at Sweeney. He'd have another man there to follow the doctor.

Eliot may have been able to see the humor in the situation, but at the same time, his frustration with the case — and with Sweeney — ran deep. Late in the summer, that frustration took a turn for the worse. He figured the weeklong grilling at the hotel and the constant surveillance that followed would put a stop to Sweeney's rampage, but on Tuesday, August 16, 1938, the same day Eliot reached a divorce settlement with Edna, three men scavenging for scrap at Lakeshore Drive and East Ninth Street came upon a human torso wrapped in butcher paper. Police soon found more remains in the vacant lot, including the severed head, the thighs (strapped together by a rubber band), and the arms and legs. It was a young white woman, dead about four months. And that wasn't all. Later in the day police found remains of another person in the garbage-filled lot, this one a man. Victims eleven and twelve. Detective Merylo, who knew nothing about the safety department's investigation of Sweeney, was one of the first officers on the scene. "He's changing his technique," he told a reporter. "Why, I don't know. But for the first time since the two bodies we found in September 1935, he has left two victims together."

It would turn out that the killer was changing his method more than Merylo yet realized. The murderer — perhaps because investigators followed him day after day, making it difficult for him to do his bloody business — was using a kind of sleight of hand. Victim number eleven, the coroner would discover, had been embalmed and might not have been murdered. The corpse may have been stolen from a mortuary.

Still, the discoveries hit Eliot hard. He'd had his chance to break Sweeney, but he couldn't do it. He couldn't impress him — or charm him or scare him — like he had with so many other suspects over the years. The press had begun pounding the war drums again, calling for accountability from the police and city hall, disgorging an array of new theories about the killer. Congressman Sweeney issued a statement decrying the latest murder or murders and the police department's inability to stop the killings. Eliot felt like a failure. Worse, he felt responsible. This was the first time the killer had left bodies downtown. The dumping ground was within easy view of the window in Eliot's city hall office. The Mad Butcher of Kingsbury Run, as the papers were now calling the killer, was taunting the safety director, Eliot was sure of it. The detainment and interrogation of Dr. Sweeney, rather than scaring him straight, may have spurred him on. Eliot, always so careful and deliberate, made a snap decision.

Two days later, in the dead of night, twenty-five policemen stood along the top of a ridge near Commercial and Canal Roads. They hefted axes, truncheons, and hammers. The safety director, about a hundred feet ahead of them, waved a flashlight. The men began to move out. As they closed in on the string of hobo camps that stretched along Kingsbury Run's high ground, big lights attached to fire trucks clapped on. The lights caught many of the officers holding their breath. The stench of sweat, food scraps, and excrement washed over them as they approached their quarry. The detectives and patrolmen knocked over tents and used crowbars to split open makeshift homes built from cardboard and tin.

Officers pulled disheveled, bleary-eyed men

out of the huts, many of them drunk or in a permanent haze. Yelling at them to keep quiet and not to resist, the policemen herded everyone into a big huddle and began searching their pathetic homes. Eliot strode into this human wreckage in a crisp suit, his hair slicked perfectly into place. He looked through many of the hovels and questioned some of the shantytown residents, taking notes in a little black book. One man, in a state of shock, began to cry as Eliot asked him questions. The safety director patted him on the shoulder and led him to the lieutenant charged with gathering up the homeless men.

The officers moved farther down the embankment to another collection of makeshift homes. It was now past one in the morning. Dozens of men in this second shantytown had rushed out of their tents and cardboard houses when they heard scuffling and dogs barking at the other hobo camp, but they didn't get far. Squads of officers covered all available exits. As the raiders began to search this second encampment, a large, bellowing man emerged from a hut swinging a shovel. Eliot, leading the officers, dropped to the ground to avoid the attack. The shovel missed the top of his head by inches. Officers jumped on the man, pummeling him with truncheons until he toppled and his body went limp. Blood poured out of his ear when they lifted him onto a cot. Using axes, clubs, and shovels, policemen pounded the encampment into splinters.

Police placed about sixty shantytown residents in paddy wagons for the trip to Central Police Station. As the wagons trundled away from the area, the Animal Protective League came through and rounded up the homeless men's pets. Fire officials moved in last, soaking everything with oil. The safety director stared at what remained of the shantytowns for a long time before turning to his fire chief. "Burn it," he said. "Burn it to the ground."

Huge orange flames soon snapped into the sky, visible from blocks away. Clevelanders awakened by the flash of light leaned out their windows and wondered if there'd been a terrible third-shift accident at one of the city's great factories. Eliot had convinced himself this was the right thing to do. The killer needed Kingsbury Run's homeless camps — Eliot believed they were his best hunting ground — and so they had to be destroyed. The safety director ordered that all of the shantytown residents be fingerprinted so they could be identified if they ended up becoming murder victims. The men who could prove they had jobs were then released. The rest were held, without charges.

Eliot thought he was being responsible and sympathetic by destroying the homeless camps and holding dozens of men in hopes of finding family members who would take them in, but not everyone saw it that way. An editorial in the *Press* lambasted Eliot "for the jailing of jobless and penniless men and the wrecking of their miserable hovels without permitting them to collect their personal belongings." The paper, slapping him for his "misguided zeal," added: "That such Shantytowns exist is a sorrowful reflection upon the state of society. The throwing into jail of men broken by experience and the burning of their wretched places of habitation will not solve the economic problem. Nor is it likely to lead to the solution of the most macabre mystery in Cleveland's history." Piling on, the *News* and the *Plain Dealer* called for Eliot to release the shantytown men from police custody immediately.

This was a new development. No newspaper had seriously criticized the safety director since his first weeks on the job. He'd always held the moral high ground, and he'd always appeared to be on top of the situation, whatever it was. But now, with the torso murders, he was flailing, desperate. The newspapers had finally noticed. They mused in print over whether he had too much power. Eliot remained immensely popular in Cleveland, but his cloak of invincibility was suddenly gone.

The bad press made Eliot even more determined to show results in the torso case. On Monday, August 22, Eliot teamed police officers with fire wardens — a clever way around the need for search warrants. For the next five days the teams went door to door in a ten-square-mile area around Kingsbury Run. They were officially looking for fire-code violations, and there were plenty of them. They poked through dilapidated buildings where they frequently found up to a dozen people living in one room. They searched basements where frayed wiring hung from the ceiling like tinsel. But they issued few citations, for they actually were looking for a killing room — the murderer's "death laboratory." Eliot was sure it existed. But even though officers and fire wardens pawed through hundreds of homes, they didn't find anything of the sort.

The fevered activity wasn't for nothing, though. With the Kingsbury Run shantytowns destroyed and the door-to-door searches getting started, Dr. Francis Sweeney showed up in Sandusky, where he committed himself to the veterans' hospital. Eliot couldn't boast of an arrest, but he had managed to remove from the streets the man he believed responsible for the gruesome murders.

Of course, Sweeney still could sign himself out of the facility whenever he wanted to.

CHAPTER 28
FULL OF LOVE

Eliot loved to fall in love, and Evaline was easy for fall for. He had no idea what he was getting himself into.

The woman he had met on a train nearly two years before was flirtatious and sexy and smart, with a wit as dry as Death Valley. She was unlike any woman Eliot had ever known. What he didn't know was that it was all an act. Evaline's confidence — her belief in herself and in the power of romance and possibility — depended on willpower. And it couldn't be maintained. She was a talented artist. She painted and sketched, made her own clothes and furniture and tapestries, but this overflow of creativity was her way of fighting off ghosts. A low-boil dissatisfaction roiled constantly inside her, though she refused to acknowledge it, even with intimates. She struggled to keep her composure — that was something she admired about Eliot, his composure, calling him "the most controlled man I ever met." The pressure she put on herself to live up to Eliot's example would become intense — unbearable. "She was an extraordinarily beautiful and talented woman, but she had demons," said Steve Resnick, her step-grandson. "God knows what they were. It wouldn't surprise me if she was abused as a child." Ann Durell saw the same darkness in her. "Oh, what was it about Eve?" she mused, calling Evaline by her nickname. "She was very elegant, very aware, but it was hard being around her. She was not a relaxed person."

Her first few months in Cleveland offered few opportunities for relaxation.

"Cleveland wasn't New York but my life was exciting, busy, and full of love," Evaline would write of her introduction to Ohio's biggest city. It was all because of Eliot. He was her dashing "fair-haired boy." She thrilled at the late-night calls that sent him charging out the door, at the newspaper stories describing his latest attacks on corruption, at the interruptions at restaurants from people who just wanted to shake his hand. She would even attend an extortion trial to see him in action. She sat in the front row wearing an exotic turban, intent on being noticed. She listened carefully to the testimony of mobsters and "stool pigeons," now and again sneaking a look at Eliot and smiling. She was in love, but more than that, Eliot made her proud.

She'd never really been proud of anyone before — certainly not of herself — and she enjoyed the novelty of it.

During his brief singlehood, Eliot had grown accustomed to closing up his office at eight or nine (instead of the usual eleven or twelve) and heading over to one of downtown Cleveland's grand hotels, where he'd drink and dance and schmooze, sometimes until it was time to go back to work in the morning. It turned out that this work-hard-and-play-harder lifestyle suited Eliot far more than the dull-boy routine he'd stuck with for so long. Drinking loosened him up, pulled him out his shell. It liberated him. "Eliot was a gay, convivial soul who liked nothing better than to sit around till all hours, drinking with friends, or dancing," recalled Phillip Porter. "It seemed to unwind him to visit night clubs and hotel dance spots. He was not a heavy drinker, but he could keep at it for long periods without giving any appearance of being swacked."

Edna had wanted only to stay at home with her husband in the evening, to have him all to herself for a few hours a day. Not Evaline. Eliot had found someone who enjoyed the nightlife as much as he did. "That may have been the best part of his life," Evaline said years later. "He loved it." They'd go to the Vogue Room at the Hollenden Hotel or the Bronze Room at the Hotel Cleveland. They became regulars at the Statler's Terrace Room. When the Terrace Room's bandleader, Manny Landers, saw them come through the doors, he'd stop the band midsong and launch into "I Live the Life I Love," the couple's favorite. Inevitably, Eliot would run into men on his hit list: the Statler was still the Mob's hotel of choice. This wasn't nearly as awkward as one might expect. Eliot and Evaline, and whoever else they had brought along, would settle in at the bar, and the pimps and enforcers and numbers-racket monkeys would all shift to the other side. Now and again, one of the tough boys would make a crack about Eliot or the police or the latest "trumped up" charges, and Eliot would look up and laugh along with them and offer a rejoinder. They'd parry back and forth, the women watching with bemused expressions, until one of the parties moved to a table in the main room. It might have seemed all too congenial to an outsider, but it was a vast improvement from just a couple of years before, when cops and mobsters spent night after night huddled together in back-room booths at the club.

While the gangsters on the other side of the bar put Eliot in an excellent mood, they didn't become part of dinnertime conversation. "He never really talked much about what he was doing," Evaline recalled. "We'd go out at night and have a good time, but there would never be any talk about his work." By this time Evaline had moved into Eliot's rented place on Lake Avenue in all but name; she maintained her own apartment for propriety's sake. She also began to take on some freelance illustrating work for Higbee's department store, thanks to Eliot calling in a favor. Working as an artist during the day, going out every night drinking and dancing, Evaline realized she was actually happy, consistently and truly happy. She wanted this feeling to go on forever — and Eliot promised her it could. In the fall of 1939 the couple sneaked out of town to get married. They both selected "single" on the marriage certificate, perhaps worried the minister wouldn't marry them if they admitted to being divorced. Inexplicably, Eliot listed his occupation as "Writer." (There wasn't a box provided for the wife to put down an occupation.) It was a quick, makeshift ceremony, presided over by a Methodist minister and witnessed by two men who were strangers to the happy couple. Eliot didn't mind being married by a clergyman outside his Christian Science faith. Two weeks later, when word finally trickled out that the safety director had married his young artist girlfriend, the *Plain Dealer* swooned: "The director's bride is a slender, attractive, friendly person, a smart girl and an unusual one. For example, she was reported as two years older than she is, and she isn't going to sue. She is 25." (Actually, the initial report was correct: She was twenty-seven.) The *Press,* for its part, excitedly announced, "Aside from her art work, she is interested in music, the theater and tennis."

Eliot chose a good time to get hitched again: he was seeing a revival of hero worship in the press after his handling of the United Auto Workers strike that had idled the Fisher Body plant at Coit Road and East 140th Street. On July 31, the nationwide strike had turned violent in Cleveland when five thousand union men arrived at the entrance to the General Motors factory. Carrying clubs and wearing papier-mâché helmets, they descended on non-striking workers heading into the plant. Horrific screams of pain and fear ripped the morning air; men trying to escape slipped in pools of blood. One replacement worker crawled under a parked sedan. Union men promptly set the car on fire. Eliot, unarmed, waded into the melee with a phalanx of officers. He ordered his men not to unholster their guns. Two Ohio National Guard officers on "observation duty" during the clash singled out Eliot for his leadership in the midst of battle. "Although members of the Cleveland Safety Department exercised rare qualities of patience and restraint under trying circumstances, when the need arose their prompt militancy and courage left nothing to be desired," they wrote in a report to the guard's adjutant general. Once the battle had been brought under control, Eliot declared an exclusion zone around the plant in all directions, with the exception of a nearby restaurant where the UAW's local leader had set up his unofficial headquarters. Eliot allowed up to ten union men in the restaurant at a time. That decision, criticized by police commanders in internal memos, would prove effective. Detroit and other cities continued to endure strike violence in the days ahead, but Cleveland stayed quiet. "City Acts to Keep Peace in Strike," the *Plain Dealer* triumphantly proclaimed across its front page.

This latest wave of press approval did not ease Eliot's mind about his recent nuptials. Worried that his divorce and quick remarriage reflected poorly on his character, he told people as little as possible about his relationship with Evaline. Cleveland's newspapers reported that the Nesses married in Chicago, where the bride, a native Chicagoan, was "a friend of Mr. Ness' family." The papers also revealed that the couple had met "several years before" through Eliot's sisters. What could be more wholesome than that? The problem was, none of it was true. They actually married in Greenup, Kentucky, a town Eliot discovered during his time with the ATU in Cincinnati. (One Greenup booster boasted that the tiny town on the Ohio border was "known for its beautiful women, fast horses and good whiskey.") Plus, Evaline was born in Ohio, not Chicago, and she hadn't yet met Eliot's family. Evaline recognized what drove her new husband's small lies. She, too, was often ashamed of her choices, her desires. She feared what people thought of her. She and Eliot were kindred spirits in this way. She stuck to her husband's talking points. "I'm lucky in my profession because it's the kind of work that doesn't interfere with being a housewife too," she told the *Plain Dealer*.

Eliot's social circle found Evaline as charming as the reporters did, but some were wary. "Evaline may have already been in the picture when Eliot and Edna separated," one friend suspected. No one had any way of knowing that for sure, but Eliot's new girl certainly fit the popular conception of a home wrecker. "Edna was an ordinary, simple person," the friend said. "Evaline was striking in appearance, even dramatic."

Some observers — and there were a lot of observers of the relationship early on — thought her desperate for attention. One said that "Evaline liked being Eliot's wife when he was a famous and influential public official. . . . She liked his prominence and power and fame." This was a common, catty misreading of Evaline at the time. She became outgoing when she drank, and she drank so she could keep it together when she found herself stuck in her husband's spotlight. Evaline remembered loving the attention at first, "because I felt like a star. But I hated it, too. It meant my having to make speeches to women's groups, appear before book clubs, hand out medals to Girl Scouts when they had jamborees — all those things that a public figure's wife is expected to do. I was no good at it." In fact, her experience as a public man's wife soon made her gun-shy, tetchy. This would harden into intransigence later in life, even though by then the spotlight had found her for her own accomplishments, not Eliot's. Ann Durell, who became her editor in the 1950s when Evaline took up writing and illustrating children's books, recalled that any kind of public appearance was "sheer torture" for her. For years Durell warded off librarians and event bookers, telling them: "She says the only kind of communicating that she can do is through her books!"

Evaline probably was an alcoholic before she met Eliot, and the new marriage didn't help. Their entire lives together revolved around drinking. Years later, she described her relationship with Eliot as "steamy" — but not in the good, sexually charged sense of the word. "She was an interesting, generous, creative person when she was sober," recalled Marni Greenberg, her step-granddaughter.

"And she was very unpleasant and confrontational when she was drunk."

Eliot, bumping up against the unpleasantness under Evaline's glossy surface, did his best to make her happy. Because he had his own struggles with black moods, he thought he understood her. Material possessions never meant much to him, but he thought they might keep his wife's busy brain occupied. He bought her a new car every year. And he moved them into a fortress-like, four-story boathouse in the swank Clifton Park Lagoon, the deepest mooring place on Lake Erie. Since they were right on the water, he also bought her a speedboat, which Evaline cranked up to its 35-mile-per-hour limit whenever she could. In the early years of their marriage, she would often zip over to East Ninth Street in the boat to pick up her husband after work and ferry him home.

Eliot loved that his wife was an artist. He encouraged her to submit her work to galleries and for competitions. He bought her a Mary Cassatt art book for Christmas, inscribing it, "To my wonderful and beautiful wife, the modern Mary Cassatt." Still, Evaline struggled with her confidence. She feared she had wasted her time at the Art Institute of Chicago, her alma mater, that she should have become a librarian or a teacher — or nothing at all. She had a breakthrough with a painting that was accepted in the May Show, a seminude, unofficial self-portrait called *Sunning*. (Evaline loved to lie out in the sun wearing as little as possible.) The work, with its long, blackened limbs stretched out across the canvas like a spider on its web, was by turns erotic, dreamy, and disturbing, depending on the viewer's frame of mind. The *Plain Dealer* listed *Sunning* among works in the show "worthy of special notice," but the painting failed to secure a prize and Evaline's momentum once again faltered. She had set up her easel in a small, glass-enclosed room in the boathouse that looked out at the lake, but day after day inspiration failed to come. "I floundered, all sense of direction lost," she wrote. "I despaired of ever becoming an artist."

A regular diet of drinking and dancing didn't help her artistic ambitions, but it did push her despair into the background for a while. She flirted brazenly with Eliot's colleagues, friends, city officials, waiters. At the Vogue Room and the Terrace Room, Evaline would take to the dance floor with anyone who would have her — which was everyone. She danced with a charming looseness, draping herself on her partner's hips and arms in her own embryonic version of dirty dancing. Eliot didn't seem to mind. "Eliot was a very social person who enjoyed partying with friends after work and also liked being married," remembered his aide, Arnold Sagalyn. Meaning, he put up with a lot. Eliot distracted himself from the more difficult aspects of his life with Evaline by redirecting his focus. He became a bit of a mother hen to Sagalyn, for one. Eliot had hired the gangly, moonfaced kid straight out of Oberlin College after Sagalyn had interviewed him for his senior paper, titled "Eliot Ness in Cleveland." It didn't matter that this well-brought-up Jewish boy from Springfield, Massachusetts, had no law-enforcement experience. Eliot saw something in him. And sure enough, the intelligent, imaginative Sagalyn proved to be a fast learner and exceptionally hardworking. So now Eliot worried over his unattached protégé, who often worked deep into the night with him. He began inviting him to parties at the boathouse. "I developed a warm personal relationship with both Eliot and Evaline," Sagalyn remembered. "I was a steady visitor at their evening gatherings, where I made myself useful making and serving drinks and hors d'oeuvres." He quickly learned that this entrée to the boss's personal life came with responsibilities. "Eliot was an extremely newsworthy public figure in Cleveland, and virtually anything he said or did was of interest and written about in the daily papers," Sagalyn recalled. That meant anyone with a close relationship with him took an oath of sorts. "I never talked about him, or in any other way revealed anything I heard or saw that might adversely affect or embarrass him," Sagalyn said. "I also made it a policy not to write anything about him or to describe in detail any of my own activities with anyone, including my family and friends." This could be a trial, because to young Arnold Sagalyn, Mr. and Mrs. Eliot Ness were the most fascinating, most sophisticated couple he had ever known.

They certainly knew how to have fun. Eliot's childlike giggle and Evaline's cannonball guffaw cut through the boathouse every Monday night, when they had a standing party at Clifton Park Lagoon. Evaline wasn't the only one busting a gut at every one of Eliot's witticisms. "He was a party man, a party man," remembered Corinne Lawson, his longtime housekeeper. "And all the women were just crazy about him."

Ultimately, the fun wasn't enough. Cracks began to appear in the marriage. Evaline may have been impressed by Eliot's low-key amiability, his desire to always remain in control and reasonable, but it also infuriated her. She needed the dramatic gesture: to be shaken or shouted down or boxed about the ears. *That* was passion. *That* was life. And so their marriage heaved and simmered. Sometimes, when Evaline was in one of her black moods,

Eliot would simply stay away from her — for days. That was easy enough. He made more time for a personal life now than he had during his marriage to Edna, but he still worked very long hours. And Evaline also worked, churning out advertising drawings for various local stores. She did her best work after dark, which meant Eliot sometimes found himself on his own whether he liked it or not. This was just as well, for Evaline couldn't manage even the most basic domestic tasks expected of a wife. One night, while trying to prepare dinner for a quiet evening with her husband, she knocked over a pot of boiling water while distracted. She ended up with nasty burns on her feet that required a trip to the doctor and an extended convalescence.

The kitchen accident could be seen as an omen. "Normal life" was simply beyond this unusual couple. Eliot had enjoyed success after success as safety director, and he had an alluring, intelligent wife, but a few close friends began to realize that something was deeply wrong. Eliot no longer fought his fatigue and stress by zoning out at home. He had reached the final, inevitable stage of mental burnout: recklessness. He began to slip away from work for long lunches that sometimes left him late for appointments. Evaline, unable to reach him in the middle of the day, suspected the worst. Years later she would tell a family member that he "screwed everything in a skirt." His wife's suspicions led Eliot to try to be more conscious of time. One day he blasted through a red light in his sedan, causing a pedestrian stepping into the street to jump back and scream at him in fury. Eliot pulled to the curb, climbed out of his car, and marched back to the man — perhaps to apologize, perhaps to give him the high hat. Whatever Eliot's aim, the man attacked him, sending the public safety director crashing to the pavement. This brought a policeman hustling to his aid, but Eliot refused to file a complaint or even give his name. He hurried away.

Even stranger than midday brawling, Eliot began playing unfunny practical jokes. He hired an actor to pretend to be a drug pusher at a restaurant where he was having a working lunch with Governor Martin Davey. He egged the actor on until the "drug pusher" got into a shoving match with a man at the bar, sending the governor fleeing out the back to avoid the press. "Eliot had pulled that stunt on a couple of other people, but doing it to the governor was going a little overboard," said Dan Moore, the state securities commissioner and Eliot's friend. Another time, having belatedly learned that Michael Harwood had secretly recorded one of the witnesses in his trial, Eliot bugged the boathouse before a party, carefully hiding microphones in every room. He couldn't help himself: technology fascinated him, and he probably wanted to know if Harwood's plan could have worked. "When the party was nearing the end, he told us what he had done, and he began to play back the recording," recalled Marion Kelly, a journalist and friend. "On it we heard women talking with other women's husbands. He managed to pick up quite a lot, and even though it stopped short of scandal, it wasn't a very nice thing to do. People were not amused."

Drink had begun to muddy Eliot's judgment, but the weird pranks he pulled weren't enough to keep partiers from putting the Nesses on their invitation lists. Eliot and Evaline's wit and bonhomie were too good. And there was always the thrill that came with knowing anything might happen. Evaline even led a skinny-dipping expedition in the lake one night after Eliot was called away on business. Just tossed her dress over her head and bounded into the water, leaving all the guests slack-jawed and wondering what to do. (The drunkest ones followed, of course.) The impromptu swim no doubt was a fuck-you to Eliot. He would frequently leave mid-party when a call came in — the call was "inevitable," remembered Viktor Schreckengost, who traveled the same party circuit. That meant if the Nesses were the hosts, Evaline would suddenly find herself running the show on her own. And if they were guests, she would have to bum a ride home from another partygoer. Making it worse, Eliot often took a lucky reveler — anyone who happened to be standing there when Eliot received the call — for the high-speed, siren-screaming ride to the crime scene, an experience the chosen one would relive at parties for weeks to come. Schreckengost went along once. So did another artist, Bill McVey, who had befriended Eliot. And Jo Chamberlin, the brother of Eliot's assistant. "If something was happening," remembered Chamberlin, "he'd say, 'We'd better go take a look,' and the next thing you know he'd be across town, and whoever happened to be with him went sailing along, too." Whoever happened to be with him except Evaline, that is. Eliot knew his wife liked excitement as much as anyone, and that she hated to be left out, but he never invited her along for the ride. It was still a man's world.

CHAPTER 29
CLEARING HOUSE

Captain Michael Blackwell picked up the scent each day outside Russo's Drug Store, or Bontempo's Confectionery, or sometimes Vince Dylinski's Trocadero Club. These were policy chieftain Frank Hoge's favorite hangouts.

Hoge and his bodyguard would alight sometime in the afternoon and clamber into one of his big touring sedans. Whether or not he had spotted Blackwell, Hoge acted as if he had a police tail. The sedan frequently and unexpectedly veered across lanes and jerked into turns. It would head west for miles before turning around and crossing the city again. The destination was always the same: the home of Miss Myrtle Taylor, the Hill gang's bookkeeper. They made sure that staking out Taylor wasn't easy. She kept moving to new digs.

Hoge, of course, always knew where she was. The car would pull up, the small, slim black woman would duck into the backseat, and the evasive maneuvers would begin again. At a prearranged spot, never the same as the day or the week before, they'd even switch to another car (or maybe not) and the two identical sedans would head in different directions.

If they knew Blackwell was behind them and they couldn't shake him, they'd drive in circles, maybe pick up some lunch, and then deposit Taylor back at home. If they thought they were in the clear, they'd blast past the city limits to meet up for the "clearing house" — the daily money count — with other members of the gambling racket. The gangsters always counted the "take" together and checked the books together, so everyone could keep an eye on one another.

The meeting always took place in the suburbs. They used to do it in the city, where the bulk of the business was, but Eliot's detectives — and especially Captain Blackwell — had made convenience impossible. The "home rule" policy that allowed casinos to thrive in the 'burbs also made it much safer for the stacks of cash the gang's gambling racket generated throughout the city.

The Mob had to be especially careful these days, ever since Lieutenant Ernest Molnar had been found out. For more than a year, Molnar had been in charge of finding the clearing-house meeting. He never managed to do so, even though he usually knew where it was. Eliot finally figured out what was going on. He had his investigators track Molnar, and they discovered the lieutenant was taking money from the two Angelos and running interference for them. It was a painful revelation for Eliot. Molnar had been his poster boy for the new Cleveland police; Eliot had promoted him and talked him up in the press for years. But nothing surprised the safety director anymore. He knew almost anyone could be corrupted. He called Molnar into his office and confronted him. The always ebullient lieutenant lost his smile. After some hemming and hawing, he admitted it. Eliot made him disgorge every penny that he knew the policeman had taken. Eliot turned over the $770 to Frank Cullitan, but he did not arrest Molnar. Cullitan didn't think they had the evidence. So like Barney Cloonan when the Prohibition Bureau had discovered his treachery, the lieutenant stayed on the payroll after being found out. He even prospered. Molnar's perfidy stayed between him, Eliot, the Unknowns, and Cullitan, and so an unsuspecting Chief Matowitz tapped him to head the vice bureau. Blackwell, another Ness protégé and an officer known for his honesty, took over the gambling investigation.

Within weeks, Blackwell and his men did what Molnar never officially could: they found the clearing-house meeting spot. It was in Frank Hoge's brother's house in Lynd-hurst. Soon it moved to a property in Warrenville Heights owned by businessman and "Mob goodwill ambassador" Abe Pickus. For a short time it landed at an industrial building in Independence Village. Like Myrtle Taylor, it now moved around a lot. One of Blackwell's raids on the clearing house, recalled McGill, "netted about a dozen numbers operators, thousands of number slips ranging from pennies to greenbacks, and about $25,000 in cash, the take for one day."

The police captain would have rather netted the books kept by Miss Taylor. That would make any trial a slam-dunk. But so far, Blackwell hadn't had any luck tracking down her life's work.

While the Mob sought a little peace and quiet out in the suburbs, Eliot made as much noise as he could at the county courthouse downtown. By early 1939, he had lined up the testimony of more than seventy policy operators for a grand jury Cullitan had empanelled. For two months he brought witnesses to a hotel suite to secretly meet with the county prosecutor. He made several copies of the notes and affidavits from these interviews, with each copy kept in a different place "to insure against theft." No one was surprised that it had taken two years to convince witnesses, by persuasion and coercion, to talk.

"That they 'talked' was almost incredible," the *Plain Dealer* marveled when the depth of the witness list became clear.

The fact was, many of the witnesses talked because they wanted to. When the Mayfield Road Mob took over the gambling racket, the gang's leaders had figured they were being smart by leaving veteran policy operators in place. Doing so eliminated the headaches and drudgery of running the games themselves. But now they realized that it also meant their business came into close contact with men who had no loyalty to the gang, men who were resentful and angry at their treatment. And unlike legitimate business owners paying protection, the policy operators often didn't have the assets, families, and roots in the community that made speaking out so dangerous. When Director Ness offered to relocate them and to pay living expenses until a trial, some eagerly ratted out their overlords.

The grand jury wasn't the only problem the Hill gang faced. The sustained crackdown — the raids, the arrests, the perpetual search for a safe haven for the clearing house — had made Cleveland's gambling syndicate vulnerable to competition. Sensing the Cleveland gang's weakness, the Pittsburgh Mob, long-time partners with the Mayfield Road outfit, decided to move into Cleveland themselves — before someone else did. The Pittsburgh gamblers arrived in town during the summer of 1938 and began offering significantly better odds than the Hill gang. They set up shop around Woodland Avenue and East Fifty-fifth Street, the heart of the black neighborhood where the games had first thrived. They specialized in the daily "bank clearing house" lottery, but there was no doubt about their plans to expand.

Cleveland's gangsters reacted like scorned lovers. They busted up furniture at the new gambling shops and ended various long-established business arrangements with the Pittsburgh Mob. When that didn't accomplish much, they fed threats to the newspapers in hopes of scaring the out-of-towners into seeing sense. "There'll be killings, if those Pittsburgh punks don't get out of town," one hoodlum told a *Cleveland News* reporter. Another told a hack: "There's going to be something done about those chiselers, and plenty soon. They'll be told to get out or be wiped out. I'm surprised there hasn't been any shooting yet, but perhaps there's nothing being done right now because the men who run the racket work smooth, just like the federal government."

In late April 1939, Eliot returned from an overnight trip to Florida and went straight from the airport to a downtown hotel, where Cullitan and others were poring over the policy-racket case files and plotting how best to proceed. Blackwell never had been able to get his hands on Miss Taylor's books, but the amount of evidence investigators had accumulated was overwhelming anyway. They all realized how close they were to the finish line. (Incredibly, the secretly disgraced Lieutenant Molnar took part in the meeting.) Eliot, arriving at the summit late, weighed in. It was time for them to make their move, he said. The meeting broke up with handshakes and backslapping all around.

On Wednesday, April 26, two years after Eliot had turned his attention from police corruption to the Mob, Cleveland's newspapers crashed banner headlines across their front pages, heralding a staggering blow to the Mayfield Road Mob. Wrote Clayton Fritchey in the *Press:*

> In the most sweeping assault on gang-dom in Cleveland's history, the County Grand Jury today returned extortion and blackmail indictments against 23 men named as key figures in the policy racket.
>
> The action resulted from months of secret and dangerous work on the part of Safety Director Eliot Ness and trusted associates and followed a parade, during the last four weeks, of 60 unnamed and closely guarded witnesses.
>
> The indictments struck at the heart of the

legendary Mayfield Road or "Hill" mob which for years, seemingly immune from detection or prosecution, has spread its web of blood, violence and terror through every phase of Cleveland's crime and rackets.

The list of the indicted included every major policy racketeer connected with the Cleveland Mob, including Angelo Lonardo, Angelo Scerria, Frank Hoge, Shondor Birns, Joe Artwell, and Albert (Chuck) Polizzi. The ambition of the indictments shocked observers: Eliot Ness and Frank Cullitan clearly wanted to wipe out almost the entire leadership of the gang that had dominated Cleveland for more than a decade.

Eliot believed that taking down the Hill gang would be his greatest legacy in the city, and a far greater accomplishment than his role in the Capone case. The press, accustomed to mayors and safety directors under the thumb of the city's mobsters, agreed. The *Plain Dealer* wrote that the "investigation . . . in years past could have existed only as a figment of the imagination." Men and women stopped Eliot on the street to shake his hand, sometimes with tears in their eyes. Finally, an honest man, they said. Finally, someone with the courage to do something about the murderous thugs who ran Cleveland.

The newspapers covered every possible

angle of the indictment. They revealed that Oscar Williams was the prosecution's key witness, forcing Eliot to hustle the numbers runner out of town. As it would turn out, Williams might have been safer in Cleveland. The city all but emptied of gangsters as soon as the indictments were revealed. (Many of them had taken off days before, most likely tipped off by Molnar.)

The police arrested six of the twenty-three indicted men within a day of the indictments' announcement. By the end of the week, they'd collared six more, including Hoge and Birns. But the arrests dried up after that. The biggest names — specifically, the two Angelos and Joe Artwell — remained at large as spring pushed into summer. Eliot, frustrated, asked for the FBI's assistance in the manhunt.

The weeks ahead saw a series of raids on suspected hideouts around the Cleveland metropolitan area, none of which turned up Lonardo, Scerria, or any of the other missing men. Eliot took it personally that so many mobsters had successfully lammed it. He devoted most of his days to the hunt. On May 15, planning to stake out a house after receiving a tip on Lonardo, he replaced his well-known personalized license plates with a set of plates from a car being held at the police yard. He hadn't gone far when Patrolman Joseph F. Prucha spotted him. Prucha was known around the department as "Camera Eye" because of his photographic memory, which he put to use memorizing the license plates of the department's constantly changing list of stolen cars. He pulled Eliot over, and when the safety director jumped out of the driver's seat and marched determinedly toward the patrolman, Prucha leveled a rifle.

Eliot, surprisingly calm with the barrel of an elephant gun pointed at him, identified himself. When the gun stayed where it was, he barked: "Officer, I am your boss."

Prucha wasn't buying it. This wouldn't be the first time someone he had pulled over claimed to be the famous safety director. "If you're Eliot Ness," Prucha replied, "I'm President Roosevelt."

Eliot carefully produced his ID and said that, with FDR's approval, he would like to be on his way. Prucha watched the peeved safety director drive off, certain he would be suspended or fired the next day. Instead, later in the week, the patrolman received a letter of commendation from the director's office.

Eliot wasn't monomaniacal about the gangster hunt. He continued to take the long view with crime, which meant putting precious resources into preventing kids from growing up to be gangsters. After the Tremont youth-gang campaign back in the fall of 1936, Eliot established a crime-prevention bureau that would focus on juvenile delinquency.

The new bureau, headed by Captain Arthur Roth, was unlike anything the Cleveland Police Department had ever tried before. Officers in the bureau undertook work typically associated with social workers. They conducted detailed surveys of neighborhood "assets": churches, clubs, playgrounds, swimming pools, and other facilities. They talked with parents, teachers, and community leaders, and became a familiar presence in schools. Eliot made it clear that, for smaller offenses, officers should keep kids out of the system. "No member of the Bureau is permitted to appear in uniform," he wrote. "Every effort is made to have the juvenile delinquent regard the members of the Bureau as sympathetic friends who are there to help them, rather than as cops. Juveniles are not brought into police stations or transported in official police vehicles. Their names are not entered upon the police records. This prevents delinquents from building up police records about which they may boast."

Eliot and a professor at Cuyahoga Community College developed techniques for interviewing juveniles. One recommendation indicated just how new this approach was for the police. Eliot felt he had to instruct officers to "be friendly." He added: "Many juveniles feel that the world is against them. Do not let your conduct further the development of an anti-social attitude in the child. Many juveniles are discouraged. They believe they are failures though they have not had time enough to develop. You wouldn't expect a half-completed airplane to fly. You can't expect an undeveloped child to function as an adult."

Being friendly, of course, was just a start. "Keep them off the street and keep them busy" became Eliot's mantra. He lobbied the mayor and the city council for help in making that happen. To many people, in and out of the police department, the crime-prevention effort smacked of coddling — maybe even communism. The police were supposed to respond when crimes happened and arrest the offenders. End of story. They shouldn't try to act like parents or priests. But Eliot remained undeterred. He believed, as Vollmer did, that the best way to make a community safer wasn't to fill up the jails but to provide positive, meaningful opportunities for those most likely to commit crimes. In short, to make better citizens. "Millions have been spent in efforts to cope with the problem of adult crime," he said in a speech. "I think the time is at hand when police officials, teachers and educators should join to prevent problem children from becoming criminals."

Slowly, he won over many of his critics. Despite facing severe budget problems, the city council found money to build baseball diamonds and basketball courts in the most depressed neighborhoods in the city. When Eliot's revamp of the police force left the department with a handful of abandoned precinct houses, the safety director convinced the city to turn them over to the privately funded Boys Town. Kids from the neighborhood ran the former police stations as clubs and activity centers, using a system of self-government provided by the safety department. The department paid for the utilities and provided a security guard at each building.

More significant still, the crime-prevention bureau followed through on Eliot's promise to the Tremont gangs by launching its own youth-employment agency. Establishing programs with some of the city's largest companies, the bureau placed more than five hundred boys in three years. It also worked with the federal Works Progress Administration to create and fund a vocational training curriculum, with some of the classes held at the former precinct houses. Next Eliot helped start up Boy Scout troops in the worst neighborhoods, with police officers and former gang leaders as Scout masters. Eliot became a troop leader himself. Having cops and former gang leaders as Scout masters, he said, "overcame any feeling that scouting was 'baby' stuff and gave the activity an additional attraction." The Scouts had given up on

462

Cleveland's inner-city neighborhoods years before, after youth gangs beat up many of their boys, often tearing the uniforms off their backs. Now there were waiting lists for troops.

The success was undeniable. In three years, juvenile crime in the city dropped by more than 60 percent. Mayor Burton became a true believer in what he called "the experimental field of crime prevention." He praised Eliot as the effort's "originator" and leading light in Cleveland. He even began to parrot his safety director's scientific-policing language. "For centuries, we have fought crime primarily by seeking to catch the criminal after the crime has been committed and then through his punishment to lead or drive him and others to good citizenship," the mayor said in his keynote address to the 1938 Rotary International Convention in San Francisco. "Today, the greater range of operation and greater number of criminals argue that we must deal with the floodwaters of crime as we now deal with the destructive flood of our great rivers. We must prevent the flood by study, control and diversion of the floodwaters at their respective sources. To do this we must direct the streams of growing boys in each community away from fields of crime to those of good citizenship."

Eliot couldn't have been surprised when, six months after privately calling out Lieutenant

Molnar on his collusion with the Mob, new allegations about the officer arose. A bar owner, Anthony Zappone, told the state liquor control board that Molnar had targeted him for harassment. The board wasn't investigating Molnar; it was determining whether to renew Zappone's liquor license after a pinball machine had been found in his bar. Pinball machines, along with all other forms of gambling, were illegal in Cleveland. Zappone brought up his dealings with Molnar as an indictment of the entire regulatory system in the city.

"For three and a half years I have been persecuted by Molnar because I refused to put him on my payroll," he testified before the liquor board. "He is supposed to be a great raider, but I can show you a hundred and five bookie joints that are operating and twenty-six 'vest pocket' slot machines in places where liquor is sold." He added: "There have been twenty-five or thirty convictions in Municipal Court for having pinball machines in cafes. Why is it that I am the only one of the proprietors who is called before the board because of a conviction? Molnar saw to it that I was called here. For years he has been trying to get me. His men come into my place and chase customers out. They come in after closing hours and try to get my bartenders to sell them liquor so they can get a charge that will put me out of business."

On June 6, with Zappone's charges appearing in all of the papers, Eliot ordered a departmental inquiry into Molnar. But the bar owner had used up all of his courage before the liquor control board. When police interviewed Zappone about the allegations, with Molnar present, he recanted his earlier testimony. He said he'd been misunderstood. The police department cleared Molnar of any wrongdoing.

Distracted, Eliot let it go. Less than a week after he ordered the official investigation into Molnar's conduct, police found Angelo Lonardo, arresting him at an apartment in suburban Shaker Heights. When detectives brought Lonardo into the county jail, Eliot was waiting for him. The safety director personally interrogated the numbers king, but nothing would come of it. Lonardo, lounging in an expensive green suit and two-toned shoes, insisted he didn't know the whereabouts of the remaining fugitives. Nine major players remained at large, including Little Angelo Scerria.

In July, with his key witnesses in hiding on the safety department dole but any potential trials on hold, Eliot opened another front in the policy war. He worked with police from the town of Bedford Township to arrest Myrtle Taylor, Frank Hoge (Frank was out on bail on the April charges), and Frank's brother, among others, on entirely new gambling charges. Fritchey, meanwhile, was still doing his part for both Eliot and the *Cleveland Press,* hectoring known gambling associates about the whereabouts of Scerria and the others. "Why doesn't the *Press* go after the legalized racketeers in Washington?" Abe Pickus asked him before slamming a door in his face.

Late in 1940, Michael Harwood walked out of the London Prison Farm near Columbus after serving two years and seven months. The other convicted former police officers would soon join him back in the free world. For Eliot, it must have been like seeing the ghost of Christmas past — the successes of his early years come back to taunt him. Such high-profile victories were increasingly difficult to come by.

After four years of thrills, Eliot had settled into a routine. Waiting for his policy fugitives to surface, he did his best to fill time with small-scale investigations. He arrested Howell Wright, a member of the Cleveland Library board, for extracting bribes from binderies that hoped to secure or hold onto the library's business. Wright was convicted and sentenced to two to twenty years. Eliot also went after the city's marijuana dealers, recruiting a young female high school teacher to work undercover for him. "She's real sharp, knows her way around," he enthused to McGill. He would net convictions of two large-scale pushers and guilty pleas from three other dealers who turned state's witness. The teacher wanted to keep working for Eliot, but Evaline, jealous of the woman, put the kibosh on that.

Early in 1940, Francis Sweeney had popped up again. He checked out of the Sandusky Soldiers' and Sailors' Home to visit an ailing niece in a Cleveland hospital. Cowles sent Merylo and Zalewski to interview him, to make sure Sweeney realized that the police knew his every move. This appears to be the first time the torso case's lead detectives had heard the name Francis Sweeney; Eliot had never shared the safety department's files on the doctor. "During our questioning, Dr. Sweeney was pacing the floor forward and back, as though he were dictating a business letter," Merylo wrote in his report. He added that he did not consider Sweeney a suspect in the torso murders; he believed the doctor was just one more kook. Eliot took the report as a sign of success. Merylo described Sweeney as "fat and soft," "delicate," and not "the type of person" who could overpower, kill, and dismember a man. To Eliot, the report proved that Sweeney had lost his murderous edge in the two years since the safety department had targeted him. The

Mad Butcher hadn't struck since 1938, and Clevelanders were beginning to forget about him. Eliot made sure Sweeney returned to the veterans' home in Sandusky and then put the case out of his mind, too. Soon, Chief Matowitz would take Merylo and Zalewski off the torso case and put them back in the regular homicide rotation. The torso murders were officially over.

Despite these successes, Eliot's inability to track down the remaining Mob fugitives weighed on him — and his reputation. The city council and the Civil Service Commission had become increasingly hostile to the safety department's budget, with its padded "common labor" expenditures for witness protection and the Unknowns. Eliot told his investigators they might have to find other jobs in the coming year. Considering this possibility, his assistant Bob Chamberlin began encouraging Eliot to go after a new job himself. The previous fall Mayor Burton had run for the U.S. Senate and, with Eliot's support in Cleveland, won a thumping victory. Before leaving office, he appointed the city's little-known law director, Edward Blythin, to finish out his term as mayor. Chamberlin told Eliot that the appointment was Burton's way of encouraging Eliot to run for the office in 1941. The Welsh-born Blythin's slurry accent and bookish personality made him ill-suited to being anything but a placeholder mayor.

Chamberlin believed that if Eliot declared himself a candidate early, the Republican machine would back him and the Democrats would essentially concede the race, offering up little more than token opposition. Another friend, municipal court judge and Democrat Frank Lausche, also urged him to run, insisting he would win in a walk. But Eliot waved away the suggestion. Evaline recalled it becoming a kind of game Eliot and Lausche played when they got together for drinks or dinner. "Eliot would tell Frank that he ought to run for mayor and Frank would insist that Eliot run. I never thought that Eliot was seriously interested in politics. He was not a political person." Jack Kennon, a longtime Cleveland reporter, believed politics bored the safety director. He considered Eliot a detective in temperament as well as training. "The constant excitement of his job is what keeps him there and is one chief reason the mayoralty post has no appeal for Ness," he wrote.

Unlike Eliot, Lausche was a political person. He'd become publicly known in the city by vocally supporting Eliot's gambling crackdown, signing off on warrants for many of the city's highest profile policy operators. When Eliot declined to run for mayor, Lausche jumped into the race, and he breezed to the Democratic nomination. Eliot was close with Lausche personally, but in the general election he felt duty-bound to support the Republican Blythin, who was his boss and represented the continuation of the Burton administration. When Lausche won and decided to keep Eliot in the safety director's job, it caused a major break between the new mayor and the head of the Cuyahoga County Democratic Party.

Eliot tried to stay out of it, and to lower his profile. He turned his attention to the fire department, asking for new firefighting equipment and funding for a training school. The proposal didn't go anywhere, because a month after the election, the Japanese bombed Pearl Harbor, slinging the United States into the Second World War. Within weeks, Chamberlin, Wilson, and Clothey — Eliot's closest friends in the safety department — headed for Washington, DC, or boot camp. Mayor Lausche was a friend, too, but Eliot recognized that the new mayor couldn't support him like Burton had. The city council finally brought the ax down on his budget, ending the era of the Unknowns. It was official: the fun was gone.

Chapter 30
L'Affaire Ness

At 4:45 on an icy March morning in 1942, Eliot and Evaline hurtled down Bulkley Boulevard, heading home after a long night of drinking at the Hotel Hollenden. The couple was laughing, with Evaline telling her husband about how she had "told off" a rude reporter, when the car began to slide. Eliot didn't realize what was happening at first. He pumped the brake, but it didn't do any good. The car crossed into the oncoming lane. Eliot shut his eyes against a sudden glare of light.

The impact slammed Evaline against the passenger-side door. Eliot cracked his face against the steering wheel, loosening his front teeth. He then spun into the door, his elbow cracking against the handle. When the car came to a rest, Eliot turned to find his wife slumped down in her seat, unconscious. He frantically shook her until she opened her eyes. She groggily insisted she was all right, that she just had the wind knocked out of her.

Eliot climbed out of the car to check on the other driver. Robert Sims, a twenty-one-year-old machinist at the Addressograph-Multigraph plant, appeared to be OK. His knee hurt, he said, that was all. He'd find out later the kneecap was broken.

Eliot told Sims to stay in the vehicle; he was going to move his own car off the road and then return. He eased the sedan down Bulkley a few hundred feet to an open area. He walked back to the crash site, where he found Sims's car on the side of the road, empty, the door hanging open. Another car appeared out of the early-morning gloom, inching along. The driver told him that a motorist had taken Sims to the Fairview Park Hospital. Eliot, wiping blood from his mouth, thanked the man and walked back to his auto. Evaline was still groggy — from drink or the accident, or both. She insisted on being taken home, not to the hospital. She then passed out again.

At the boathouse, after putting his wife to bed and cleaning himself up, Eliot called the hospital. A nurse told him Sims couldn't come to the phone — he was giving an accident report to the police. She handed the phone to Patrolman Joseph Koneval. The officer asked for the caller's name, but Eliot, not expecting to be talking to a policeman, panicked and refused to give it. Later in the day, Eliot called his traffic commissioner,

Martin Blecke, and gave an accident report over the phone.

The official report wouldn't be filed for more than two days, and when it finally was, it was incomplete. The statements of the drivers — and the name of one of them, Eliot — were missing from the record. The only tip-off that the accident involved an important person was the inclusion of Eliot's personalized license plate, EN-1. That was all a reporter from the *Press* needed. He caught up with Blecke and asked about the missing information. "If the report wasn't filled out correctly, I will call in the patrolman who made it," Blecke said. He disappeared into his office and closed the door.

The reporter could smell a big story. He kept digging, and the *Press* soon published a damning little expose on the "Ness Cover-Up." The story suggested that the accident report got "lost" on Blecke's desk, perhaps at Eliot's direction. The traffic commissioner admitted he'd had the report in his office for a day after talking to the director, "but I wasn't covering anyone then and I am not covering anyone now," he said. Eliot didn't do himself any good by keeping his head down and trying to brazen it out. "As for Director Ness' explanation of the unusual handling of the accident report," the paper wrote, "Ness said there was 'no mystery' about the report because it was 'always available.' "

Once the *Press* published its broadside, the story took on an unstoppable momentum. Radio stations and the city's other papers weighed in with righteous clucking about the behavior of the man who had done more than his share of righteous clucking over the past six years. Sims's father called reporters, declaring himself "dumbfounded" that on the day of the accident the police couldn't tell him who the other driver was. "I had to get in touch with the Cleveland Automobile Club to find who it was listed to," Ralph Sims said. The press's accusations about a cover up led to conspiracy theories, with some city hall insiders speculating that a very drunk Evaline, not Eliot, was driving the car.

Stung by the press reports and by everyone's apparent willingness to believe the worst, Eliot agreed to be interviewed by a reporter in his city hall office. He knew he had made a mistake by refusing to tell the officer at the hospital his name — and that his attempt to set things right by calling Blecke had only made the situation worse. As the reporter began the interview, Eliot sat at his desk, fidgeting, his eyes jumping about the room. He sighed, long and deep.

"It was very slippery and the thing just happened like *that,*" he said, snapping his fingers. "My first thought was for my wife, because I thought she was the most seriously injured.

She had had the wind knocked out of her. After she regained consciousness I got out of my car and went over to the other driver and told him who I was.

"I had told Mr. Sims that we would follow him to the hospital but Mrs. Ness said she was feeling better and would rather go home," he continued. "After I got home I immediately called the hospital and talked to someone. I didn't know who he was. The person at the other end of the wire asked who was talking and I said the other party. . . . I wanted to make sure that the injured man was all right, but I didn't identify myself. I said that I would have my insurance adjusters on the job in the morning. . . . At no time did he say he was a policeman."

Eliot gazed at the reporter for a long time, trying to gauge his sympathies. "I have never regretted anything more in my life," he said. "I felt I was discharging my duties to the others involved. Obviously, I was trying to avoid publicity."

The interview did not shut down the scandal. The battering in the press continued, the accident rehashed time and again in editorials and gossip columns. Newsmen and politicians who had long tired of Eliot's golden-boy image embraced the vicious stories. It wasn't until nearly a week later that the official police report reached the newspapers, where it was buried on the back pages. Written by Koneval's partner, Patrolman James Webster, and submitted before he knew the safety director was involved in the collision, the report declared:

The injured man [Sims] stated that after the collision the other driver stopped and came back to his auto and asked if he were injured, and assisted in every way to get him to the hospital and told him he would be taken care of.

In considering the fact that there was no liquor involved and that the injured man showed no desire to prosecute, and also the time of day and condition of the pavement, I did not think it was necessary to make any further investigation . . .

After a short meeting with Eliot, Mayor Lausche tried to put an end to what the *Press* was calling "L'Affaire Ness." "So far as I am concerned, it is a closed matter," the mayor told reporters. "If there was any delinquency about filing the report, Mr. Ness already has more than paid the penalty. If it were not for the position he occupies, the accident would not have commanded the attention it did and would have called only for a routine investigation."

Six days later, Eliot attempted to change the subject by announcing an updated plan for improving the fire department. This

476

included replacing a station house, building a maintenance facility, and purchasing two thirty-foot fireboats. It wasn't enough to turn the tide. Just as newspaper columnists were running out of ways to tweak Eliot over the car accident, news broke of four white teenage schoolgirls having sex with black nightclub entertainers, possibly with money exchanging hands. The newspaper story shocked the city. The scandal worsened when rumors circulated that one of the girls had also had sex with Cleveland police officers. Charges now flew that Eliot hadn't done anything to clean up prostitution during his long tenure as safety director, leading to a culture of promiscuity in many Cleveland neighborhoods. Prostitution was "just as deep and just as open as it was during the regime of Mayor Harry L. Davis," said Jane Hunter, a prominent African American activist in the city and founder of the social-service organization the Phillis Wheatley Association.

Mrs. Hunter was trying to keep blame from falling on the black community, but her accusation was true enough. Eliot had targeted brothels controlled by the Mob, but otherwise he'd paid little attention to lifestyle sex crimes such as fornication, sodomy, and bigamy. Eliot agreed with August Vollmer that sexual deviancy was an issue for social workers and doctors, not the police. A student of police history, he believed that a crackdown on vice for its own sake was doomed to fail in a big city and was a good way for a police department to get bogged down. He didn't want to make the same mistake Police Commissioner Theodore Roosevelt had made in New York and Police Chief Francis O'Neill had made in Chicago. Both of them had led unsuccessful vice campaigns that had damaged their careers. As a result, Eliot had ended up doing too little — and now it had come back on him. Underage white girls were being corrupted in the city — by Negroes, no less — and the safety director had done nothing about it. A new wave of condemnation washed through the newspapers.

Eliot read every word printed about him. He cut out and saved even the most damning and unfounded accusations. The way coverage of the teen-sex scandal focused on him, rather than on the men actually involved in the aberrant behavior, showed him that he had lost his moral authority in the city. He fell into a depression. As far as he was concerned, this latest brouhaha served as proof that the criticism he'd faced over the car accident had been deserved and probably had been a long time coming. He had always assumed he would suffer cosmic retribution for failing to live up to his own expectations; now it had arrived. He stopped going out to the nightclubs after work. He stopped taking meetings with anyone but his safety department staff. With Evaline working long hours on a Higbee's campaign every evening, he holed up at the boathouse, drinking alone and listening to recordings of Shakespeare's tragedies from his extensive record collection. He took long drives, too. He had always liked to drive — his high school yearbook had proclaimed him "an automobilist" — but it wasn't speed he was after but simply the feeling of motion, the illusion that he was going somewhere. When, after a few weeks, he finally surfaced from his self-imposed social and professional exile, he had made a decision: it was time to leave the best job he'd ever had.

CHAPTER 31
THIS IS WAR

Eliot wanted to do his bit for the war effort, just like everyone else. He'd been issued a national draft order number — 1359 — but he wouldn't be joining the army. He was about to turn forty. He instead decided to pursue the directorship of the Social Protection Division in the federal Office of Defense Health and Welfare Services (ODHWS), an opportunity he'd been mulling since it first came up in January. The division was charged with reducing the venereal-disease rate among military personnel, a mission that included working with police departments across the country to suppress prostitution near military bases and war-related industries. He had been volunteering with the agency part-time since September, making him an obvious candidate now that war had been declared and the operation needed a full-time leader. He believed that if he could land the job it would prove that criticism of his

Cleveland record on prostitution was misplaced.

Federal spending for military preparedness had reached nearly $75 million a day by the end of 1941, but the Social Protection Division remained strictly small-time, with a staff of just twenty-four. Still, the government sought out high-profile men for the directorship — including August Vollmer, former Chicago police superintendent (and Vollmer protégé) O. W. Wilson, Houston police chief Ray Ashworth, and former California assistant health director H. D. Chope. There was a good reason for this ambitious recruitment: managers at the Office of Defense Health and Welfare Services needed a dynamic leader in the Social Protection Division who could do a lot with a little — and fast. No one really wanted to talk about the venereal-disease problem in the military, but it couldn't be ignored. The service branches would reject more than sixty thousand of the first million men called in the draft because they showed symptoms of VD. Thousands more would miss training time or deployment because they had to undergo treatment. On top of that, the arsenic-based cure was lengthy, brutal, and no sure thing. (Newly developed penicillin was just making its way onto the market.) With the Nazis in almost total control of Europe and the Japanese sweeping across the Pacific, America's generals needed every man they could get. Congress underlined the seriousness of the problem by passing the May Act, which gave the federal government the power to take over the policing of towns or districts "deemed to be hazardous to the troops by the secretary of war or the secretary of Navy."

Eliot fought hard for the position. He argued passionately for complete repression of prostitution, dismissing the worries of some doctors (and some of the other candidates for the job) that this would lead to "the spread of illegitimate sex and disease among the better class of girls in the community." Eliot wanted to shut down red-light districts and launch an education campaign to encourage enthusiastic "amateurs" — "victory girls," "good-time Charlottes" — to rethink their behavior. He listed Lausche and Burton as references, as well as Illinois governor Dwight Green and former Unknown Frank Wilson, who had just joined the U.S. Secret Service. The hiring committee contacted his references, and then went in search of more. Arthur Miles, assistant regional coordinator of the Defense Housing Administration, wrote to the committee that "Mr. Ness is a very good man. . . . He is one of the best half-dozen legal administrators in the country. I certainly would rate him very close to [O. W.] Wilson. He would do very well, probably as well as Wilson." Cleveland Trust Company chairman Delo Mook offered an explanation for the one significant stain on Eliot's character: his divorce. "From the publicity and from various private information available to me," Mook wrote, "I form the opinion that the trouble in Mr. Ness's first marriage was due to character defects in the lady and not to any fault of his."

The hiring process showed that, though he may have been the biggest name in the country's sixth-largest city, Eliot remained small potatoes on the national stage. Wilson and Vollmer were stars in police circles everywhere; Eliot was still viewed as the smart-aleck kid who had hassled Al Capone. But Eliot's prospects brightened when the pursuit of his more eminent competitors ran into hurdles. The Public Administration Service's executive director David L. Robinson Jr. visited Vollmer in Chicago and concluded that "the old gentleman's health . . . would not permit him to undertake any kind of a full-time job." He also lamented the difficulty of luring Wilson into government service unless the veteran police chief could be assured that it would not affect his professorship at the University of California. As a result, the job seemed to come down to Eliot and Ashworth. In his official report on the hire, Robinson wrote:

Both Wilson and Ashworth are highly intelligent, broad in their concepts and interests, and possess a forceful, but pleasing, personality. I haven't the slightest question that either would be an excellent choice for the position of director of the division. I doubt if either would accept a position as assistant director.

Elliot [*sic*] Ness is earnest and sincere, has a good personality, and is reputed to have done a splendid job in Cleveland. He possibly has more "savoir faire" than either of the other two men, but not to any significant extent. He probably would be slightly less acceptable to police authorities through the country than would the others because he has been a civilian director of public safety rather than having come up through the military ranks in a police department. . . .

In summary, I am inclined to think that any one of the three would do a good job. If I were responsible for filling the position, I probably would offer it first to Ashworth, next to Wilson, if he could secure leave of absence [from the University of California], and next to Ness.

On Friday, April 10, the Bataan Death March began in the Philippines. In her nationally syndicated newspaper column that morning, Eleanor Roosevelt wrote, "The war news is bad today. Even though it has been hanging over us for weeks, so many of us had hoped that courage could dominate hunger and weariness and over-powering numbers." A couple of hours after reading the First Lady's grim report, Eliot received word that he had been chosen for "War Service appointment as Director of Social Protection P-8 $8,000 per annum." Somehow he had prevailed over Wilson and Ashworth. He would be hired as a temporary employee "for a period not to exceed the duration of the war and six months thereafter." Eliot exulted. He hugged Evaline and spun her around. She hadn't seen him so excited in months. The next morning, he called Mayor Lausche with the news.

Nearly two weeks later, on April 23, Eliot turned in his official resignation as safety director, to "fulfill my duty to the nation in the work to which I have been assigned in connection with this country's armed forces." He wrote that "it has been my privilege to have been allowed to work unhampered" as safety director. In a summary memo about his term, which he submitted with his resignation letter, he heralded the new professionalism of the police department, declaring — with some validity — that it had become a model for big cities across the country. "At the beginning of my tenure in office the police department was at a low ebb, morally and in efficiency," he wrote, adding that the police-corruption trials he spearheaded had served a valuable purpose. "The so-called purge which was undertaken at that time had three very good results. It raised the morale of the officers and men who had been doing an honest job and who resented the conduct of their dishonest superiors. It established the confidence of the public in the police department. And it revealed that the number of persons implicated in dishonest practices was a small percentage of the whole force."

Eliot did not meet with reporters or issue a public statement. After turning in his resignation, he drove home and stayed out of sight with Evaline. The newspapers did not take offense at the snub. After pillorying him for the past six weeks, all three daily papers rediscovered their admiration for Eliot now that he was headed out the door.

"Taking Mr. Ness's record as whole, including all the errors and omissions, we think he is the best safety director Cleveland has ever had, and we have no doubt that his term of office will gain increasing luster by future comparisons," the *Press* wrote.

Under the header "Six Eventful Years," the *Plain Dealer* wrote that "Burton never regretted [appointing Ness safety director]."

In fact, Ness became the star performer in the Burton cabinet and added greatly to the mayor's political strength.

In his six-year career under three mayors, Ness displayed personal courage, initiative and ingenuity. . . . The task of finding a successor to Ness will not be easy.

Clayton Fritchey, horrified at the way his paper had attacked Eliot over the car accident, weighed in as well with a stirring tribute to his friend's work.

Cleveland is a different place than it was when Eliot Ness became Safety Director. Ness restored a sense of hope and pride to a beleaguered community. Cleveland was in desperate need for a lawman with the talent and integrity of Eliot Ness. Today, policemen no longer have to tip their hats when they pass a gangster on the streets. Labor racketeers no longer parade down Euclid Avenue in limousines bearing placards deriding the public and law enforcement in general. Motorists have been taught and tamed into killing only about half as many people as they used to slaughter.

More personally meaningful to Eliot than even Fritchey's public accolade was the benediction of the man who had taken a chance on him when Eliot was just thirty-three years old. A week after he announced his resignation, Eliot received a letter from Senator Burton.

Dear Eliot:

Now that you are leaving Cleveland and taking up your full-time work in Washington, I wish to add a personal word of appreciation of the extraordinary public service which you rendered to Cleveland during the past six years.

When you accepted the appointment in 1936 [sic] as Director of Public Safety, under my administration as Mayor, you tackled the most difficult situation in the City Government. You more than met expectations and throughout the past six years, you have repeatedly moved into one field after another where you have cleared up a particular matter at hand.

The safety forces of a City are a key to its good government. Under your direction, these safety forces in Cleveland were changed from a bad to a good influence. . . .

Under your directorship, there grew up in the Department a high standard of integrity and of professional performance. I hope that you feel that the sustained effort which you put into this work has been worthwhile. It has contributed benefits not only to the City of Cleveland but to municipal government in general in this country.

The men and women who worked directly

with Eliot didn't need the press's reevaluation any more than Burton did. They had never wavered in their admiration of their boss. The secretaries in city hall appreciated his shy, low-key manner, which ran counter to the usual barking management style of safety directors. Some of them left work in tears on the day of his resignation. Eliot had also bonded particularly well with the young investigators and police officers assigned to the safety department. "Eliot was a great man to work with," Luther DeSantis, a detective in the department, said years later. "We all loved him and learned a great deal from him."

"Eliot was a wonderful guy to work for," recalled Arnold Sagalyn. "He was very affable, very bright and innovative. Cleveland was a corrupt city — a lot of officers taking bribes. There was no real training at that time for police officers. He changed that. In many ways, he modernized that police force. He made Cleveland a better place."

Eliot left one significant piece of unfinished business when he turned in his city hall credentials: the policy and clearing house case. But he never gave up on it, and neither had Cullitan. Three months after Eliot left Cleveland, many of the accused finally received their day in court. On July 3, kicking off a series of trials, ten men were convicted of extortion, including Angelo Lonardo and

489

Willie Richardson. Eliot sent the county prosecutor a congratulatory telex.

A surprise came a month later, when a jury acquitted Shondor Birns of extorting some $4,000 from the former policy operator Oscar Williams. Williams, who hadn't seen Birns in ten years, misidentified the defendant from the witness stand. He pointed to the wrong man after Birns and one of his attorneys surreptitiously switched places at the defendant's table. Birns and the lawyer wore identical suits, shirts, ties, and shoes. This kind of stunt was exactly why Eliot had always sat in the courtroom for trials. McGill, the prosecutor, derided the seat-switching trick as the "Notre Dame shift," but he couldn't help but feel it wouldn't have happened if Eliot had still been around.

Stepping out of the courthouse, Birns told a reporter he was "greatly relieved by the verdict. I've been carrying that charge over my head for more than three years and it sure feels good to be able to forget about it now." He eased into the backseat of a car and, with a wave and a smile, was gone.*

Birns wasn't the only gangster to escape justice. Angelo Scerria and a handful of other senior gang members remained fugitives. It

---

* Birns continued to ply his trade in Cleveland for another thirty years — until a car bomb killed him in 1975 at age seventy.

bothered Eliot that so many of the top men managed to evade capture, but in a sense this turned out to be even better for Cleveland. Those who went to trial and were convicted served a few years in the pen and then returned to the city's streets. The indicted mobsters who fled the area, however, were gone for good. A clutch of the fugitives settled in Las Vegas, where they took pieces of the Desert Inn and Stardust casinos. They found the money so good in the desert that they had no reason to ever go back home. Never again would organized crime hold the kind of power in Cleveland that it did in the 1920s and '30s.

The Mob had been so weakened, in fact, that a cop was able to step into the breach. With the gang in turmoil, Ernest Molnar took over Cleveland's numbers racket. He ran it for six years, until he was finally arrested in 1948. A police reporter who'd known Molnar for a decade was so shaken by the arrest he found himself unable to ask the lieutenant a coherent question. "Buck up, kid," Molnar said as he left Central Police Station after his booking. "It isn't the end of the world."

PART III
FALLING STAR

"With regard to women I never had any information or indication that Ness had an interest in women excepting his own wife." Some of Ness's former colleagues would spend years protecting his reputation.

Chapter 32
Girls, Girls, Girls

Evaline was miserable. Every morning she woke up with a silent scream in her head — *Let me out of this* — but there was nowhere to go.

She had no home. The boathouse, and Cleveland, had been abandoned after Eliot secured the wartime job. Their furniture sat in storage. They lived out of suitcases in a succession of hotels in Washington, DC. Eliot dived into his work, as always, but the car accident and its fallout still weighed on him like wet winter wool. He worried that the scandal, the shame of it, could resurface at any time and undermine his reputation among the military officers and police chiefs he had to work with every day. "I don't think he could stand criticism that well, especially when it came to his job," Evaline recalled. "That's why he tried to avoid publicity with the accident. It was just one of those things."

Just one of those things. That sounded like Eliot talking, not Evaline. She long before had stopped trying to match her husband's smiling, come-what-may shrugs in the face of adversity, his cool, detached reasonableness. She needed to scream, to get the blood pulsing through her veins like Niagara Falls. Every month or so she would embrace this need. She cried and broke plates and let herself be swept away by it all. It was *necessary.* By now she recognized that her husband could use a good scream, too. She believed that instead of letting his frustration out, he allowed it to eat him alive. It was his blindness to how trivial the car accident really was that had plopped him down in wartime Washington in a rinky-dink job. Eliot surely would have been in the running for any big-city police-chief position that opened up, but he had rushed to make his part-time VD gig a permanent one, lest he never receive another offer. When the Social Protection job didn't come to him quite as easily as it probably should have — O. W. Wilson seemed to have been everyone's first choice for the position — he no doubt saw it as confirmation that his career had gone into the deep freeze. On top of all that, he faced the terror of midlife's official arrival. He was now forty years old. He had suddenly aged out of his boy-wonder status, that cherished part of his identity that had set him apart from the crowd for years.

Despite his shaky confidence, Eliot still

refused to do anything in his professional life halfway. He hired Arnold Sagalyn as his information and reports specialist, and together they "designed a systematic, comprehensive program," Sagalyn wrote, "that made it virtually impossible for a prostitute to meet and pick up a serviceman; and if she did succeed, impossible to find and transport him to a hotel or a motel that would give them a room." Every serviceman diagnosed with VD had to fill out a form that helped the Social Protection Division track down how and where he had been infected. Eliot strong-armed alcohol distributors into discontinuing deliveries to bars where soldiers had met prostitutes, which led the bars to self-police the local sex trade in their establishments. A cab driver found to cart around "chippies" and their johns faced the forfeiture of his license or the cancellation of his gas-ration card. Sagalyn marveled at how Eliot attacked the military's venereal-disease problem the same way he had attacked Cleveland's corruption problem.

As he had done in Cleveland, Eliot created a corps of undercover investigators who would identify the active prostitution operations near Army, Navy and Air Force bases and urban installations, to provide the OSP [Office of Social Protection] with the names of the principals and individual prostitutes involved.

The undercover men would arrive in a town and insinuate themselves into the hotels, bars, and restaurants that served soldiers. They reported their findings directly to Eliot and made special note of whether police or mobsters played a role in the sex industry. The problem was, there were army bases and defense plants all over the country. His handful of new Unknowns couldn't investigate them all. Eliot had to rely on local sheriff and police departments to carry out his program, which meant he had to convince them of its importance. With his division's miniscule budget taken up by his investigators, Eliot decided to sell his anti-VD program himself in towns and cities across America. Even if he could have farmed it out to staffers, he really wouldn't have wanted to. He was determined that the effort not have "any suggestion of a moral crusade," and he didn't want to threaten anyone with invocation of the May Act unless absolutely necessary. He didn't trust anyone else to make the pitch.

Though he hit hard at businesses that allowed prostitution to thrive, he showed an unusually enlightened attitude toward the professional girls whose livelihood he was determined to stamp out. Sagalyn recalled Eliot being moved almost to tears by research that indicated the average prostitute had been abused by a parent or husband "and was often unable to read or write." Disturbed by the tendency of local authorities to blame the prostitutes themselves for their community's vice problem, Eliot pushed beyond the purview of the division's mission by creating an unofficial network of social workers and health officials. Girls found to be infected were detained and treated, but Eliot didn't want to incarcerate hundreds of women for the duration of the war. He wanted to give them better options. He hadn't focused on prostitution when he was safety director in Cleveland, but now he would try to save girls across the country from the sex industry. "Many of them have come from broken homes, deprived families," he wrote in a report justifying his efforts. "Often their education has been limited, and they have had no specialized job training. They have simply drifted from one poorly-paid, dead-end job to another, and — lacking both emotional and economic stability — have eventually taken the path of least resistance." He insisted that "sympathetic, trained case workers should be available in each town or vice district for personal interviewing of women arrested in enforcement of repression." Whenever possible, he sent prostitutes to Civilian Conservation Corps camps for vocational training.

Evaline sometimes went on the road with Eliot, "living in dreary hotels in towns near army bases where Eliot conferred with the mayors," she remembered. Eliot, the city boy, found he liked small-town America. He appreciated the easy, natural friendliness of the people, the no-nonsense, let's-roll-up-our-sleeves attitude to whatever problem they faced. These people weren't whiners, and they didn't put on airs. Better still, they liked him back. His reserved, unpretentious amiability allowed him to fit right in. "Eliot liked that job," Evaline said. "We'd go to all of those small towns and he'd advise them on how to get rid of their red-light districts. We met a lot of funny people in those towns, believe me." There can be little doubt about that. Not just anyone went down to the town hall to hear a man from Washington talk about sex diseases. Eliot would give his lecture, show some gross pictures, and then spend hours patiently answering questions from the kooks and the civic-minded alike. The actual useful conversations, with town councilors and the police on how to implement his program, took place before or after the public meetings. After each trip, he and Evaline would return to DC and try to find a hotel that had a room for them.

For Evaline, returning "home" was the worst part of Eliot's work. Wartime mobilization had obliterated almost every niggling vestige of the Great Depression; by the second year of the war the federal budget on its own exceeded the nation's total gross national product from just a decade before. Lingering high unemployment disappeared completely across the country. But the capital city boomed like nowhere else. The population of the metropolitan area had doubled since 1930 and continued to rise fast. And all the newcomers seemed to be women — eager single women, married women whose husbands were in Europe or the Pacific, and even teenage girls looking for adventure. Washington had become a modern-day Amazon nation. Women drove cabs, operated jackhammers, put out fires, asked "Which floor?" when you stepped into an elevator. Lured by splashy employment ads that ran in all the glossy national magazines, the women arrived day after day, heading directly from Union Station to a massive intake department that, working with very nongovernmental efficiency, parceled them out to federal agencies as quickly as the newcomers proved they could type.

The growth was so explosive and continuous that the women found there was no place for them to live. The city issued more than fifteen hundred building permits each month, and yet it seemed to barely put a dent in the housing shortage. Women would arrive on trains in the morning, and by the afternoon they'd be working at a government agency they hadn't known existed before they walked in the door. That night they'd sleep on the couch in the office's lobby. When they finally got a day off to look for a room, they had no way to get around. The city had spread outward so rapidly that you couldn't possibly walk from place to place. And stepping onto a bus was like falling into a black hole. Rush hour didn't exist; traffic was paralyzed almost around the clock.

This was the chaos to which Eliot and Evaline returned time and again. Coming out of the train station, they would store their luggage in a locker, and then Eliot would head to his office while Evaline began searching for a room. The government had forced the city's hotels to restrict bookings — after three consecutive nights, you were out on the street — to help ease the jam-up. But a room seeker had no way to know which hotels would have availability on a given day or how many people were seeking to claim the available spots. Evaline usually ended up sitting on park benches for hours, grinding her teeth as she waited for a room to open up. She hated the waiting, hated the uncertainty of it. It made her even angrier when she learned that many well-to-do "dollar-a-year" men working in the federal bureaucracy stayed on in suites for months at a time by slipping the room clerk a little something extra every week, or, better yet, by having a congressman friend call the hotel's manager. Eliot wasn't willing to do either, not even for Christmas week. Frustration would build up until Evaline could barely stand to be in her own skin. "I would have said 'War is Hell!' if General Sherman hadn't already said it," she joked years later about this period, long after the anger — but not the memory of it — had burned off.

Waiting for hotel rooms wasn't her only source of frustration. She felt "useless." She had no place to paint, no commercial assignments to work on, nothing to do but play secretary for Eliot on his trips to military bases. The war effort, visible everywhere around her, made her feel guilty and selfish. Women rushed past her on the street every day, on their way to important jobs. Every woman in the capital seemed to be in uniform. It was a sign of the new feminism. "The uniform," wrote *Vogue,* "stands for our spine of purpose . . . it is time to stop all the useless little gestures, to stop being the Little Woman and be women." That sounded good to Evaline. The outbreak of war gave focus and meaning to her interminable, opaque longing to belong. She finally decided to join the American Women's Voluntary Services, which was on its way to becoming the largest wartime women's service organization in the country. One of the reasons for its success:

volunteers had eight attractive uniforms to choose from. The AWVS girl was immediately identifiable, a wartime trendsetter. Evaline cut her hair short and classically, "up off the neck," as directed, and got to work. "I paid for a snappy navy-blue uniform with brass buttons and a hat to match," she remembered. "I volunteered our car and gas rations and drove admirals, generals and lesser brass here and there, waited for them, and drove them back again."

Eliot was supportive — at first. He liked that his wife had become involved in the war effort — he thought it only right — but he also knew that all was not well in their marriage. When he realized she was spending her evenings escorting self-important officers to cocktail parties and that she wouldn't be going with him on trips anymore, he told her to quit. Evaline did not like being told what to do, but she also couldn't have been surprised by the demand. No doubt she flirted with her admirals and generals and lesser brass. She couldn't help herself. Her sex appeal was important to her; it always would be. She insisted to Eliot that she usually waited out in the car during the soirees, but that could have given him only more reason to worry. His wife was unhappy and lonely, and with the lodging shortage in DC, the automobile had become the favored trysting spot not just for teenagers but for everyone. He put his foot down. She would have to find another way to occupy herself.

"Go to art school," he told her, a knee-jerk response. "If Renoir could paint through *two* wars, you are allowed to paint through *one*."[*]

"Some comparison — Renoir and me . . . me and Renoir," Evaline thought. But she did it. She had recently stumbled upon the Corcoran School of Art "tucked between the exhibition rooms" of the Corcoran Gallery. It was a small operation, with just five artists on the faculty, nothing at all like her ambitious, wide-ranging alma mater, the Art Institute of Chicago. And that was just fine with her. It seemed like a comfortable little school, almost like it needed her. In October 1943, she put down $35 to enroll in unlimited "Day Life" classes and another $2 for locker number 256 to store her equipment. Just like that, she was a student again.

Going back to school turned out to be exactly what she needed.

"As I climbed the steps to my first class," Evaline recalled later, "I couldn't have guessed what lay ahead: that day the walls of Jericho came down . . . the Red Sea

[*] Eliot was spot-on with his art history. Renoir sat out the Franco-Prussian War in his late twenties and, shortly before his death at seventy-eight, he painted through World War I, too.

parted . . . manna fell from Heaven! All because I met the right teacher at the right time."

The teacher was Richard Lahey, a romantic, white-haired Irishman who had made the unlikely transition from newspaper cartoonist to respected painter and art instructor. The fifty-year-old Lahey was having a bad war. All of his best students had joined the military, leaving him with dotty old ladies and one untalented hunchback the army wouldn't take. So he quickly homed in on Evaline. Her work was uncertain, but it also showed great promise — and just enough maturity to make her passion for art useful. He hovered behind her during class, watching her strokes, her decision-making. He kept her after class for one-on-one discussions and pep talks. The attention quickly paid off. "My painting flourished because he urged me to experiment," she recalled. "With his sensitive perception, he led me to express feelings that I never knew I had."

Evaline believed she was finally becoming a real and true artist. "It was here that everything gelled for me," she said of her work at Corcoran. She spent night after night lost in her painting. It provided a "peace and enjoyment" she hadn't been able to find through any other activity, not even drinking. At the end of the term, she won the school's highest award for painting — which came with a $50 prize — in a competition open to students and faculty alike.

Eliot had always encouraged his wife's artistic ambitions, but he couldn't take this new Evaline. His wife had changed, suddenly and dramatically. "He said I was no longer the woman he married," she recalled. Eliot thought she'd become "dull." For the first time in Evaline's adult life, that word might actually have applied. Creating art had become her only interest. She had to create, and she did so constantly, in every kind of medium. Her main focus was painting, but she also worked in woodcutting, lithography, etching. She found the physicality involved with woodcutting perfect for taking out her frustrations. She loved the "infinite possibilities for making texture in wood by pounding, gluing, scratching. Nails, screws, paper clips, wire mesh, or anything else which will make a dent are for pounding."

Through Lahey's guidance Evaline began to focus anew on the human form. She had learned years before at the Art Institute of Chicago that any decent artist could master technique. "It was adding part of yourself to your work that made the difference." That was where she'd always come up blank. That was what had kept her work no more than adequate, solidly competent but uninspired. Now that elusive inspiration had arrived. She realized she must create for herself, and only for herself, not for anyone else's approval.

The turning point came in a life-drawing course. On the first day of the spring term, a young woman entered the classroom, carefully disrobed, and stood before the artists. This was nothing unusual. Even some of the school's students earned cigarette money by posing in the nude for classes. But something about this woman was different. Evaline stared at her dark hair, her heavy breasts, her long legs and big feet. She felt herself blushing. The woman, so comfortable with her body, with her nakedness, fascinated her. No, it was more than that. Evaline was "extremely attracted to her."

She tried hard to reproduce the woman on her sketchpad, but it didn't work. She threw page after page to the floor. Her newfound confidence as an artist couldn't help her with this assignment; there was no way art could satisfy the artist. At the end of class one day she approached the model. The woman never ducked into an empty room to change. She brought her clothes in a bag, and as the students filed out, she stood in a corner, adjusting her slip, hiking up her dress. She turned and smiled at Evaline.

"In order to have that beauty I saw in her, I had to have her," Evaline would tell a friend years later. "So I left Eliot to be with her."

■ ■ ■ ■

The Allies were slowly making up ground in Europe and the Pacific, but for Eliot, the good news in the papers didn't penetrate. He had begun to slip into depression again. A friend from Cleveland, in Washington on business, was shocked at the former safety director's appearance. The discipline of Eliot's face — so stark and intense early in his career — had broken down. He looked old and bloated and worn out.

He was hardly alone. Heavy drinking had become epidemic in the District of Columbia. The Allies may have gained some momentum, but it was still a cataclysmic world war, with no end in sight. After the disaster of Prohibition and the economic catastrophe that swallowed the 1930s, you couldn't help but see a world falling apart forever. Millions of people had been hollowed out by the Depression; many would never emotionally recover from it. The world war, the second in twenty years, would exact an even greater toll. Eliot followed the crowd to the bar every evening to try to forget it all. He began to black out, and wake up at the office the next morning in a rumpled suit.

Careening headlong into middle age, professionally adrift, he needed his wife as never before — but it was too late. Evaline got up

509

one morning when Eliot was out of town and slipped on trousers and her favorite blouse. She put her champagne bucket and mink coat in their Cadillac, left everything else, and pointed the car north. Her new lover had decided to move to New England, and Evaline decided to follow her. The odd items she chose to take with her suggest she was not acting entirely rationally, but, out on the open road, she felt a weight lift off of her. She didn't tell Eliot she was leaving. It would be days before he realized she wasn't coming back.

In October 1945, nearly a year after Evaline had taken her bucket and left, Eliot quietly returned to Cleveland and filed for divorce, citing "gross neglect and extreme cruelty." The legal proceedings must have mortified him. In court documents, he said he was seeking a divorce because his wife "refused to live with her husband here because she wanted to study art in Maine under the tutelage of a Cleveland artist." Worse, he was forced to testify that he'd been cuckolded, that there was "another person" in Evaline's life. Eliot left town straight from the courthouse.

Reporters rushed to the county clerk's office when word of the divorce petition reached the city's newsrooms. Three years after he had left the safety director's office and Cleveland, Eliot Ness continued to be newsworthy — especially if it involved scandal. The hacks verified that the $11 fee had been paid, but they found no paperwork for the divorce. Eliot still had friends in the county bureaucracy. An almighty roar went up, the outraged cry of a frustrated reportorial herd on deadline. The reporters cornered County Clerk Leonard Fuerst and demanded to know where the petition was. "As far as we're concerned, it was filed properly and indexed," he said.

"Where is it, then?" a reporter demanded.

"Isn't it in the files?" he responded defensively — or evasively. "Nothing is ever hidden from anybody."

In their next editions, the newspapers tried to raise a stink about the "concealment" of court papers. "The mystery of Eliot Ness's missing divorce petition apparently will remain a mystery at Lakeside Avenue Courthouse," the *Plain Dealer* grumbled. "No official wants to ask questions or hunt for it."

This left a very public information void. No one had any idea what had gone wrong with the city's one-time golden couple. Their Cleveland friends had thought they were happy together. They recalled that Eliot always called Evaline "Doll" and gazed lovingly at her, and that Evaline's barking laugh resounded with every quip he offered up. She'd sketched sweet domestic portraits of her husband that showed him lounging around their home, attractively lost in thought. Even Sagalyn, witness to the marriage in Washington, believed they had "a good and close relationship." He thought they were the perfect couple. "It was a mystery to me why they broke up," he said.

Of course, there had been hints for those paying close attention. Eliot's friend Marjorie Mutersbaugh remembered Evaline as "a kind woman, gregarious and fun. She loved Eliot for who he was, but it always seemed more like they were best friends or buddies than husband and wife." And then there was the leggy blond woman at Evaline's side for several months in 1940 and '41. Evaline introduced the blond as her bodyguard, though she never said why she needed a private protector — especially when Eliot had the whole police department at his command. The woman claimed to be married — to a dwarf who lived in Florida. No one knew whether she was joking. One night, Eliot invited "a seven-foot-tall woman" to one of their Monday night parties at the boathouse, a silly (or petulant) jab at his wife's close companion.

But lesbianism was too far "out there" for it to cross anyone's mind as a possibility. Homosexuality was a taboo subject. It didn't exist in polite society. And besides, there was a better explanation for the marriage's demise. Rumors of Eliot's womanizing had first come up in Cleveland when he and Edna separated and he began going over to the big hotels after work to drink and dance. Now, even though he'd left public office in the city, the local press felt duty-bound to write about his partying ways. "His social habits, which included living in a Lakewood boathouse and entertaining in a most sophisticated manner, had tongues wagging most of the time," wrote the *Plain Dealer*'s Bud Silverman. The *News* reported that he'd had an unusually close relationship with one of his secretaries at city hall.

His friends would defend him against such rumors for years — even long after his death. In 1973, Neil McGill, at ninety, reacted in outrage to a proposed article about Eliot that claimed "drink and women were his downfall." In a private letter to *Cleveland Press* editor Thomas L. Boardman, he wrote that he had worked closely with Eliot for years and wished "to assert without equivocation, mental reservation or any doubt in my mind that nothing could be further from the truth." He added: "I can say from personal knowledge and observation that Eliot Ness was not a heavy drinker or a moderate drinker. The fact is that Ness was a light drinker. With regard to women I never had any information or indication that Ness had an interest in women excepting his own wife. It is unfortunate that so many years after his death anyone would undertake to assassinate the fine character of Eliot Ness even for profit." More than three decades after that rousing defense, Arnold Sagalyn, at ninety-four, insisted Eliot didn't have the time — and was too well known — to mess around with women while he was safety director. "Where could he go with a woman?" he said. "Everyone recognized him. And I always knew where he was."

That line of reasoning might have held up during Eliot's tenure in Cleveland, but of course the war years were a different matter. As the Social Protection director he traveled to dozens of cities and towns, usually without Evaline. He would later boast that he was "attached to the Canadian army in 1944 and visited every province in Canada." He had the opportunity to stray like he never had before, meeting anxious war brides and bored waitresses across the land. His friend Marion Kelly recalled that "Eliot had a tremendous line" — and there had never been a better time for a tremendous line. Illicit romance had suddenly become socially acceptable. People didn't come right out and say that, but everyone understood. It was the price of winning the war. "The entire female population was for an odd slip of time effectively single," pointed out the journalist Betsy Israel. "No one knew if their fiancés, boyfriends, lovers would ever return."

Eliot believed his own official warnings about the risks of promiscuity, but he was hardly a prude. He read the work of the radical psychoanalyst Wilhelm Reich, coiner of the phrase "sexual revolution," in an effort to understand the arguments against complete suppression of prostitution. Reich, who studied under Sigmund Freud, believed that eye-popping orgasms were the best path to physical and emotional wellbeing. He also believed prostitution should be legal — indeed, that it should be encouraged, socially legitimized. Healthy, thoughtful sex should take the place of shameful sex or no sex. "Reich shared the moralist's distaste for the kind of sexuality that flourished in brothels," wrote the critic and essayist Kenneth Tynan. "He distinguished between primary drives, which were natural and wholly benevolent, and unnatural or secondary drives, which came into being when primary drives were frustrated." Reich believed that urges like sadism or masochism "were not biologically innate in man, as Freud was tending to believe; instead they were caused by the repression of basic desires that were inherently life-enhancing."[*]

[*] Reich would eventually spin out of control, inventing an "orgone energy accumulator" — essentially an orgasm machine — that was supposed to jack up the universe's good vibes and thus increase "orgas-

For Eliot, as with so many other people, alcohol piqued those inherently life-enhancing desires. And he was drinking more and more during the war years. A snapshot from this period finds Eliot in a dark bar, gazing into the mists, eyelids closing like sodden umbrellas. Leaning toward him but looking warily at the camera is a woman who is not his wife. She sports a smart hat and an authoritative half profile. Her hand is extended on the table, reaching for Eliot's hand — or maybe she's reaching for her drink. Eliot would realize that he looked a bit out of it in the photo. He scribbled on it, "The flash light got me!! It was 10:30 a.m. and the first drink — and that's my story."

---

tic potency." He would be put on trial for fraud in the 1950s.

CHAPTER 33
STARTING OVER

When the war began to wind down, Eliot decided to return to Cleveland. He was starting over and determined to set aside his law-enforcement career and remake himself into a businessman. His wartime work had been low profile but successful. He had closed down more than seven hundred red-light districts and sent hundreds of prostitutes to training camps to learn vocational skills. When he took over the Social Protection Division, prostitutes were responsible for 75 percent of soldiers' venereal-disease infections. Two years later, that infection rate had dropped to 20 percent, leading the director of Community War Services, Mark A. McCloskey, to tell him: "You had one of wartime's tough jobs. You have done it well." But Eliot knew all along it was a wartime job only, not a career. And by this point he wanted to make some real money, build up a nest egg for his old age. So when an opportunity arose at the Diebold Company — he'd been acquainted with the controlling Rex family for years — he jumped at it. He would be chairman of the board of the Canton, Ohio–based safe maker. Never one to do anything halfway, he also picked up a job on the side, becoming vice president of the Middle East Company, a new, small-time import-export business based in Cleveland. He submitted his resignation to McCloskey two months after D-Day.

Eliot's old crowd in Cleveland wasn't surprised when he returned to town with an impressive new career in the private sector. Everyone had figured he'd end up in an executive suite sooner or later. They were surprised, however, that he brought with him an impressive new wife. As the newspapers made all too clear, this third marriage for Eliot came soon after his second divorce — very soon. Eliot was granted a divorce from Evaline on November 17, 1945. Two months later, he married Elisabeth Andersen Seaver. Neither Betty nor Eliot ever revealed when exactly their relationship started, but it undoubtedly became serious sometime during the latter stages of the war, when they were both living in Washington. (Betty's husband, Hugh, had a wartime job in the capital, while she made camouflage at a factory thirty miles away in Baltimore.) The marriage may have surprised their friends but it had been a long time coming. After catching sight of him from her perch above the grounds of the Great Lakes Exposition in 1936, the young sculptor had decided she wanted to meet Cleveland's dashing safety director, and so a few weeks later she staged an introduction — without their respective spouses in attendance — through New Deal bureaucrat Dan Moore and his artist wife. Eliot turned out to be even more interesting than she expected. She found herself drawn to his "delightful, off-beat sense of humor." He wasn't anything like his reputation as an intense, steely-eyed crime-buster. "He laughed easily and a lot," she recalled of that first meeting. He didn't talk much about his "old adventures" in Chicago, but when they did come up, Betty said, "his stories were very funny, and usually on himself." She would admit years later that she fell for him immediately.

By the time they married, nearly a decade later, Eliot wasn't dashing anymore — age and booze had softened his face into a lumpy pillow — but he was sweet and kind, and that was exactly what she needed. Marjorie Mutersbaugh called them "so congenial." Years later Betty told her she had never been so happy in her life as when she was married to Eliot.

Hugh and Betty's divorce became final on January 10, 1946, two weeks before she and Eliot married. Upon returning to Cleveland, however, Betty told friends there had been no romance between her and Eliot until both of their marriages had officially ended. Being seen as a respectable woman meant a lot to her. Betty had left Hugh in August 1943, but she couldn't bring herself to file for divorce. She feared her parents' opinion of her. Hugh eventually filed himself, citing abandonment, "gross neglect of duty, and extreme cruelty." (He filed the petition on November 15, 1945, two days before Eliot and Evaline's divorce was granted.) There were whispers that Hugh, known for his temper, had banged Betty around some, but they were only rumors. Something someone heard from somebody. Such a harsh charge never could be traced back to Betty. Members of Cleveland's art and social scene circulated the story because, well, there had to be a reason. People didn't get divorced simply because they had drifted apart or squabbled a lot.

It wasn't just Betty's respectability that appealed to Eliot. At thirty-nine years old, she was beautiful in the kind of natural, unadulterated way Evaline never could be. She had been a beautiful child, with a perfect round face and large, heartbreaking eyes, and she never grew out of it. Even more remarkable was how little her striking good looks seemed to mean to her. She had a boyish, practical stride, artless compared to Evaline's, but seductive, too, the willful amateurishness of it. She pulled her hair back into a bun even for formal occasions. Betty, not Evaline, was born to be a model, but doing such a thing never crossed her mind when she was growing up in Sioux Falls, South Dakota. She fished. She hunted with her daddy. She wore overalls around the house and didn't mind getting plaster in her hair and clothes when she worked in the high school's art studio.

This ingrained lack of affect faced a challenge once she moved to the big city to attend the Cleveland School of Art. Her tiny frame and pixie smile caught the Jazz Age zeitgeist, and she soon came across people who nudged — or shoved — her in a new direction. Not long after Betty landed in Cleveland, the city's foremost art photographer, Clifford Norton, convinced her to pose. The eighteen-year-old immediately became his favorite subject. Teachers and students at the school asked her to pose for them, too, and she always obliged. She had been taught never to be rude.

All of this attention inevitably led to an evolution in her look. She chopped her unruly long hair into a pageboy. She squeezed into form-fitting dresses provided by her photographer patron. Men did double takes in the street. The more ambitious mugs reversed course midstride and chased her down.

That she had transformed herself wouldn't

have been a surprise to anyone who knew her back in South Dakota. She had always loved to create, to make something new and alive out of whatever she had at hand — blank pieces of paper or lumps of clay or herself. Her father, somewhat befuddled by his daughter's talent, agreed to send his little Betty Lee away to school because he didn't know what else to do with her. She had too much ambition to marry a farmer and settle down in Sioux Falls. In 1924, he prevailed upon J. A. Derome, an esteemed local clergyman and newspaper editor, to write a letter of recommendation for Betty to the Cleveland School of Art. Derome wrote, "Miss Andersen is peculiarly gifted along the lines of art, especially in sculpture. I have no doubt she has before her a brilliant future as an artist."

The Reverend Derome's words would soon appear prophetic. Betty was an excellent student in Cleveland, and she made a splash right out of art school. She won first-place awards time and again at the May Show. Her winning piece for the 1932 show sold for a jaw-dropping $1,500. Later that year, New York's Metropolitan Opera Company hired her to produce a statuette of its premiere danseuse, Rita De Leporte. Four years later, she landed the sculpture commission for the Great Lakes Exposition. By then she was one half of a celebrated artistic couple, having married Hugh Seaver, a well-known watercolorist. But in the teeth of the Great Depression, success proved difficult to maintain. Despite continued raves for their work, commissions dried up for the Seavers; their paintings and sculptures sold at galleries for less and less — and then not at all. Betty followed her husband to Minneapolis, then to Michigan (where she studied under the great sculptor Carl Milles at the Cranbrook Academy of Art). The wanderlust was for naught: Hugh couldn't find a secure teaching position anywhere, nor could Betty get her career momentum back. Finally, the couple returned to Cleveland, where their struggles continued. Childless, with their careers floundering, the marriage started to fall apart.

The couple ended up on the city's relief rolls, until Betty landed a job with the Works Progress Administration's ceramics project, headed by the artist Edris Eckhardt, with whom she'd once worked at the now-defunct Cowan Pottery. Betty considered herself lucky to be earning $109 a month making art for public schools and government buildings, but the WPA proved to be a contentious place to work. Extreme dysfunction and internecine battles — Eckhardt faced near-constant threats of sit-down strikes from her artists — soured Betty on continuing her career. By the time war broke out and she and Hugh moved to Washington, she wanted nothing more than to be a wife and a mother.

Now, with a new husband and both the Depression and the war in the past, Betty would get her wish. In January 1947, a year after she and Eliot married, the couple adopted a baby boy. They named him Robert. Eliot had wanted to be a father for years, and now finally he felt like he had the time for it. Just days after he and Betty brought Robert home, Eliot received a jolt from his morning paper. His long-ago nemesis, Al Capone, had died of a heart attack at his estate in Florida. The former gangster, released from prison in 1939 and suffering from advanced syphilis, was forty-eight years old.

CHAPTER 34
NESS IS NECESSARY

Eliot tried to make the best of a bad situation.

He hired a band to sit in an open car and bang out jaunty tunes as the car rolled slowly down the street. Behind the band came a shiny new automobile with Eliot's picture stuck on every available surface. A local radio personality, George Kilbride, rode in a truck with a large megaphone strapped to the top. He called himself the "Voice of Tomorrow." Next came another open car, this one with Eliot and Betty in the backseat.

Tony LaBranche, a former boxer and a longtime handball and tennis buddy of Eliot's, was the operation's ringleader. Ten years earlier, a drunk LaBranche had invoked Eliot's name at a police station to avoid spending the night in jail after a car accident, sparking the first bad press of Eliot's Cleveland tenure. He now had a way to make up for it. He chose the neighborhood and cleared traffic each time they conducted their small parade. He seeded the route with supporters to assure waving and cheering when Eliot and Betty rolled by. Behind Eliot and Betty's car came the "beauty squad" — three attractive young women with big smiles and even bigger brassieres, assuring still more waving and cheering.

"This is the Eliot Ness caravan," the Voice of Tomorrow boomed from the megaphone. "In the car immediately behind the sound truck are Eliot Ness, candidate for mayor of Cleveland, and Mrs. Ness. They are going today to discuss Cleveland problems with Cleveland people."

The Diebold Company chairman and new father had decided, against all sensible advice, to run for mayor against a popular incumbent. And he was doing it in his own way. *The Plain Dealer*'s Bud Silverman heralded the mini-parades as an idea that had "revolutionized major political campaigning in Cleveland. This is the caravan about which thousands of citizens are talking with such enthusiasm that some professional campaigners here already sense the end of the venerable ward meeting as a forum of candidacy."

It certainly was something different. Eliot was the featured attraction, of course, but Silverman pointed out that Kilbride almost always stole the show, expertly riffing on the campaign's themes and the sights and sounds of the neighborhood around him.

Is that group of persons waiting for a streetcar?

"Eliot Ness has a plan for a transportation system that works, not jerks," comes the voice.

See those children playing tag around their mothers on the crowded sidewalk?

"Cleveland needs playgrounds. For action now, Ness is necessary."

The caravan halts at an important intersection. The band busts loose again. Out of the cars spill the occupants. The beauty squad, armed with Ness literature and buttons, disappears into the side streets for door-to-door visitations.

The campaign's managers worried about one of the beauty squad members — willowy, brown-eyed Winifred Higgins. The concern was well placed. The thirty-two-year-old Higgins had been Eliot's secretary at the Social Protection Division, where the two developed a close bond. After the war she divorced her husband and followed Eliot to Cleveland. On business trips, Eliot wrote to "Winnie Darling" — ostensibly the letter would be about his itinerary and hotel arrangements but somehow he would manage to work in praise for his secretary's smile and "sex appeal." He often closed out telegrams to her with an emphatic "Love and Kisses."

Not that he gave anything away in public.

527

Stepping out of the car, he always clasped Betty's hand. They strolled down the sidewalk alongside LaBranche, who would guide potential voters into their orbit. "Meet the next mayor and his wife," he'd say, time and again.

These outings offered nothing of substance, which worked out for the best. Eliot was unexpectedly having difficulty with his speeches. He tended to lose his way even with the text right in front of him. He would trail off in the middle of a sentence, distracted by a face in the crowd or a plane flying overhead. Red-faced and watery-eyed, he proved much better at playing the greeter. Campaign polling showed that older women were his best block of voters, and so LaBranche sought out ladies over forty. They always seemed thrilled to shake the former safety director's hand.

At one caravan event in Ward 12, veteran councilman Herman H. Finkle rode with Eliot and Betty. Stopping at a central intersection, the three climbed out together in front of a small crowd.

"Do you know who that is?" precinct captain Bill Blackman asked a preteen boy standing at the curb.

The boy consulted the campaign literature Blackman had just handed him.

"Sure, that's Mr. Ness," he said.

"Kee-rect," Blackman declared with his best carnival-barker drawl. "And do you know who that is?" he continued, now indicating Finkle, a key Ness supporter.

The boy again perused his handouts. He was flummoxed.

"That," Blackman happily heaved, "is our distinguished city councilman, the Honorable Herman H. Finkle."

" 'Tis not," the boy said.

"Why certainly it is."

The boy, put on the spot, grimaced. "Have him take off his hat," he said.

Finkle, smiling, did so, displaying his shiny bald dome. The boy again flipped through his campaign literature. Blackman, feeling the happy democratic moment slipping away, pointed to the picture of Finkle.

"Now I know it ain't Mr. Finkle," the kid triumphantly announced. "Mr. Finkle's got hair."

That brought a good laugh, for Finkle had used the same campaign photo for twenty years. With Blackman sending the boy off to hand out the literature, Eliot, Betty, and the councilman, hat firmly back in place, headed down the sidewalk, shaking hands and smiling. Here and there, they'd duck into a store to offer campaign handbills for the front counter and to cluck over the hardworking proprietors, the backbone of America. When they came to a store that sold liquor, Betty, careful of propriety, stayed outside.

■ ■ ■

It didn't matter that Eliot hadn't voted in seven years.* It didn't matter that for most of his adult life he had been registered as an independent voter. He was the Republican Party's choice for mayor of Cleveland. The same day the newspapers reported his candidacy — "Eliot Ness it is," The *Plain Dealer* declared on July 30, 1947 — he and Betty had gone down to the board of elections office to register to vote. It would be the first time Betty had ever done so. They listed their residence as Wade Park Manor, a hotel in University Circle. The couple had been renting a house in the nearby town of Bratenahl.

The announcement that Eliot would run for mayor surprised most political observers. The *Plain Dealer* reported that the "heavy contributors to the Republican party, naturally, are practically delirious with enthusiasm that a person of ability, stature and appeal is about to challenge the formidable incumbent, Thomas A. Burke." In actuality, the heavy contributors were glad to have *any* candidate to take on Burke, the former city law director

* In 1941, faced with a choice between his boss, the Republican incumbent Edward Blythin, and his friend, Democrat Frank Lausche, Eliot had publicly supported Blythin but couldn't bring himself to vote.

who had succeeded Lausche in 1944. At least six prominent Republicans — including the notoriously corrupt former mayor, Harry L. Davis, and even Eliot's former assistant, Robert Chamberlin — had turned aside inquiries from a committee tasked with finding a credible candidate. Cleveland, after all, was a Democratic city and Burke a popular Democratic mayor. More than that, the Republican organization in Cleveland had collapsed since Burton's departure for the U.S. Senate. The state party now focused primarily on the city's suburbs.

Eliot acknowledged to reporters that he had been drafted by Republican muckety-mucks, but he insisted: "Nobody has told me what to do, and, of course, nobody can." Chamberlin and another longtime friend, reporter-turned-PR-man Ralph Kelly, Marion Kelly's husband, would run the campaign, not party hacks.

No one was quite sure why Eliot had decided to make the race. He himself judged his chances as "slight." Was he bored with the business world already? Probably. But some old friends worried it was worse than that. They wondered if he was pursuing a quixotic political campaign in an effort to jolt himself out of an alcoholic torpor, a desperate attempt to reclaim his old life, his old drive and ambition. That did sound like Eliot, always one to make bold, even fatalistic gestures. Eliot was self-aware, perhaps too much so for his own good. He surely sensed he was slipping. The evidence was right there on his campaign posters. His once perfectly cut and slicked hair was now slightly askew. His eyes, always tinged with sadness, now also had a heaviness, as if he were straining to stay awake. He looked at least a decade older than his forty-five years.

Something was definitely up. The desire to run for public office required a certain kind of egotism that Eliot simply did not possess. Everyone in Cleveland politics knew he could have become mayor back in 1941 without much effort. Heck, he could have sandbagged Burton and declared for the U.S. Senate the year before. He would have had a good shot at it. One night late in 1940, he and Lausche, joking around, had flipped a coin to decide which of them would run for mayor. Eliot won the toss — and immediately insisted on best two of three. As comfortable as he was with reporters, and as much as he enjoyed speaking before admiring crowds, Eliot just didn't like the idea of being one more huckster on the hustings. He believed there were other, better ways to do his civic duty.

Now, seven years later, Eliot realized he would need to run an active, "news-producing" campaign if he had any hope of beating a popular and personable incumbent who had won two-thirds of the vote two years before. His team came up with catchy, alliterative slogans — "Vote Yes for Eliot Ness," "Ness Is Necessary" — and printed up a four-page tabloid, the *Ness News.* Eliot made pitches on the radio and stood in front of factory gates with an armful of campaign leaflets.

His chief theme, however, was negative. "This town used to have a forward spirit," he said, coming out of the election board office with Betty after registering to vote. "It has gotten listless, apathetic and careless. Anyone wanting to have proof of this can look in any direction and see evidence of it: uncared for playgrounds; the air full of smoke; streets full of holes; a noisy, inadequate, poorly maintained transportation system. . . . What we are seeing is the natural result of five years in office on the part of any administration. Accomplishments are difficult to achieve in public service. It takes a lot of energy and a lot of desire, and it has to be accompanied, in order to add up to success, by a thrill of doing and a thrill of accomplishment."

This was the best he could come up with. That the current administration lacked adequate get-up-and-go. That there was smog in one of the country's foremost industrial cities. His opponents would hit much harder than that. Local CIO leader A. E. Stevenson told union members that as safety director Eliot "ordered police on horses to charge defenseless men, women and children during a strike at the Fisher Body plant in 1939." The charge was an outrageous lie, but that hardly mattered. The Democrats kept repeating it. Eliot wanted Clevelanders to remember him as the heroic public safety director who had cleaned up the police force, run the Mob out of town, made the roads safer, and given city hall a youthful dazzle. But that had been a long time ago — or at least it felt like a long time ago to most people. At one campaign stop, a man asked Eliot about the torso-killer investigation, still officially open even though it had been nearly a decade since a murder had been attributed to the Mad Butcher. It was the biggest black mark on Eliot's six-year directorship, and it annoyed him that he couldn't tell all he knew about the case. Those murders had been "solved," he snapped. He moved on without elaborating.

Eliot eventually started being specific about his plans for the city if elected, sticking mainly with issues right in his wheelhouse. It rankled him that the police department's crime-prevention bureau, one of his proudest accomplishments, had languished since he left office, and he brought it up at every opportunity. In a fifteen-minute radio broadcast on WTAM, he promised that Cleveland women would be safer under a Ness administration because he would refocus police priorities. "Our purpose should not be to fill our jails with people who have committed crimes," he said. "Our purpose should be to prevent crimes." At rallies, he held up photographs of pothole-pitted streets and neighborhood squares awash in litter. "It is a difficult problem to keep a large city clean and to keep its streets repaired," he said. "The present administration, which I have called the 'ho-hum administration,' has done a much poorer job than might be expected."

This was deadly boring stuff. The *Plain Dealer* put it mildly (appropriately enough) when it called Eliot "no ball of fire as a candidate." Eliot was even boring himself. He may have jumped into the race to rejuvenate himself, to reignite his fire, but it wasn't happening. He soon began to lose interest in the campaign. After downtown campaign rallies, he'd sometimes slip away from his handlers and head over to city hall, where he'd pop his head into the office of Safety Director Alvin Sutton, a longtime acquaintance.

"What are you doing here?" Sutton asked him more than once. "You're running for mayor and I'm working for Burke. He's about fifty feet from here. Why don't you come back after work, so we can have a drink or something?"

Eliot would offer his lazy, affable smile and encourage Sutton to duck out for that drink now rather than later. He'd even suggest inviting Burke along. For years afterward, Sutton would shake his head at the memory. "I think he was just innocent and unaware of the political realities," he said.

The nonpartisan primary vote arrived on September 30 and, as expected, Burke breezed to victory, scoring 47 percent of the vote to Eliot's 30 percent, with former councilman Eddie Pucel taking 23 percent.

Burke and Eliot moved on to the general election. Pucel's strength in the primary surprised everyone, and Eliot's only hope in November would be to take most of the insurgent Democrat's votes. No one had to tell him there wasn't much chance of that, seeing as Pucel's support came mostly from union members and hard-core lefties. *Plain Dealer* columnist Philip Porter summed up the first phase of the election: "The most notable thing about the primary campaign is that . . . it was a bore. The 'outs' can't get much of a hearing unless they are at least interesting." He would later add that Eliot was a "wretched public speaker."

One of Porter's colleagues used baseball language (the World Series was coming up) to offer advice: "It is time now for Ness, in fact for the Republican party, to send for the professionals before all chance of winning in the Cleveland political league is kicked away. The campaign the former safety director just concluded was so distinguished by bush league political performance that in the absence of replacements it is horrible to contemplate what Mayor Thomas A. Burke will do to him in the championship series."

Faced with an embarrassment at the polls in November, Eliot finally did get desperate. He called on Burke "publicly to disavow Communists and Communist sympathizers who are supporting his political camp." There had been no indication that communists had infiltrated city government or had any love for Burke, a middle-of-the-road, business-friendly Democrat. The *Plain Dealer* called it a "sleazy insinuation." Burke mostly ignored it.

Eliot then promoted a goofy idea to devolve power in the city, saying he would set up thirty or so branch city halls around the city. He followed that with an accusation that the Burke administration was using bulldozers to push garbage into the lake to give the appearance of competence with basic services. Porter cut him with a particularly fine knife, writing that Eliot "believes himself to be running for mayor of Cleveland."

Rain came on Election Day, but the bad weather seemed to keep only Eliot's supporters at home. The incumbent scored a staggering landslide victory, taking 67 percent of the vote. Burke even won the traditional Republican wards. The Democrats expected the big victory, but at the same time they gave a sigh of relief. They couldn't know for sure that the old Ness magic was gone until the final vote came in. "Eliot missed the boat," Burke's executive secretary John Patrick Butler observed. "He should have run for mayor in 1941, against Frank Lausche, who was then a comparative unknown with a name hard to pronounce. He could have beat Lausche then because at that time Ness was the most famous man in the city and the most admired."

Early in the evening on Election Day, Eliot stepped up to the front door of the mayor's twelve-room home on the East Side. He knocked softly. When Burke opened the door, Eliot, hat in hand, smiled and gave a little wave. "Naturally, I am disappointed," he told the mayor. "But it is more important that the democratic process has taken place. There were some things I wanted to do in this town." He sighed and smiled again. "Congratulations," he added, as if just remembering why he'd come.

Burke, trying to recover from his surprise at finding Eliot on his doorstep, stammered, "Nice campaign," and invited him in. The mayor was hosting a victory party for staff and supporters. Radio station WGAR was broadcasting from the sunroom, and Eliot sat down and gave his concession speech, with the mayor watching.

Tomorrow Eliot would have to return to the boredom of the Diebold boardroom, so he quickly got drunk. The large, brick house, which once belonged to Harold Burton, rocked with cheering and applause. Eliot soon embraced the spirit of the party. He slapped backs and accepted flutes of champagne. At the height of the festivities, he toasted the victor and cheerfully lamented his failed expedition into political life.

"Who'd want an honest politician anyway?" he cracked.

CHAPTER 35
ELIOT-AM-BIG-U-OUS NESS

The election proved to be the tipping point. Eliot would never really be taken seriously again.

In 1951, the Diebold board dumped him as chairman. The decision had been a long time coming. Eliot had pushed the company into new product areas, such as office equipment, and he'd led the takeover of York Safe & Lock Company, but all that ambition and activity had come early in his tenure. He hadn't been on top of things for quite a while. Managers complained about his inability to focus on details. His directives and goals sometimes contradicted each other. He often seemed distracted, out of his depth. At the same time that Diebold cut him loose, the Middle East Company, where Eliot served as vice president and treasurer, was slowly flaming out. He put some of his own cash into the operation in hopes of propping it up, a big mistake. Eliot had made a hefty $24,000 per year at Diebold, but he had never been very good with money. Almost overnight, his financial situation turned dire.

He had to scrabble for work. His corporate career was deader than Al Capone, so he turned to retail. He sold electronics and frozen hamburger patties. He worked at a bookstore. One day, he paid a visit to Alvin Sutton, hoping there might be some consulting or investigative work he could do for his old department. Sutton liked and respected Eliot; he recognized that the police department — indeed, the entire city — was much better off because of Eliot's time as safety director. But he couldn't help him as long as Burke was mayor. Eliot then showed up at the public-relations firm that had handled his mayoral campaign. "I'd regard it as a favor if you could put me on the payroll for about sixty dollars a week," he told his former flack. He left the office without a job offer.

Eliot had gotten out of law enforcement at the wrong time. Science and technology were triumphant after the war. Americans conquered polio and broke the sound barrier. Vernon Stouffer, Eliot's former witness against the Cleveland Mob, helped pioneer the frozen dinner. Scientific thinking spread through policing, too. Training academies, crime labs, internal-affairs bureaus, and crime-prevention programs became the norm in big-city police departments. Clannishness in the ranks began to fall away, and more men with college degrees joined the profession. Organized crime didn't disappear but it definitely was on the run. To survive, mobsters were increasingly forced to embrace something novel: anonymity.

Eliot observed this transformation with satisfaction, knowing he'd played a part in setting it in motion. Betty would say that "he was always serious about law enforcement." He viewed it as the highest calling. But by the time he reached fifty in 1952, he seemed to recognize that he no longer had what it took to run a police department. While he was still at Diebold, he'd shown interest in becoming Detroit's police chief, but the city's mayor, Albert Cobo, had been put off by Eliot's run for office in Cleveland. Cobo didn't want a man with political ambitions in the job. That was the last serious attempt Eliot made at restarting his old life. After his visit with Sutton, he stopped trying to find police work, his one true love.

Eliot had given up on policing, but his crime-busting past still periodically reappeared, like a haunting. Francis Sweeney found out where Eliot lived and began sending him letters and postcards, addressing them to "Eliot (Esophogotic) Ness" or "Eliot-Am-Big-U-ous Ness." These messages offered nothing but nutty, childish wordplay, but they terrified Betty. Eliot told her to ignore them.

The torso murders in Cleveland had officially stopped in 1938 at twelve. Detective Merylo, however, had reached the conclusion that the case was much bigger than Cleveland, that the murderer rode the rails and used boxcars as a traveling "murder laboratory." In his final report on the torso case, in 1943, he wrote that he "believed and still do at this time that one person is responsible for all of these murders between here and Pittsburgh, Pa., including New Castle, Pa. and Youngstown, O. which now figure to 27 victims." This was a minority opinion. Panic about the serial killer had dribbled away as World War II began to dominate both the newspapers and people's lives. Many Clevelanders, remembering an old headline, believed the Mad Butcher of Kingsbury Run had been caught. In 1939 Cuyahoga County sheriff Martin O'Donnell had arrested a ratty fifty-two-year-old Slav immigrant named Frank Dolezal. After a two-day interrogation in which the suspect was beaten and denied food, Dolezal confessed to murdering Flo Polillo, an acquaintance of his. The confession hit the front page of every newspaper in the region, but ultimately prosecutors lost faith in its accuracy. The case went before a grand jury, but only on a manslaughter charge. A month later, with the case in free fall, guards found Dolezal hanged in his cell, quite possibly after another brutal interrogation. The press had moved on to other subjects by then. Dolezal's death wouldn't garner anything close to the media attention his arrest had.

Sweeney, meanwhile, increasingly spent his time in veterans' hospitals, lost in his delusions. By the early 1950s, along with the letters to Eliot, he was peppering the press and various law-enforcement agencies with nonsensical missives. He declared himself Ness's "Paranoidal-Nemesis." He even sent a letter to the FBI, warning J. Edgar Hoover of "Nessism." From at least 1956, Sweeney's stays in the hospital became compulsory. He would die in 1964 at the age of seventy.

It took Eliot nearly four years to secure a meaningful position after Diebold. He was finally hired as president of both Guaranty Paper Corporation and Fidelity Check Corporation, subsidiaries of the North Ridge Industrial Corporation. He, Betty, and Bobby soon would move from Cleveland to Coudersport, Pennsylvania, where North Ridge set up its headquarters in two rented buildings downtown. Eliot fit in easily in the town: like him, the small rural community had been in decline for years. "He was dead broke, just like the rest of us," said Coudersport storeowner Lewis Wilkinson, whose wife, Dorothy, landed a secretarial job at North Ridge. Eliot found he loved the small-town life. Everyone was friendly, if not necessarily open, and Eliot reciprocated. He had lunch most weekdays at Mackey's Restaurant downtown, either by himself or, during the summer, with Bobby. He said hello and smiled at folks but he didn't try to strike up conversations. He felt both at home and hidden away.

Now he just needed North Ridge Industrial to take off. The company's chairman and founder, G. Frank Shampanore, had come up with a new chemical formula for watermarking paper to prevent fraud. North Ridge was a small, unproven company just getting up on its feet, but its directors didn't want Eliot for his management experience. They hired him — at $150 a week, plus company stock — for his name value and his address book. That was fine with Eliot, who threw himself into sales calls. He spent weeks making phone calls and writing letters in search of clients and investors. He put the arm on many of his old associates in Cleveland, offering them stock options and exclusive franchises, but no one took him up on his pitch. He set up a meeting with longtime friend Delo Mook, the bank executive, but Mook didn't sign up for the product, either. He told Eliot the watermarks on his samples weren't as good as the current standard. These Cleveland-area power brokers had once respected or feared Eliot, but now they pitied him. He seemed so pathetic in his rumpled suit, his face puffy and red. "Eliot had run out of gas," said an old friend. "He was still a fairly young man, but he simply ran out of gas. He didn't know which way to turn."

Betty, accustomed to being admired for her looks and her talent, tried to keep up appearances. The strain began to show around her eyes, in the way she would purse her lips when she fell into thought. "She was quite vivacious, but she was somewhat subdued except for people she knew," said Franny Taft, a friend of Betty's. "So there were two Bettys. She was certainly very popular with the friends she had. They were protective of her, especially after she started to drink too much. She became a little depressed later in her life. She had a problem with alcohol."

This was an occupational hazard for any wife of Eliot Ness. "They were partying people," acknowledged their housekeeper, Corrine Lawson. By that Lawson meant they went out drinking a lot. They didn't throw parties like Eliot and Evaline had. That took too much effort. By now, drinking had undeniably become central to Eliot's life. He didn't just drink every day. He got drunk every day. "He always had scotch and soda," said Lawson. "He loved his Cutty Sark." A drinking buddy from this period, Jack Foyle, called him "a very lonesome man" who clearly was in the grip of alcoholism. "I would have two drinks and he'd have twenty-two,"

Foyle said. Eliot became a regular at the Old Hickory Tavern in Coudersport, but he usually sat by himself and stayed out of conversations. When he had his fill, he would find his way home, settle in on the couch in the living room, and put on recordings of Paul Robeson reciting Shakespeare. He'd listen to the actor's sonorous voice echo around the room until he passed out.

North Ridge Industrial had begun to take on water even before Eliot arrived on the scene. The company suffered through a series of aborted attempts to get a production facility up and running, with the chief problem being Shampanore's insistence on handling everything himself. North Ridge's vice president, Joseph E. Phelps, would later claim that Shampanore was a charlatan. "He surrounded the entire activity with a great deal of secrecy and mystery," he wrote in a report to the Pennsylvania Securities Commission. "He stated that he had been pledged by various departments of the Federal Government such as the State Department, Central Intelligence Agency and the Defense Department to keep the process and operation absolutely secret, so that he was not free to disclose the entire process to even his own officers and directors and employees." William Ayers, North Ridge's director of research and development, called Shampanore "a spellbinder . . . who was able to captivate all who came along with his grandiose schemes." Shampanore's stories of secret meetings with government officials had certainly fascinated Eliot. When Eliot started to figure out that they were all just hot air, he couldn't hide his shock. His relationship with North Ridge's founder fell apart; the two men began to avoid each other in the office. Eliot suspected Shampanore wanted to force him out of the company.

"Eliot was very depressed and felt victimized. He went out of his way not to let others see it," recalled a Coudersport acquaintance. "Deep down inside, he felt guilty and ashamed for failing to adequately provide for his wife and son."

Eliot's increasingly desperate attempts to save the company — a company he no longer really believed in — took him out on the road a lot, which frustrated him. He wanted to be a better father to Bobby than he believed his own father had been to him, but he didn't have much time to spend with the boy. When he was home, he was so exhausted — mentally and physically — he could barely move. He would sit down with a drink and promise Bobby that tomorrow he would play catch with him, tomorrow they would go fishing. He always meant it when he said it. But tomorrow would come and as often as not he'd put on a suit, get in the car — a five-year-old Ford convertible with the back window missing — and head out of town for more sales calls. "Betty tried to be understanding," a friend recalled, "but she felt abandoned at times."

EPILOGUE:
LITERARY LIFE

Late in 1955, North Ridge Industrial managed to get a printing facility into operation. The company finally had a real product — not just a promise — it could sell. Eliot and Joe Phelps headed to New York for a series of sales meetings.

On their first night in town, a school friend of Phelps met them at their hotel. His name was Oscar Fraley; he was a reporter for United Press International. "Ness sat listening while Phelps and I enjoyed one of those good old 'long-time-no-see' bull sessions," Fraley would remember. It was late and the men were drunk when Phelps nodded toward Eliot and told Fraley that this was "the guy who dried up Al Capone." He'd been involved in raids and shootouts and much more during the Prohibition days, Phelps insisted.

Fraley turned to his old friend's colleague, waiting for the punch line. After all, Eliot didn't look like much. He was soft and puffy, with heavy bags under his eyes. He had been a pleasant enough companion all night, but he hadn't really said anything, focusing chiefly on ordering drinks for himself and the others. Now Phelps egged him on. Eliot waved away the encouraging noises, embarrassed at being put on the spot, but he was smiling. Downing another drink, he began to talk.

As Eliot's story took shape, Fraley found himself listening intently.

The "words rushed out in a smooth flood which mixed wit, perception and warmth," Fraley recalled. It was clear that Eliot enjoyed transporting himself into the past, back to a time when he led a more exciting — and more useful — existence. When success seemed so easy and natural. The men ended up in Eliot's hotel room, where Eliot collapsed on the floor and kicked off his shoes. He kept talking. He told Fraley and Phelps about secretly hitching a ride on the back of a beer truck to ride into a hidden brewery. He told them about standing at the bottom of a telephone pole, gun drawn, as a fellow agent tapped the line to Ralph Capone's place. He told them about Frank Basile, dead on the side of the road at twenty-seven. Eliot's eyes welled with tears.

"Let's knock this off and get some breakfast," Eliot said, embarrassed at the narrative's mawkish turn. He shook himself and climbed to his feet. It was six in the morning.

The three men started to put themselves together, combing their hair, shaking out their jackets.

"Someday, you should write a book on your experience," Fraley said, finally voicing what he'd been thinking for hours. "You might make some money with it."

Eliot looked over at Fraley, a rueful smile on his face. "I could use it," he said.

Over breakfast, Fraley persisted with the idea. He told Eliot he would write the book for him. Slowly, he won over his new friend. He pointed out that Al Capone, who died a gibbering loon, had become a legend in the years since Prohibition; he was Casey at the Bat for the criminal class. Everyone knew the mighty Al Capone. But what of the men who laid him low, who turned his overconfidence against him? They were forgotten. Fraley was a newspaperman and a history buff, and yet even to him the Untouchables and Eliot Ness had meant nothing. Eliot agreed with Fraley that the agents who had worked day and night to bring down the Capone syndicate deserved some recognition. After returning home, he typed up a handful of stories from memory, packed up his scrapbooks, and sent them off to New York. In the accompanying letter, he wrote, "Am enclosing additional background and incidents of the Capone case. If you find parts sketchy on which you would like more detail, please drop me a note." Fraley, reading through the material, felt like he'd stumbled upon a hidden treasure chest. He'd been looking for a promising book project for years, and now one had fallen right in his lap. Working feverishly, he wrote half a dozen sample chapters, inventing dialogue and simplifying the narrative, and sent them to his literary agent. Within days he had a deal for a memoir about the Untouchables' crusade against Capone. When Fraley called and said the publisher Julian Messner Inc. wanted his life story, Eliot was stunned. He had figured he'd never hear from Fraley again.

Fraley flew to Cleveland and later Coudersport to work on the book with Eliot, but it didn't go well. Eliot's mind was muddy. The confident storytelling the newsman witnessed in New York had disappeared. "Eliot knuckled his brow, stamped about the room and berated himself as he groped for names, places and incidents half forgotten," Fraley would recall. The two men took long walks so Eliot could clear his head in the fresh air. Eliot talked about the Cleveland Mob, the torso killer, reforming the Cleveland Police Department, hobbling labor racketeers. His years as safety director — that's what he was most proud of. That's when he made a lasting difference. He pounded his fist as he listed his accomplishments. Why didn't a publisher care about *that* story? Why didn't Cleveland voters care about it back in '47? Fraley had a hard time getting Eliot back on topic. The Capone operation remained hazy. Eliot didn't seem very interested in revisiting those days anymore. The reporter, after returning to New York, would ultimately decide to fill in the gaps with his imagination.[*]

However conflicted he may have been about a book on the Capone squad, Eliot loved the idea of the literary life, of being a writer, as he had claimed to be back when he and Evaline got married in Kentucky. He was aware of his ex-wife's burgeoning career in publishing. She now lived in a swank apartment in Manhattan thanks to her work on children's books. Eliot didn't know that Evaline's long-sought creative success did not bring her happiness, though he wouldn't have been surprised. She would soon marry again, to an engineer named Arnold Bayard, but he was not her third True Love. She'd given up on such childish ideas. She continued to drink heavily, just like Eliot, her alcohol consumption becoming the one certainty to every day. Slowly and methodically, her drinking would destroy every relationship in her life. When she died, in 1986 at seventy-five, her husband had her cremated and told the owner of the

[*] Fraley would eventually use Eliot's Cleveland years as the subject of his highly fictionalized sequel, *4 Against the Mob*.

funeral home to throw the ashes in the trash.

Eliot probably didn't expect the literary life to bring him happiness either. He would be satisfied with some financial security, or even a brief cash infusion. He began to spend his evenings telling Capone stories at the Old Hickory Tavern in an effort to corral memories that fit with the draft chapters Fraley was sending him. The other patrons thought he was telling tall tales. On some evenings, he would walk over to the Wilkinsons' house on Ross Street and ask Dorothy to take notes while he talked. "He wrote the book on the backs of unused [Fidelity Check Corporation] checks, and Dorothy would type them up and then throw the originals in the wastebasket," Lewis Wilkinson recalled years later.

Eliot began to think of those wild years chasing Capone as a beautiful dream, colorful and alive and yet somehow frustratingly unclear. He thought about tracking down some of the old gang to ask about their memories, but he never got around to it. It probably wouldn't have helped anyway. More than two decades after the Capone squad's last mission, those glory days seemed no more plausible to the other Untouchables than they did to Eliot. Most of them were closing out government careers in anonymity. Not many had distinguished themselves in the years since they'd helped send the world's most powerful gangster to federal prison. In

1951, Paul Robsky's career ended in shame after a drunk-driving arrest. The fifty-four-year-old ATU agent was driving a government car without permission, having disconnected the speedometer cable to avoid detection. In the agency's last efficiency report on Robsky, submitted a month before his arrest, his supervisor wrote "that at one time he was regarded as a capable Special Investigator but that for the last two years he has not been regarded as even a mediocre character." Barney Cloonan also worked for the ATU for two decades after Prohibition, even though his supervisors knew he had probably taken bribes from the Chicago syndicate during the dry years. He would never get promoted above the special investigator level at which he'd entered the agency. The FBI kept a "Derogatory Data" file on him. William Gardner continued to struggle with drink, wrecking his career, driving off a succession of wives and alienating his children. He hadn't held a regular job since before the war. He was in the process of moving to Arizona, where he'd live off a small pension and sink into ill health.

Of course, not every member of the team peaked with the Capone hunt. Marty Lahart enjoyed a long, fruitful career in the ATU. Sam Seager and Joe Leeson rose rapidly in the federal bureaucracy after Prohibition, though neither would get to fulfill his potential. Leeson died suddenly of a heart attack in 1944. He was just forty-six. Seager died two years before him, at fifty-two. Lyle Chapman was run out of the federal government after repeal, but he made an impressive recovery. After World War II, he put his mathematical mind to work on a rating system for college football. By the 1950s he was forecasting game results on the radio. He still liked to brag about his connection to Al Capone, showing off a 150-page file on the case that he really shouldn't have had in his possession. "I often find myself looking it over," he admitted. "It brings back exciting memories."

Eliot's exciting memories, filtered through and expanded by Fraley, landed on his doorstep in Coudersport in the spring of 1957. Opening up the manuscript, he found himself filled with foreboding. He'd been stuck in a low-level depression for months, maybe years. He had never really expected anything to come of the book project. He didn't believe that his story — his life — was worth writing down. William Ayers would recall that as Eliot read through Fraley's manuscript "he was many times on the verge of chucking the whole project because the book made him out to be a hero, which he honestly didn't consider himself to be."

But he didn't chuck the whole project. He conscripted Walter Taylor, the editor of Coudersport's newspaper, and Betty to read the manuscript and help him choose "what to leave in and what to leave out." Eliot tried not to think too much about it. He still had a day job to worry about. North Ridge was still struggling along, teetering on the edge of bankruptcy. On May 16, he decided to leave the office early and finish up some work at home. He packed up his briefcase and headed out on foot, strolling down Main Street. Sweat rushed down his forehead; it was a warm, sticky day. As he passed the newspaper's small office, he glanced in the front window and noticed that Taylor was at his desk, perhaps reading Fraley's manuscript. He stuck his head in the door and suggested they have "a cool one." Taylor begged off; he had an appointment in an hour. Eliot gave him a smile and continued on to Third Street. His colleagues in the office had noticed that he'd been in "exceptionally fine spirits" all day, but by the time he reached his house's front walk he had begun to flag. The humid weather really took it out of him. He walked through to the kitchen, calling out to let Betty know he was home. He turned on the faucet in the sink and was reaching for a glass in the cupboard when a shock rolled through him. He wavered, losing his grip on the glass, which smashed into the sink. He dropped to the floor. Betty, out in the backyard watering the flowerbeds, found him a few minutes later. It was too late. He was dead at fifty-five.

Over the next few days, as telegrams arrived from U.S. senator Frank Lausche, former Illinois governor Dwight Green, and Harold Burton, now a U.S. Supreme Court justice, many of his friends and acquaintances in Coudersport expressed surprise that Eliot Ness once had been such an important man. One local resident called him someone "you probably haven't given a second look on the street." Taylor, who had sent out the news of Eliot's death on the wires, described him in affectionate but prosaic terms. He was "an understatement, a giggler, a man 'you knew from somewhere,' a man you'd pick out if you were looking for a fellow elbow-bender, a face in the crowd." These friends would be even more surprised six months later when his slam-bang memoir reached bookstores. In the twenty-five years between the disbanding of the Capone squad and his first meeting with Fraley, Eliot had never presented himself or his accomplishments as anything special. Former Cleveland political insider John Patrick Butler, like so many others who knew him, would remember Eliot as the very opposite of a braggart. "He talked to me about his Chicago days but took no personal claim in doing more than having helped expose the size of the Capone empire and its widespread activities," he said.

Worried about the book, Eliot had talked through his memories of the Untouchables with Betty during the last days of his life. He never dwelled on heroic action in these long, meandering monologues. He had grown sentimental, maudlin. He admitted to his wife that he was often scared during the Capone squad's short existence. He told her about the time in the Cozy Corner when one of the goons had said in Italian: "Shall I put a knife in him now?" Eliot wasn't proud of his reaction. He had been useless when he needed to be courageous, he told her. The mournful look in his eyes as he said it broke Betty's heart. Eliot asked his wife if he could get rid of her target pistol and hunting rifle. He didn't want guns in the house anymore. Hunting was a popular pastime in the Coudersport area, but Eliot wouldn't teach their son to hunt. "I've seen enough killing in my life," he said.

Eliot's doubts about himself didn't make it into the book. Fraley understood what would sell and what wouldn't. "Don't get scared if we stray from the facts once in a while," he wrote to Eliot. Ultimately, Eliot couldn't argue. He needed the money. He was more than $9,000 in debt. The book's advance hadn't arrived in time to prevent him from bouncing a $10 check. Talking about the book to a friend in Coudersport, he parroted Fraley, saying: "If you want it to be interesting you have to embellish it a little."

Just a few weeks before his death, Eliot received some proof that Fraley knew what he was talking about, that everything might turn out all right for him and Betty and Bobby. He was in Cleveland for a business meeting. North Ridge Industrial was spiraling down, in desperate need of customers to stay afloat. He checked into the Pick-Carter Hotel and met up with an old friend, Milton Bowman. They had dinner in the Frontier Room, the décor of which featured old rifles and shotguns hung on the wood-paneled walls. Afterward, the two men went to Eliot's room for a drink. The phone rang just as they stepped into the room. Eliot's eyes widened as he listened to the voice on the line.

"No kidding," he said before cheerfully signing off.

"What was that?" Bowman asked.

Eliot couldn't wipe the smile off his face. "They just told me Hollywood is nibbling on the book idea."

He wouldn't live to see it, but he was about to become an American icon.

ACKNOWLEDGMENTS

My agent, Jim Donovan, helped get me started on this project and provided invaluable insight all along the way. My editor, Brittney Ross, improved this book in many ways both large and small.

Barbara Osteika, the staff historian at the Bureau of Alcohol, Tobacco, Firearms and Explosives, tirelessly aided my research. She patiently answered questions about the ATF's history and work; helped me track down key documents, such as government personnel files; and led me through the agency's archives.

I also must express my thanks to the following for research and other assistance:

James Badal; Mark Bassett; Peter Bhatia; Maria Brandt; Jerry Casey; James Ciesla; the Cleveland Police Historical Society staff; the Cleveland Public Library staff; the Cleveland State University Special Collections staff; Anne Collier; Jonathan Eig; Susan Gage; Abby Gilbert; Marni Greenberg; Daniel M.

Huff; Carol Jacobs; Méira King; Joe Kisvardai; the Library of Congress staff; Alessandra Lusardi; the Multnomah County Library interlibrary loan staff; Adrienne Pruitt; Michelle Regan; Steve Resnick; Arnold Sagalyn; Rena Schergen; Ellen Seibert; Cindy Shifflett; and especially Scott Sroka.

And, of course, this book would simply not have been possible without the love and support of my beautiful and talented wife, Deborah King.

NOTES

AI — Author interview

ATF — Bureau of Alcohol, Tobacco, Firearms and Explosives historic archives

Berardi — "Prohibition: Tony Berardi: About Eliot Ness and 'the Untouchables.' " Video interview with Tony Berardi. Produced in 1999: onlinefootage.tv/video/show/id/7684. Accessed February 28, 2011.

CN — *Cleveland News*

CP — *Cleveland Press*

CPD — Cleveland *Plain Dealer*

CPHS — Archives at the Cleveland Police Historical Society

CT — *Chicago Tribune*

ENP — Eliot Ness Papers, 1928–1960, MSS 3699; and Eliot Ness Scrapbooks, 1931–1947: Microfilm Collections, Western Reserve Historical Society

ENP/MS — Ness's original draft summary for his memoir, *The Untouchables:* Eliot Ness Papers, Microfilm Collections, Western Reserve Historical Society

HHB — The Papers of Harold H. Burton, Manuscript Division, Library of Congress

Johnson — "Prohibition: George E. Q. Johnson: About Eliot Ness and 'the Untouchables.' " Video interview with George E. Q. Johnson Jr. Produced in 1999. www.online footage.tv/video/show/id/7733. Accessed February 28, 2011.

Lonardo — Statement of Angelo Lonardo before the U.S. Senate Permanent Subcommittee on Investigations of the Committee on Governmental Affairs, United States Senate, 100th Congress, Second Session, U.S. Government Printing Office, Washington: 1988

NPRC — U. S. government civilian personnel records (by name of employee): Official Personnel Folders, The National Personnel Records Center, National Archives at St. Louis

Vollmer — August Vollmer Historical Project, 1983, Regional Oral History Office, The Bancroft Library, University of California, Berkeley

Introduction: The Real Eliot Ness

The death scene in the Ness kitchen was recreated using the following sources: "End Comes Quickly: Eliot Ness, Resident Here Only Eight Months, Passes Away," *Potter Leader-Enterprise,* May 23, 1957;

"Walter Taylor Reminisces on Eliot Ness's Last Years," *Potter Leader-Enterprise,* Mar. 22, 1961; "Film Crews Tracking Eliot Ness: Famous Crime Fighter Died Unheralded — But of Natural Causes — in Potter County," *Pittsburgh Post-Gazette,* Dec. 1, 1996; Elisabeth Seaver file, unlabeled news clippings, Cleveland Museum of Art archives; ENP, unlabeled obituary clippings, reel 3.

He walked out of the kitchen: Cleveland Public Library photo collection, Eliot and Elisabeth Ness living room.

It got his age wrong: "Eliot Ness, 53, Dies; Helped Jail Capone," CT, May 17, 1957.

Ness had taught Sagalyn how to: AI, Arnold Sagalyn, May 22, 2011.

Sagalyn sent her some money: Ibid.

But unlike Sagalyn, he didn't owe: *Something About the Author: Autobiography Series,* vol. 1, (Detroit, MI: Gale, 1985), 227.

"The last time I saw Eliot . . .": David Cowles oral history, 1983, CPHS.

The young, irrepressible top cop: "What They Are Saying," CPD, Feb. 7, 1937.

As one of the resident experts: Peter Jedick, "Eliot Ness," *Cleveland,* April 1976.

"He really captured the imagination . . .": George E. Condon, *Cleveland: The Best Kept Secret* (Garden City, NY: Doubleday, 1967), 243.

During a lull in the conversation: Oscar Fraley, "The Real Eliot Ness," *Coronet,* July 1961.

"It was dangerous": Ibid.

"I can hardly believe it": Ibid.

Worried about what he considered: Roger Borroel, *The Story of the Untouchables, as Told by Eliot Ness* (East Chicago, IN: La Villita Publications, 2010), 1; Fraley, "The Real Eliot Ness."

George E. Q. Johnson Jr., son of: Johnson.

"Eliot changed . . .": Paul W. Heimel, *Eliot Ness: The Real Story* (Nashville, TN: Knox Books, 1997), 81.

Thirty years after Ness's death: "The Death of Eliot Ness Was Exaggerated," *Los Angeles Times,* June 14, 1987.

Ken Burns, promoting his: " 'Prohibition' Gives Lie to Era's Chicago Myths," *Chicago Sun-Times,* Sept. 26, 2011.

"I am going to be out . . .": "Ness to Fight in Front Lines," CP, Dec. 13, 1935, ENP, reel 2.

Marion Kelly, a longtime Cleveland: Laurence Bergreen, *Capone: The Man and the Era* (New York: Simon & Schuster, 1994), 598.

Louise Jamie, who was related: Ibid., 345.

"There is nothing about Ness' appearance . . .": "Crime Buster Ness Shares

Trial Spotlight," CN, Oct. 2, 1940, ENP, reel 2.

"Tell me, what kind of guy . . .": Fraley, "The Real Eliot Ness."

Chapter 1: Hardboiled

Edna Stahle opened her eyes: AI, Maxine Huntington, a longtime friend of Edna's, Sept. 5, 2011.

The gangsters had figured out that: Studs Terkel, *Hard Times: An Oral History of the Great Depression* (Pantheon Books, 1970), 169–70.

"So [gangsters] took these yachts and decorated them . . .": Ibid.

One saloon regular put it succinctly: Ibid., 187.

He'd come because he was: "Eliot Ness Colleague Marguerite Downes, 90," CT, Dec. 23, 1986.

On the weekend, she clattered around town: AI, Maxine Huntington, Sept. 5, 2011.

"We used to double-date": "The Real Eliot Ness," *Tucson Citizen,* July 17, 1987, Scott Sroka personal collection.

"Women threw themselves at Eliot": Condon, "The Last American Hero," *Cleveland,* Aug. 1987.

This dichotomy — between the "very modest man . . .": "The Real Eliot Ness,"

569

Tucson Citizen, July 17, 1987, Scott Sroka personal collection.

The division oversaw: "Federal Prohibition Enforcement: A Report to the National Commission on Law Observance and Enforcement," Justice Department, 1930, 168.

The Chicago Prohibition office had recently: Laurence F. Schmeckebier, "The Bureau of Prohibition: Its History, Activities and Organization" (Washington, DC: The Brookings Institution, 1929), 50.

In 1922, two years after the arrival: Ibid., 45.

He and Chicago's Prohibition administrator: "Bailiff Shot By Dry Squad," CT, Mar. 30, 1928.

The newspapers dubbed him "Hard-boiled Golding": unlabeled *Chicago Tribune* clipping, Oct. 12, 1927, ENP, reel 1.

"The agents swooped down on unsuspecting Chicago . . .": Elmer L. Irey, as told to William J. Slocum. *The Tax Dodgers: The Inside of the T-Men's War with America's Political and Underworld Hoodlums* (New York: Greenberg, 1948), 20.

In March 1928, one of Golding's men shot: "Indict Bailiff After Drys Shoot Him," CT, Mar. 31, 1928; "Get Warrant for Dry Agent," CT, April 1, 1928; "Seized as Deneen Bomber," CT, April 3, 1928.

He said the wounded man, under guard:

"Bailiff Shot by Dry Squad," CT, Mar. 30, 1928.

When the police showed up: "Bailiff Shot by Dry Squad," CT, Mar. 30, 1928; " 'Ace' Golding's Police Clash Not His First," CT, Mar. 31, 1928; and "Get Warrant for Dry Agent," CT, April 1, 1928.

Irey recalled that the special agent: Irey, *Tax Dodgers,* 20.

On April 5, Caffey surrendered: "U.S. May Yield Dry Agent Who Shot Bailiff," CT, April 5, 1928; " 'Hardboiled' Facing Pressure," *Chicago Daily News,* April 5, 1928.

"The situation here is so tense . . .": "Seized as Deneen Bomber," CT, April 3, 1928.

In his meeting with Willebrandt: Irey, *Tax Dodgers,* 20.

He believed in Golding and his hard-boiled tactics: ENP/MS.

From their initial interview, Golding pegged: NPRC, George Golding.

He was a college boy: University of Chicago Office of the Registrar, Eliot Ness student transcript.

He'd started his career at the consumer-reporting: Eliot Ness personnel file, ATF.

And he was among the few agents in the office: "Drys Bob Up at Illinois U. and Stop Speakeasies," CT, May 26, 1927; Ness personnel file, ATF.

Golding put down that Eliot had landed: NPRC, George Golding.

He carried the Prohibition Bureau's rule book: ATF. The historic archive at the Bureau of Alcohol, Tobacco, Firearms and Explosives is not like the Library of Congress. It is a large, long storage room inside a much larger warehouse in industrial Washington, DC. Inside this room are rows and rows of rickety metal shelves, on which sit unmarked or often incorrectly marked cardboard boxes. Inside the boxes are hundreds of pieces of the agency's history. Nothing is in any discernible order. A box might have Prohibition Bureau ledgers documenting confiscated beer in Pittsburgh in 1928 along with ATU public-information pamphlets from the 1950s and the diaries of an agent from World War II. ATF staff historian Barbara Osteika allowed me to spend hours in the room going through box after box, taking notes as I went. An ATF intern, Daniel M. Huff, assisted in the search and made photocopies of whatever I wanted. Once we were done with a document, the original would go back in the cardboard box and disappear back onto the nondescript shelf, like a reenactment of the last scene of *Raiders of the Lost Ark.*

A memo from Washington the week before: Ness personnel file, ATF.

On June 5, Golding personally gave: Ibid.

"The way of the transgressor is hard . . .": "$4,000 Offered to Bribe Dry Agents Seized," CT, May 3, 1928.

The narrative for the City Hall Square operation and its aftermath comes from: "Shot by U.S. Drys in Loop," CT, Aug. 22, 1928; "Panic as Federal Agents Raid Loop Tower," *Chicago Daily News,* Aug. 22, 1928; "Dry Raiders Held for Loop Shooting," CT, Aug. 25, 1928; "Disband U.S. Dry Gunmen," CT, Aug. 29, 1928; "Golding's Squad 'Dry Cleaned' in Shakeup Order," CT, Sept. 12, 1928; George Golding's federal personnel folder, NPRC.

"All previous records for brutality, depravity . . .' ": "3 Killed, Dozens Hurt in 60 Day Drive by Drys," CT, Oct. 1, 1928.

The Prohibition Bureau dismissed a handful: "Dry Advocate of Terrorism Evades Rebuke," CT, Sept. 8, 1928.

Two weeks later, Yellowley named Jamie: NPRC, Alexander Jamie.

At one stop in 1922 a reporter asked: "The First Woman Federal Prohibition Agent," *A.I.U.,* December 1922, ATF.

She loved to quote "the highest authority . . .": Ibid.

In the second half of the nineteenth cen-

tury: *Longview Daily News,* Nov. 11, 2012.

Yet even decades later, after years of: Daniel Okrent, *Last Call: The Rise and Fall of Prohibition* (New York: Scribner, 2010), 36.

"The whole world is skew-jee . . .": Ibid., 3.

The notoriously corrupt William "Big Bill": Jonathan Eig, *Get Capone: The Secret Plot That Captured America's Most Wanted Gangster* (New York: Simon & Schuster, 2010), 24–25.

A visit the following year showed: Okrent, *Last Call,* 141.

Trying to enforce the law, she said: Geoffrey C. Ward, *Prohibition,* Florentine Films, directed by Ken Burns and Lynn Novick.

She freely admitted that she'd "had liquor . . .": Herbert Hoover Presidential Library and Museum, Papers of Herbert Hoover, Clippings File, 1928 Subjects. File: Prohibition, Articles by M. Willebrandt

"The skies were black with smoke . . .": Irey, *Tax Dodgers,* 19.

"Chicago, the world's Fourth City . . .": Edward Dean Sullivan, *Chicago Surrenders* (New York: Vanguard, 1930), xii–xiii.

When Torrio's forces, led by young Capone: Bergreen, *Capone: The Man and the Era,* 106-109.

The election, wrote another paper: Edward Dean Sullivan, Rattling the Cup on Chicago Crime (New York: Vanguard, 1929), 24.

Jamie "is lazy and takes three hours . . .": NPRC, Alexander Jamie.

When Eliot was in college, Jamie helped: NPRC, Alexander Jamie; "Where the Trails Cross," 1985–90, vol. 16–20, 19:3, 99, Michelle Regan personal collection.

The dry law, the Tribune declared: "Prohibition Blamed for Booze Gangs' Long Reign of Guns and Terror in Chicago Heights," CT, Jan. 7, 1929.

The Outfit's influence stretched across: Bergreen, Capone: The Man and the Era, 347.

The police believed him to be responsible: "Seized as Deneen Bomber," CT, April 3, 1928.

Earlier in the year, gangsters had shot to death: "War Rages in Chicago Heights," unlabeled magazine article, ENP, reel 1.

Instead of classical skyscrapers: Bessie Louise Pierce, ed., As Others See Chicago: Impressions of Visitors, 1673–1933 (University of Chicago Press, 2004), 430.

"I would not want to live there . . .": Ibid., 276–77.

He was a mama's boy, the youngest: AI, Arnold Sagalyn; Heimel, Eliot Ness: The Real Story, 16–20; Ness personnel file,

ATF; various pages from unknown edition of the *Fenger Courier* and the privately published local history "Where the Trails Cross," Michelle Regan personal collection.

Chapter 3: The Special Agents

So he wasn't surprised in the fall: ENP/MS.

Years later he would describe Albert: ENP/MS.

Emma disapproved of her youngest son's: Heimel, *Eliot Ness: The Real Story,* 20.

"If there's anything you taught me . . .": Heimel, *Eliot Ness: The Real Story,* 20; Kenneth Tucker, *Eliot Ness and the Untouchables: The Historical Reality and the Film and Television Depictions,* second edition (Jefferson, NC: McFarland, 2011), 13.

Peter had more than twenty bakers: NPRC, Alexander Jamie. Jamie worked at his father-in-law's bakery before joining the FBI and detailed his work experience on his application for federal employment.

"He never had a lot to say . . .": Heimel, *Eliot Ness: The Real Story,* 16.

Kooken took charge of the conversation: ENP/MS; "War Rages in Chicago Heights," ENP, reel 1.

Eliot couldn't help but swell with pride: ENP/MS.

The bureau wanted to build a conspiracy case: Ibid.

Their chauffeur was Frank Basile: *Homicide in Chicago 1870–1930: Interactive Database,* Frank Basile entry, case number 9507, accessed May 4, 2013, homicide .northwestern.edu/database/9163/.

Basile, who spoke fluent Italian: "U.S. Joins Hunt for Murderers of Dry Informer," CT, Dec. 13, 1928.

"They would leave their cars . . .": ENP/ MS.

Even Basile joined in, pretending: "War Rages in Chicago Heights," ENP, reel 1.

The men found more than a dozen: ENP/ MS.

"Come and talk . . .": "War Rages in Chicago Heights," ENP, reel 1.

Eliot, "the hungry one": ENP/MS.

He and Martino "had quite . . .": ENP/ MS; "Indicted Fugitive Burned to Death as Still Explodes," CT, Dec. 1, 1928.

Finally, they grudgingly agreed on a weekly payment: "U.S. Shuns Concession and Spurs Gang Drive," " 'Untouchables' Rewarded," *Washington Evening Star,* ENP, reel 1; " 'Untouchables' Hazard Death in Campaign against Capone," *Washington Evening Star,* June 18, 1931, ENP, reel 1.

"The silk-shirted Italian has just asked . . .": ENP/MS.

"I felt young and alone . . .": "TV Brings Father Back for Son of Eliot Ness," CPD, Oct. 17, 1959.

Moving quickly, shouting over one another: Bergreen, *Capone: The Man and the Era,* 347. It's not clear whether the truck-jacking was sanctioned by Jamie or was done on the QT by the ambitious young agents — or even whether it was something mistakenly attributed to the legendary Eliot Ness long after the fact.

They also began pocketing $100: " 'Untouchables' Hazard Death in Campaign against Capone," *Washington Evening Star,* June 18, 1931, ENP, reel 1.

"It was apparent," Eliot wrote: ENP/MS.

That meant hitting the Cozy Corners: Narrative for raid on the Cozy Corners comes from Bergreen, *Capone: The Man and the Era,* 349, and ENP/MS.

Late that night, Eliot showed up on: "The Real Eliot Ness," *Tucson Citizen,* July 17, 1987; unlabeled *Santa Fe New Mexican* clipping, July 23, 1987; letter from Dorothy Hauck (Marty Lahart's widow) to Marie Sroka, Scott Sroka personal collection.

"He became deathly sick . . .": ENP/MS.

Martino understood what his arrest: "Indicted Fugitive Burned to Death as Still Explodes," CT, Dec. 1, 1928.

"He apparently had not been . . .": ENP/ MS.

Assistant District Attorney Dan Anderson: "Indicted Fugitive Burned to Death as Still Explodes," CT, Dec. 1, 1928.

Ten days later, an unidentified man: "Gunmen Kill New Victim in Chgo. Heights," CT, Dec. 10, 1928.

At 7 a.m. on Wednesday, December 12: *Homicide in Chicago 1870–1930: Interactive Database,* Frank Basile entry, case number 9507, accessed May 4, 2013, homicide .northwestern.edu/database/9163/.

They fished a calendar: "U.S. Joins Hunt for Murderers of Dry Informer," CT, Dec. 13, 1928.

"Basile was a government witness . . .": Ibid.

When he saw Basile: Eliot Ness with Oscar Fraley, *The Untouchables: The Real Story* (New York: Pocket Books, 1987), 189.

They kept at it even after the police: *Homicide in Chicago 1870–1930: Interactive Database,* Frank Basile entry, case number 9507, accessed May 4, 2013, homicide .northwestern.edu/database/9163/. Nearly thirty years later, in his notes to Oscar Fraley, Eliot would simply say, "The evidence on him was positive enough to make us feel that the person who had gotten [Basile] had been brought to justice." See ENP/MS.

At restaurants, Eliot recalled: Bergreen, *Capone: The Man and the Era,* 349.

He quietly, bashfully: AI, Dave Deming, Sept. 7, 2011.

Three days after Christmas: unlabeled newspaper clipping; CT, Jan. 3, 1929; ENP, reel 1; ENP/MS.

Chapter 4: Flaunting Their Badness

The narrative for the Chicago Heights operation is derived from: "Prohibition Blamed for Booze Gangs' Long Reign of Guns and Terror in Chicago Heights," CT, Jan. 7, 1929; "Chgo. Heights Raided by U.S.," CT, Jan. 7, 1929; "Chicago Heights Rum Quiz Brings 81 Indictments," CT, May 4, 1929; Eig, *Get Capone,* 83, 111, 236; ENP/MS; "War Rages in Chicago Heights," ENP, reel 1.

"George E. Q. Johnson and State's Attorney . . .": "Indict Suspect in Plot to Kill Two Dry Agents," CT, Jan. 3, 1929.

He added: "There would be a lot of emotion . . .": "TV Brings Father Back for Son of Eliot Ness," CPD, Oct. 17, 1959.

Chapter 5: The Capone Fans

Kids and mothers loved him: Bergreen, *Capone: The Man and the Era,* 15–16.

"We're big business . . .": Eig, *Get Capone*, 81.

Another local bootlegger, Terry Druggan: Okrent, *Last Call*, 274.

The social worker Jane Addams: Eig, *Get Capone*, 81.

"Morally," the writer Nelson Algren: Ibid., 147.

"They dream of the Forty Two's . . .": Terkel, *Talking to Myself*, 14–15.

One night at the Paramount Club: Terkel, *Hard Times*, 172.

He told the *Chicago Tribune*'s Genevieve: Eig, *Get Capone*, 272.

" 'Public service' is my motto": Ibid., 123.

The novelist Mary Borden: Pierce, *As Others See Chicago*, 492.

The fifty-six-year-old Iowan's: Johnson; ENP, reel 1.

"You'd have to be crazy, right?": Bergreen, *Capone: The Man and the Era*, 15.

The St. Valentine's Day Massacre: Ibid.

New York's Lucky Luciano: Geoffrey C. Ward, *Prohibition*.

He wrote a long, defensive reply: Eig, *Get Capone*, 294–95.

As the Internal Revenue agents working the case: Internal Revenue Service memo dated July 8, 1931, National Archives, record group 58, 1791–1996.

President Hoover, and so Attorney General Mitchell: Eig, *Get Capone,* 219–21.

Chapter 6: Good-Hearted Al

Willebrandt had once said: Okrent, *Last Call,* 141.

The Justice Department had been encouraging Johnson: Eig, *Get Capone,* 239.

"As Mr. Kooken and myself are leaving . . .": NPRC, Alexander Jamie, letter dated Oct. 22, 1930.

He noted that the agent: Ness personnel file, ATF.

When Johnson told him: Ness and Fraley, *The Untouchables,* 23; ENP, reel 1.

"The success of the entire venture": Ness and Fraley, *The Untouchables,* 27–28.

Good men were hard to come by: Ness personnel file, ATF.

In November and December 1930: NPRC: Lyle Chapman, William Gardner, Alexander Jamie, Martin Lahart, Joseph Leeson, Samuel Seager (W. E. Bennett, Department of Justice memo, various dates); Ness personnel file, ATF.

Eliot, via his cowriter Oscar Fraley: Ness and Fraley, *The Untouchables,* 27.

Twenty-five years later, in his memoir: Ibid., 19.

Johnson had worked with Marty Lahart: Bergreen, *Capone: The Man and the Era,*

349; ENP/MS.

Jamie instead sent him on temporary assignment: NPRC, Samuel Seager.

He was known in the bureau: ENP/MS; NPRC, Joseph Leeson.

On December 15, William Jennings Gardner: NPRC, William Gardner.

"I am exceedingly interested in the case . . .": Ibid.

Johnson also tapped another Detroit agent: NPRC, Joseph Leeson.

A week before receiving Nye's letter: *Time,* Sept. 19, 1927.

Prohibition Bureau commissioner J. M. Doran: NPRC, William Gardner.

"Frankly, I pondered how to get out of it": "Member of 'Untouchables' Who 'Broke' Capone Recalls Exploits," *Los Angeles Times,* Oct. 4, 1962.

Six months before Johnson requested Chapman: NPRC, Lyle Chapman.

Eliot would describe him as "a barrel-chested giant . . .": Ness and Fraley, *The Untouchables,* 32.

Rounding out what would become the core group: Bureau Bulletin, June 20, 1931, ATF; Ness and Fraley, *The Untouchables,* 33–34; Tucker, *Eliot Ness and the Untouchables,* 16.

pharmacist and World War I–era baseball: "Lawrence S. Ritter," *New York Times,*

Feb. 17, 2004; the obituary quoted from Ritter's *The Glory of Their Times.*

Gang violence had spiked again: Eig, *Get Capone,* 106.

Homicide detectives and a morgue truck: Frank Deford, *The Best American Sports Writing: 1993* (Boston: Houghton Mifflin Co., 1993), 241.

A friend remembered him frequently: "The Real Eliot Ness," *Tucson Citizen,* July 17, 1987.

"The Depression was *so* real . . .": Terkel, *Hard Times,* 164.

"Suddenly, all the copybook maxims . . .": Terkel, *Hard Times,* 169–71.

"The bread line outside of Al Capone's . . .": Pierce, *As Others See Chicago,* 490–93.

As she headed upstairs: Ibid.

Chapter 7: The First Step

The brewery business made for a prime target: " 'Untouchables' Hazard Death in Campaign Against Capone," *Washington Evening Star,* June 18, 1931, ENP, reel 1.

He'd even had time for a real personal life: Heimel, *Eliot Ness: The Real Story,* 57; AI, Michelle Regan personal collection, Aug. 6, 2012; ENP, reel 2.

they had married on August 9, 1929:

Cook County (Ill.) Clerk, certificate 12466, Michelle Regan personal collection.

"We knew that regularity was necessary . . .": " 'Untouchables' Hazard Death in Campaign Against Capone," *Washington Evening Star,* June 18, 1931, ENP, reel 1.

"The first observation we made . . .": ENP/MS.

Sometimes they would follow by: "Puts Raids Up to Chief," CPD, July 14, 1935.

"The garage was on Cicero Avenue . . .": ENP/MS.

On January 18, a Sunday, Gardner called: NPRC, William Gardner.

One high school friend remembered him: Heimel, *Eliot Ness: The Real Story,* 17.

On January 20, just six weeks after being assigned: NPRC, William Gardner.

The long, detailed memo impressed Avis: Ness personnel file, ATF.

Chapter 8: Kid Stuff

The narrative of the raid on the South Cicero Avenue brewery is constructed from: AI, Pam Sroka, June 28, 2011; Bergreen, *Capone: The Man and the Era,* 409–10; "Capone Brewery, Huge Beer Supply Raided in Cicero," CT, Mar. 26, 1931; unlabeled news clippings, ENP, reel 1; ENP/MS; Fraley, "The Real Eliot Ness."

Years later, Eliot would call his mission: Ness and Fraley, *The Untouchables,* 85.

The team's agents continued tailing trucks: ENP/MS; Bergreen, *Capone: The Man and the Era,* 412; ENP/MS; unlabeled news clippings, ENP, reel 1.

The seizure of the two breweries: ENP, reel 1.

"We were to arrest him again . . .": ENP/MS.

"At 11 o clock four sedans swept . . .": ENP, reel 1.

He was directing the two men: Bureau Bulletin, June 20, 1931; "Hold 4 Capone Aids Seized at Raided Brewery," CT, April 14, 1931.

Two days later, jacked up on success: "Nab Five in Raid on Capone Stills; Alky Stock Seized," *Chicago Heights Star,* April 15, 1931, ENP, reel 1.

That meant Eliot would get to make: NPRC, Paul Robsky.

Almost every day in Greenville: "Last of the Untouchables," *National Star,* April 20, 1974.

The squad rented a basement apartment: Sources used to reconstruct the phone-tap operation include: unlabeled news clippings, ENP, reel 1; Ness and Fraley, *The Untouchables,* 112–14; Ness personnel file, ATF; NPRC, Paul Robsky; Tucker, *Eliot Ness and the Untouchables,*

18–19. Robsky's recollections of the event come from his 1962 memoir, *Last of the Untouchables* (New York: Pocket Books, 1962), 77–82. The book, cowritten with Oscar Fraley, generally is not a reliable document, though Eliot's own memories and official Prohibition Bureau records support some of Robsky's version of the Montmartre operation.

At last he hit one — Chapman: ENP/MS; NPRC, Paul Robsky. In Robsky's telling in *Last of the Untouchables,* Lahart gets inside the Montmartre and makes a call out to "Edna" while Robsky is raking the line. Eliot's memory, which appears to be supported by official memoranda, has the call coming into the Montmartre.

"The federal men found 140 barrels . . .": unlabeled *Chicago Daily News* clipping, ENP, reel 1.

Calloway was already under indictment: Bureau Bulletin, June, 20, 1931.

The agents ran a car off: "Dry Raiders Cost Capone Half Million in Six Weeks," *Chicago Herald and Examiner,* Sept. 26, 1931, ENP, reel 1.

On his own Eliot chased: "Seize Beer Truck after Chase in Streets of Loop," CT, May 12, 1931.

A few weeks later, the team took down: "Dry Raiders Cost Capone Half Million in Six Weeks," *Chicago Herald and Examiner,*

Sept. 26, 1931, ENP, reel 1.

Chemist John R. Matchett remembered: Unpublished internal ATF history, 87, ATF.

"I have never met such a hostile group . . .": Vollmer, "Fred E. Inbau: Scientific Crime Detection: Early Efforts in Chicago," in "August Vollmer: Pioneer in Police Professionalism," vol. 2, 10–11.

Years later, in another life: AI, Scott Sroka personal collection, June 25, 2011.

Agents and support staff noticed how: "Eliot Ness Tipped Off His Big Raids," CT, Mar. 1, 1970.

Stanley Slesick, one of the Prohibition agents: Ibid.

"He and the six or seven other people . . .": Berardi.

"They have information that you got your job . . .": "U.S. Uncovers True Story of Capone's Rise," CT, June 14, 1931.

He knew the Mob must be approaching: NPRC, Alexander Jamie; Ness personnel file, ATF.

Leeson would later tell his second wife: AI, Pam Sroka, June 28, 2011.

"Capone's men would pop up . . .": "Member of 'Untouchables' Who 'Broke' Capone Recalls Exploits," *Los Angeles Times,* Oct. 4, 1962.

Gardner's college football career: Lars Anderson, *Carlisle vs. Army: Jim Thorpe, Dwight Eisenhower, Pop Warner, and the Forgotten Story of Football's Greatest Battle* (New York: Random House, 2007), 19; 158–59; Crawford, 83.

He would later describe Gardner admiringly: ENP/MS.

"You appear in the newspapers . . .": NPRC, William Gardner.

"His boss in Indianapolis had . . .": NPRC, Lyle Chapman.

"Her greatest wish was not to be known": "Eliot Ness' First Wife Quietly Dies," *St. Petersburg Times,* Nov. 19, 1994.

He'd sometimes shudder at "how close . . .": Fraley, "The Real Eliot Ness."

By late spring, saloon owners had noticed: Eig, *Get Capone,* 318; unlabeled newspaper clipping, CT, May 12, 1931; ENP, reel 1.

The Mob stole their cars: "U.S. Uncovers True Story of Capone's Rise," CT, June 14, 1931; "Member of 'Untouchables' Who 'Broke' Capone Recalls Exploits," *Los Angeles Times,* Oct. 4, 1962.

"I remember twice Ness and I . . .": "Member of 'Untouchables' Who 'Broke' Capone Recalls Exploits," *Los Angeles*

Times, Oct. 4, 1962.

One night Eliot caught a junior gangster: "U.S. Uncovers True Story of Capone's Rise," CT, June 14, 1931; Robert J. Schoenberg, *Mr. Capone* (New York: Perennial, 1993), 297–98.

Chapter 10: The Untouchables

Sources for the tax and Volstead cases against Capone include: Bergreen, *Capone: The Man and the Era,* 430; "U.S. Uncovers True Story of Capone's Rise," CT, June 14, 1931; Eig, *Get Capone,* 318–19, 330; "U.S. Brings 'Chief Foe' to Bar Upon Two Charges," unlabeled newspaper clipping, ENP, reel 1; other unlabeled news clippings and memos, ENP reel 1; ENP/MS; Frank Wilson memo dated Dec. 21, 1933, Internal Revenue Service archives.

Sources for Ness and Untouchables celebrity include: Berardi; Bergreen, *Capone: The Man and the Era,* 343–44; Bureau Bulletin, June 20, 1931; "8 New U.S. Heroes! They Resisted Capone's Gold," CPD, June 15, 1931; "Capone Allies See His Finish and Dispute for Gang Throne," CT, June 15, 1931; Condon, *Cleveland,* 236; "Capone's Power Is Destroyed by Fearless Eight," unknown date and publication, ENP, reel 1; letters to Eliot Ness and unlabeled news clippings, ENP, reel 1; "Al's

Nemesis Boasts Ph.B.; Finds Humor in Dry Work," *Chicago Herald and Examiner,* June 15, 1931; Heimel, *Eliot Ness: The Real Story,* 16; "Capone Dynasty Falls Under Incessant Hammering of United States Officials," *Lowell Sun,* June 17, 1931; Schoenberg, *Mr. Capone,* 297; " 'Untouchables' Rewarded," *Washington Evening Star,* Washington, June 15, 1931.

They stormed the Lexington: ENP, reel 1.

Eliot would spot dashing Mob associate: "Capone Allies See His Finish and Dispute for Gang Throne," CT, Nov. 15, 1931; unlabeled newspaper clipping, "Gang Playboy Meets Fate at Football Game," ENP, reel 1.

Wrote the *Tribune:* "Capone Allies See His Finish and Dispute for Gang Throne," CT, June 15, 1931.

"Out: Is Johnny there? . . .": ENP, reel 1.

"Well, boys, it looks like . . .": newspaper clippings: "Dry Raiders 'All Wet,' " *Chicago Evening American,* July 17, 1931; "Dry Flips a Half Dollar; Uncovers $15,000 Rum," *Chicago Evening Post,* undated; "Missing 'Clink' of Coin Bares Liquor Cache," unknown publication, ENP, reel 1.

On the night of September 21, 1931: Berardi; ENP, reel 1.

In the weeks that followed, the phone company: "Al Capone's Gang Taps Phone

Wires, Federal Agents Say," CT, Aug. 12, 1931.

the young leader of the Capone squad: Ness and Fraley, *The Untouchables*, 135–36.

"From the inception of the organization . . .": Bergreen, *Capone: The Man and the Era*, 411.

The *Chicago Daily News* wrote that Eliot Ness: unlabeled news clipping, *Chicago Daily News*, Sept. 23, 1931, ENP, reel 1.

The Outfit was getting hit with a double whammy: "S. Side Bars Lower Beer Price to 15c; first Cut in Dry Era," CT, Mar. 31, 1932.

On a Sunday in July, truck drivers: "Beer Drivers' Strike Goes Up in Foam," CT, July 14, 1932.

Chapter 11: A Real and Lasting Impression

On October 5, 1931, Al Capone: Eig, *Get Capone*, 343–44.

"That's the first [time] that Eliot Ness ever saw . . .": Berardi.

George Johnson had been nervous enough: Eig, *Get Capone*, 340–42.

Frank Wilson had broken the code: "Legendary Lawmen, Part 7: Four Who Got Capone," CT, Jan. 15, 2012.

"Did this Robin Hood buy $8,000 worth . . .": Ibid.

"It was a blow to the belt . . .": Eig, *Get Capone,* 369.

In June, a machine-gun volley eviscerated: "Machine Gunners Kill 'Red' Barker," CT, June 17, 1932.

Six months later, another potential boss: "Capone Brother, Pals Quizzed on Newberry Death," CT, Jan. 17, 1933.

"Did you ever think you wanted something . . .": Heimel, *Eliot Ness: The Real Story,* 11.

M. L. Harney, Chicago's new Prohibition: NPRC, Paul Robsky.

On January 21, with Capone: "Dry Agents Arrest Five in Raid on Capone Brewery," CT, Jan. 22, 1932; "44 Arraigned After 33 Raids by Dry Squads," CT, May 29, 1932; unlabeled news clippings, ENP, reel 1.

"The automobile was a Ford coach . . .": "Even Beer Trade's Hard Up; Deliver Now in Small Cars," *Chicago Daily News,* Sept. 12, 1932, ENP, reel 1.

So he called Armand Bollaert: "The Real Eliot Ness," *Tucson Citizen,* July 17, 1987.

The assignment took Eliot's "pencil detective" to: NPRC, Lyle Chapman.

Johnson told the press that the Volstead: "New Rum Case Blasts Capone Parole Chance," CT, Mar. 8, 1932; "U.S. Will Seek New Liquor Indictment for Capone Gang," CT, Sept. 26, 1932; Eig, *Get Capone,* 377.

Back in Chicago, Chapman shut himself: NPRC, Lyle Chapman.

In February 1932, according to a personnel memo: NPRC, Bernard Cloonan.

Eliot could never take a bribe — *never*: AI, Arnold Sagalyn, June 9, 2011.

A month later, Eliot was promoted: Ness personnel file, ATF; "Exposed Capone; Wins Promotion," CPD, April 25, 1932; "Capone Nemesis Promoted," *New York Times,* April 25, 1932.

A few months later, the bureau also booted: NPRC, Paul Robsky, termination letter dated Aug. 9, 1933.

Every dry agent in the city: "Chicago Chiefs of Dry Bureau on Anxious Seat," CT, Aug. 7, 1933.

"It is most peculiar that . . .": NPRC, Albert Wolff.

He called himself "the last . . .": *People,* July 13, 1987.

Chapter 12: It's Just Tuesday Night

"Crowds were gathered in a few . . .": "Prohibition Era Ended! Loop Crowds Hail Repeal," *Chicago Herald and Examiner,* Dec. 6, 1933.

Joe Leeson moved over to the Treasury Department's: "New Agent Was One of First Assigned to Al Capone Probe," *Cincinnati Times-Star,* Jan. 12, 1940, Scott Sroka

594

personal collection; NPRC: Bernard Cloonan, William Gardner, Martin Lahart, Joseph Leeson, Paul Robsky.

The unit's Midwest administrator: Ness personnel file, ATF.

But what he really wanted: "A Brief History of the FBI," accessed May 4, 2013, fbi.gov/about-us/history/brief-history.

"Dear Mr. Hoover . . .": ENP, reel 1.

Eliot thanked Johnson: Ibid.

Even ten years later, with: Borroel, *Story of the Untouchables,* 70.

Chapter 13: Chasing Moonshine

In late August 1934: James Jessen Badal, *In the Wake of the Butcher: Cleveland's Torso Murders* (Kent, OH: Kent State University Press, 2001), 22–28; unlabeled news clipping: CN, Sept. 6, 1934; CPD, Sept. 5–7, 1934; CP, Sept. 5, 1934, ENP reel 2.

He and Edna had moved to Cleveland: Ness personnel file, ATF; "City's Bootleg Output Tops Legal Liquor," CN, Jan. 8, 1935.

Sixty-five percent of the population: "Labor: Jobless," *Time,* Feb. 24, 1930.

In February 1930, some two thousand men: Ibid.

By the end of the year, a hundred thousand: Badal, *In the Wake of the Butcher,* 6; Philip W. Porter, *Cleveland: Confused City* *on a Seesaw* (Columbus: Ohio State University, 1976), 73–74; John Vacha, *Meet Me on Lake Erie, Dearie! Cleveland's Great Lakes Exposition, 1936–1937* (Kent, OH: Kent State University Press, 2011), 23.

Broke, out-of-work Clevelanders: Vacha, *Meet Me on Lake Erie,* 1.

"Cleveland's bootleg output today . . .": unlabeled news clippings, CN, Jan. 8–9, 1935, ENP, reel 2.

"He was a very great person": "Woman 'Graduates' From NASA Center," CPD, Nov. 3, 1966.

George Mulvanity, a Georgetown University: *Today* show interview with Mulvanity, Feb. 10, 1972.

Eliot "was a real eagle eye": "Last of Ness Men Leaving Duty Here," CPD, Jan. 19, 1972.

Bruner crowed to his superiors: unlabeled news clippings, CPD, Oct. 8, 1934; unlabeled clipping, CPD, Mar. 17, 1935, ENP, reel 2.

Years later Mulvavity told his son: AI, Francis Mulvanity, July 7, 2011.

Eliot had been in the building: "Feds Here Smash New $75,000 Still," CPD, July 11, 1935; "Crashing Ohio's Greatest Bootleg Hideout," CPD, Jan. 19, 1936; ENP, reel 2.

Eliot's charge as chief investigator: "Feds Here Smash New $75,000 Still," CPD, July 11, 1935; "Crashing Ohio's Greatest Bootleg Hideout," CPD, Jan. 19, 1936; "George D. Mulvanity, Last Untouchable," CPD, Oct. 16, 1976; Ness personnel file, ATF.

Months of interrogations, wiretaps: "Feds Here Smash $75,000 Still," CPD, July 11, 1935; unlabeled notes and clippings, ENP, reel 2.

One time, after raiding a small distillery: "Gets Into a Bad Sweat," CPD, Aug. 29, 1935.

Another time, he stopped to chat: "Raiders Nab 3 in 'Haunted House,' " CPD, Sept. 3, 1935.

As the agents stood smoking: "Crashing Ohio's Greatest Bootleg Hideout," CPD, Jan. 19, 1936; ENP, reel 2.

After the agents finished up: "Crashing Ohio's Greatest Bootleg Hideout," CPD, Jan. 19, 1936; AI, Francis Mulvanity, July 7, 2011.

Chapter 14: Real Work

The narrative for the day Eliot became safety director and resulting press coverage comes from: "Ness Sworn In as Safety Head," CN, Dec. 11, 1935; "Police Shakeup Seen in Chief's Check on Men," CN, Dec. 14, 1935; Condon, *Cleveland,* 231; "Police Politics Will End, Is Burton Pledge; Lake Front Action, Is Miller Promise," CPD, Oct. 29, 1935; "Facts First,

Then Talk, Says Ness," "The Inside of the News in Cleveland," "Ness Is Nemesis of Crooked Cops," CPD, Dec. 12, 1935; "Ness Is Seen as City's New Safety Chief," CP, Dec. 7, 1935; "Eliot H. Ness Takes Oath as City Safety Director," "Ness — Safety Director," CP, Dec. 11, 1935; "The Cleveland Scene," "The New Safety Director," CP, Dec. 14, 1935; unlabeled news clippings, ENP, reel 2.

The director oversaw the police, fire: "Fight to Stop Labor Rackets in Cleveland," CT, Nov. 24, 1937.

The second meeting between the mayor: "Keenan to Decide on City Job Today," "Keenan's New Opportunity," CPD, Nov. 20, 1935.

The mayor himself admitted: "Burton Reports City On Way Up," CPD, Dec. 13, 1935.

The new mayor, sighed a *Plain Dealer:* "Keenan Says No," CPD, Nov. 21, 1935.

For the second week running, midday: "Cleveland on Way to Win Title of 'The Dark City,' " CP, Dec. 14, 1935.

Under Mayor Harry L. Davis, whose administration: Porter, *Cleveland,* 87.

Just days after becoming mayor: "Job Slash Reprisals Threaten Burton," CP, Nov. 15, 1935.

The most recent director, Martin: "Brother Sat Up for Drowned Girl,"

"Lavelle Won't Resign; Coroner Gets Stories of Drinking and Death," "Many Lies Told, Truth Does Out," CPD, July 2, 1935; "Puts Raids Up to Chief," CPD, July 14, 1935.

"Ness would be just the kind of guy . . .": Porter, *Cleveland,* 97.

"He is Eliot Ness . . .": "Ness Leads Field for Safety Post," " 'Untouchable' Who Spurned Capone's Bribes Willing to Smash Crime Here," CP, Dec. 8, 1935, ENP, reel 2.

Colleagues with longtime experience: Arnold Sagalyn, *A Promise Fulfilled: The Memoir of Arnold Sagalyn* (privately published, 2010), 45.

He was now arresting people simply: "Makes First Arrest Here for Unbroken Used Liquor Bottles," CPD, Mar. 8, 1935.

"I've served under five safety directors . . .": "Policy Raid Stops 5 Big-Time Games," CPD, Jan. 7, 1938.

He drew "doodlegrams": "Eliot Ness: The Cosmopolite of the Month," *Cosmopolitan,* Aug. 1940, ENP, reel 2.

Vollmer background information comes from: Ken Alder, *The Lie Detectors: The History of an American Obsession* (New York: Free Press, 2007), xiii, 19, 66, 72; "Police: Finest of the Finest," *Time,* Feb. 18, 1966; August Vollmer, *The Police and*

Modern Society (Berkeley: University of California Press, 1936), 118.

Sitting down to his typewriter: August Vollmer Papers, box 44, The Bancroft Library, University of California, Berkeley, letter dated Dec. 16, 1935.

During that first full day on the job: Newspaper clippings (CN, Dec. 14, 1935; CPD, Dec. 15, 1935), ENP, reel 2.

The next night, determined to prove: "Ness Turns Raiders on Night Tour," CPD, Dec. 14, 1935; "Crimefighter With a Passion," CPD, Oct. 4, 1998; "First 'Bookie Raid' by Ness is Fizzle," "Ness Quits Game of Cops and Robbers," "Police Shakeup Seen in Chief's Check on Men," CN, Dec. 14, 1935; unlabeled news clippings, ENP, reel 2.

A sergeant loaned him a gun: ATF.

But Eliot, undaunted, told the mayor: Porter, *Cleveland,* 97.

He wrote to Vollmer: August Vollmer Papers, box 24, The Bancroft Library, University of California, Berkeley, letter dated Jan. 4, 1936.

Chapter 15: Tough Babies

The narrative for the Harvard raid is constructed from: Condon, *Cleveland,* 233–34; "Cullitan, Ness Shut Harvard Club; Gamblers Block Raiders 6 Hours,"

"You Can't Do That to Us, 'Boys' Cry," " 'Let's Go,' Ness Says, as He Shows His G-Man Training," "Prosecutor's Sudden Attack Also Closes Thomas Club Layout," "Sheriff Refuses to Raid; Ness Does It as Citizen," CPD, Jan. 11, 1936; "Ness Roasts Sulzmann's Denial of Aid," CPD, Jan. 14, 1936; "Calls Sum Portion of Week's Cut," CPD, Mar. 1, 1936, ENP, reel 2; "Refused Aid As He Faced Guns," CP, Jan. 11, 1936; memorandum for the director, "Re: Police Corruption in Cleveland, Ohio," May 12, 1936, "FBI Records: The Vault," accessed May 4, 2013, vault.fbi.gov/Eliot%20Ness; Jedick, "Eliot Ness."

"Long before there was a Las Vegas . . .": Condon, "The Last American Hero."

The police found Fergus buried: "Whatever Happened to the Gambling Palaces of the Great Depression?" CPD, Nov. 27, 1977.

The Harvard Club boasted some eighteen: "Cullitan, Ness Shut Harvard Club; Gamblers Block Raiders 6 Hours," CPD, Jan. 11, 1936.

Forty years later, one member would recall: "Whatever Happened to the Gambling Palaces of the Great Depression?" CPD, Nov. 27, 1977.

"They may wear all the shorts . . .": "Ness Stamps Women's Shorts O.K. for Street," CN, July 10, 1936.

601

"Eliot Ness last night showed . . .": " 'Let's Go,' Ness Says, as He Shows His G-Man Training," CPD, Jan. 11, 1936.

"It was a highly credible thing . . .": unlabeled news clippings, CN, Jan. 11, 1936 and CP, Jan. 11, 1936, ENP, reel 2.

"About the time we got there . . .": "Crimefighter with a Passion," CPD, Oct. 4, 1998.

Flynn "found six deputies . . .": Condon, *Cleveland,* 236; "Ness Roasts Sulzmann's Denial of Aid," CPD, Jan. 14, 1936.

"In any city where corruption continues . . .": Ibid.

He told Lieutenant Michael Blackwell: "Officer, Noted for Valor, Wins Promotion Chance," CP, April 30, 1936; ENP, reel 2.

"The excitement generated in these raids . . .": Sagalyn, *A Promise Fulfilled,* 48–49.

The police moved out every girl: Memorandum for the director, "Re: Police Corruption in Cleveland, Ohio," May 12, 1936, "FBI Records: The Vault," accessed May 4, 2013, vault.fbi.gov/Eliot%20Ness.

A local manufacturer of negligees: ENP, reel 2, undated letter to Ness.

The *Plain Dealer* exulted that: "Harassing Gamblers," CPD, Mar. 9, 1936; Letter to the editor, CPD, July 26, 1936.

Even the Harvard Club was up and run-

ning: "Held in Canada in $6,800 Shortage," CPD, Aug. 26, 1936; "Marshall Out, So No Raid on Harvard Club," CPD, Sept. 1, 1936; unlabeled news clippings, ENP, reel 2.

Chapter 16: This Guy Ness Is Crazy

Cleveland "was well on its way. . .": "Cleveland on Way to Win Title of 'The Dark City,' " CP, Dec. 14, 1935.

In the early morning blackness: Badal, *In the Wake of the Butcher,* 49–52.

The city's smallest paper: Badal, *In the Wake of the Butcher,* 52–53.

Four months before, in September 1935: Ibid., 30–32, 37.

Dudley McDowell, a security officer: Ibid., 35–39.

He declared that the traffic: "Traffic 'Siberia' Displeases Ness," CPD, Dec. 14, 1935, ENP, reel 2.

He declared that when they weren't fighting: Sagalyn, *A Promise Fulfilled,* 46.

"People resent change": "Ness Hopes to Place Fire Department in No. 1 Spot With Newest Experiment," CN, Nov. 14, 1936.

Throughout the winter and spring: Martin L. Davey Papers, box 1, folder 55, Kent State University Special Collections and Archives.

"If people have been accustomed to . . .":

Jedick, "Eliot Ness."

The *Press* ran a series of photos: "A Ness
Grip Beats the Trigger!" CP, April 30, 1936,
ENP, reel 2, unlabeled news clipping.

"You have a badge just like mine . . .":
unlabeled news clipping, CN, April 4,
1936, ENP, reel 2.

**At about the same time, an unshaven
man:** "Says He's Ness, Held," CPD, May
28, 1936.

Chapter 17: The Boy Wonder

**The Ness, Cullitan, and McGill meeting
is detailed in:** Neil W. McGill and William H. Perry, *Court Cases of Eliot Ness: An
Exciting True Story in the Life of Eliot Ness
Told by the Cleveland Prosecutor Who
Worked with Him* (Fullerton, CA: Sultana
Press, 1971), 23–25.

The team became known around: Porter,
Cleveland, 98.

Flynn told the city's financial officers:
"Flynn to Have Investigator Check Police,"
CPD, Dec. 29, 1935.

"No fox hound ever hit the trail . . .":
McGill and Perry, *Court Cases of Eliot Ness,*
25.

"Time meant nothing to him . . .": "Ness
Recalled as Quiet Enforcer," CPD, April
30, 1960.

"We have no place for traitors . . .":
"What They Are Saying," CPD, Feb. 7, 1937.

Then the safety director himself scored: unlabeled news clippings, ENP, reel 2.

Chapter 18: Right to the Heart of Things

When Clayton Fritchey arrived at his desk: "Cleveland Versus the Crooks," *Reader's Digest,* Feb. 1939, 48–51.

He'd grown up in Baltimore: "Clayton Fritchey, Columnist and Adviser to Democrats, Dies," *Washington Post,* Jan. 24, 2001.

The lumbering cop, weighing in: "Cadek Is Cop Who Saved $109,000," "Grand Jury Hears 9 in Police Case," CPD, April 14, 1936.

"Clayton was the best investigative reporter . . .": AI, Arnold Sagalyn, June 9, 2011.

His attorney, Gerard J. Pilliod: "Cadek Stand Challenges Ness' Power," CPD, April 15, 1936.

Some said they had paid him: "Grand Jury Hears 9 in Police Case," CPD, April 14, 1936.

"The gang told me to tell him . . .": "Lawyer Ordered Out in Cadek Quiz," CPD, April 16, 1936.

"Two and two make four . . .": "Court Is Told Cadek Wished For Car; Got 2," CPD,

May 22, 1936.

Other former bootleggers told of: "6 Policemen Back Cadek On Defense," CPD, May 26, 1936; "Cadek Silent as Bribe Case Goes to Jury," CP, May 26, 1936.

"A good guy always gets kicked . . .": "Cadek Guilty of Bribery, Is Jailed," "Cadek Guilty," CPD, May 27, 1936; "Conviction Sours Cadek Stomach," CPD, May 28, 1936; "Capt. Cadek Gets 2 to 20 Years in Pen," CP, May 29, 1936.

Chapter 19: Victim No. 4

A little after midnight: Badal, *In the Wake of the Butcher,* 63–64; news clipping, CN, June 7, 1936, various unlabeled news clippings, ENP, reel 2; AI, Arnold Sagalyn, May 22, 2011.

Chapter 20: The Original Mystery Man

In the first sign that the economy: Vacha, *Meet Me on Lake Erie,* 5–6, 9–10, 75.

Scheduled to open on June 27: "Steel Drama to Flare for Expo Throngs," CPD, June 1, 1936.

"The pressure has been so great . . .": Vacha, *Meet Me on Lake Erie,* 131–35.

At the Expo's revival: Vacha, *Meet Me on Lake Erie,* 170.

"The enormous statues . . .": unlabeled

news clipping, Cleveland Museum of Art, Elisabeth Seaver file.

Her signature work for Cowan: Mark Bassett and Victoria Naumann, *Cowan Pottery and the Cleveland School* (Atglen, PA: Schiffer Publishing, 1997), 117.

Her success became a source: AI, Rebecca McFarland, May 19, 2011.

Elisabeth nevertheless graduated to: "Alexander Blazy and Some of Former Students Exhibiting at Ruth Coulter's," CPD, Oct. 27, 1935.

Hugh didn't like it: Cuyahoga County Common Pleas Court, Hugh D. Seaver v. Betty A. Seaver, no. 557135.

That's a very attractive man: AI, Franny Taft, July 1, 2011.

Officers manning the stall: Memo dated Dec. 22, 1937, to Sgt. E. G. Frankfather, CPHS.

Eliot also prominently displayed: Badal, *In the Wake of the Butcher,* 66.

"Vehovec has made a mountain . . .": "Vehovec Snips and Harwood Snaps Him Up," CPD, June 1, 1936.

In a report, Eliot would call: Cuyahoga County Common Pleas Court, State of Ohio v. Michael J. Harwood, no. 46553.

He'd later tell an associate: "Says He Saw Capt. Harwood in Bet Joint," CPD, July 2, 1936.

"Didn't Harwood telephone you . . .":

"Ness Raids, then Yanks Harwood," CPD, June 7, 1936.

"You were a damn fool . . .": "Says He Saw Capt. Harwood in Bet Joint," CPD, July 2, 1936.

Early in July, Tom Clothey and: "The Inside of the News in Cleveland," CPD, July 26, 1936.

On Monday evening, while some: " 'Misjudged,' Says Capt. Facing Probe," CPD, July 31, 1936; unlabeled news clippings, CPD, July 22–23, 1936, ENP, reel 2.

The safety director kept the pressure: "Charge Harwood Aided in Bootleg Competition," CP, Oct. 7, 1936; " 'DP' in Gambler' Books Is Mystery," CPD, July 24, 1936; "Police Get 56 in 2 Gambling Raids," CPD, July 25, 1936; "Raid Like Rookies, Police Are Told," CPD, Jan. 10, 1937.

Late in the summer, Eliot disappeared: Condon, "The Last American Hero;" "Jurors Hear Evidence of Police Graft," CP, Oct. 8, 1936.

In August and September, Eliot quietly left: Cuyahoga County Common Pleas Court, no. 46553; "G-Men Capture Key Witnesses," CP, Oct. 14–15, 1936; "Ness Air Trip Nets Witness in Burns Case," CPD, Mar. 4, 1937.

When Eliot heard that patrolmen: "Ness Hits at Undercover Foes in 15th," CPD, Sept. 2, 1936.

"My investigation shows that . . .": Ibid.

With the press cheering him on: "Bravo, Eliot Ness!" CPD, Sept. 2, 1936; Porter, *Cleveland*, 98.

At city hall functions, suburban: Condon, *Cleveland*, 237.

Chapter 21: The Sadistic Type

On the morning of September 10: Badal, *In the Wake of the Butcher*, 75–85; "Sixth Hacked Body Found in Kingsbury Run," CP, Sept. 10, 1936; "Fear Hangs over Kingsbury Run Where Butcher Leaves His Dead," CP, Sept. 11, 1936; "Clean Out Haunts of Mad Killer," CP, Sept. 12, 1936; Martin, *Butcher's Dozen and Other Murders*, 60–62.

"The killer is apparently a sex maniac . . .": Badal, *In the Wake of the Butcher*, 79.

The better reason for his reluctance: AI, James Jessen Badal, June 12, 2011.

The *Plain Dealer* called the killer: "Calls Torso Killer New Insane Type," CPD, Sept. 16, 1936.

The *News* wrote, "Of all horrible . . .": Badal, *In the Wake of the Butcher*, 92.

The safety director was known for his soft touch: AI, James Jessen Badal, June 12, 2011; Badal, *In the Wake of the Butcher*,

156; unlabeled news clippings, CPHS.

He felt he was being called to account: AI, James Jessen Badal, June 12, 2011.

"You can't bring up Eliot Ness . . .": Badal, *In the Wake of the Butcher,* 89.

In one report, he wrote: "I am of the opinion . . .": Cleveland Police Department report on torso murder investigation, dated Mar. 15, 1943, CPHS.

Merylo's theories about the killer: Badal, *In the Wake of the Butcher,* ix.

A bartender at a grimy dive told of: "Butcher's Dozen: The Cleveland Torso Murders," *Harper's,* Nov. 1949.

Perhaps it was someone who reached "sexual . . .": Cleveland Police Department report on torso murder investigation, dated Mar. 15, 1943, CPHS.

Merylo would write in an unpublished: Badal, *In the Wake of the Butcher,* 96.

"All is infinite Mind . . .": Mary Baker Eddy, *Science and Health, with Key to the Scriptures* (Boston: First Church of Christ, Scientist, 1994), 468.

The indictments charged that during Prohibition: "Harwood, Burns, 6 Others Indicted for Police Graft," CP, Oct. 29, 1936; "Seven Police Deny Guilt in Graft Charge," CP, Oct. 30, 1936.

Reporters rushed to Harwood's home: "7 Policemen Deny Ness Had Cause to Take Them Off Duty," "20 Policemen Hit

by Ness Graft Report," CPD, Oct. 6, 1936.
Just as with the Cadek trial, the bootleggers: Sources for the Harwood trial and its press coverage include: "Tell of Price Harwood Set on Protection," CP, Dec. 9, 1936; "Relates Midnight Raid by Harwood," "Testimony Heard in Harwood Case," CPD, Dec. 10, 1936; "No Payoff, Cites Raid by Captain," CPD, Dec. 11, 1936; "Captain Ends Defense with Bribe Denial," CPD, Dec. 15, 1936; "Harwood Jury Deliberates Again Today," CPD, Dec. 16, 1936; "Guilty Pleas Offer Hinted in Bribery," "Victorious Safety Director; Aid Who Is Out," CPD, Dec. 17, 1936; "The Inside of the News in Cleveland," CPD, Dec. 20, 1936; "Says Harwood Pocketed $50," CP, Dec. 10, 1936; "Says Harwood Encouraged Bootlegging after Repeal," CP, Dec. 11, 1936; "Harwood Sobs as Prosecutor Denounces Him," CP, Dec. 15, 1936; "Police Captain Convicted on Six Counts Charging He Took Graft from Bootleggers in Collinwood," CP, Dec. 16, 1936; "Crime Buster Ness Shares Trial Spotlight," CN, Oct. 2, 1940; Cuyahoga County Common Pleas Court, State of Ohio v. Michael J. Harwood, no. 46553; Heimel, *Eliot Ness: The Real Story,* 142.
Without informing his lawyer, the newly: "Women Used in Trap to Lure Witnesses," CP, Oct. 12, 1937; ENP, reel 2, unlabeled

news clippings.

As the jury filed out of the room: "Jury Finds Burns Guilty of Bribery," "No Hard Feelings, Burns Tells Ness at Trial End," CPD, Mar. 11, 1937.

Neil McGill prided himself: McGill and Perry, *Court Cases of Eliot Ness,* 27–28.

The second time around, Eliot brought: news clipping, CPD, May 26, 1937, ENP, reel 2.

Flynn admitted privately to a friend: news clipping, CPD, Dec. 17, 1936, ENP, reel 2.

When Eliot returned to the office: "Flynn Overruled On Police Choice," CPD, Aug. 4, 1936.

In just a few short months in the job: "Three Out," CPD, July 31, 1936; "Victorious Safety Director; Aid Who Is Out," CPD, Dec. 17, 1936.

Reporters surrounded him: magazine clipping, *Investigator,* May 1988, ATF.

When he began to gear up: Container 383, Notes folder, HHB.

Eliot, though he had never been involved: "Slogan," CPD, Oct. 14, 1937.

With Burton safely ensconced in office: "The Inside of the News in Cleveland," CPD, Nov. 28, 1937.

"By now the entire department knew . . .": Porter, *Cleveland,* 99.

Even the Ohio Supreme Court, after re-

jecting: Condon, "The Last American Hero;" "Ness' Cases Win Weygandt Praise," CPD, Feb. 19, 1938.

When the judge read the verdict: "Stotts Wins Acquittal in Bribe Trial," CPD, May 6, 1938.

Chapter 22: Social Workers

"Please remember," he told: "Calls Sum Portion of Week's Cut," CPD, Mar. 1, 1936; "Talk Up and Oust Gangs, Says Ness," CPD, Feb. 5, 1937.

Eliot would rent a fleet: "Stotts Wins Acquittal in Bribe Trial," CPD, May 6, 1938.

Each patrol car would be equipped: Unlabeled radio contract, CPHS.

Thirty-two new cars, Eliot announced: Ness, Eliot, "Radio-Directed Mobile Police," *American City,* Nov. 1939.

He thought policemen should be intimately: Alder, *Lie Detectors,* 21.

As an experiment, he sent: "Cleveland Woos Its Young Gangs into Clubhouses," CT, July 21, 1939.

"The leader is 24 years old . . .": Container 372, folder 1937–1942, subfolder Youth, Statement for Rotary International Convention, June 22, 1938, HHB.

"They meet in a pool room . . .": Ibid.

He cornered gang members: "Cleveland

Woos Its Young Gangs into Clubhouses," CT, July 21, 1939; container 372, folder 1937–1942, subfolder Youth, Statement for Rotary International Convention, June 22, 1938, HHB.

A tough kid from the Flats: "Nab Filkowski, 5 Others in Break," CPD, Dec. 8, 1936.

Eliot, the scientific policeman: unlabeled news clipping, CPD, Mar. 3, 1932, ENP, reel 2; container 372, folder 1937–1942, subfolder Youth, Statement for Rotary International Convention, June 22, 1938, HHB.

"He had an instinct about children . . .": "My Husband, Eliot Ness," *TV Guide,* May 11, 1961.

Vollmer had kept a city map: Alder, *Lie Detectors,* 21.

He established an accident-prevention: "Traffic Death Toll Slashed over America," *Cumberland Evening Times,* Dec. 30, 1938; unlabeled news clippings and memos, ENP, reel 2.

"At the end of the month or at a designated . . .": "Contemplated Division of Territory for Policing the City of Cleveland/Reorganization Police Department," by Eliot Ness, 1938, CPHS; "Supplementary Order Relating to the General Duties of Patrol Car Crews/Reorganization Police Department," 1938, CPHS.

Philip Porter wrote that: Porter, *Cleveland,* 95.

"He was not too opinionated . . .": "Ness Recalled as Quiet Enforcer," CPD, April 30, 1960.

An internal history of the: Untitled department history, CPHS.

Just eighteen months after: "Crime in Cleveland: The Law Finally Catches Up With Labor Racketeers," *Newsweek,* Mar. 21, 1938.

Chapter 23: The Virtues of Courage

On a piercing June day in 1937: *Something About the Author: Autobiography Series,* vol. 1, 226.

"She wasn't beautiful . . .": AI, Ann Durell, June 2, 2011.

Evaline had bought a train ticket: *Something About the Author: Autobiography Series,* vol. 1, 226–27; AI, Ann Durell, June 2, 2011.

She had long suspected: AI, Maxine Huntington, Sept. 5, 2011.

The job communicated something: AI, Arnold Sagalyn, June 9, 2011.

Eliot's dedication to his work: unlabeled news clipping, CP, Dec. 12, 1935, ENP, reel 2.

On good nights, he would stretch out: Tucker, *Eliot Ness and the Untouchables,* 13.

When Matowitz assigned Eliot a body-guard: Jedick, "Eliot Ness."

Eliot's obsessive commitment: "Ness Goes to Chicago," CPD, Nov. 8, 1937; unlabeled news clippings, ENP, reel 2, news clippings.

"WHEREAS, it is at a mother's knee . . .": ENP, reel 2.

Chapter 24: Gun, Blackjack, and Brass Knuckles

"In the old days, it was nothing . . .": "The Inside of the News in Cleveland," CPD, Jan. 31, 1937.

he had turned his staff's attention: David Cowles oral history, Sept. 6, 1983, CPHS; "Obtain Extortion Confession," CPD, Jan. 19, 1938; McGill and Perry, *Court Cases of Eliot Ness,* 49–51; AI, Arnold Sagalyn, May 22, 2011.

"We had never heard of . . .": "Herman Pirchner," CPD, Dec. 4, 1983.

George Mulvanity, still over at: AI, Francis Mulvanity, July 7, 2011.

The gangster Angelo Lonardo: Lonardo.

The most basic policy game: McGill and Perry, *Court Cases of Eliot Ness,* 30.

Policy and clearing house had started: "Grand Jury Acts Today on 'Policy,' " "Hill Mob Bullets Won Policy War," CPD, April 26, 1939; "Indict 23 of Mayfield Mob in

Policy Extortion Racket," "Policy Conquered with Guns, Force," "Records of Mayfield Mob Indicted in Policy Probe," CP, April 26, 1939.

Jacob Collins, a thirty-one-year-old: "Testimony Links Sciria to Policy," CPD, Nov. 3, 1938.

The *Press* labeled them: "Indict 23 of Mayfield Mob in Policy Extortion Racket," "Angelo Sciria Beat Killing 'Rap,' " CP, April 26, 1939.

"Killings were followed by retaliatory . . .": McGill and Perry, *Court Cases of Eliot Ness,* 20.

The "thick-necked,thick-fingered. . .": "Policy Conquered with Guns, Force," "Angelo Sciria Beat Killing 'Rap,' " CP, April 26, 1939.

The men conducting the initiation: Lonardo.

By the early 1930s, in fact: Ibid.

"It is debatable whether gambling . . .": Condon, *Cleveland,* 236; "Choke Crime by Its Purse, Ness Urges," CPD, Jan. 23, 1936.

"Two hundred thousand dollars . . .": "Calls Sum Portion of Week's Cut," CPD, Mar. 1, 1936.

"The mild, unorganized and personal . . .": "Dice at Clubs Are Loaded, Ness Says," CPD, Oct. 4, 1940.

"He got information from informers":

"Ness Recalled as Quiet Enforcer," CPD, April 30, 1960.

In one interview session: "Admits Mistaking Lawyer for Birns," CPD, Aug. 6, 1942; "State Ready to Bring Gang History Up to Recent Days," CPD, Dec. 8, 1949.

Birns cultivated a pleasant, roguish: news clipping, CN, Feb. 12, 1937, ENP, reel 2.

Eliot decided to harass Birns: "Shondor Birns, in Jail, Sings Blues," CPD, Feb. 11, 1937.

On January 6, 1938, police took over: "Policy Raid Stops 5 Big-time Games," CPD, Jan. 7, 1938.

"Cleveland situation very critical": Ibid.

"To the Editor of the *Press* . . .": "To the Editor of the *Press,*" CP, May 23, 1937, ENP, reel 2.

He snipped Pony Boy's letter: Ibid.

Chapter 25: Against Racketeers

Back in September 1936: "Cullitan Pledges Study of 'Racket,' " CPD, Sept. 3, 1936.

Eliot had met Campbell: "Testifies of Added 'Gift' to Campbell," CPD, Feb. 19, 1938.

"Being union officials gives . . .": McGill and Perry, *Court Cases of Eliot Ness,* 32–33.

He believed Campbell, McDonnell: "Convict Labor Racketeers of Extortion Plot,"

CT, Mar. 9, 1938.

Over several months, the safety director and: "Jury Will Sift Labor Rackets in Cleveland, O.," CT, Nov. 18, 1937.

"These people had us just where . . .": "Fight to Stop Labor Rackets in Cleveland," CT, Nov. 24, 1937.

A critic once described Arthur: Grann, 15.

Campbell snarled, "Go to hell . . .": "Four Union Chiefs Indicted in Racket," *New York Times,* Dec. 21, 1937.

"When I approached them . . .": "Jury Will Sift Labor Rackets in Cleveland, O.," CT, Nov. 18, 1937.

On December 1, 1937, McGee stood: "Ness Bluffs, M'Gee Tells Federation," CPD, Dec. 2, 1937.

Workers had violently struck: "Ness Sets Steel 'Peace Areas,' " CP, July 27, 1937; "40 Hurt in New Strike Riot," CT, July 27, 1937; "One Dead, 40 Hurt in Strike Battles at Cleveland Mill," *New York Times,* July 27, 1937; "Police Bring Peace to Steel Area," CPD, July 28, 1937; see also "The Little Steel Strike of 1937," by Donald Gene Sofchalk, PhD dissertation, 1961, Ohio State University.

When asked about the charge: Condon, "The Last American Hero."

Campbell and McGee came to trial: "Convict Labor Racketeers of Extortion

Plot," CT, Mar. 9, 1938; "Four Union Chiefs Indicted in Racket," *New York Times,* Dec. 21, 1937.

Vernon Stouffer dominated: "Fail to Keep Ness Out of Racket Trial," CPD, Feb. 18, 1938.

Cutting off requests for bail: "M'Gee-Campbell Parade Ends in Pen," CPD, Mar. 9, 1938; "Claims Chicago Money Donated to Bribe Juror," CT, Mar. 10, 1938.

"I was one of the spectators . . .": ENP, reel 2.

"Campbell and McGee asked for it": "M'Gee-Campbell Parade Ends in Pen," CPD, Mar. 9, 1938.

***Newsweek* wrote that Eliot had:** "Crime in Cleveland: The Law Finally Catches Up With Labor Racketeers," *Newsweek,* Mar. 21, 1938.

***Cosmopolitan,* then a literary:** "Eliot Ness: The Cosmopolite of the Month," *Cosmopolitan,* Aug. 1940; ENP, reel 2.

***Reader's Digest* noted that Eliot:** "Cleveland Versus the Crooks," *Reader's Digest,* Feb. 1939, 51.

Chapter 26: The Doctor

The story of Ness and his team zeroing in on Dr. Sweeney as a suspect and interrogating him is derived from: AI,

620

James Jessen Badal, June 12, 2011; Alder, *Lie Detectors,* 82, 109; *In the Wake of the Butcher,* Badal, 128; 214, 218–20; David Cowles oral history, Sept. 6, 1983, CPHS; AI, Arnold Sagalyn, May 22, 2011; Sagalyn, *A Promise Fulfilled,* 50.

Even though the campaign season: Badal, *In the Wake of the Butcher,* 93.

Eliot figured that he and his Unknowns: AI, James Jessen Badal, June 12, 2011.

One example: in September 1935: Badal, *In the Wake of the Butcher,* 36.

"We played on him for a long time": Cowles refused to use Sweeney's name when discussing the interrogation, but there was no mistaking who he was talking about. AI, James Jessen Badal, June 12, 2011; David Cowles oral history, Sept. 6, 1983, CPHS.

After releasing Dr. Sweeney back: AI, Maxine Huntington, Sept. 5, 2011; Pinellas County, Fl., Divorce Index, vol. 139, no. 5771, 1939; "Eliot Ness' First Wife Quietly Dies," *St. Petersburg Times,* Nov. 19, 1994.

He even considered stepping down: Jedick, "Eliot Ness."

"The director says he'll do this . . .": "Ness Fires Word Barrage at Young," "Ness to Reassign All Police in City," CPD, Sept. 20, 1938.

He'd been seen at a nightclub: "Remembering Eliot Ness," CPD, Feb. 21, 2000;

AI, Arnold Sagalyn, June 9, 2011.

"Don't let 'em get your goat": Caption for photo of Ness and Chamberlin, CPD, Sept. 26, 1938.

He hadn't been removed: "Ness and Young Hurl Charges," CP, Sept. 19, 1938.

"We have sort of agreed . . .": "Nesses Separated, Divorce Is Planned," CP, Sept. 20, 1938; Condon, "The Last American Hero."

word began to leak out: "Capone Reported as Mentally Ill," CPD, Feb. 9, 1938.

"I was looking for a big fellow": "A Bad End for a Good Guy," CPD, Sept. 7, 1997.

Eliot began showing up: "Behind-the-Scenes Campaigner," CN, Sept. 18, 1947; CIA Scrapbook, vol. 14, p. 98, Cleveland Institute of Art; AI, Joe Kisvardai, June 24, 2011.

One night he took Betty Seaver: Undated fundraising pamphlet, Cleveland Museum of Art, Elisabeth Seaver file.

"Women were attracted to him": Porter, *Cleveland,* 102.

He would tell a secretary or: Bergreen, *Capone: The Man and the Era,* 598.

"Few people really knew him": "An Image Retouched," CPD, June 16, 1966.

"He was handsome and charming . . .": "A Bad End for a Good Guy," CPD, Sept. 7, 1997.

One woman confided to a friend: Porter,

Cleveland, 102.

He never called for a date: AI, Rebecca McFarland, May 19, 2011.

Chapter 27: An Unwelcome Surprise

When Eliot Ness left her: *Something About the Author: Autobiography Series,* vol. 1, 226; AI, Steve Resnick, June 5, 2011.

Her father, Albert Michelow: *Something About the Author: Autobiography Series,* vol. 1, 223–31.

***Newsweek* magazine had accidentally:** "Benes for Ness," *Newsweek,* Mar. 28, 1938.

Day after day an investigator fell in behind: AI, Arnold Sagalyn, May 22, 2011; Sagalyn, *A Promise Fulfilled,* 50–51.

One rookie investigator: AI, Arnold Sagalyn, May 22, 2011.

Police soon found more remains: Badal, *In the Wake of the Butcher,* 135–36, 142.

The corpse may have been stolen: AI, James Jessen Badal, June 12, 2011.

Two days later, in the dead of night: Badal, *In the Wake of the Butcher,* 146–48; "Torso Killer Hunt Centers Near Market," "Derelicts Worry as City Plans to Burn Shantytown," CP, Aug. 8, 1938; unlabeled news clipping, CPHS; news clipping, CN, Aug. 19, 1938, ENP, reel 2; Steven Nickel, *Torso: Eliot Ness and the Hunt for the Mad*

Butcher of Kingsbury Run: A True Story (New York: Avon, 1990), 142–43.

The killer needed Kingsbury Run's: unlabeled CN news clippings, ENP, reel 2; "Butcher's Dozen: The Cleveland Torso Murders," *Harper's,* Nov. 1949.

The paper, slapping him for: Nickel, *Torso,* 145.

On Monday, August 22, Eliot: ENP, reel 2, unlabeled news clippings; Nickel, *Torso,* 148.

With the Kingsbury Run shantytowns destroyed: AI, James Jessen Badal, June 12, 2011.

Chapter 28: Full of Love

A low-boil dissatisfaction roiled: AI, Ann Durell, June 2, 2011; AI, Marni Greenberg, June 7, 2011; AI, Steve Resnick, June 5, 2011.

She struggled to keep her composure: Jedick, "Eliot Ness."

"Cleveland wasn't New York . . .": *Something About the Author: Autobiography Series,* vol. 1, 227. Also: "Crime Buster Ness Shares Trial Spotlight," CN, Oct. 2, 1940.

"Eliot was a gay, convivial soul . . .": Porter, *Cleveland,* 102.

"That may have been the best . . .": Jedick, "Eliot Ness."

When the Terrace Room's bandleader:

"Robberts and White Make Alpine's New Show Lively, Ernie Taylor Clicks Again," CPD, July 7, 1940.

Eliot would run into men: Ted Schwarz. *Cleveland Curiosities: Eliot Ness & His Blundering Raid, a Busker's Promise, the Richest Heiress Who Never Lived, and More* (Charleston, SC: The History Press, 2010), 9–11.

Now and again, one of the tough boys: AI, Joe Kisvardai, relating stories Edris Eckhardt had told him, June 24, 2011.

"He never really talked much . . .": Jedick, "Eliot Ness."

They both selected "single": ATF.

Two weeks later, when word finally: news clippings, University of Chicago Special Collections Research Center, Harold Swift Papers, box 156, folder 7.

On July 31, the nationwide strike had turned: "Gas and Clubs Fell 100 in Auto Strike," *Daily Mirror,* ENP, reel 2; "46 Hurt as Pickets of Auto Union Fight Cleveland Police," *New York Times,* Aug. 1, 1939.

In a report to the guard's adjutant general: Ohio Historical Society, FEIN 314389673.

Cleveland's newspapers reported: "Eliot Ness Weds Fashion Artist," CN, Oct. 26, 1939.

One Greenup booster boasted: ENP, reel 2.

"I'm lucky in my profession . . .": unlabeled newspaper clipping, University of Chicago Special Collections Research Center, Harold Swift Papers, box 156, folder 7.

"Evaline may have already been . . .": Condon, "The Last American Hero," 139.

One said "Evaline liked being . . .": Heimel, *Eliot Ness: The Real Story,* 165.

Ann Durell, who became her editor: Letter from Durell to Beulah Campbell, April 22, 1965, box 24, folder 2, Lloyd Alexander Papers, 1941–95, Free Library of Philadelphia, Children's Literature Research Collection.

Years later, she described her relationship: AI, Steve Resnick, June 5, 2011.

"She was an interesting, generous . . .": AI, Marni Greenberg, June 7, 2011.

He bought her a new car: Jedick, "Eliot Ness."

Since they were right on the water: news clipping, CPD, July 7, 1940; ENP, reel 2; "Galley Gossip," CPD, Sept. 29, 1940.

He bought her a Mary Cassatt art: AI, Marni Greenberg, June 7, 2011.

The *Plain Dealer* listed "Sunning" among: "Powerful Oils Section Rivals May Show's Best in 27 Years," CPD, May 6, 1942.

"I floundered, all sense . . .": *Something*

About the Author: Autobiography Series, vol. 1, 227.

"Eliot was a very social person . . .": Sagalyn, *A Promise Fulfilled,* 54–55, 58–59.

"He was a party man . . .": "A Bad End for a Good Guy," CPD, Sept. 7, 1997.

She ended up with nasty burns: "Burned Cooking Dinner," CPD, May 22, 1941.

He had reached the final, inevitable stage: AI, Marni Greenberg, June 7, 2011; AI, Arnold Sagalyn, June 9, 2011; Bergreen, *Capone: The Man and the Era,* 599; undated memo, ENP, reel 2.

"Eliot had pulled that stunt . . .": Heimel, *Eliot Ness: The Real Story,* 157.

"When the party was nearing . . .": Bergreen, *Capone: The Man and the Era,* 598.

And there was always the thrill: AI, Rebecca McFarland, May 19, 2011; AI, Steve Resnick, June 5, 2011; AI, Franny Taft, July 1, 2011; Heimel, *Eliot Ness: The Real Story,* 160.

Making it worse, Eliot often took: AI, Dave Deming, Sept. 7, 2011; AI, Rebecca McFarland, May 19, 2011; "A Bad End for a Good Guy," CPD, Sept. 7, 1997.

Chapter 29: Clearing House

Captain Michael Blackwell picked: "City Line Ends Policy Chase," CP, Sept. 17, 1940.

The Mob had to be especially: "Demand 3 on Force Resign in Police Probe of Rackets," CPD, Mar. 24, 1948.

One of Blackwell's raids: McGill and Perry, *Court Cases of Eliot Ness,* 31.

He made several copies: "Grand Jury Acts Today on 'Policy,' " CPD, April 26, 1939.

"There'll be killings, if those . . .": "Seek Torso Slayer's Workshop," CN, Aug. 18, 1938; ENP, reel 2.

On Wednesday, April, 26: "Indict 23 of Mayfield Mob in Policy Extortion Racket," "Policy Conquered with Guns, Force," CP, April 26, 1939; "Grand Jury Acts Today on 'Policy,' " "Hill Mob Bullets Won Policy War," CPD, April 26, 1939.

The police arrested six of the: "Indict 23 Ohioans in Numbers Game," "Hoge Expected to Surrender Today," CPD, April 29, 1939.

He hadn't gone far when Patrolman: "Prucha, Nemesis of Car Thieves, End 39-Year Career," CPD, Feb. 4, 1962.

"No member of the Bureau . . .": "The Participation of Boys," *Phi Delta Kappan,* 339, ENP, reel 2.

Eliot and a professor at Cuyahoga: CPHS.

More significant still, the crime-prevention: "The Participation of Boys," *Phi Delta Kappan,* 338–39, ENP, reel 2.

Next Eliot helped start up: Container 372,

folder 1937–1942, subfolder Youth, Statement for Rotary International Convention, June 22, 1938, HHB.

A bar owner, Anthony Zappone: : "Demand 3 on Force Resign in Police Probe of Rackets," CPD, Mar. 24, 1948.

When detectives brought Lonardo: "Nine Still Evade Racket Roundup," CPD, June 10, 1939.

"Why doesn't the *Press* go . . .": ENP, reel 2.

Late in 1940, Michael Harwood: "Harwood to Leave Prison Farm Today," CPD, Nov. 1, 1940.

He arrested Howell Wright: Supreme Court of Ohio: State of Ohio v. Howell Wright, no. 28,227.

"She's real sharp . . .": AI, Marni Greenberg, June 7, 2011; "Ness Asks Jury Marijuana Probe," CN, May 18, 1939; "12 in Marijuana Ring Sentenced," CPD, July 6, 1939; McGill and Perry, *Court Cases of Eliot Ness,* 49, 51.

"During our questioning . . .": AI, James Jessen Badal, June 12, 2011; Badal, *In the Wake of the Butcher,* 231.

Eliot told his investigators: AI, Arnold Sagalyn, June 9, 2011.

"Eliot would tell Frank . . .": Jedick, "Eliot Ness."

Jack Kennon, a longtime Cleveland re

porter: news clipping, CPD, Feb. 4, 1941, ENP, reel 2.

Chapter 30: L'Affaire Ness

The car accident and its aftermath are constructed from: Condon, "The Last American Hero;" "Ness Incident Is Now Closed, Lausche Says," CN, Mar. 9, 1942; "Asks 'Why' in Ness Cover-Up," CP, Mar. 6, 1942; " 'I Had a Few Drinks' — Ness," CP, Mar. 7, 1942; "Report on Ness Crash Written 60 Hours Late," CPD, Mar. 6, 1942; "Mayor Gets Story of Ness' Accident," CPD, Mar. 8, 1942; unlabeled news clippings, ENP, reel 2, Jedick, "Eliot Ness."

Six days later, Eliot attempted to: "Ness Asks Triple in Fire Program," CPD, Mar. 12, 1942.

Prostitution was "just as deep . . .": "Probe Police Link in 'Jitterbug' Vice," CPD, April 9, 1942.

With Evaline working long: "Behind-the-Scenes Campaigner," CN, Sept. 18, 1947.

He had always liked to drive: *Fenger Courier,* 1920.

When, after a few weeks: undated letter, ENP, reel 2; Jedick, "Eliot Ness."

Chapter 31: This Is War

He'd been issued a national draft order: "2850 and 441 Top Draft List Here," CPD, Mar. 18, 1942.

Federal spending for military: William H. Chafe, *The Unfinished Journey: America Since World War II, Second Edition* (New York: Oxford University Press, 1991), 7.

Still, the government sought out: Ness personnel file, ATF.

The service branches would reject: Eliot Ness, "The National Program of Social Protection," *Public Welfare: The Journal of the American Public Welfare Association,* April 1943.

Congress underlined the seriousness: Allan M. Brandt, *No Magic Bullet: A Social History of Venereal Disease in the United States Since 1880* (New York: Oxford University Press, 1987), 166.

He listed Lausche and Burton: Ness personnel file, ATF.

Public Administration Service's executive director: Ibid.

In her nationally syndicated: unlabeled news clipping, ENP, reel 3, news clippings.

Nearly two weeks later, on April 23: "Celebrezze Leading in Open Safety Job Race," CPD, April 24, 1942.

"Taking Mr. Ness's record as whole . . .":

Condon, "The Last American Hero."

Under the header "Six Eventful Years": "Six Eventful Years," CPD, April 25, 1942.

"Cleveland is a different place than . . .": Heimel, *Eliot Ness: The Real Story,* 169–70.

"Dear Eliot: Now that you are leaving . . .": ENP, reel 3.

"Eliot was a great man to work . . .": "Veteran Mediator Here Found a Smile the Best Persuasion," CPD, July 19, 1970.

"Eliot was a wonderful guy . . .": AI, Arnold Sagalyn, May 22, 2011.

On July 3, kicking off a series of trials: "10 in Policy Ring, Guilty, to Appeal," CPD, July 4, 1942; Cuyhoga County Common Pleas Court, State of Ohio v. Angelo Scerria et al., no. 49836.

Williams, who hadn't seen Birns: "Admits Mistaking Lawyer For Birns," CPD, Aug. 6, 1942; "Birns Acquitted on Policy Charge," CPD, Aug. 7, 1942; "State Ready to Bring Gang History Up to Recent Days," CPD, Dec. 8, 1949; McGill and Perry, *Court Cases of Eliot Ness,* 42–43.

Birns continued to ply: "Shondor Birns Is Bomb Victim," CPD, Mar. 30, 1975.

Chapter 32: Girls, Girls, Girls

Evaline was miserable: *Something About the Author: Autobiography Series,* vol. 1, 229.

"I don't think he could stand criti-

cism . . .": Jedick, "Eliot Ness."

She needed to scream: AI, Marni Greenberg, June 7, 2011; AI, Steve Resnick, June 5, 2011.

He hired Arnold Sagalyn: Sagalyn, *A Promise Fulfilled,* 70–71.

"As he had done in Cleveland . . .": Ibid.

He was determined that the effort: Ness, "Venereal Disease Control in Defense," *Annals of the American Academy of Political and Social Sciences,* March 1942.

"Many of them have come from broken . . .": Ness personnel file, ATF; Ness, "National Program of Social Protection."

"Eliot liked that job": Jedick, "Eliot Ness."

Washington had become a modern-day: David Brinkley, *Washington Goes to War* (New York: Ballantine Books, 1996), 107–9, 119.

"I would have said 'War . . .' ": *Something About the Author: Autobiography Series,* vol. 1, 227.

"The uniform," wrote *Vogue*: "Civilian Defense: The Ladies!" *Time,* Jan. 26, 1942.

She couldn't help herself: AI, Steve Resnick, June 5, 2011.

"Go to art school": Evaline's return to art school and artistic awakening are derived from AI, Marni Greenberg, June 7, 2011; "Evaline Ness: the Caldecott Medalist for 1967," *American Artist,* June 1967; Evaline

Ness official records, Corcoran College of Art and Design, Office of the Registrar; "Evaline Ness's Centenary," April 21, 2011, Free Library of Philadelphia blog, libwww.freelibrary.org/blog/index.cfm?post id=1311; *Something About the Author: Autobiography Series,* vol. 1, 227–28.

Evaline was "extremely attracted . . .": AI with longtime friend of Evaline Ness who asked not to be named.

A friend from Cleveland: ENP, reel 3, undated letter, signed "Bruce," ENP, reel 3.

Evaline got up one morning: AI, Marni Greenberg, June 7, 2011; AI, Steve Resnick, June 5, 2011.

In October 1945, nearly: Condon, *Cleveland,* 242; "Ness Papers in Divorce Invisible," CPD, Oct. 19, 1945.

Worse, he was forced to testify: undated news clipping, Eliot Ness file, Cleveland State University Special Collections.

Reporters rushed to the county clerk's: Condon, *Cleveland,* 242.

"The mystery of Eliot Ness's missing . . .": "Ness Papers in Divorce Invisible," CPD, Oct. 19, 1945.

They recalled that Eliot always: Heimel, *Eliot Ness: The Real Story,* 165; AI, Arnold Sagalyn, June 9, 2011.

Of course, there had been hints: AI, Steve

Resnick, June 5, 2011.

Marjorie Mutersbaugh remembered: AI, Rebecca McFarland, May 19, 2011.

And then there was the leggy: Bergreen, *Capone: The Man and the Era,* 600.

One night, Eliot invited: "A Bad End for a Good Guy," CPD, Sept. 7, 1997.

"His social habits, which included . . .": Condon, *Cleveland,* 239.

In 1973, Neil McGill, at ninety: Letter from McGill to Edward Winter dated May 8, 1973, Personal Correspondence folder, Edward and Thelma Frazier Winter Papers, manuscript collection no. 4503, WRHS.

"Where could he go . . .": AI, Arnold Sagalyn, June 9, 2011.

He would later boast: 1947 mayoral campaign flyer, ENP, reel 3.

His friend Marion Kelly recalled: Condon, "The Last American Hero."

"The entire female population . . .": Betsy Israel, *Bachelor Girl: 100 Years of Breaking the Rules: A Social History of Living Single* (Perennial, 2003), 165.

"Reich shared the moralist's . . .": Kathleen Tynan, *The Life of Kenneth Tynan* (New York: William Morrow & Co., 1987), 414.

A snapshot from this period: ENP, reel 3.

Chapter 33: Starting Over

She found herself drawn to: "TV Brings Father Back for Son of Eliot Ness," CPD, Oct. 17, 1959; "My Husband, Eliot Ness," *TV Guide,* May 11, 1961.

Marjorie Mutersbaugh called them: AI, Rebecca McFarland, May 19, 2011.

Hugh and Betty's divorce became: AI, Rebecca McFarland, May 19, 2011; AI, Franny Taft, July 1, 2011; Cuyhoga County Common Pleas Court, Hugh D. Seaver v. Betty A. Seaver: no. 557135; undated letter to Edris Eckhardt, Joe Kisvardai personal collection.

In 1924, he prevailed upon J. A. Derome: Elisabeth Andersen's official student file, Cleveland Institute of Art.

Her winning piece for the 1932: library.clevelandart.org/search/search_mayshow.php.

Betty considered herself lucky: Edris Eckhardt interview, Nov. 1972, Joe Kisvardai personal collection.

Chapter 34: Ness Is Necessary

Ness Caravan narrative derived from: "Inside of the News in Cleveland," CPD, Nov. 26, 1947; news clipping, CPD, Oct. 29, 1947, ENP, reel 3.

The thirty-two-year-old Higgins: Undated letters from personal collection of Winifred Higgins. The collection was purchased by the National Law Enforcement Museum in Washington, DC, in Aug. 2012. **The narrative for the 1947 Cleveland mayoral campaign draws from:** AI, James Jessen Badal, June 12, 2011; AI, Rebecca McFarland, May 19, 2011; AI, Arnold Sagalyn, June 9, 2011; Bergreen, *Capone: The Man and the Era,* 603; Condon, *Cleveland,* 243; "Inside of the News in Cleveland," CPD, July 30, 1947; "Ness Will Liven Race for Mayor," "There Will Be a Contest," CPD, July 31, 1947; "Porter on Eliot Ness," CPD, Aug. 2, 1947; "Ness Files in Race For Mayor, Pledges 'Rebirth' for City," CN, Aug. 8, 1947; "Burke Rips Finkle; Police for Me, Ness Says; Pucel Hits Big Money," CPD, Sept. 23, 1947; "Inside of the News in Cleveland," CPD, Sept. 24, 1947; "Fire Department Slips, Ness Says," "Sample Vote Shows Burke Leading Foes," CPD, Sept. 24, 1947; "Burke and Ness Collide on City's Housekeeping; Pucel in Price Fight," CPD, Sept. 26, 1947; "Ness Hits 'Confusion'; Pucel Drives On with Taft Issue; Burke Sums Up," CPD, Sept. 27, 1947; "Burke, Ness Named in Cleveland," *New York Times,* Oct. 1, 1947; "Burke and Ness Are Nominated," CPD, Oct. 1, 1947; "Porter on the Elections," CPD, Oct. 2, 1947; "The Inside of the News in Cleveland," Oct. 5, 1947; "Ripon Clubmen Offer Ness Bushels of Tips for Victory," CPD, Oct. 9, 1947; "Tactics of Desperation," CPD, Oct. 20, 1947; "Porter on Silly Statements," CPD, Oct. 27, 1947; "Ness' 34 City Halls," CPD, Oct. 28, 1947; " 'False Issues' Blasted by Burke; Safety Jobs Rigged, Ness Charges," "Inside of the News in Cleveland," CPD, Oct. 29, 1947; "Burke Wins by Record Majority," CPD, Nov. 5, 1947; "Cleveland Returns Democratic Mayor," *New York Times,* Nov. 5, 1947; "Inside of the News in Cleveland," CPD, Nov. 26, 1947; Heimel, *Eliot Ness: The Real Story,* 185; "Selling Ness to Cleveland," *Newsweek,* Oct. 13, 1947; Porter, *Cleveland,* 104–6.

Chapter 35: Eliot-Am-Big-U-ous Ness

Narrative of Ness's last years in Coudersport constructed from: AI, Franny Taft, July 1, 2011; Condon, "The Last American Hero;" Fraley, "The Real Eliot Ness;" "A Bad End for a Good Guy," CPD, Sept. 7, 1997; Pennsylvania Department of Banking and Securities investigation report on North Ridge Industrial, ENP, reel 3; Heimel, *Eliot Ness: The Real Story,* 83, 188–93, 198–202; Jedick, "Eliot Ness;" "Film Crews Tracking Eliot Ness: Famous Crime Fighter Died Unheralded — But of Natural Causes

— in Potter County," *Pittsburgh Post-Gazette,* Dec. 1, 1996; *Potter Leader-Enterprise,* Nov. 24, 1971.

In 1951, the Diebold board: undated letters, ENP, reel 3; "There Goes Eliot Ness," *Fortune,* Jan. 1946; "Executive Changes," *New York Times,* April 14, 1951.

He had to scrabble for work: AI, Rebecca McFarland, May 19, 2011; Condon, *Cleveland,* 243; Heimel, *Eliot Ness: The Real Story,* 192–93; Jedick, "Eliot Ness."

Betty would say that: "TV Brings Father Back for Son of Eliot Ness," CPD, Oct. 17, 1959.

Cobo didn't want: Bergreen, *Capone: The Man and the Era,* 603; ENP reel 3.

Francis Sweeney found out: postcards from Sweeney, ENP, reel 3.

Detective Merylo, however, had reached: Cleveland Police Department report on torso murder investigation, dated Mar. 15, 1943, CPHS.

In 1939 Cuyahoga County sheriff: Badal, *In the Wake of the Butcher,* 184–93.

Epilogue: Literary Life

Narrative of Ness's collaboration with Fraley and Ness's last days are constructed from: AI, Rebecca McFarland, May 19, 2011; Borroel, *Story of the Untouch-*

ables, 11; Fraley, "The Real Eliot Ness;" "TV Brings Father Back for Son of Eliot Ness," CPD, Oct. 17, 1959; various unlabeled documents, ENP, reel 3; Heimel, *Eliot Ness: The Real Story,* 202; Jedick, "Eliot Ness;" "The Man Who Booked Eliot Ness," *Miami Herald,* June 19, 1987; "Film Crews Tracking Eliot Ness: Famous Crime Fighter Died Unheralded — But of Natural Causes — in Potter County," *Pittsburgh Post-Gazette,* Dec. 1, 1996; "We're Still Touched by the Untouchable," *Pittsburgh Post-Gazette,* Sept. 11, 1997; "Walter Taylor Reminisces on Eliot Ness's Last Years," *Potter Leader-Enterprise,* Mar. 22, 1961; "As I Knew Eliot Ness," *Potter Leader-Enterprise,* Nov. 24, 1971; "My Husband, Eliot Ness," *TV Guide,* May 11, 1961.

When she died, in 1986: AI, Steve Resnick, June 5, 2011.

Career wrap-ups of Untouchables derived from: AI, Barbara Osteika, who interviewed Gardner family members; Benjey, 131; "Member of 'Untouchables' Who 'Broke' Capone Recalls Exploits," *Los Angeles Times,* Oct. 4, 1962; NPRC, Paul Robsky, Bernard V. Cloonan, William Gardner, Martin Lahart, Joseph Leeson, Paul Robsky, and Samuel Seager; various news clippings, Scott Sroka personal collection.

Former Cleveland political insider John

Patrick Butler: "Ness Recalled as Quiet Enforcer," CPD, April 30, 1960.

BIBLIOGRAPHY

Books

Abbott, Karen. *American Rose: A Nation Laid Bare: The Life and Times of Gypsy Rose Lee* (New York: Random House, 2012).

Adams, Henry. *Viktor Schreckengost and 20th-Century Design,* revised edition (Cleveland Museum of Art/Viktor Schreckengost Foundation, 2005).

Alder, Ken. *The Lie Detectors: The History of an American Obsession* (New York: Free Press, 2007).

Anderson, Lars. *Carlisle vs. Army: Jim Thorpe, Dwight Eisenhower, Pop Warner, and the Forgotten Story of Football's Greatest Battle* (New York: Random House, 2007).

Badal, James Jessen. *In the Wake of the Butcher: Cleveland's Torso Murders* (Kent, OH: Kent State University Press, 2001).

Bassett, Mark and Victoria Naumann. *Cowan Pottery and the Cleveland School* (Atglen, PA: Schiffer Publishing, 1997).

Benjey, Tom. *Doctors, Lawyers, Indian Chiefs: Jim Thorpe & Pop Warner's Carlisle Indian School Football Immortals Tackle Socialites, Bootleggers, Students, Moguls, Prejudice, the Government, Ghouls, Tooth Decay and Rum* (Carlisle, PA: Tuxedo Press, 2008).

Bergreen, Laurence. *Capone: The Man and the Era* (New York: Simon & Schuster, 1994).

Borroel, Roger. *The Story of the Untouchables, as Told by Eliot Ness* (East Chicago, IN: La Villita Publications, 2010).

Brandt, Allan M. *No Magic Bullet: A Social History of Venereal Disease in the United States Since 1880* (New York: Oxford University Press, 1987).

Brinkley, David. *Washington Goes to War* (New York: Ballantine Books, 1996).

Buford, Kate. *Native American Son: The Life and Sporting Legend of Jim Thorpe* (New York: Alfred A. Knopf, 2010).

Burrough, Bryan. *Public Enemies: America's Greatest Crime Wave and the Birth of the FBI* (New York: Penguin, 2009).

Chafe, William H. *The Unfinished Journey: America Since World War II, Second Edition* (New York: Oxford University Press, 1991).

Collins, Max Allan. *Butcher's Dozen* (New York: Bantam, 1988).

Condon, George E. *Cleveland: The Best Kept*

Secret (Garden City, NY: Doubleday, 1967).

Crawford, Bill. *All American: The Rise and Fall of Jim Thorpe* (Hoboken, NJ: John Wiley & Sons, 2005).

Deford, Frank, ed. *The Best American Sports Writing: 1993* (Boston: Houghton Mifflin Co., 1993).

Eddy, Mary Baker. *Science and Health, with Key to the Scriptures* (Boston: First Church of Christ, Scientist, 1994).

Eig, Jonathan. *Get Capone: The Secret Plot That Captured America's Most Wanted Gangster* (New York: Simon & Schuster, 2010).

Ferrell, Robert. *The Strange Deaths of President Harding* (Columbia: University of Missouri, 1996).

Fraley, Oscar. *4 Against the Mob* (New York: Popular Library, 1961).

Fraley, Oscar, with Paul Robsky. *Last of the Untouchables* (New York: Pocket Books, 1962).

Grann, David. *The Devil and Sherlock Holmes: Tales of Murder, Madness, and Obsession* (New York: Vintage, 2011).

Griffith, George P. *Life and Adventures of Revenooer No. 1* (Birmingham, AL: Gander Publishers, 1975).

Heimel, Paul W. *Eliot Ness: The Real Story* (Nashville, TN: Knox Books, 1997).

Hoffman, Dennis E. *Scarface Al and the*

Crime Crusaders: Chicago's Private War against Capone (Carbondale: Southern Illinois University Press, 1993).

Irey, Elmer L., as told to William J. Slocum. *The Tax Dodgers: The Inside of the T-Men's War with America's Political and Underworld Hoodlums* (New York: Greenberg, 1948).

Israel, Betsy. *Bachelor Girl: 100 Years of Breaking the Rules: A Social History of Living Single* (New York: Perennial, 2003).

Kellner, Esther. *Moonshine: Its History and Folklore* (Indianapolis: Bobbs-Merrill, 1971).

Kobler, John. *Capone: The Life and World of Al Capone* (New York: Da Capo Press, 1992).

Larson, Erik. *In the Garden of Beasts: Love, Terror, and an American Family in Hitler's Berlin* (New York: Crown, 2011).

Martin, John Bartlow. *Butcher's Dozen and Other Murders* (New York: Signet, 1952).

Maurer, David W. *The Big Con: The Story of the Confidence Man* (New York: Anchor Books, 1999).

McGill, Neil W. and William H. Perry. *Court Cases of Eliot Ness: An Exciting True Story in the Life of Eliot Ness Told by the Cleveland Prosecutor Who Worked with Him* (Fullerton, CA: Sultana Press, 1971).

McLoughlin, Maurice. *Tennis as I Play It* (New York: George H. Doran, 1915).

Murray, George. *The Madhouse on Madison Street* (Chicago: Follett, 1965).

Napoli, Tony, with Charles Messina. *My Father, My Don: A Son's Journey from Organized Crime to Sobriety* (Silver Spring, MD: Beckham, 2008).

Ness, Eliot, with Oscar Fraley. *The Untouchables: The Real Story* (New York: Pocket Books, 1987).

Nickel, Steven. *Torso: Eliot Ness and the Hunt for the Mad Butcher of Kingsbury Run: A True Story* (New York: Avon, 1990).

Okrent, Daniel. *Last Call: The Rise and Fall of Prohibition* (New York: Scribner, 2010).

Pierce, Bessie Louise, ed. *As Others See Chicago: Impressions of Visitors, 1673–1933* (Chicago: University of Chicago Press, 2004).

Porter, Philip W. *Cleveland: Confused City on a Seesaw* (Columbus: Ohio State University, 1976).

Reik, Theodore. *The Unknown Murderer* (New York: Prentice-Hall, 1945).

Rollyson, Carl. *Beautiful Exile: The Life of Martha Gellhorn* (London: Aurum Press, 2001).

Sagalyn, Arnold. *A Promise Fulfilled: The Memoir of Arnold Sagalyn* (privately published, 2010).

Schoenberg, Robert J. *Mr. Capone* (New York: Perennial, 1993).

Schwarz, Ted. *Cleveland Curiosities: Eliot Ness*

& His Blundering Raid, a Busker's Promise, the Richest Heiress Who Never Lived, and More (Charleston, SC: The History Press, 2010).

St. John, Robert. *This Was My World* (Garden City, NY: Doubleday, 1953).

Sullivan, Edward Dean. *Chicago Surrenders* (New York: Vanguard, 1930).

———. *Rattling the Cup on Chicago Crime* (New York: Vanguard, 1929).

Terkel, Studs. *Hard Times: An Oral History of the Great Depression* (New York: Pantheon Books, 1970).

———. *Talking to Myself: A Memoir of My Times* (New York: The New Press, 1994).

Tippins, Sherill. *February House* (Boston: Houghton Mifflin, 2005).

Tucker, Kenneth. *Eliot Ness and the Untouchables: The Historical Reality and the Film and Television Depictions,* second edition (Jefferson, NC: McFarland, 2011).

Tynan, Kathleen. *The Life of Kenneth Tynan* (New York: William Morrow & Co., 1987).

Vacha, John. *Meet Me on Lake Erie, Dearie! Cleveland's Great Lakes Exposition, 1936–1937* (Kent, OH: Kent State University Press, 2011).

Vollmer, August. *The Police and Modern Society: Plain Talk Based on Practical Experience* (Berkeley: University of California Press, 1936).

Watts, Jill. *Mae West: An Icon in Black and White* (New York: Oxford University Press, 2001).

Wendt, Lloyd and Herman Kogan. *Bosses in Lusty Chicago: The Story of Bathhouse John and Hinky Dink* (Bloomington: Indiana University Press, 1968).

Other Sources

Condon, George. "The Last American Hero," *Cleveland,* August 1987, 88–91 and 138–42.

Covering History: Revisiting Federal Art in Cleveland 1933–43, Cleveland Arts Foundation/Cleveland Public Library, 2006.

Durell, Ann. "Evaline Ness," *Library Journal,* Mar. 15, 1967, 1298.

Edris Eckhardt: Visionary and Innovator in American Studio Ceramics and Glass, Cleveland Artists Foundation, 2006.

"Evaline Ness's Centenary," Free Library of Philadelphia blog, posted April 21, 2011.

"Federal Prohibition Enforcement: A Report to the National Commission on Law Observance and Enforcement," Department of Justice, 1930.

Fraley, Oscar. "The Real Eliot Ness." *Coronet,* July 1961, 25-30.

Helvering, Guy T. "Intelligence Unit Bureau of Internal Revenue Treasury Department:

Organization, Functions and Activities: A Narrative Briefly Descriptive of the Period 1919 to 1936," United States Treasury, 1938.

Jedick, Peter. "Eliot Ness," *Cleveland,* April 1976, 48–57, 91–95.

"The Method of Training Enforcement Personnel upon Their Duties and Limitations Under the Law: a Factual Outline of the Training Program," United States Treasury Department, Bureau of Prohibition, 1930.

Michel, Joan Hess. "Evaline Ness: the Caldecott Medalist for 1967," *American Artist,* June 1967, 32–37 and 69–73.

Ness, Eliot. "Community Policing: Vital to Victory," *True Detective,* October 1942, 49 and 70.

———. "How to Curb Prostitution in Hotels," Social Protection Division, Office of Defense Health and Welfare Services.

———. "The National Program of Social Protection," *Public Welfare: The Journal of the American Public Welfare Association,* April 1943, 115–18.

———. "Venereal Disease Control in Defense," Annals of the American Academy of Political and Social Sciences, March 1942, 89–93.

———. "What About Girls?" Social Protection Division, Office of Defense Health and Welfare Services.

Ness, Elisabeth. "My Husband, Eliot Ness,"

TV Guide, May 11, 1961, 5–7.

Ness, Evaline. "Evaline Ness," *Something About the Author: Autobiography Series,* vol. 1 (Detroit, MI: Gale, 1985), 223–33.

Richard, George E. "The Last Boy Scout: Eliot Ness' Tenure as Cleveland, Ohio's Public Safety Director," *International Journal of Humanities and Social Sciences,* September 2011, 14–20.

Schmeckebier, Laurence F. "The Bureau of Prohibition: Its History, Activities and Organization." Washington, DC: The Brookings Institution, 1929.

Watson, Ernest W. "Ness: Rising Star in the Illustration Firmament," *American Artist,* January 1956, 29-31 and 80–82.

ABOUT THE AUTHOR

Douglas Perry is the author of *The Girls of Murder City: Fame, Lust, and the Beautiful Killers Who Inspired Chicago*, which the *Wall Street Journal* hailed as "a sexy, swaggering historical tale." He is an award-winning writer and editor whose work has appeared in the *Chicago Tribune*, the *Oregonian*, the *Faster Times*, *Tennis*, and many other publications. He lives in Portland, Oregon.